Intermediate Japanese

REVISED EDITION

AN **INTEGRATED** APPROACH **TO** LANGUAGE **AND** CULTURE

Michael L. Kluemper & Lisa Berkson

TUTTLE Publishing

Tokyo | Rutland, Vermont | Singapore

Contributing authors:
Fumiko Chiuini, Mai Fujii, Hiromi Hollett, Fumiko Kikuchi, Akiko Miyamoto, Masumi Reade, Kyoko Shoji, Noriko Wachowski

Editing assistance:
Mai Fujii, Manami Imaoka, Fumiko Kikuchi, Kyoko Shoji

Illustrations:
Boya Sun and Keiko Murakami

Audio assistance:
Special thanks to: Keio Academy of New York High School, Teachers Fumiko Kikuchi and Tomonori Inugai as well as Keio Academy of New York High School students Kaoru Doi, Shota Yoshimura, Minami Kenmochi, Takayasu Kato, Shunta Orimoto, Kengo Nagano, Rei Adachi, Yuki Murai and Yuki Hirose, and Satoshi Fukushima. Also thanks to: Kaho Hoshino, Sumiko Imai, Takuya Kawamura, Sachiko Kuwakubo, Hiroko Morita, Tomoe Nakamura Tomohiro Urita, Kazuhide Shimizu, Keiko Uchiyama, Chikayo Yamakoshi, Akiko Yokomitsu

We would like to dedicate this book to the never-ending support, inspiration, and patience of our families and friends, sensei, and students—past and present. Special thanks for the generous cooperation given by Paul and Miriam Ash, Zaq Berkson, Steve Bokenkamp, Julie Cain, Akiko Ogasawara, Michio and Taeko Oyagi, the Hiromi and Emiko Sasaki family, and Yasuko Watt.

Published by Tuttle Publishing, an imprint of Periplus Editions (HK) Ltd.

www.tuttlepublishing.com

Copyright © 2011, 2016, 2022 Michael L. Kluemper and Lisa Berkson

Library of Congress 2011045147

ISBN 978-0-8048-4864-0 (paperback edition)

Distributed by

"Books to Span the East and West"

Tuttle Publishing was founded in 1832 in the small New England town of Rutland, Vermont |USA|. Our core values remain as strong today as they were then—to publish best-in-class books which bring people together one page at a time. In 1948, we established a publishing office in Japan—and Tuttle is now a leader in publishing English-language books about the arts, languages and cultures of Asia. The world has become a much smaller place today and Asia's economic and cultural influence has grown. Yet the need for meaningful dialogue and information about this diverse region has never been greater. Over the past seven decades, Tuttle has published thousands of books on subjects ranging from martial arts and paper crafts to language learning and literature—and our talented authors, illustrators, designers and photographers have won many prestigious awards. We welcome you to explore the wealth of information available on Asia at www.tuttlepublishing.com.

North America, Latin America & Europe
Tuttle Publishing
364 Innovation Drive, North Clarendon, VT 05759-9436 U.S.A.
Tel: 1 (802) 773-8930 Fax: 1 (802) 773-6993
info@tuttlepublishing.com; www.tuttlepublishing.com

Japan
Tuttle Publishing
Yaekari Building, 3rd Floor
5-4-12 Osaki Shinagawa-ku Tokyo 141 0032
Tel: (81) 3 5437-0171 Fax: (81) 3 5437-0755
sales@tuttle.co.jp; www.tuttle.co.jp

Asia Pacific
Berkeley Books Pte. Ltd.
3 Kallang Sector #04-01 Singapore 349278
Tel: (65) 6741-2178 Fax: (65) 6741-2179
inquiries@periplus.com.sg; www.tuttlepublishing.com

25 24 23 22   5 4 3 2 1   2208TP
Printed in Singapore

To the Learner

Welcome to *Intermediate Japanese*. You have learned much in your studies to this point about Japanese language, culture, and history. This is your second step along the path to language and cultural proficiency in Japanese.

This book is organized in a manner similar to *Beginning Japanese*, to allow you to continue your historical exploration of Japan.

You will learn about and be able to discuss:
- wants and needs
- artistic traditions of Japan—musical, performing, and visual
- local flavors including dialects, foods, and festivals
- certain literary figures and some of their works
- opinions about a variety of topics
- how something is done or should be done
- weather, geography, and geology of Japan's islands
- travel, transportation, and accommodation details
- some details about important historical persons

You will be able to:
- tell stories
- give and ask directions
- make comparisons using a variety of methods
- talk about cause and effect
- make conditional statements or imply that something should/must be done
- understand and/or use basic informal, formal, and women's speech
- write informal and introductory letters
- use appropriate verbal and non-verbal signals, sounds, and words during conversations
- have a deeper understanding of the makeup and use of kanji and their radicals
- use at least an additional 150 kanji, making a total of 300

The Authors

Contents

1   Hokkaido 1908: Migration and Indigenous Peoples   17

2   Ryukyu Islands (Okinawa) 1608: Travel and Music, Past and Present   60

3   Edo 1830: Visual Aesthetics of Edo and Beyond   97

Goals and Guidelines

	Performance Goals	Language Points	Culture	Kanji
Chapter 1: Hokkaido 1908: Migration and Indigenous Peoples	• talk about using various means of transportation • introduce yourself and others • talk generally about Hokkaido and its culture	• self-introduction and introduction • review particles, adjectives, verbs, etc. • 〜て−form review • 〜ましょう form review • kanji radicals	• Japanese education system • Hokkaido • zodiac animals • the poet Ishikawa Takuboku	漢 字 子 森 川 州 館 雪 才 歳 自 重 動 働 駅 歩 杯 読 勉 王 主 住 田 町 教 習 入 出 (28)
Chapter 2: Ryukyu Islands (Okinawa) 1608: Travel and Music, Past and Present	• give and ask directions • make basic reservations for travel, lodging, and meals	• review 〜ませんか • giving and understanding basic directions • use of multiple adjectives to describe a noun • use of counters for travel and overnight stays (泊 and 日)	• Okinawa geography • using maps and finding locations • Okinawan traditional performing arts and music • Okinawan traditional music today • Okinawan food	北 南 西 番 東 右 左 乗 降 首 道 枚 的 新 古 線 横 個 後 注 文 晩 宿 少 多 調 皆 階 会 付 肉 酒 (32)
Chapter 3: Edo 1830: Visual Aesthetics of Edo and Beyond	• talk about the locations of people or objects in a room • make comparisons using 〜の方が…より and もっと • talk about cause and effect using から • use the potential form of verbs • make negative comparisons using 〜ほど	• particle usage for location • comparison using 〜の方が…より • comparison using もっと • use of から、ですから、だから for cause and result • adverbs なかなか、けっこう、逆に • potential form of verbs • negative comparison using ほど	• Ueno Park • the European art trend of Japonisme • Western vs. Eastern ideals of beauty in the 19th c. • the history of manga • stories about Kintarou	公 園 前 紙 絵 飛 刀 方 空 地 竹 所 速 然 簡 単 弱 難 早 力 (20)
Chapter 4: Edo 1815: Traditions in Performing Arts	• use informal and formal speech • say that you can do something • use それで and ので to express cause and effect	• review of 持って行く and 連れて行く, etc. • introduction to keigo • informal statements and questions • "what kind of" using 何の〜 • 事が出来る to say that you "can do 〜" • はず (is expected to) and つもり (intend to) • それで and ので to talk about cause/effect	• kamishibai • kabuki and the play 義経千本桜 よしつねせんぼんざくら • other dramatic arts during the Edo period • lucky and unlucky colors • honorific and humble language • あいづち (verbal signals)	連 形 合 茶 変 品 葉 忘 度 非 悲 (11)

	Performance Goals	Language Points	Culture	Kanji
Chapter 5: Izu 1922: Ryokan and Onsen	• make presentations in Japanese • talk about the way something is done • use modifying clauses • use から to express cause and effect • talk about the temperature of objects and weather	• the verb stem + 方 (かた) to refer to the way of doing something • modifying clauses • から to show cause and effect	• author 川端康成 (かわばたやすなり) • the short story 伊豆の踊り子 (いず おど こ) • Japanese inns (旅館 りょかん) and hot springs (温泉 おんせん) culture • the 伊豆 (いず) Peninsula and 静岡 (しずおか) Prefecture • regional dialects • useful temperature vocabulary • Japanese-style rooms (和室)	浴 散 洗 泳 氷 湯 温 男 女 冷 若 泉 暖 遠 近 浜 忙 比 危 止 (20)
Chapter 6: Oga Hanto 1951: Positive Connections Out of a Troubled Past	• say something will become bigger, taller, more delicious, etc. • write basic informal and introductory letters • say that something is "more than ~" or "less than ~" • say that something is "only/just/just that (and nothing else)" • make prohibitive commands • ask if it is all right NOT to do something • say "if it is so, then" or "well then" • say you have had the experience of doing something	• い adj. + くなる • writing styles in informal letters • ばかり • 〜ないで下さい to make a prohibitive command • 〜なくてもいいですか to ask if it's OK not to do something • それでは、それじゃ to say if it is so…, then, or well then • 〜した事がある to say that something has been experienced • 〜たら ending to say "if" or "when"	• お正月 (Japanese New Year) • the 男鹿 (おが) Peninsula and 秋田 (あきた) Prefecture • a little about the American Occupation after WWII	朝 内 夕 正 夜 昼 鬼 第 様 配 以 怖 知 (13)
Chapter 7: Tokyo 1892: The Identities Behind the Pen Names	• make "if X then Y" statements • state that something must be done • say you or someone else wants something • ask someone to do something for you • say that it is all right not to do something • suggest someone try doing something	• the conditional 〜ば form • the 〜ほしい and ほしがる forms • the 〜しなければなりません pattern • 〜してほしい to ask someone to do something for you • 〜なくてもいい • 〜てみてください	• the 明治 (めいじ) period • the author 樋口一葉 (ひぐちいちよう) • the geography of Edo • brief history of poetry in Japan • Japanese emoticons	疲 代 治 由 画 漫 飯 松 庭 初 願 (11)

	Performance Goals	Language Points	Culture	Kanji
Chapter 8: Tokyo 1960: Effects of Geology and Weather	• use some transitive and intransitive verbs • say that something seems or appears + adj. • use だけ to say "only ~ " or "just ~ " • talk about when something happens • say you do this and also do that • say something is completely finished	• transitive and intransitive verbs • the pattern ～そうです to indicate something seems + adj. • だけ • ～の時 • the verb て form + しまいました pattern	• the "Ring of Fire" • responses to natural disasters and Disaster Prevention Day • dancing as a popular pastime in Japan • earthquakes and animals • NHK Broadcasting Network	関 開 閉 台 始 次 集 伝 考 困 走 (11)
Chapter 9: Hiroshima 1958: Rising up from Tragedy and Moving Forward	• state your opinion or the opinion of others • talk about the way of doing something • say "for the sake of" something	• ～と言いました；～と思います；～と聞きました • verb stem + 方 • ～のために	• the 中国 region and the city of 広島 • women's speech • Sadako and 千羽鶴 • お好み焼き • grass-roots peace efforts in Japan and around the world	覚 式 急 (3)
Chapter 10: Tokyo Present Day: Moving Forward and Planning for the Future	• state that you want to become something	• ～になりたい	• 手塚治虫 and Astro Boy • ～ことわざ (proverbs)	牛 匹 馬 鳥 虎 (5)

Please visit TimeForJapanese.com for detail on how *Intermediate Japanese* aligns with the standards set forth by organizations such as the Japanese National Standards Task Force, ACTFL (American Council on the Teaching of Foreign Languages), and others.

🎧

How to Download the Online Audio of this Book.

1. Make sure you have an Internet connection.
2. Type the URL below into your web browser.

https://www.tuttlepublishing.com/intermediate-japanese-textbook

For support, you can email us at info@tuttlepublishing.com

Historical Timeline

日本		中国	世界 せ かい
710 奈良時代 な ら じ だい 752 東大寺 dedication 774 空海 born く う かい		618–907 Tang Dynasty	668 Korea unified under Silla
794 平安時代 へ い あん じ だい	794 藤原 ふじわら		800 Charlemagne crowned emperor
1008–1021 Murasaki Shikibu finishes *Tale of Genji*		960–1279 N., then S. Song Dynasty	
1189 Benkei dies			1150 Angkor Wat expanded 1167 Oxford Univ. established
1185 鎌倉時代 か ま くら じ だい			
1252 鎌倉大仏 (Great Buddha) か ま くら だい ぶつ		1271–1368 Kublai Khan conquers China, forms Yuan Dynasty	1240 Mongols invade Poland and Hungary 1271 Marco Polo begins his journey
1398 金閣寺 built きん かく じ	1392 室町 むろまち or 足利 あしかが 時代 じ だい	1368–1644 Ming Dynasty	1345 Notre Dame cathedral completed 1400 Machu Picchu construction begins; Chaucer dies before completing *Canterbury Tales* 1492 Columbus lands in Americas 1503 Leonardo da Vinci begins *Mona Lisa* 1557 Portuguese land in Japan 1600 William Adams lands in Japan 1616 Shakespeare dies
1603 徳川 or 江戸時代 とく がわ え ど じ だい 1620 兼六園 established けん ろく えん 1694 松尾芭蕉 dies まつ お ば しょう 1707 Mt. Fuji's most recent eruption 1823–29 Hokusai's *Great Wave* ukiyo-e 1853 Commodore Perry's first landing 1854 Japan and U.S. sign agreement		1644–1912 Qing Dynasty	1653 Taj Mahal completed 1776 U.S. declares independence 1788 First Fleet arrives at Sydney Cove 1789 French Revolution 1840 Founding of New Zealand
1868 明治時代 めい じ じ だい 1873 Ueno Park made public 1895 Higuchi Ichiyo's *Takekurabe* (Growing Up) 1910 Ishikawa Takuboku's *Ichiaku no suna* 1912 大正 reign period begins			1861 U.S. Civil War begins 1889 Van Gogh's *Starry Night* Eiffel Tower built 1891 Gauguin goes to Tahiti
1923 Great Kanto earthquake 1926 昭和 reign period begins しょう わ 1926 Kawabata's "Dancing Girl of Izu" 1928 手塚治虫 born て づか おさむ		1912 Republic of China (Taiwan) founded	1938 Superman action comic published
1951 Astro Boy appears 1955 Sadako dies 1958 Tokyo Tower built 1989 平成 reign period begins へい せい		1949 People's Republic of China founded	1952 American Occupation of Japan ends 1960 Beatles formed 1973 Sydney Opera House opens

Introduction

In Volume 1 of this series, *Beginning Japanese*, you met the main characters: Kiara, Ben, Jun, and Tomo. You traveled with them, learning along the way about a variety of historical and legendary figures who have impacted Japan's culture and history in interesting ways. You met William Adams, the "warrior monk" Benkei, Murasaki Shikibu, Basho, and others. You've been introduced to locations around Japan where events took place that were instrumental in shaping Japan into the country it is today. These sites include Nagasaki, Nara, Hiraizumi, Kyoto (Heian-kyo), Amanohashidate, Tokyo (Edo), and Kanazawa. These are only a few of the personalities, locations, and times that were important in Japan's history, up through the pre-modern time period (the mid-1800s).

Here in Volume 2 of this series, *Intermediate Japanese*, your journey with the four main personalities continues, exploring more of the language, history, and culture of Japan.

Using This Book

Anyone who has experienced a new language can testify that you don't have to be fluent in a language to communicate. Conversations about what time your flight departs, the location of the restroom, or the cost of a souvenir happen every day between people who are not mutually fluent in the other's language. If the speaker and the listener are good communicators, basic information can be shared and understood. In fact, this sort of exchange can be a memorable experience. A higher level of skill with another language, however, allows you to expand your cultural horizons, to more easily make new friends, and to join the global community of the twenty-first century.

Intermediate Japanese is the second step in a language learning series designed to give you a more natural experience in Japanese language acquisition.

This series aims to introduce the framework of the language (vocabulary, grammar points, grammar patterns, etc.) in natural and contextualized situations and scenarios. Social, historical, and cultural aspects of Japan are embedded in these scenarios, giving you, the learner, more exposure to the varied and complex society within which you will be utilizing your Japanese language skills.

This approach also provides opportunities for you to experience being "in" Japan by closely interacting with certain moments in Japan's history and culture. There will be many occasions in your career as a language learner when you will not understand perfectly and completely everything that you read and hear. With study and practice, however, you can become skilled at picking up cues and clues that help you decode and interpret information and then respond appropriately. To give you that practice, there are aspects of this text, and the accompanying web and audio resources, that include language and patterns designed to challenge your linguistic skills at any given point in your learning process. The 会話 (Dialogue) and メール (Mail) sections of this text (as was the case in *Beginning Japanese*) are carefully constructed to be at a learning level just beyond the language level of the learner. This mild challenge helps to develop some of the intuitive skills important to becoming a successful speaker of any language. Do not panic! This is a natural way of learning a language and, although it may on occasion be uncomfortable or even frustrating, you will ultimately benefit from practicing speaking, hearing, and reading language that challenges your abilities.

This series differs from other learning sources in that:

❶ KANJI characters (non-phonetic Chinese characters) are taught from the first lesson of *Beginning Japanese*. In traditional materials, often students are expected to master the two phonetic "alphabets," hiragana and katakana, prior to the introduction of kanji.

As in *Beginning Japanese*, *Intermediate Japanese* continues this practice of introducing kanji as they appear in the context of each chapter. The kanji characters include FURIGANA, phonetic guides below each kanji to help you read the new characters and to give assistance where needed. To challenge yourself, don't just rely on the furigana guides; rather, consciously cover up the furigana readings with your hand or a piece of paper while reading. This will help your reading skills improve enormously. Eventually, the furigana disappear from the kanji that you are expected to learn. If you have been weaning yourself off of them as you progress, you will not even miss them and in fact will realize that it is much easier to read Japanese without this aid. For many, learning to read kanji and exploring new ways to use them in writing is an enjoyable part of the process.

❷ This series is explicitly visual. The visual nature of this book, with its many drawings and photos, helps you make more immediate connections and contributes to your mastery of the language. The manga at the beginning of each section bring the characters in the story to life. The photographs provide an authentic glimpse of what Japan really "looks" like. These illustrations also offer a starting point for expanded conversations and a chance for you to creatively interpret the cultural aspects of the text.

❸ *Intermediate Japanese* continues the engaging story of characters travelling through time and place in the pages of the book and website. The story incorporates cultural and historical information as it offers carefully spiraled levels of language learning that increase in difficulty as your language skills improve. Opportunities for practicing real-life skills in situational contexts help reinforce these skills.

Learning Strategies

As an intermediate language learner, you understand that organizing the new information you will be absorbing is crucial to making progress in the language. This organizational process is useful not just for learning Japanese, but when studying any new content area.

Remember that, whatever type of learning strategy works best for you, trying to use as many of your senses as you can is most effective. For example, writing down AND saying aloud what you have written uses more than one sense. When you do this, your hand is moving, your eyes see the words on paper, your mouth speaks the words, and your ears hear them. Expanding your favorite learning strategy in this way will help you retain the information more intuitively and speed up your learning so that you can more quickly and naturally integrate new vocabulary and grammatical structures in your repertoire of linguistic tools. Here are some ideas for studying material effectively and producing it from memory when needed.

• Take a Learning Skills Inventory to determine the type of learner you are: visual, auditory, kinesthetic, logical, verbal, inter- or intra-personal. Then make your strengths work for you. You can find examples of these at **TimeForJapanese.com**.

• Use flash cards. Visual and verbal flash cards for the kanji and vocabulary in *Beginning Japanese* and in *Intermediate Japanese* can be downloaded from **TimeForJapanese.com**.

• Type your vocabulary words in Japanese. Typing a word in Japanese helps you better understand unique Japanese language characteristics such as long and short vowels and double consonants.

Graphic Organizers

Use graphic organizers to continue categorizing vocabulary to help you clarify patterns and to aid you in making connections between newly acquired vocabulary and previous knowledge. This is one good way to place new material in your long-term memory.

Think of a graphic organizer as a means of making new information accessible for you to use whenever you need it. When you want to find a language book in a bookstore, you go to the language section. A graphic organizer is the same idea, in that you can consistently recall a given item.

Here is a sampling of graphic organizer ideas. Try grouping new material by:

• Sound: first, last, or overall sound
• A-i-u-e-o order
• Parts of speech (verbs, adjectives, nouns, etc.)

- Meaning (things that move, that you eat, that you drink, that are blue, etc.)
- Mapping (making a story map on paper) or drawing a web
- Charts or graphs
- Songs or raps

Visit **TimeForJapanese.com** regularly for additional downloads, practice exercises, review games, and other activities. Be sure to send us any ideas that were particularly helpful to you, so we can share them with other language learners.

The Components of This Series

Intermediate Japanese consists of several component parts designed to assist you in gaining proficiency in the four aspects of language: speaking, listening, reading, and writing. Each chapter includes:

漫画 Manga

Each section begins with a manga. These manga generally include a dialogue or conversation between characters, designed to provide context through visual clues. The dialogue is written to be adaptable to situations you may experience in your own Japanese language learning.

会話 Dialogue

In the Dialogue section, the manga dialogue appears in a basic text format. This component allows you to view the conversations with more furigana included to support easier reading.

単語 New Words

In *Beginning Japanese*, most new vocabulary words were introduced through images. Visual imagery helps the beginning language student associate a particular word with an image suggestive of the meaning of that word. In contrast, here you will notice fewer images included in New Words, because at the intermediate level, students generally have established a foundation of linguistic cues, drawing on these to quickly associate new vocabulary with prior knowledge. Another important factor that's changed is that you developed an understanding of the most efficient way for you, as an individual, to acquire new vocabulary.

In New Words, you will find gray type used for the kanji that are either taught in that section or in previous sections. This should help you as you write the vocabulary on your flash cards. Be sure to learn both the hiragana pronunciations and the kanji for these words.

漢字 Kanji

As in *Beginning Japanese*, *Intermediate Japanese* provides kanji reading and writing practice from the start. Pronunciation subscripts (furigana) are inserted where necessary to help you develop your reading skills.

Each kanji is introduced first by a large-sized example, with numbered stroke order, a guide to common pronunciations (the on-yomi in katakana, and the kun-yomi in hiragana), examples of kanji usage in compounds, and a learning hint or mnemonic device to help you learn the kanji.

As you advance through this series, you will learn how and when it is appropriate to use kanji. You will also learn strategies to help you use contextual cues to make more educated assumptions about the meaning of kanji and kanji compounds.

Japanese, both spoken and written, is a living, changing language. Usage and production of written Japanese, as with English and other languages today, is in continuous flux. One example of this change is that Japanese in the 21st century is often written with the aid of electronic devices such as computers and handheld devices. *Intermediate Japanese* takes these technological developments into account as far as expectations for passive and active kanji knowledge and reading abilities are concerned. The degree to which you are required to use kanji increases gradually as you progress through the series. Written workbook exercises and tests where kanji are to be produced will include kanji banks where needed, offering you a supportive tool. Kanji that you see and write often will become very familiar to you, though you will probably refer to the kanji banks for kanji that are less commonly used by you personally.

For example, if you have used *Beginning Japanese*, you probably already know all three of the kanji in the name 高山君 though you've only been taught the first two. Exposure to an increased number of kanji has allowed you to read the last kanji as くん without having furigana included. Gradually, as you work your way through *Intermediate Japanese*, you will be able to produce still more kanji from memory.

言葉の探索 Language Detection

Unlike many other language books, this component is not limited to grammatical explanations. It also offers contextual, social, and cultural cues for how, when, and why the words and phrases being introduced are used.

自習 Self Check

This component is designed as a quick test for you to complete orally on your own, to confirm your understanding of the patterns covered in the Language Detection section above. Conducting this check orally lets you read, speak, and hear the new vocabulary and patterns.

Follow the directions and test yourself. If you are unsure or unclear about some point, reexamine the Language Detection section and ask your instructor for clarification. Complete this section before moving on to practicing with a partner, in small groups, or as a class.

練習時間 Practice Time

This section allows you to apply the material introduced in the Language Detection component. With a partner, in a small group, or as a class, here is your opportunity to cement your new knowledge in your long-term memory. By the time you have completed this component, you should have a good understanding of the material covered in the Language Detection component and feel comfortable using new vocabulary. If you are unclear about any aspect of the new material, do not hesitate to ask your instructor for additional examples and explanations.

文化箱 Culture Chest

Study of a language cannot exist independently of an understanding of culture and context. This component explores a broad range of cultural phenomena, from geography to the intricacies of Japanese social interactions, from traditional drama to the artistic and creative details of contemporary culture.

メール Mail Messages

In *Beginning Japanese* you met Kiara, and got to know her through her journal entries. In *Intermediate Japanese*, this reading component includes various sorts of communications (letters, email, posters, texts) written by a variety of contributing authors. These are sent to Kiara, Ben, Jun, and Tomo from a wide range of friends, family, and acquaintances. The goal of this section is twofold: to offer you a glimpse of a range of writing styles and voices; and to provide you with a review of vocabulary and patterns learned up to that point in a reader-friendly yet challenging manner.

When you travel to Japan as a non-native speaker, you are bombarded with visual and auditory stimuli that must be decoded to make them comprehensible. Essentially, this decoding speeds up and improves as you strengthen your translating and interpreting skills and become a better communicator. Sifting through authentic sights and sounds to figure out the gist, or the core element required to answer your needs, is the process through which language is internalized and learned. As would happen in an actual experience in Japan, you will probably not understand everything you read in these messages. You will, however, practice negotiating skills and learn to sort out the main points, ideas, and details most important to you at that point in time.

The manga and the Mail messages in *Intermediate Japanese* are designed to provide insight into aspects of Japanese history and culture. In this textbook series, we have taken care to be as historically accurate as possible; however, some liberties have been taken with language and culture in order to present Japanese as it is spoken today. We have tried our best to blend the past and present to give you, the learner, an engaging tale and a powerful learning experience.

Digital Dictionary

One of the greatest challenges for any level of language learner is to remember vocabulary terms. You are most likely already utilizing strategies practiced in *Beginning Japanese*—such as making and using flash cards and repeatedly writing (or typing) kanji—to facilitate memorization of new vocabulary. Throughout this series, you will be asked to keep a Digi-Dictionary (digital dictionary). This dictionary will help you understand subtle differences in the spelling and pronunciations of words, especially words with elongated vowels or doubled consonants. It will also serve as your own personal reference glossary and checkpoint. Periodically review the vocabulary you collect here. That way, you will be able to see just how far you have come and just how much new vocabulary you have learned!

Online Materials and Workbook

The Workbook and online materials that accompany this book are designed for your use. Use the Workbook regularly to check your understanding and to practice and apply previously learned and new material. Audio files and additional activities can be found online. Look for this icon as a reminder to check the Tuttle website for important material:

www.TimeForJapanese.com

The web-based resource for this series, **TimeForJapanese.com**, contains additional learning content and practice tools, to help learners and teachers alike. **TimeForJapanese.com** is continually updated. Bookmark or save it to your favorites list on your computer and visit it often.

北海道　1908年
ほっかいどう

Migration and Indigenous Peoples

Kiara, Ben, Jun, and Tomo have left Basho in Kanazawa, at the end of *Beginning Japanese*, and arrived in snow-covered Hokkaido. Here, they meet one of Takuboku Ishikawa's middle school students and his friends. Many here have resettled from other parts of Japan to Hokkaido. The port city of Hakodate, where our group arrives, was home to many Japanese who migrated there during the Meiji Period. These immigrants were hoping to explore the opportunities offered by the vast island of Hokkaido.

Learning and Performance Goals

This chapter will enable you to:
- review introducing yourself and others
- review particles and their usage
- review adjective and verb conjugation
- review using the 〜ましょう form (let's ~)
- talk about travel and various means of transportation
- talk about a friend's birthplace and hometown
- learn about the life of the author Takuboku Ishikawa
- learn about Hokkaido, its people, culture, and history
- learn about the zodiac calendar used in Japan
- use 28 additional kanji

初めまして。私は小原良和です。
おはらよしかず

How do you do? I am Yoshikazu Ohara.

会話 Dialog

Setting: The four characters travel through the 時の門 and arrive at a 神社 in Hakodate. Here they meet Yoshikazu, a student of the teacher and author Takuboku Ishikawa.)

1. ベン　：うわあ。寒い！雪が降っています。ここはどこですか？

2. じゅん　：あの男の子に聞いてみましょう。すみません。

3. 良和　：うわあ。皆さんは外国人ですね。そこに入ってはだめですよ。そこは神社の中です。
皆さんはだれですか？

4. キアラ　：初めまして。キアラです。ここはどこですか？

5. 良和　：ここは北海道の函館です。神社の名前は函館八幡宮です。侍の神社です。

6. 友　：ああ、函館八幡宮は有名な神社ですね。

7. 良和　：私は小原良和です。弥生中学校の生徒です。僕の*担任は石川啄木先生です。

8. じゅん　：へっ、石川先生って・・・

9. ベン　：初めまして。僕はベンです。良和君の中学校に行ってもいいですか？

10. 良和　：はい。でも、授業は難しいですよ。

11. ベン　：大丈夫です。僕は歴史が得意ですから。

12. 良和　：じゃあ、一緒に来て下さい。

13. 友　：もうすぐ晩ご飯でしょう。函館で一番美味しい食べ物は何ですか？

14. 良和　：かにです。

* 担任 – person in charge, person responsible

単語 New Words

おきなわ 沖縄 (pn) – Okinawa (island of, or island chain of)

きゅうしゅう 九州 (pn) – Kyushu (southernmost of the four main islands of Japan)

こおり 氷 (n) – ice, shaved ice (snow cone)

さっぽろ 札幌 (pn) – Sapporo (city in Hokkaido)

しこく 四国 (pn) – Shikoku (smallest of the four main islands of Japan)

しゅっしん 出身 (n) – person's origin (hometown, country, etc.)

しょうかい 紹介 (n) – introduction

じこしょうかい 自己紹介 (n) – self-introduction

じぶん 自分 (n) – myself, yourself, oneself

じんこう 人口 (n) – population

なか 中 (n/adv.) – in, inside, middle, center

はこだて 函館 (pn) – Hakodate (city in Hokkaido)

りょうしん 両親 (n) – parents

へん 辺 (n) – vicinity

ほっかいどう 北海道 (pn) – Hokkaido (northernmost of the four main islands of Japan)

こっち (pron.) – this way (close to or toward the speaker), this direction, informal for こちら

あっち (pron.) – that way (direction distant from both speaker and listener), over there, informal for あちら

そっち (*pron.*) – that way (distant from the speaker, close to the listener), that direction (close to listener), informal for そちら

ほんしゅう 本州 (*pn*) – Honshu (largest of the four main islands of Japan)

(お)いくつ (*inter.*) – how many years (are you), how old

いちばん 一番 (*counter*) – first, number one

にばん 二番 (*counter*) – second, number two

さんばん 三番 (*counter*) – third, number three

よんばん 四番 (*counter*) – fourth, number four

ごばん 五番 (*counter*) – fifth, number five

ろくばん 六番 (*counter*) – sixth, number six

ななばん 七番 (*counter*) – seventh, number seven

はちばん 八番 (*counter*) – eighth, number eight

きゅうばん 九番 (*counter*) – ninth, number nine

じゅうばん 十番 (*counter*) – tenth, number ten

なんばん 何番 (*counter*) – What number?

漢字 Kanji

漢 13 strokes	カン – Sino-, Han (Chinese dynasty)	丶	冫	氵	汁	汁	汁	汁
	漢字 – Chinese characters; 漢朝 – Han Dynasty (China); 漢方薬 – traditional Chinese medicine	泞	泸	湛	漢	漢	漢	
	Water (氵) is the main radical for this kanji. The top right is the grass radical (艹) while below are some of the first CHINESE characters/KANji you learned: 口, 一, and 大.							

字 6 strokes	ジ, あざ – character, letter, section of village	丶	丷	宀	宀	字	字
	ローマ字 – Latin alphabet (romanization); 数字 – numeral						
	A roof with a handle (宀) here can be lifted off to allow the child inside to learn to read LETTER(s) or CHARACTER(s).						

子 3 strokes	シ, ス, ツ, こ, 〜こ, ね – child, sign of the rat	了	了	子
	子供 – child; 男の子 – boy; 電子 – electronic			
	The three strokes of CHILD look like a baby, arms outstretched, wrapped up in a blanket.			

森 12 strokes	シン, もり – forest, woods	一	十	才	木	木	本
	森 – forest, woods; 森本 – Morimoto (family name); 青森市 – Aomori City	森	森	森	森	森	森
	Two trees (林) would be a woods, while three or more would surely be a FOREST.						

川	セン, かわ, がわ – river	ノ	川	川			
	川 – river; 西川 – Nishikawa (family name); 小川 – Ogawa (family name)						
3 strokes	The three strokes of this kanji flow out like a RIVER or STREAM.						

州	しゅう – province, state	'	)	少	州	州	州
	本州 – Honshu; 九州 – Kyushu; イリノイ州 – state of Illinois						
6 strokes	The main islands of Japan are like distinct STATE(s), with three bits of land in the middle of the river (川) representing STATE(s).						

館	カン, たて, やかた – large building	ノ	人	今	今	今	食	食
	函館 – Hakodate; 図書館 – library; 体育館 – gymnasium	食	食'	館	館	館	館	館	館
16 strokes	The left radical (食) means food, the right half (官) means bureaucrat or government. Both are related to food, and both are often housed in large BUILDING(s) or facilities.							

雪	セツ, ゆき – snow	一	厂	戶	冊	乕	乕
	雪 – snow; 大雪 – heavy snow; 雪国 – snow country	冊	雪	雩	雪	雪	
11 strokes	Rain (雨) on the top half of this kanji is the radical. It is on top of really cold thick layers of SNOW on the ground.						

才	サイ – genius, years old	一	十	才			
	三才 – three years old: 天才 – genius, natural gift; 才能 – talent, ability; 才気 – wisdom						
3 strokes	This kanji looks like a ten 十 with a slash through it: this person is now 11 YEARS OLD.						

歳	サイ, セイ, とし, とせ, よわい – year-end, age, occasion	᠂	ト	止	止	芹	芦	芦
	三歳 – three years old; 歳を取る – to grow old; お歳暮 – year-end gift	芦	芦	芹	歳	歳	歳	
13 strokes	Some parents may stop (止) and stand next to a wall (or cliff 厂) and mark an "X" (戊) for their child's YEAR-END height, noting with a line or a mark how small (小) or big the child is at each AGE.							

NOTE ▶ Note that the kanji 歳 is the official kanji for "age." However, the less-complicated kanji 才 is more commonly taught in elementary schools.

言葉の探索 Language Detection
ことば　たんさく

1. 紹介／自己紹介 – Introductions/Self-introductions
しょうかい　じこしょうかい

You have learned how to include a wide variety of details in an introduction or self-introduction. In Japan, you will find yourself giving a self-introduction on many different occasions. For a casual or more brief introduction, you need only say your name, _____ です.
your name

Remember, NEVER use さん after your own name; however, be sure to use さん after someone else's name.

A slightly longer self-introduction might include your name and where you are from: "(私は) _____ です。シカゴからです。" A more formal introduction might include things like your favorite color, class, movie, or book; or your class schedule, club, family members, and hobbies.
your name

Here are two sample introductions. As you read these, pay attention to the words that show a humble attitude on the part of the speaker.

例A：紹介
れい　しょうかい

こちらは友達のエミさんです。オーストラリアから来ました。ご家族は四人です。お父さんとお母さんと弟さんとエミさんです。エミさんのお誕生日は六月二十日で、今年十七オです。日本語と テニスが得意です。エミさんの一番好きな色は紫です。だから、時々、エミさんを「紫さん」と呼びます。私とエミさんはいい友達です。

例B：自己紹介
れい　じこしょうかい

僕の名前は ダヴィです。ブラジルから来ました。家族は五人です。母と父と姉二人です。十六オで、高校一年生です。趣味は水泳と歌を歌う事です。でも、あまり上手ではありません。どうぞよろしくお願いします。

2. オ or 歳 – Expressing Age
さい　さい

To refer to the age of people or animals in Japanese, add either of these suffix kanji after the age (number): オ or 歳. The official kanji for age is 歳, but オ is generally taught in elementary schools and is more commonly handwritten.

When asking how old someone is, use either 何オ(何歳)ですか。(How old are you?) or おいくつですか (specifically — How many years are you?).
なんさい　なんさい

When using 何オ, the answer should include the kanji オ as the counter. Conversely, if (お)いくつ is used, the generic counters can be used in the response (一つ、二つ, etc.). If the person is presumably older than you, use おいくつですか, since 何オ can be considered more informal.
なんさい　さい

_____ は ____ です。 – (person's/animal's name) is (age).
person's name　age

例ア： A-さん: 何才ですか。
B-さん: 十六才です。

例イ： (*A is asking about B's sibling*)
A-さん: 弟さんは何才ですか。
B-さん: 弟は四才です。

例ウ： (*A is presumably not younger*)
A-さん: 何歳ですか。
B-さん: 今、二十歳 です。

例エ： (*B is presumably older*)
A-さん: おいくつですか。
B-さん: 私ですか。二十八です。

自習　Self Check

1. Introduce each of the following people in Japanese. Include all of the given information.

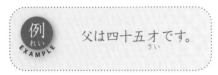

例 父は四十五才です。

(ア) 友子 (12 years old), likes art
(イ) 良和 (6 years old), has 4 family members
(ウ) 山口先生 (55 years old), teaches Japanese
(エ) 兄 (20 years old), studies at university

(オ) 姉 (18 years old), is in high school
(カ) 弟 (11 years old), is an elementary student
(キ) 祖母 (93 years old), likes reading
(ク) 木村さんの猫 (4 years old), is a little fat

2. Introduce each of these people. Pretend you know them well. Include personal details such as where they are from, where they live, likes and dislikes, or sports or subjects they are good or bad at.

練習時間　Practice Time

1. Asking Age

Form groups of three or four. Each person should use scrap paper or a notebook to copy the form below. Ask each partner in your group his/her age. Next, pair up with someone from another group and inquire the ages of the people in that group. Continue pairing up with students from new groups until you are told to stop or you finish. You may be asked to report on your classmate's ages to the class.

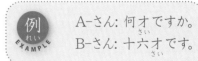

例 A-さん: 何才ですか。
B-さん: 十六才です。

自分のグループのメンバー	～才	友達のグループのメンバー	～才

2. Introducing Yourself

Copy the chart below onto a piece of scrap paper or in your notebook. Practice asking and answering the example questions, then interview/respond to six classmates, or until your 先生 says 時間です. Be prepared to report some of your findings to the class. Substitute answers for the underlined words to create responses that are true for you.

Question	Answer
A. お名前は何ですか。	ア. ユンファです。
B. 何才ですか。	イ. 十七才です。
C. 何年生ですか。	ウ. 高校二年生です。
D. お国はどちらですか。	エ. 韓国人です。
E. 何が得意ですか。	オ. サッカーが得意です。
F. 何が嫌いですか。	カ. バスケが嫌いです。

名前	何才	何年生	何人	得意な事	嫌いな事

文化箱 Culture Chest

The modern-day Japanese education system was developed during the Meiji Period (1868–1912), and it was further standardized after World War II. The national government determines the curriculum, while teachers have some freedom to develop their own teaching styles. Students attend 小学校 for six years and 中学校 for three years, for a total of nine years of compulsory education. Nearly all continue their studies in 高校 for a final three years. During 中学校 and 高校, many students also attend 塾, or cram school, in the evenings and on weekends. Students might also take off one year and attend 予備校, a preparatory school where they get their grades up before moving to the next level.

Uniforms, or 制服, are very common in 中学校 and 高校 and English language study is compulsory for nearly all students from the fifth grade on. English language (including a listening section) is one of five categories tested on nearly all college entrance exams. The focus of many students' lives in their final year of high school is studying for this exam. Japanese language (国語), social studies (社会), science (科学), and math (数学) are the other tested subjects.

After high school, students may attend 専門学校 (specialty trade/vocational schools), 短期大学 (junior colleges), or 大学. Some of the most well-known universities in Japan are 東京大学, 京都大学, 慶応大学, and 早稲田大学. Their graduates often go on to prestigious and powerful careers. Many of these schools have sister schools in other countries. Do colleges and universities in your region have study abroad programs in Japan?

地図 Map Skills

Hokkaido is the northernmost of the four major islands of Japan. Refer to the map in the back of your book and other resources to answer the questions below.

❶ What is the prefectural capital of Hokkaido?

❷ Name three cities in other parts of the world that fall within the same latitude as Hokkaido.

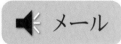 メール

This is a letter to Jun from Colin, a student at Jun's sister school in Bristol, England.

Points to consider as you read:

❶ How old is Colin? How many are in his family?

❷ Where are his parents employed?

❸ How often does Colin practice soccer?

❹ What are Colin's plans for next summer and how is he preparing for them?

❺ In the last paragraph, what is Colin talking about?

じゅん君へ

　僕の名前はコリン・ベッセルです。イギリスのブリストルにある、じゅん君の学校の姉妹校のコルストンズという学校の生徒です。初めまして！

　僕は17才で三人兄弟の長男です。*両親の名前はウィリアムとマーガレットです。妹はエリザベスで弟はマシューです。エリザベスは小学生で10才です。マシューは来年から学校に行きます。今5才です。父は銀行で*働いていて、母は僕の学校の美術の先生です。

僕の趣味はサッカーとビデオゲーム、それに読書です。テレビを見るのも好きです。サッカーは、学校のクラブでほとんど毎日放課後練習しています。

　来年の夏に日本に行くのを楽しみにしています。その為に2年間お金を*貯めています。家の近くのスーパーでアルバイトをしています。

　今年アメリカ人の女の子がホームステイをしているのですか？（ホームステイをしていると聞きました。）きっと毎日楽しい時間を過ごして、日本の事や日本語を勉強していると思います。

ではまた！
コリン

* 両親 – parents; 働いていて – is working; 貯めています – saving (money)

えーっと… 車で来ました。
Uhmm…I came by car.

1) 皆さん、静かにして下さい。

2) 起立。礼。おはようございます。着席。

3) 皆さん、今日は新しい友達がいます。こちらはベンさんとキアラさんとじゅんさんと友さんです。

4) ベン君とキアラさんはどこから来ましたか？

5) 遠い国から来ました。

6) 何で来ましたか？

7) えーっと。。。車で来ました。

8) そうですか。

9) 私は飛行機で来ました。

10) 飛行機って何ですか？

11) えーっと。。。

12) 私は四国の森から来ました。私は歩いて来ました。

13) 皆さんは何で学校に来ますか。歩いて来ますか。

14) 僕は自転車で来ます。

15) 私の家は遠いですから、電車で来ます。そして駅から学校まで歩いて来ます。

会話 Dialog
かい

(Setting: Yoshikazu has escorted the group to Ishikawa's classroom.)

1. 石川先生　：皆さん、静かにして下さい。
　　　　　　　みな　　しず

2. 生徒　　　：起立。礼。おはようございます。着席。
　　と　　　　きりつ　れい　　　　　　　　　　　ちゃくせき

3. 良和　　　：皆さん、今日は新しい友達がいます。こちらはベンさんとキアラさんとじゅんさ
　　よしかず　　みな　　　きょう　あたら
　　　　　　　んと友さんです。

4. 石川先生　：ベン君とキアラさんはどこから来ましたか？
　　　　　　　　くん

5. ベン　　　：遠い国から来ました。
　　　　　　　とお　くに

6. 生徒　　　：*何で来ましたか？
　　と　　　　なに

7. ベン　　　：えーっと…車で来ました。(thinking of a 21st century car)
　　　　　　　　　　　くるま

8. 生徒　　　：そうですか。(thinking of a contemporary 馬車 or 人力車)
　　と　　　　　　　　　　　　　　　　　　　　ばしゃ　　じんりきしゃ

9. キアラ　　：私は飛行機で来ました。
　　　　　　　　　ひこうき

10. 良和　　　：飛行機って何ですか？
　　　よしかず　ひこうき

11. じゅん　　：えーっと…(trying to avoid answering the question)

12. 友　　　　：私は四国の森から来ました。私は歩いて来ました。
　　　　　　　　　しこく　もり　　　　　　　　　ある

13. じゅん　　：皆さんは*何で学校に来ますか？歩いて来ますか。
　　　　　　　みな　　　なに　　　　　　　　ある

14. 良和　　　：僕は自転車で来ます。
　　　よしかず　ぼく　じてんしゃ

15. 生徒　　　：私の家は遠いですから、*電車で来ます。そして駅から学校まで歩いて来ます。
　　　と　　　　　　いえ　とお　　　　　でんしゃ　　　　　　えき　　　　　　　ある

*何で来ましたか？ can be replaced with どうやって来ましたか？; The first train station in Sapporo opened in 1880.

単語 New Words
たん

えき　駅 (n) – station (subway/rail)	ひこうき　飛行機 (n) – airplane	あるいてかえる　歩いて帰る (v) – return by walking (to)
きっぷ　切符 (n) – ticket	ふね　船 (n) – boat, ship	
くうこう　空港 (n) – airport	タクシー (n) – taxi	うんてん(を)する　運転(を)する (v) – drive (to)
しごと　仕事 (n) – job, occupation	バス (n) – bus	
じてんしゃ　自転車 (n) – bicycle	あるく　歩く (v) – walk (to)	のる　乗る (v) – ride (to)
じどうしゃ　自動車 (n) – car, automobile	あるいていく　歩いて行く (v) – go by walking (to)	はたらく　働く (v) – work (to)
ちかてつ　地下鉄 (n) – subway	あるいてくる　歩いて来る (v) – come by walking (to)	つとめる　勤める (v) – employed [at] (to be)
でんしゃ　電車 (n) – electric train		

漢字 Kanji

自 6 strokes	ジ, みずか(ら) – oneself, self	` ´ ` ` ⼁´ ` ` ⼌ ` ` 白 ` ` 自 ` ` 自 `
	自ら – for oneself, personally; 自動 – automatic; 自由 – freedom, liberty; 自分 – myself, yourself	
	This is an eye (目) with a small arrow pointing to it, as if to say that this is the window to the SELF.	

重 9 strokes	ジュウ, チョウ, え, おも(い), かさ(なる) – heavy, pile up	` 一 ` ` 二 ` ` 三 ` ` 盲 ` ` 盲 ` ` 盲 `
	重い – heavy, massive, serious; 重なる – to be piled up	軍 重 重
	This kanji looks similar to 車, but there are extra weights on the ends of the axles. One axle is bent under the HEAVY weights PILED UP on each end.	

動 11 strokes	ドウ, うご(く) – move, motion, change	` 一 ` ` 二 ` ` 三 ` ` 盲 ` ` 盲 ` ` 盲 `
	動く – to move; 動かす – to move (something); 動物 – animal; 運動 – exercise; 自動 – automatic	軍 重 重 動 動
	Heavy (重) is on the left, with strength (力) on the right. To MOVE heavy objects often requires great strength.	

働 13 strokes	ドウ, はたら(く) – work	` ノ ` ` イ ` ` イ ` ` イ ` ` 仁 ` ` 信 ` ` 信 `
	働く – to work; 働かせる – to put someone to work	信 俥 俥 俥 働 働
	When a person (イ) moves (動) something, it involves WORK.	

駅 14 strokes	エキ – station	` 1 ` ` ⼖ ` ` Π ` ` 厍 ` ` 厍 ` ` 馬 ` ` 馬 `
	駅 – station; 駅前 – in front of station; 駅員 – station attendant; 駅弁 – boxed lunch bought at a station	馬 馬 馬 馿 馿 馿 駅
	Here is a horse (馬) and a shaku (尺), a traditional measurement for length. Imagine traveling on horseback and trying to count the distance from STATION to STATION.	

歩 8 strokes	ボ, ブ, フ – counter for steps; ある(く) – walk	` 1 ` ` ⼞ ` ` 止 ` ` 止 ` ` 半 ` ` 歩 ` ` 歩 `
	歩く – to walk; 百歩 – 100 steps	歩
	To stop (止) is on top of "a little" (少). When you WALK, stop a little here and there to enjoy the sights.	

杯 **8 strokes**	ハイ, バイ, パイ, さかずき – wine glass, glass, counter for cupfuls	一	十	才	木	杯	杯	杯
	一 杯 – 1 cupful _{いっぱい}	杯						
	A tree (木) with the four strokes of a negative (不) looks like one tree, plus one CUPFUL that is about to overflow.							

言葉の探索 Language Detection
_{こと　ば　　たん さく}

1. **Review of previously introduced particles**
   - は – used after the sentence topic. This particle generally appears near the beginning of the sentence, and can be omitted if the topic is understood.
   - か – signifies a question when appearing at the end of a sentence
   - に – "in" or "at", denotes location where someone/thing exists
     - "at" or "on", used with specific time words
     - "to", used after the recipient of an action
   - に or へ – either of these can be used to mean "to" before a verb of motion
   - の – indicates possession (used after the name of the possessor and before the object being possessed); shows a relationship, as in 日本の着物
   - が – used after the subject; used with あります/います
     - new information marker, accentuating previously unknown or important information
     - "but", conjunction used to combine two contrasting sentences
     - used after the giver of an action or object
   - と – "and", used to connect more than one noun
     - quotation particle, used after a direct quotation
   - を – used after the direct object
   - も – "too", "also"; replaces the particles は, が, and を
   - でも – "but", "however"; comes at the beginning of a sentence
   - で – by means of, marks the "tool" used to do something
     - for, used when shopping or ordering food
     - used after the place of action when used with a transitive (action) verb
   - から – "from"; used with specific facts (locations, times, etc.)
   - まで – "until"; used with specific facts (locations, times, etc.)

2. **Using the particle で**
   Three uses of the particle で have been previously introduced. The particle で can be used:

   A) after the "tool" used for an action (that is, the means by which an action is done). The "tool" can be the mode of transportation (自転車で, バスで, etc.), the method through which something is communicated (英語で, 日本語で, メールで, 電話で), or a tool by means of which something is
   _{じ てんしゃ}　_{でん わ}

accomplished (コンピューターで, 鉛筆で, ペンで).

B) to indicate the place where some action takes place (図書館で勉強しました).

C) when shopping or ordering food, use で to refer to the "total" of more than one item (ハンバーガー二つで３００円です。).

3. **Using "means of transportation" particles に, で, and を**
   Note that each of these particles has a specific and distinct usage:

   A) に – To state that you "ride/rode" (in) something such as a bus, car, etc., use the particle に. For example, バスに乗ります – I ride the/a bus.

   B) で – To state that you traveled by means of a vehicle, such as a bus, use the particle で. For example, バスで行きます – I go by bus.

   C) を – In the example バスを運転しました, the bus is the direct object, receiving the action of the verb "driving." – I drove the bus.

自習 Self Check

1. Identify the function of each word (topic, subject, verb, etc.) and then insert the correct particle in each blank, according to the English translation. Use X if no particle is necessary.

   A) 七時半 ___ 妹 ___ 私 ___ 学校 ___ 車 ___ 来ます。
      = At 7:30 my little sister and I come to school by car.

   B) 友子さん ___ 猫 ___ ミルク ___ 飲んでいます。 = Tomoko's cat is drinking milk.

   C) こちら ___ ベン君 ___ キアラさん ___ じゅん君 ___ 友さんです。
      = They are Ben, Kiara, Jun, and Tomo.

   D) 四時ごろ ___ 私達 ___ 電車 ___ 帰ります。 = About 4:00, we will return home by train.

2. Use the orders and menu prices below to restate the order and say how much each item will cost. Remember to use で after quantities and after the order is placed, before the price is given. Use と between items (after the counters if applicable).

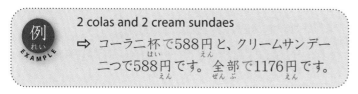

例 EXAMPLE 2 colas and 2 cream sundaes
⇒ コーラ二杯で588円と、クリームサンデー二つで588円です。 全部で1176円です。

   A) 2 coffee floats

   B) 3 colas and 2 chocolate sundaes

   C) 1 ice coffee, 1 lemon squash, and 2 coffee floats

   D) 2 ice coffees, 1 cream sundae, and 1 blueberry sundae

練習時間 Practice Time
れんしゅう

1. Pair Practice

Take turns making sentences using the cues. Be careful to choose the correct particle. The first one is done for you.

ア)

(Hiroko) + (bus) + (Himeji) + (hamburger)

博子さんはバスで姫路へ行って、ハンバーガーを食べました。
ひろこ　　　　　　　ひめじ

イ)

(Akiko) + (festival) + (fishing) + (takoyaki)

ウ)

(mother and child 親子) + (swim) + (see the ocean) + (ride a boat)
おや

エ)

(Yuusuke) + (ride Shinkansen) + (Tokyo) + (eat tempura)

オ)

(Hiro) + (ride a bicycle) + (go to school) + (read a book at the library)

2. Pair Practice

Take turns filling in the missing particles in the following sentences: if a particle should go in the blank, add it. Make sure that the Japanese matches the English. Then, with your partner, create four more sentences that contain at least four particles each. Leave blanks for each particle, and exchange your newly created sentences with another group, to fill in.

A) 先生＿＿＿＿鉛筆＿＿＿＿書いて下さい＿＿＿＿言いました。 ＝ The teacher said, "Please write in pencil."

B) 私＿＿＿＿家＿＿＿＿学校＿＿＿＿遠いです＿＿＿、電車＿＿＿＿来ます。
   ＝ Because my house is far from school, I come by train.

C) パーティー＿＿＿＿どこ＿＿＿＿やりますか。私＿＿＿＿家＿＿＿＿しますよ。 ＝ Where is the party? It's going to be at my house, you know.

3. Group Practice

As a class, create a menu. Include at least four Japanese foods and drinks as well as their prices. In groups, stand in two lines facing each other. お客さん is a customer, and 店員 is the waiter/waitress. Use your menu and the dialog below as a model. Be sure to practice counters for cupfuls (杯), objects (個), bottles (本), and generic counters (一つ、二つ、三つ, etc.). Remember to use the particle で for more than one item.

例 EXAMPLE

店員　　　：　いらっしゃいませ。
　　　　　　　何にしますか。
お客さん　：　ええと、コーラ一つとハンバーガー二つにします。
店員　　　：　コーラは一つ２００円、ハンバーガーは二つで４００円です。
　　　　　　　全部で６００円です。

文化箱 Culture Chest

Rail Travel

Japan has a wide range of rail options for travel. There are 地下鉄 (subway lines), and 普通列車 (local), and 特急列車 (express commuter trains) for those traveling longer distances, as well as the famous 新幹線 (bullet train lines), that speedily deliver passengers throughout the country. Faster and faster 新幹線 lines and others are being built all the time.

　　　Traveling to and within 北海道 by rail can be enjoyable, even though its distances can take a relatively long time to cover. The island of 北海道 seems vast in comparison to the other islands of Japan. Japanese often think of the island, with its extensive farmlands, as being as spacious as the plains of the United States. 北海道 also boasts large mountains and grand sea vistas. Many travelers see these landscapes as a sharp contrast to other parts of Japan, which can be quite intimate in scale.

After choosing your destination, ask the staff at the rail station for the best way to travel there, and for your ticket. (Or, until you actually go to Japan, try searching online for video footage of Japanese train ticket purchasing, to watch clerks complete "your" ticket purchase. Their skill at using their particular computer terminals is quite impressive!)

Using your Japanese language skills to communicate your travel needs is of course the best way to get what you want. Here are a few phrases to get you started on your trip:

_____ にXからYまで行きたいです。 = I would like to go from X to Y at _____.
　　date and time　　　　　　　　　　　　　　　　　　　　　　　　　　　　　　　　　　　　　date and time

_____ から _____ まで、どのぐらいかかりますか。
　　place name 1　　　　　place name 2
= How long does it take to travel from _____ to _____?
　　　　　　　　　　　　　　　　　　　　　　　place name 1　　　　　　place name 2

切符はいくらですか。 = How much is the ticket?
きっぷ

地図 Map Skills
ちず

Study the map and charts. Then use them to answer the following questions:

❶ What time does the earliest train leave 札幌 for 函館?
　　　　　　　　　　　　　　　　　　　　　さっぽろ　　　はこだて

❷ What is the latest you could arrive in 函館 according to this schedule?
　　はこだて

❸ If you ride the 特急 スーパー北斗 10号, what time will you arrive in 函館? How long will the trip take?
　　とっきゅう　　　　　ほくと　ごう　　　　　　　　　　　　　　はこだて

❹ Why do you think that the 特急 スーパー北斗8号 does not stop in 室蘭?
　　　　　　　　　　　　　とっきゅう　ごう　　　　　　　　　　むろらん

❺ How much would the ticket be from 札幌 to 東室蘭?
　　　　　　　　　　　　　　　　　　さっぽろ　ひがしむろらん

❻ Train service in 北海道 began in the 1880s. List several ways you think goods and people were transported to, from, and around 北海道 before that time.

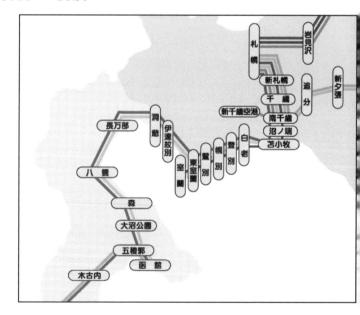

	特急スーパー 北斗8号 とっきゅう　ほくと　ごう	特急すずらん 2号 とっきゅう　ごう	特急スーパー 北斗10号 とっきゅう　ほくと　ごう	特急スーパー 北斗12号 とっきゅう　ほくと　ごう
札幌 さっぽろ	9:19	9:51	10:37	12:22
南千歳 みなみちとせ	9:47	10:24	11:05	12:48
苫小牧 とまこまい	10:03	10:41	11:20	13:04
白老 しらおい	10:12			13:12
登別 のぼりべつ	10:25	11:08	11:42	13:25
東室蘭 ひがしむろらん	10:38	11:23	11:53	13:37
室蘭 むろらん	・	11:36	・	・
長万部 おしゃまんべ	11:04	…	12:15	14:00
大沼公園 おおぬまこうえん	11:30	…	12:39	・
五稜郭 ごりょうかく	12:10	…	・	・
函館 はこだて	12:49	…	13:50	15:31

NOTE▶ The numbers in the body of this chart are times.

円 えん										
札幌 さっぽろ	260	290	320	350	400	420	460	510	520	550
南千歳 みなみちとせ		260	290	320	370	390	430	480	490	520
苫小牧 とまこまい			250	280	330	350	390	440	450	480
白老 しらおい				260	310	330	370	410	420	450
登別 のぼりべつ					280	300	340	390	400	430
東室蘭 ひがしむろらん						260	300	350	360	390
室蘭 むろらん							260	310	320	350
長万部 おしゃまんべ								270	280	310
大沼公園 おおぬまこうえん									250	280
五稜郭 ごりょうかく										250
函館 はこだて										
	南千歳 みなみちとせ	苫小牧 とまこまい	白老 しらおい	登別 のぼりべつ	東室蘭 ひがしむろらん	室蘭 むろらん	長万部 おしゃまんべ	大沼公園 おおぬまこうえん	五稜郭 ごりょうかく	函館 はこだて

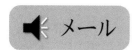

This letter to Ben is from an Ainu friend, talking about where he lives and how he gets to school.
Points to consider as you read:

❶ What is Masato's living situation?

❷ List three ways students at Masato's school commute to school.

❸ What might Masato do during his free time in the summer and then in the winter?

ベンさんへ

　私は北海道の札幌市の高校に*通っています。私はアイヌ人で、父と母は遠くに住んでいます。だから、学校の近くの寮に住んでいます。週末は、父と母の住む二風谷町に帰ります。札幌から二風谷までは電車で帰ります。四時間ぐらいかかります。

　私達は寮から学校に歩いて通いますが、バスや地下鉄で*通う生徒もいます。友達の一人は電車で一時間以上もかけて学校に通っています。

　休み時間は友達と皆で遊びます。夏には、海へ行ったり、冬には*雪合戦をしたりします。

　ベンさんは、どこに住んでいますか?学校へはどうやって通っていますか?

　返事を待っています。

正人より

* 通う – to commute; 寮 – dormitory; 雪合戦 – snowball fight

先生は短歌を書くのが好きで、昨日短歌を書いて、新聞社に送りました。

Since the teacher likes writing tanka, yesterday he wrote a tanka and sent it to the newspaper.

1) 良和君の趣味は何ですか？

2) 俳句を作る事です。先生は短歌を書くのが好きで、昨日短歌を書いて、新聞社に送りました。

3) すごい！

4) そして毎日公園に行って野球をします。

5) 私の趣味は雑誌を読む事です。毎月「子供の国」を買って読みます。

6) 私も読書が好きです。

7) 僕の祖父はアイヌです。祖父は木で熊の像を作って売っています。僕はアイヌの昔話と歌を聞く事が好きです。好きな昔話は「カムイ」です。

8) 「カムイ」はアイヌ語で「神様」ですよ。

9) 僕は「カムイ」のビデオゲームを持っています！

会話 Dialog

(Setting: Talking to Yoshikazu and some of his friends after school.)

1. じゅん　　　：　良和君の趣味は何ですか？

2. 良和　　　　：　俳句を作る事です。先生は短歌を書くのが好きで、昨日短歌を書いて、新聞社に送りました。

3. ベン　　　　：　すごい！

4. 良和　　　　：　そして毎日公園に行って野球をします。

5. 女子生徒　　：　私の趣味は雑誌を読む事です。毎月「子供の国」を買って読みます。

6. キアラ　　　：　私も読書が好きです。

7. 男子生徒　　：　僕の祖父はアイヌです。祖父は木で熊の像を作って売っています。僕はアイヌの昔話と歌を聞く事が好きです。好きな昔話は「カムイ」です。

8. 友　　　　　：　「カムイ」はアイヌ語で「神様」ですよ。

9. ベン　　　　：　(Whispers to Kiara) 僕は「カムイ」のビデオゲームを持っています！

単語 New Words

あいぬ　アイヌ (n) – peoples indigenous to Hokkaido, Sakhalin, and the Kuril Islands

いのしし　猪 (n) – wild boar

うさぎ　兎 (n) – rabbit

かみ　神 (n) – God

かみさま　神様 (n) – God, god, spirit

くに　国 (n) – country

くま　熊 (n) – bear

こうえん　公園 (n) – park

こども　子供 (n) – child

さる　猿 (n) – monkey

ざっし　雑誌 (n) – magazine

しんぶん　新聞 (n) – newspaper

とら　虎 (n) – tiger

ぶた　豚 (n) – pig

へび　蛇 (n) – snake

むかしばなし　昔話 (n) – folktale

りゅう　龍 (n) – dragon

うし　牛 (n) – cow

すごい　い (adj.) – terrible, amazing, wonderful

〜さま　〜様 (suffix) – polite suffix for Mr., Miss, or Mrs. when writing letters

ちょうだい(する) 頂戴(する) (v) – receive (to), be given (to)

漢字 Kanji

	ドク, よ(む) – read	`	二	三	言	言	言	言
読	読む – to read; 読書 – reading (n) よ　　　　　　　どくしょ	言	計	訃	訃	詩	詩	読
14 strokes	Speech (言) is important to sell (売) things, but before many could READ, town criers had to READ out loud the news they would "sell" to listeners.							

	ベン, つと(める) – exertion	ノ	ク	々	么	各	各	免
勉	勉強 – to study べんきょう	免	勉	勉				
10 strokes	An 8-stroke character that means to avoid (免) is next to power (力). You must EXERT yourself to study (勉強) some things that you would rather avoid.							

言葉の探索 Language Detection
ことば　　たんさく

1. **Review of the て-form for sequential actions**

   When listing a series of actions, use the て-form to link the verb phrases. The tense of the final verb determines the tense of the entire sentence.

> 朝、シャワーを浴びて、朝ご飯を食べて、学校に来て、友達と話して、先生に
> あさ　　　　　あ　　　　あさ　はん
> 「おはようございます。」と言って、漢字をちょっと練習して、本を読んで、
> 　　　　　　　　　　　は　　　　かんじ　　　　　れんしゅう　　　　よ
> 日本語のクラスに来ました。
>
> In the morning I took a shower, ate breakfast, came to school, talked with friends, said "Good morning" to the teacher, practiced kanji a little, read a book, and came to Japanese class.

自習 Self Check
じしゅう

Practice combining these separate actions into one sentence. Remember that the final verb determines the tense of the entire sentence.

A) 友達と話しました。テレビを見ました。晩ご飯を食べました。
　　　　　　　　　　　　　　　　　　　　　　　ばん　はん

B) お水を飲みました。兄にメールを送りました。寝ました。
　　　　の　　　　　　　　　　　　　おく　　　　ね

C) テニスを練習します。家へ帰ります。音楽を聞きます。宿題をします。
　　　　れんしゅう　　　うち　かえ　　　おんがく　　　　しゅくだい

練習時間 Practice Time

In small groups, create the longest sentence you can, trying to outdo your classmates in terms of interest and quality. Be sure to include a time expression, direct objects followed by the particle を, and several different verbs in the て-form showing a variety of successive actions. Share your sentence with the class.

地図 Map Skills

Though the perception of Japan is that it is small, the country is actually made up of almost 7,000 islands. Geographically, the total area of Japan is just slightly smaller than that of California. Japan is one-third larger than New Zealand, and more than double the size of England. The islands of Japan are extremely diverse in climate, including everything from a cold, wintery climate in the north to tropical, palm-covered islands in the south. Look at a map of East Asia. Can you find the Japanese islands that are on the extreme edges of the country? Some of these islands lie close to other countries; some are even claimed by both Japan and its neighbors. Locate several such islands, and then find 2 or 3 facts about them to report to your class.

文化箱 Culture Chest

Ainu Culture

The Ainu were the earliest known inhabitants of the island of Hokkaido, or Ezo (蝦夷), as it was known in Japanese. The Ainu are a race distinct from the Japanese. Hokkaido was formally annexed by the Japanese government in 1868 through a policy of advancement into the northern island. Newcomers pushed westward, displacing Ainu at roughly the same time as First Nations' peoples of the United States, Canada, and Australia were displaced or assimilated. The distinct language and culture of the Ainu barely survived total assimilation.

A recent surge of interest in traditional Ainu culture has helped to save much of what was nearly lost forever. Evidence of this resurgence can be seen in the founding of schools to teach the Ainu language, and cultural museums and centers devoted to the preservation of Ainu culture.

As with many other First Nations' peoples, the Ainu had no written language. For centuries, they maintained their cultural heritage through traditional oral tales known as yukar, or epic stories. These were passed down from generation to generation, chanted by both men and women to the accompaniment of beating sticks. Many of these stories involve カムイ, or "spirits." The Ainu people believed that the world rested on the back of a fish. Can you imagine what the Ainu would say was the source of earthquakes?

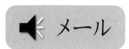 メール

This is a letter to Jun, from his cousin Yuriko, who visited Hokkaido on her school trip.

Points to consider as you read:

❶ When did Yuriko travel to Hokkaido?

❷ What did Yuriko do after she studied Ainu culture according to her letter?

❸ What does Yuriko want Jun to do?

じゅん君へ

　今北海道にいるそうですね。

　私も去年、修学旅行で北海道に行きました。札幌の他に北海道*開拓の村へバスで行きました。開拓の村では*19世紀から20世紀の北海道の*暮らしやアイヌの人のことを勉強して、学校新聞に書きました。

　じゅん君もアイヌの文化を勉強していますか。良かったら、私の学校の新聞を読んで下さい。面白いかもしれません。また、じゅん君が東京に帰ってから、アイヌについて話しましょう。

じゃまたね。

由理子　より

* 開拓の村 – pioneer village; 19世紀 – 19th century; 暮らし – living, livelihood

1.3 Since the teacher likes writing tanka, yesterday he wrote a tanka and sent it to the newspaper.　41

今は家族皆函館に住んでいます。
かぞくみんなはこだて　す
Now my family lives in Hakodate.

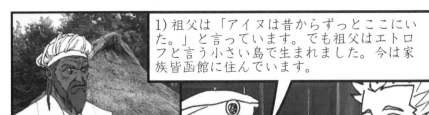

1) 祖父は「アイヌは昔からずっとここにいた。」と言っています。でも祖父はエトロフと言う小さい島で生まれました。今は家族皆函館に住んでいます。

3) 僕は1886年2月20日に岩手で生まれました。戌年生まれです。岩手は平泉で有名です。弁慶が亡くなった町です。

2) 僕はオーストラリアのメルボルンで生まれました。でも、今はシドニーに住んでいます。祖父はイギリスのマンチェスターで生まれました。

4) 僕は四国の高知で生まれました。坂本龍馬も高知で生まれて、そこに住んでいました。坂本龍馬は未年生まれです。

5) 私は青森で生まれて、父と母と兄と一緒に函館に来ました。誕生日は7月7日です。青森はねぶた祭りで有名です。

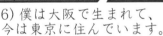

6) 僕は大阪で生まれて、今は東京に住んでいます。

7) 大阪には美味しい食べ物がたくさんありますね。

8) キアラさんはどこで生まれましたか？

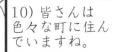

9) 私はサンフランシスコで生まれました。でも、今はシカゴに住んでいます。

10) 皆さんは色々な町に住んでいますね。

会話 Dialog

(Setting: A group of children listens patiently to the other students talking about where their families come from.)

1. 男子生徒 ：祖父は「アイヌは 昔 からずっとここにいた。」と言っています。でも祖父は*エト ロフと言う小さい 島で生まれました。今は家族皆函館に住んでいます。

2. ベン ：僕はオーストラリアのメルボルンで 生まれました。でも、今はシドニーに住んでい ます。祖父はイギリスのマンチェスターで生まれました。

3. 良和 ：僕は1886年2月20日に岩手で生まれました。戌年生まれです。岩手は平 泉 で有名です。弁慶が亡くなった町です。

4. 友 ：僕は四国の高知で生まれました。坂本龍馬も高知で生まれて、そこに住ん でいました。坂本龍馬は未年生まれです。

5. 女子生徒 ：私は青森で生まれて、父と母と兄と一緒に函館に来ました。誕生日は 7月7日です。青森はねぶた祭りで有名です。

6. じゅん ：僕は大阪で 生まれて、今は東京に住んでいます。

7. 友 ：大阪には美味しい食べ物がたくさんありますね。

8. 良和 ：キアラさんはどこで生まれましたか?

9. キアラ ：私はサンフランシスコで生まれました。でも、今はシカゴに住んでいます。

10. 良和 ：皆さんは色々な町に住んでいますね。

*エトロフ – one of the Kuril Islands

単語 New Words

いぬどし 犬年 or 戌年 (n) – n year of the dog

ひつじどし 羊年 or 未年 (n) – year of the sheep

まち 町 (n) – town, city block
むら 村 (n) – village
とかい 都会 (n) – city

漢字 Kanji

王 4 strokes	オウ, 〜ノウ – king, ruler, magnate	一	丁	干	王		
	王様 – king; 女王 – queen; 王手 – checkmate おうさま／じょおう／おうて						
	The three horizontal strokes here are three steps of power up to the KING's throne.						

主 5 strokes	シュ – lord, chief, master	`	二	亍	主	主	
	主人 – head (of a household); 家主 – landlord しゅじん／やぬし						
	The dot on top of the hat of a king (王) signifies that this person is not a king, but the LORD or MASTER of a smaller piece of property or land rather than a large kingdom (国).						

住 7 strokes	ジュウ, す(む) – dwell, reside, live	ノ	イ	亻	仁	行	
	住みます – to live (in a place); お住まい – dwelling, house; すむ 住吉 – a district of Osaka; 住所 – address すみよし／じゅうしょ	住	住				
	A person stands (亻) next to his/her master/landlord (主). Attendants usually RESIDE close to their master, but could not LIVE close to the king (王).						

田 5 strokes	デン, た – rice field, field	丨	冂	冂	田	田	
	田んぼ – paddy field, farm; 田舎 – rural area, countryside; た／いなか 田園– country(side), rural district; 秋田犬 – Akita (breed of でんえん／あきたけん dog)						
	When viewed from above this character looks like a FIELD (田).						

町 7 strokes	チョウ, まち – town, village, block	丨	冂	冂	田	田	田
	町 – town; 田和町 – Tawa Town; 下町 – まち／たわちょう／したまち shitamachi, lower-lying or traditional section of a town, downtown	町					
	A rice field (田) sits on the corner of a TOWN or ward (丁). Small TOWNS and VILLAGES in Japan often have rice fields within their boundaries.						

言葉の探索 Language Detection

1. **Review and differentiation of location particles dealing with places: に/へ for location, で for place of action.**

   - Verbs of existence – に shows where something exists (sleeps, resides, etc.).
   - Verbs of motion (go/come/return) – に is generally used if going/coming/returning to a place for a purpose; へ is generally used though if the verb is simply going/coming/returning.
   - Action verbs – で follows the place of action.

   Read the following examples carefully, noting the use of particles に, へ, and で.

A) 花子さんは京都に住んでいます。	= Hanako lives in Kyoto.
B) 絵里子さんは学校に (or へ) 行きます。	= Eriko goes to school. -or- Eriko is going to school.
C) 私は家に (or へ) 帰ります。	= I return home. -or- I am returning home.
D) 友子さんは京都で生まれました。	= Tomoko was born in Kyoto.
E) 絵里子さんは昼ご飯を学校で食べました。	= Eriko ate lunch at school.
F) 私は家で母を手伝います。	= I help my mother at home.
G) 鉛筆はテーブルの上にあります。	= The pencil is on the table.

2. **Action verb + ています – is doing (an action)**

   To say that someone "is doing" something (the present progressive tense), use the て-form of the verb followed by います.

A) まいさんは数学を勉強しています。	= Mai is studying math.
B) 豊君は朝ご飯を食べています。	= Yutaka is eating breakfast.
C) 花子さんはケーキを作っています。	= Hanako is making a cake.
D) 先生は面白い本を読んでいます。	= The teacher is reading an interesting book.
E) 父は車を運転しています。	= Father is driving a car.

自習 Self Check

Fill in the correct particle for each blank below. Note that there may be multiple answers.

(ア) 七月＿母＿函館＿行きました。

(イ) 長崎＿住んでいますか。

(ウ) 今体育館＿います。

(エ) 図書館＿本＿読んでいます。

(オ) 妹＿小学校＿います。

(カ) 筆＿机＿上＿あります。

(キ) ロンドン＿＿生まれましたか。

練習時間 Practice Time
れん しゅう

1. Information gap activity.

A-さん looks at the pictures in chart A while B-さん looks at the pictures in chart B. Take turns asking and answering questions about what each person in the bottom row of your chart is doing.

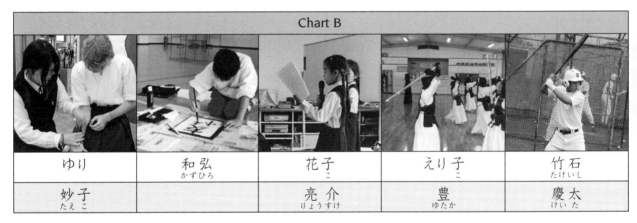

Chart A				
妙子 たえこ	亮介 りょうすけ	アシュリー	豊 ゆたか	慶太 けいた
ゆり	和弘 かずひろ	えり子 こ	花子 はなこ	竹石 たけいし

Chart B				
ゆり	和弘 かずひろ	花子 こ	えり子 こ	竹石 たけいし
妙子 たえこ		亮介 りょうすけ	豊 ゆたか	慶太 けいた

地図 Map Skills
ち ず

Japan is officially divided into eight regions, all of which are then separated into prefectures except for Hokkaido and Okinawa. Refer to the map on the inside cover of your text and state which regions the following cities are located in.

1. Sapporo
2. Kanazawa
3. Nagoya
4. Takamatsu
5. Nagasaki
6. Hiroshima
7. Kyoto
8. Sendai
9. Tokyo
10. Fukuoka
11. Osaka
12. Yokohama
13. Hiraizumi
14. Naha
15. Akita
16. Nagano
17. Nara

What's Your Zodiac Sign?

1) **Birth year:** When you ask someone's birth year in Japanese, you can say 何年生まれですか. To ask
なんねん う
what day they were born, say either 誕生日はいつですか (When is your birthday?) or 誕生日は
たんじょう び   たんじょう び
何月何日ですか (What date is your birthday?). If you are stating your entire birth date, remember to
がつ にち
start with the year (the largest unit of time) and work back to the day (the smallest unit of time). For instance, if you were born March 31, 1990, you would say 誕生日は1990年3月31日です.
たんじょう び

2) 十二支 (the Zodiac): The Japanese borrowed the traditional 12-year zodiac calendar from the Chinese.
し
These animals appear often on calendars, in almanacs, and are used to ask someone their birth year (
何年ですか。– What zodiac year are you?). The chart below lists both the traditional and modern kanji
なにどし
used for the twelve animals. Note that different kanji are used for each animal sign (丑 for 牛, for ex-
うし
ample). The first kanji of each pair is the traditional kanji used specifically when referring to the zodiac
animal. The second kanji in the list is used to talk about the animal as you might see it in the wild, on
a farm, or as a pet. Certain personality traits are said to be associated with certain animals. Find your
own animal. Then ask your partner 何年ですか.
なにどし

十二支 し (the Zodiac)	Trad. and Modern Character	Characteristics/Traits	Year
	子/鼠 ね ねずみ	Year of the rat/mouse people are charming and ambitious, witty, have excellent observation skills, and are honest. 子年生まれの人は、魅力的で、野心家。利口で、優れた観察力を持っていて、正直である。	1960, 1972, 1984, 1996, 2008
	丑/牛 うし うし	Year of the bull/cow people are patient, skillful, strong-willed, healthy, and dependable. 丑年生まれの人は、我慢強く、器用で、強い意志を持っている。また、健康で、信頼できる。	1961, 1973, 1985, 1997, 2009
	寅/虎 とら とら	Year of the tiger people are courageous, sensitive. They are often leaders who enjoy a challenge. 寅年生まれの人は、勇気があり、神経質。チャレンジを好むのでリーダーになりやすい。	1962, 1974, 1986, 1998, 2010
	卯/兎 う うさぎ	Year of the rabbit people are ambitious, talented, and friendly. They are often seen as stylish. 卯年生まれの人は、野心家で、才能があり、友好的。よく流行の最先端を行く。	1963, 1975, 1987, 1999, 2011

十二支し (the Zodiac)	Trad. and Modern Character	Characteristics/Traits	Year
	辰／龍 たつ りゅう	Year of the dragon people are brave, energetic, and passionate. They are risk takers and hard working. 辰年生まれの人は、勇敢で、活発で、情熱的である。危険を恐れず、勤勉である。	1964, 1976, 1988, 2000, 2012
	巳／蛇 み へび	Year of the snake people are determined and deep thinkers. They are very analytical and can be materialistic. 巳年生まれの人は、決意が固く、思慮深い。分析的で、実利主義である。	1965, 1977, 1989, 2001, 2013
	午／馬 うま うま	Year of the horse people are wise, skillful, and outgoing. They are often humorous and gregarious. 午年生まれの人は、賢明で、器用で、外交的である。ユーモアがあり、社交的である。	1966, 1978, 1990, 2002, 2014
	未／羊 ひつじ ひつじ	Year of the sheep people are passionate, elegant, and calm. They can be quiet and reserved. 未年生まれの人は、情熱的で、気品があり、おだやかである。また、無口で、控え目である。	1967, 1979, 1991, 2003, 2015
	申／猿 さる さる	Year of the monkey people can be clever and curious, smart and good at practical jokes. They often have active lifestyles. 申年生まれの人は、いたずら好きだが、利口で好奇心旺盛である。活発な生活を好む。	1968, 1980, 1992, 2004, 2016
	酉／鳥 とり とり	Year of the rooster/cock people are devoted, deep thinkers, and trustworthy. They are often opinionated and enjoy being the center of attention. 酉年生まれの人は、献身的で、思慮深く、信頼できる。頑固で、注目の的になりたがる。	1969, 1981, 1993, 2005, 2017
	戌／犬 いぬ いぬ	Year of the dog people are loyal and honest. They can be very determined and stubborn though extremely ethical. 戌年生まれの人は、忠実で、正直。善悪に対して敏感。非常に意志が強く、頑固である。	1970, 1982, 1994, 2006, 2018
	亥／猪 い いのしし	Year of the boar/pig people are brave and affectionate. They also enjoy spending money. 亥年生まれの人は、勇敢で、情が深い。浪費家でもある。	1971, 1983, 1995, 2007, 2019

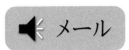 メール

This is a letter to Tomo from his nephew Shirou, who lives on Sado-jima in the Sea of Japan. Shirou heard a story at his school, Sado-jima Kita Tanuki Preschool, and retells it here. The story is about the 12 zodiac animals and how they came to be listed in the order they are.

Points to consider as you read:

❶ What animal reached the Buddha first?

❷ Which animals was the rooster between?

❸ This story is about the zodiac animals. It is also about something else that happens every month. What is that?

❹ Did you find it easy to read this message? Explain any difference in readability you experience between previous messages and this one.

ともおじさんへ

　しろうです。こんにちは、ほいくえんでおもしろいはなしをきいたよ。ぼくは2006ねんにうまれたので、いぬどしにうまれたの。

　ぜんぶで12のどうぶつがいるんだよ。

　この12のどうぶつは*おしゃかさまにあいにいった*じゅんにきまったんだって。

　うしははやくいったけど、足がおそかったから、うしの*せなかにのっていたねずみがいちばんについたの。

　にわとりは、*なかのわるいさると犬をべつべつにするために、さるといぬのあいだに*入ってるんだよ。

　ねこは、ねずみにいつおしゃかさまのところにいくかきいたけど、*うそをいってねこは入れなかったんだよ。でもそのあと、ねこはねずみを*おいかけるようになったんだって。

　13ばんめについた*いたちをかわいそうにおもったおしゃかさまは、まいつきのさいしょのひを「ついたち」とよぶことにしたんだ。

ね、おもしろいでしょ？

しろう

---

* おしゃかさま – Buddha; じゅん – in order (taken from 順番 – in order); せなか – back (bone); なかのわるい – unfriendly; おいかける – to have chased after, pursued; いたち – weasel

いいえ、船でオホーツク海に行ってかにを食べましょう。

No, let's go to the Okhotsk Sea by boat to eat crab.

会話 Dialog
かい

(Setting: The characters are traveling to Sapporo on a 馬車鉄道. They come upon what they call a
　　　　　　　　　　　　　　　　　　　　　　　　　　　ば しゃてつどう
Snow Festival.) (Note that while the Snow Festival as we know it today did not start officially until the
1930s, children and adults enjoyed playing in the snow long before this.)

1. 友　　　：お腹が空きました。本当にペコペコです。今何時ですか？教えて下さい。
　　　　　　　なか　す　　　　　　　ほんとう　　　　　　　　　　　　　　　　　おし

2. キアラ　：えーっと。あそこに白い大きい*時計がありますね。昼の十二時ですよ。
　　　　　　　　　　　　　　　しろ　　　　とけい　　　　　　ひる

3. 良和　　：あれは札幌*時計台です。
　　よしかず　　　　　　　さっぽろ　とけいだい

4. ベン　　：(using cell phone) 皆の写真を撮ります。はい、チーズ！皆の後ろに時計台があり
　　　　　　　　　　　　　　　　みんな　しゃしん　と　　　　　　　　　　　みんな　うし
　　　　　　　ます。

5. キアラ　：あ、見て下さい。小学生が雪でお城を作っています。雪祭りですね。
　　　　　　　　　　　　　　　　ゆき　しろ　つく　　　　　　　ゆきまつ

6. 友　　　：雪は美味しくないです。昼ご飯は札幌ラーメンを食べて牛乳を飲んで、昼寝
　　　　　　　ゆき　お　い　　　　　　ひる　はん　さっぽろ　　　　　　　　　ぎゅうにゅう　　　　　　ひる ね
　　　　　　　をしましょう。

7. じゅん　：いいえ、船で*オホーツク海に行ってかにを食べましょう。
　　　　　　　　　　　ふね　　　　　　　かい

8. ベン　　：海は寒いです。札幌の近くに登別温泉があります。スノーボードをしてから、
　　　　　　　うみ　さむ　　　さっぽろ　ちか　のぼりべつおんせん
　　　　　　　温泉に入りませんか。
　　　　　　　おんせん　はい

9. 友　　　：はい、はい。でも、皆さん、もうすぐ、神社の時の門に入りますよ。
　　　　　　　　　　　　　　　みな　　　　　　　　　　　　　　　　　　はい

10. 良和　　：残念ですね。じゃあ、函館八幡宮に帰りましょう。これはプレゼントの俳句です。
　　よしかず　ざんねん　　　　　はこだてはちまんぐう　　　　　　　　　　　　　　　　はいく
　　　　　　　「白雪の　新しい友　森神社」。
　　　　　　　しらゆき　あたら　とも　もりじんじゃ

11. キアラ　：ありがとう。うわあ、きれいに書きましたね。

12. 良和　　：どういたしまして。僕は書道を習っているんです。じゃ、さようなら。元気で！
　　よしかず　　　　　　　　　　ぼく　しょどう　なら

*時計 – clock, watch; 時計台 – clock tower; オホーツク海 – Sea of Okhotsk
　とけい　　　　　とけいだい　　　　　　　　　　かい

単語 New Words
たん

うしろ 後ろ (n) – behind, back	プレゼント (n) – present, gift
うでどけい 腕時計 (n) – wristwatch	(お)げんきで (お)元気で (exp.) – take care, go in good health
おんせん 温泉 (n) – hot spring	おしえる 教える (v) – teach (to), tell/inform (to)
ぎゅうにゅう 牛乳 (n) – milk	すく 空く (v) – empty (to become)
しょどう 書道 (n) – calligraphy	ならう 習う (v) – learn (to)
とけい 時計 (n) – clock, watch	スノーボード(を)する (v) – snowboard (to)

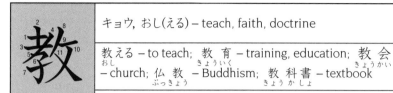

漢字 Kanji

教	キョウ, おし(える) – teach, faith, doctrine	一	十	土	耂	耂	孝
	教える – to teach; 教育 – training, education; 教会 – church; 仏教 – Buddhism; 教科書 – textbook	孝	孝	孝	教	教	
11 strokes	On the left, earth (土) is crossed by a line that reaches down to the child (子), in order to TEACH that child about the importance of the earth.						

習	シュウ, なら(う) – learn	フ	ヲ	ヲ	羽	羽	羽
	習う – to learn; 学習 – study, learning, tutorial; 自習 – self-study; 練習 – practice	羽	羽	習	習	習	
11 strokes	Here, feathers or wings (羽) sit over white (白). Birds LEARN to keep their feathers clean and white so they can succeed in flying high.						

入	ニュウ, い(れる), はい(る) – enter, insert	ノ	入				
	入る – to enter; 入れる – to insert, put in; 入り口 – entrance; 入学試験 – school entrance exam						
2 strokes	A person (人) sometimes has to ENTER a room backwards if it is a small doorway.						

出	シュツ, で(る), だ(す) – to appear, emerge; to pull out, stick out	丨	屮	中	出	出	
	出して下さい – please take out; 出口 – exit						
5 strokes	This kanji is made up of an open enclosure (凵) leaping OUT or EMERGING from the very tall mountain (山) below.						

言葉の探索 Language Detection

1. **食べましょう "let's eat"**

   In *Beginning Japanese* Chapter 10, you learned how to use the verb form でしょう – will probably/is probably. The ending 〜ましょう is conjugated the same way; however, when used with a 〜ます verb, it suggests "let's do" such and such. 食べましょう – let's eat and 行きましょう – let's go are examples. Adding the question particle か softens the meaning to "shall we?"

	A)	行きます	⇨	行きましょう	= let's go
	B)	乗ります の	⇨	乗りましょう の	= let's ride (a vehicle)
	C)	見ます	⇨	見ましょう	= let's watch/look

2. Verb Review

You have studied many verbs in *Beginning Japanese*, and might even be keeping your own verb list. You have also learned a number of conjugations, which are listed in the verb chart in the Appendix. Basic verb forms you have learned thus far include these.

Form	Conjugation/Tense	English Meaning
〜ます (present/future)	食べます	eat; will eat
〜ません (negative)	食べません	does not eat; will not eat
〜ました (past)	食べました	ate
〜ませんでした (negative past)	食べませんでした	did not eat
〜て-form	食べて（食べています）	eats (is eating); eats and...; also used for asking and granting permission
(dictionary form)	食べる	eat; will eat (informal speech)
〜ましょう (volitional)	食べましょう	let's eat; shall we eat

自習 Self Check
じ しゅう

Verb Review

Match the English verbs below with the correct Japanese conjugation.

1. to drink

2. is drinking

3. want to drink

4. shall we drink

5. does not drink

6. drank

7. is not drinking

8. let's drink

9. did not drink

A. 飲みませんでした

B. 飲みましょう

C. 飲んでいません

D. 飲んでいます

E. 飲む

F. 飲みましょうか

G. 飲みたい

H. 飲んでいます

I. 飲みました

練習時間 Practice Time
れん しゅう

1. Pair Practice: Verb groupings

Work with a partner. To make it easier to remember new vocabulary, try categorizing verbs. Write out as many verbs from *Beginning Japanese* as you can and group them according to your favorite type of graphic organizer on a page in your notebook. Your categories might include verbs of motion, activities at home, verbs of wearing, things your parents do, etc. Use the verb chart in the Appendix for more verbs, if you like. Each person should write in their own notebook for 練習 (practice). Be creative!

2.　Small Group Practice: Verb conjugation

Form groups of three or four students. You will need one six-sided die. Print out the verb conjugation cards and game board for this chapter from **TimeForJapanese.com**, *Intermediate Japanese*, Chapter 1 Section 5.

Place the cards face down on the game board and roll the die to see who goes first. The first person rolls the die and moves that number of spaces forward. The others move forward in the same manner. On the second turn, you must draw a card and conjugate the verb according to the space where you landed. If you do that correctly, you may move forward one space. If you're incorrect, you must follow the instructions on the bottom of the card. Take turns. If you disagree with another player, say 違います！ The winner is the first to reach 終わり.

地図 Map Skills

Superimposed over the eastern seaboard of the United States, it is easy to see just how long Japan is. Its landmass (378,000 sqkm) is slightly smaller than the state of California (423,970 sqkm). Use the map here and available resources to determine what Japanese and American cities are on similar latitudes.

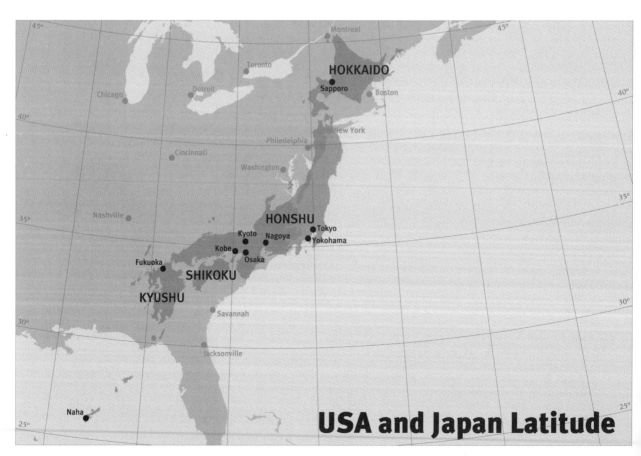

文化箱 Culture Chest
ぶん か ばこ

1. 札幌の文化 - the culture of Sapporo
さっぽろ ぶん か

Although the administrative center for 北海道 was originally 函館, in 1868 the 明治 government moved
ほっかいどう　　　　　　　　　　　　　　　はこだて　　　　　　　　めい じ
the capital to the port of 札幌, now a bustling modern city. 札幌 offers visitors a wide range of activities:
さっぽろ　　　　　　　　　　　　　　　　　さっぽろ
its 雪祭り draws millions of visitors every February. Many of these visitors eat at least one bowl of 札
ゆきまつ　　　さっ
幌味噌 ラーメン at some point during their visit. The 北海道日本ハムファイターズ regularly fill the
ぽろ み そ　　　　　　　　　　　　　　　　　　　　ほっかいどう
Sapporo Dome for nine innings. Fans of other sports can attend rugby, basketball, ice hockey, or soccer
competitions. In June, tourists visit the city to enjoy the よさこいソーラン祭り and listen to the famous
まつ
traditional Japanese 民謡, called ソーラン節. Search online for examples.
みんよう　　　　　　　　ぶし

2. The Poet 石川啄木 (1886–1912)
いしかわたくぼく

石川啄木 was born in Iwate-ken (where Benkei died), and published his first booklet as a middle school
student. In 1907, he became a teacher at Hakodate Yayoi Elementary School and a freelance reporter. He
died of tuberculosis at the age of 26. During his short life, 啄木 was very active as a poet, especially with
たくぼく
短歌 type poetry, and published many popular works. More information about 石川啄木 can be found
たん か　　　　　　　　　　　　　　　　　　　　　　　　　　　　　　　　　　　いしかわたくぼく
online.

メール

This is another letter to Jun's cousin Yuriko. She suggests some things for him to experience in Sapporo.
Points to consider as you read:

❶ What sorts of food is Hokkaido well known for?

❷ The Winter Olympics were held in Sapporo in the year Showa 47. What year is that in the Western
calendar?

❸ At the famous Sapporo Snow Festival, what sort of snow and ice sculptures does Yuriko mention?
Which would you like to see?

じゅん君

　由里子です。北海道には美味しい食べ物が沢山あります。札幌では、必ず味噌ラーメ
ゆりこ　　　　　　　　　　　おい　　　　　　　　たくさん　　　　　　　　　　　かなら　み そ
ンを食べて下さいね。それから、*ジンギスカンと、とうもろこしやじゃがいもも、とても美味し
　　おい
いです。

　そして、札幌には観光名所が沢山あります。昭和47年に冬季オリンピックが開かれた
　　　　　　　　　かんこうめいしょ　　　　　　しょうわ　　　　　とうき　　　　　　ひら
大倉山や、近くの丸山は桜で有名です。ここでジンギスカンが食べられます。
おおくらやま　　ちか　　まるやま　　ゆうめい

大通り公園の回りには、札幌市時計台や*すすきのもあります。すすきのはラーメン屋さんが沢山並んでいます。

羊ヶ丘展望台には、*「青年よ、大志を抱け」で有名なクラーク博士の像もあります。

それから、札幌と言えば、雪祭りがとても有名です。雪や氷を固めて沢山の*雪像や氷像を作ります。毎年*コンクールがあります。雪像はインドのタージ・マハルやフランスのエッフェル塔のような建物だったり、ミッキーマウスや龍のようなものもあるのよ。毎年2月にあるので、今度一緒に行きましょう！

由里子

* ジンギスカン – Mongolian stir fry barbeque; すすきの – entertainment district of Sapporo; 青年よ、大志を抱け – "Boys, be ambitious," a quotation from William Clark, American educator who founded Hokkaido Agricultural College after the Meiji Restoration; 像 – statue, sculpture; コンクール – competition

第1課の6   A Radical Path to Kanji

All kanji consist of components called radicals, although many kanji are radicals in and of themselves. The radical is the part of it that gives the character its primary meaning. Other components give the character its pronunciation. Glance at the chart on page 58 to see how many radicals you have learned in your study of Japanese so far. Knowing more about radicals, their meanings, and how they fit together can help you quickly expand the number of kanji you are able to read and use. A clear understanding of radicals will help you both better understand the kanji you already know and make it easier to learn more.

The kanji 木 was one of the first kanji you learned in *Beginning Japanese*. It was actually your first radical too. You will see this radical over and over again, used as the component part of other kanji. Knowing that 木 means "tree" will help you grasp the meaning of more complicated kanji. As an example, you learned that a person (亻) leaning up against a tree (木) means resting (休み). Other kanji with this radical include 林 woods, 森 forest, 松 pine tree, and 校 school (building).

Some very basic kanji like 木 are based on ancient pictograms that represent their meaning. For other kanji, it is more difficult to discern their origin. That is one reason why you find mnemonic hints under many kanji in this textbook series.

As a Japanese language learner, you have probably discovered that learning occurs at different speeds at different times. Sometimes, you have to work hard to learn just ten kanji; other times, you realize that you have memorized ten new ones in no time. This is most likely because you related the newer group of kanji to those previously learned. An example of this is when 木 and 日 combine to create east (東). For more complex kanji such as 達 (in 私達 and 友達), you can easily use the vocabulary you already know to grasp the meaning of the suffix 達, meaning "a group of." Though some kanji are more difficult to remember simply in terms of their component parts, mnemonic devices and hints can help.

Identifying the main radical of any given kanji is helpful when you start using a kanji dictionary. As you read more Japanese and come across more unfamiliar kanji, a good kanji dictionary is an indispensable tool. You may want to consider purchasing one at this point in your study.

Below is a sampling of the 214 traditional radicals from the *New Nelson Japanese-English Character Dictionary* (A. Nelson [revised by J.H. Haig], Tuttle, 1997), their meanings, and some example kanji where you will find that radical as a component (it might not be the primary radical). The last column has the reference number for the radicals in the smaller, yet excellent *The Learner's Kanji Dictionary* (M. Spahn and W. Hadamitzky, Tuttle, 1998). Also look for examples of the radical in its combined, or "standing", form (for example, where the water radical appears as this radical 氵 instead of 水).

Radical/ Meaning	Common Kanji				N. ref. #	S + H ref. #
一 one	上 下 五 半 正				1	–
、 dot					3	–
亠 lid	京 六 高 校				8	2j
人 (亻) person	人 休 何 体 低 伝 使 作				9	2a
儿 two legs	元 読 売				10	–
入 enter					11	–
八 eight	分 公 弟 前				12	2o
冫 ice	冷				15	2b
几 table enclosure	風				16	2s
力 power	動 働				19	2g
匕 spoon	北				21	–
十 cross	古 南				24	2k
卜 divining rod	店				25	2m
ム myself, private	私 広				28	–
又 again	友					2h
冂, 匚, 囗 These are all enclosures.	国 面 医				13, 22, 31	2r, 2t, 3s
口 mouth	口 兄 足 味				30	3d
土 earth	土 寺				32	3b

Radical/ Meaning	Common Kanji				N. ref. #	S + H ref. #
夕 evening	多				36	–
女 female/ woman	女 好 妹 姉				38	3e
子 child	子				39	–
宀 crown	字 安 家 寒				40	3m
小 little	小 当 学 歩				42	3n
弓 bow	強				57	3h
彳 moving man	行 待 後				60	3i
心 (忄) heart/spirit	悪 思 忘 悲				61	4k
手 (扌) hand	持				64	3c
攵 folding chair	枚 散				66	4i
日 sun	日 白 百 者 春 時 書 暗				72	4c
木 wood	木 桜 校 森 楽				75	4a
气 steam	気				84	–
水 (氵) water	池 海 涼				85	3a
牛 cow	物				93	4g
王 jewel	玉 主 国				96	4f
示 (礻) to show (left radical)	社 神				113	4e
禾 two branch tree or nogi (丿 plus 木)	私 和 秋				96	4f

Radical/ Meaning	Common Kanji			N. ref. #	S + H ref. #	Radical/ Meaning	Common Kanji				N. ref. #	S + H ref. #
竹 bamboo	竹	簡		118	6f	金 money	金				167	8a
糸 thread	絵			120	6a	門 gate	門 開	間 閉	問	聞	169	8e
艹 grass	花	英	薬	140	3k	雨 rain	雨	雲	雪	雷	173	8d
言 word	言	話	語	149	7a	食 food	食	飲	館		184	8b
豆 bean	頭			151	–							

NOTE ▶ N = *New Nelson Japanese-English Character Dictionary*; S & H = *Spahn & Hadamitzy's The Learner's Kanji Dictionary*

練習時間 Practice Time
れん しゅう

Radical Identification

To identify the main radical, the priority is:

- Choose a LEFT radical over a right if the radicals are more horizontal (side by side), or
- Choose the TOP radical over the bottom if they are more vertical (one over the other).

Apply these rules to the following kanji to determine the traditional radical.

1) 林 ＿＿＿

2) 僕 ＿＿＿
ぼく

3) 男 ＿＿＿
おとこ

4) 薬 ＿＿＿

5) 思 ＿＿＿

6) 読 ＿＿＿

7) 紙 ＿＿＿
かみ

8) 簡 ＿＿＿
かん

9) 洗 ＿＿＿
あら

10) 夜 ＿＿＿
よる

Now, try to match each of the above kanji with its correct English meaning, using the radical as a guide.

A) to wash

B) medicine; herbs

C) woods

D) to think

E) simple; brief

F) night

G) I, me (male)

H) male, man

I) paper

J) to read

琉　球　（沖　縄）　1608年
りゅうきゅう　　おきなわ

Travel and Music, Past and Present

The characters arrive near Naha in 1680年, its final year as the Ryukyuan capital. Since the 1300s, Ryukyu rulers had been paying tribute (money and goods) to China. After 1609, Japan demanded this tribute and assumed the Ryukyu islands under their influence and control. In 1879, the new Meiji Government changed the relationship status and established these islands as part of Okinawa Prefecture. Here, our group enjoys some aspects of the relaxed lifestyle of the islands and a performance of traditional music.

Learning and Performance Goals

This chapter will enable you to:

- review making polite invitations (〜ませんか)
- review conjunctions, adverbs, and use of な adjectives
- understand and use basic directions to get from one point to another
- describe general and specific locations
- use multiple adjectives
- use counters for days and nights (stops and stays)
- reserve hotel rooms, transportation, and a table at a restaurant
- use 32 additional kanji

ゴーヤチャンプルーを食べませんか？

Won't you eat some of this goya chanpuru?

1) わあ。海が青くてきれいですね。そして水が温かそうですね。

2) あ、男の子が釣りをしています。魚はとても大きいです。

3) あのー。手伝いましょうか？

4) はい。お願いします！

5) よいしょ。やった！

6) 皆さん、どうもありがとうございました。僕は金城けんじです。

7) 初めまして。この島は小さいですね。日本のどこにありますか？

8) ええと、ここは沖縄ですよ。北には九州があります。南と東には小さい島がたくさんあります。

9) 西には中国がありますね。

10) 僕の家は首里城の東にあります。一緒に行って魚を食べましょう。

11) 沖縄の人は魚をたくさん食べますか？

12) いいえ。あまり食べません。僕は豚肉が好きです。家でちんすこうとゴーヤチャンプルーを食べませんか？

13) 沖縄そばは世界で一番美味しいと思います。中国のラーメンと似ています。

会話 Dialog

(Setting: The characters have just crossed through the torii gate of a small shrine next to a beach in Okinawa, not far from Shuri Castle in the Ryukyuan capital. They see a young boy fishing.)

1. キアラ ： わあ。海が青くてきれいですね。そして水が温かそうですね。

2. じゅん ： あ、男の子が釣りをしています。魚はとても大きいです。

3. 友 ： あのー。手伝いましょうか?

4. 金城 ： はい。お願いします!

5. 皆 ： よいしょ。やった!

6. 金城 ： 皆さん、どうもありがとうございました。僕は金城けんじです。

7. キアラ ： 初めまして。この島は小さいですね。日本のどこにありますか?

8. 金城 ： ええと、ここは沖縄ですよ。北には九州があります。南と東には小さい島がたくさんあります。

9. 友 ： 西には中国がありますね。

10. 金城 ： 僕の家は首里城の東にあります。一緒に行って魚を食べましょう。

11. ベン ： 沖縄の人は魚をたくさん食べますか?

12. 金城 ： いいえ。あまり食べません。僕は豚肉が好きです。家で*ちんすこうと*ゴーヤチャンプルーを食べませんか?

13. 友 ： 沖縄そばは世界で一番美味しいと思います。中国のラーメンと似ています。

* ちんすこう – Okinawan sweet; ゴーヤチャンプルー – Okinawan stir-fried dish of vegetables including ゴーヤ (bitter gourd), tofu, and some kind of meat

単語 New Words

きた 北 (n) – north
にし 西 (n) – west
みなみ 南 (n) – south
ひがし 東 (n) – east
まえ 前 (n) – in front of, before
つり 釣り (n) – fishing

よいしょ ヨイショ (exp.) – effort or strain (expression of)
やった! (exp.) –We did it!
かんたん 簡単 な (adj.) – simple
ふくざつ 複雑 (な adj.) – complex, complicated
バラバラ (な adj./ono.) – scattered, in pieces, disconnected
にる 似る (v) – resemble (to), similar (to be); (common usage: 似ている)

漢字 Kanji

北 5 strokes	ホク, きた – north	一	ﾉ	ﾅ	노	北	
	東北 – northeast or northeastern region of Japan; とうほく 北京 – Beijing; 北九州 – (city of) Kita Kyushu ペキン きたきゅうしゅう						
	The left is a spoon, but looks like a table, standing on its side and pointing NORTH. The right is the katakana ヒ, a small ladder used to climb up NORTH(ward).						

南 9 strokes	ナ, ナン, みなみ – south	一	十	广	市	市	両
	南海 – southern sea; 南アフリカ – South Africa なんかい みなみ	両	両	南			
	Here, 十 is above a downward box (冂) facing SOUTH. This is on top of two blades of grass trying to break through a dry (干) patch of land to the SOUTH.						

西 6 strokes	セイ, サイ, にし – west	一	厂	冂	两	西	西
	西洋 – the west, Western countries; 東西 – east せいよう とうざい and west						
	This looks like 四 with a table on top. The 4th direction mentioned in English is WEST, so this table works best on the WEST(ern) wall.						

番 12 strokes	バン, つが(い) – turn, number in a series	一	⺊	⺈	立	平	乎
	電話番号 – telephone number; 番組 – (TV) でんわ ばんごう ばんぐみ program; 順番 – order of things, sequential order じゅんばん	采	釆	番	番	番	番
	Rice (米) with an extra stroke (釆) on top of a rice field (田) helps to divide the field into a SERIES OF NUMBER(s) or TURN(s).						

東 8 strokes	トウ, ひがし – east	一	厂	冂	戸	百	車
	東洋 – East Asia; 関東 – Kanto (a region of とうよう かんとう Honshu, including greater Tokyo)	東	東				
	previously introduced						

NOTE The kanji 東 was introduced in chapter 1 of *Beginning Japanese*. Additional pronunciations are introduced here.

1. ～ませんか – Polite invitations (review)

Previously you learned how to make polite requests with ～ます verbs by dropping ます and adding ませんか.

クッキーを食べ~~ます~~。　→　クッキーを食べませんか。

I eat cookies.　　　　　　　→　　Won't you have a cookie?

A) あめを食べます。	→ あめを食べませんか。
(I eat candy.)	(Won't you eat candy?)
B) 日本語を話します。	→ 日本語を話しませんか。
(I speak Japanese.)	(Won't you speak Japanese?)
C) 先生を手伝います。	→ 先生を手伝いませんか。
(I help the teacher.)	(Won't you help the teacher?)

2. 小さな島 – small island

Review of using the な with な-adjectives

You have been told that the two kinds of adjectives are い and な. When な adjectives are immediately followed by the nouns they modify, な is added to the end of the adjective. In the example pairs below, in the "A" lines, the adjectives follow the nouns. In the "B" lines, the adjectives precede the nouns they modify and must be followed by な.

A) この人は有名です。	This person is famous.
B) これは有名な人です。	This is a famous person.
A) そのテストは簡単でした。	That test was simple.
B) それは簡単なテストでした。	That was a simple test.
A) その問題は複雑です。	That problem is complicated.
B) それは複雑な問題です。	That is a complicated problem.

自習 Self Check

1. Change the following verbs to their 〜ましょう and 〜ませんか forms. Then, add more words to create complete sentences.

	〜ましょう	〜ませんか		〜ましょう	〜ませんか
A) 待ちます			D) 帰ります		
B) 始めます			E) 歌います		
C) 泳ぎます			F) 住みます		

2. Use the な adjective + noun pattern to make sentences with the following adjectives.

A)	不思議	D)	嫌い	G)	色々
B)	大事	E)	上手	H)	バラバラ
C)	好き	F)	スマート		

練習時間 Practice Time

1. Pair Practice

Politely suggest things to do with your partner, using the 〜ませんか pattern. Your partner should respond with a complete answer.

例 大学、行きます
A-さん: 大学へ行きませんか。
B-さん: ええ、大学へ行きましょう。
or　　いいえ、大学はちょっと…

A) ご飯、食べます
B) コーラ、飲みます
C) バスケ、します
D) ビデオゲーム、買います
E) 鉛筆、使います
F) (free choice)

2. Pair Practice

Take turns describing things around you using な-adjectives. Use the pattern な-adj. + noun.

文化箱 Culture Chest

Geography of Okinawa and Cardinal Directions

At the very southern end of the Japanese islands lies the 47th prefecture of Okinawa. Originally the independent nation of Ryukyu, the islands of the Ryukyu archipelago developed their own unique culture and have been an important link for trade routes within Asia for centuries. Use the Internet to answer the following questions.

❶ Okinawa lies between what lines of latitude (north/south)? What other locations are on the same latitude as Okinawa in Asia, Africa, and North America (name at least one place on each continent)?

❷ Describe the climate of Okinawa.

❸ What is the capital and population of Okinawa Prefecture?

❹ From Okinawa, which direction would you go to find the following?

A) 九 州
　きゅうしゅう

B) 台湾
　たいわん

C) 中 国
　ちゅうごく

D) グアム

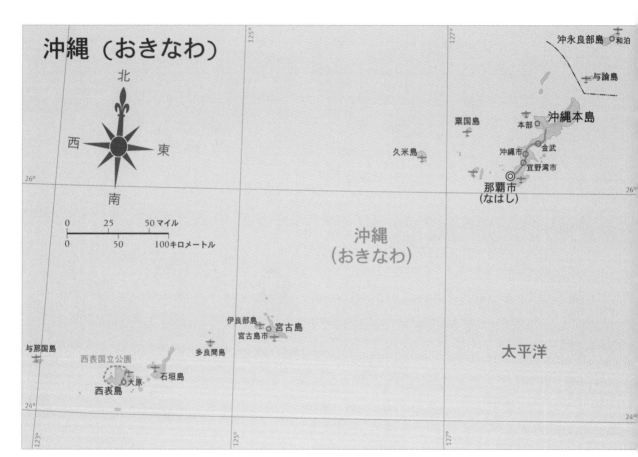

 メール

Below is a note from Ben's friend Shunichi who grew up on a small island in Okinawa-ken.

Points to consider as you read:

❶ What are two things he likes about his aunt?

❷ Name two facts about his hometown.

❸ Whose grave can be found there?

❹ What subjects is Shunichi good at? What is he poor at?

❺ Would you like to visit Shunichi's hometown? Why or why not?

こんにちは、ベン君。毎日元気にしてる？　僕は毎日クラブに、勉強に、目が回りそうなくらいに忙しいよ。でも忙しいのはいい事だな。だって、お父さんやお母さん、それからおばあちゃん達の事を思い出して悲しくなる暇がないから。

　僕の家族は伊是名島に住んでいるんだ。沖縄*本島の那覇の北東にある小さな島で、本島の一番北にある港から50分くらいフェリーに乗らないと行けない。僕の学校は那覇にあるから、今は弟と一緒に、お母さんの大叔母さんの家に住んでいるんだ。だから、伊是名には長い休みの時だけしか帰れない。大叔母さんは優しいし、料理も上手だし、学校は楽しいし、友達もたくさんいるし、とても楽しいんだけど、でもやっぱり、時々ホームシックになるよ。

　いつか、君も僕の生まれた島に来て。伊是名は那覇みたいな都会ではないけれど、海のきれいで、歴史のたくさんあるところだよ。島には『伊是名ふれあい民族館』という博物館があるんだけど、そこには縄文時代の男性の骨もあるんだよ。それから伊是名は琉球の*王様になった尚王が生まれたところだから、お城の跡もあるし、*お墓もある。学校では日本の歴史の他に、沖縄の歴史も教えてくれる。昔沖縄が琉球って言う国だったころの話が特にすごく面白い。テレビドラマでも時々やってる。着物も髪型も日本とは違っていて、僕らは沖縄人なんだっていう気がすごくするよ。僕は沖縄に生まれたから、歴史オタクになったのかもしれない。

　来週からテスト！*嫌だなあ。オーストラリアもテストがたくさんある？僕達の学校は厳しくて、毎回テストの結果を学校の廊下の壁に*貼り出すんだよ。たまんないよ。僕は歴史と国語はけっこう得意だけど、数学が苦手だから、10番までに入った事なんか一度もない。まあ、いっか。

　じゃあまたメールするよ。

玉城俊一
たまきしゅんいち

---

* 本島 – literally "original/main island"; 王様 – king; お墓 – a grave; 嫌だ – disagreeable, unpleasant; 貼り出す – to post, to display

沖縄の料理は辛くて美味しいですね。

おきなわ　りょうり　から　　おい

Okinawan cooking is spicy and delicious, isn't it!

会話 Dialog
かい

(Setting: The group has just finished eating at a small restaurant near the beach.)

1. 皆　　　：ごちそうさまでした。
   みんな

2. 友　　　：沖縄の料理は辛くて美味しいですね。
   　　　　　おきなわ　りょうり　から　　おい

3. 金城　　：これから皆さんはどこに行きますか？
   きんじょう　　　　　みな

4. ベン　　：那覇の町に行きます。でも、道が分かりません。
   　　　　　なは　まち　い　　　　　　みち　わ

5. 金城　　：大丈夫です。僕が*水牛車で連れて行ってあげますよ。
   きんじょう　だいじょうぶ　ぼく　すいぎゅうしゃ　つ

6. じゅん　：水牛車？うわあ。大きい牛が車を引いていますね。すごい！
   　　　　　すいぎゅうしゃ　　　　　　うし　くるま　ひ

7. 金城　　：友さん、牛に乗ってはだめですよ。降りて下さい。車に乗って下さい。
   きんじょう　　　　うし　の　　　　　　　　お　　　　　くるま　の

8. キアラ　：牛はゆっくり歩きますね。のどかですね。
   　　　　　うし　　　　　　ある

(Arrive at City Center)

9. キアラ　：ありがとうございました。ここから歩いて行きます。首里城はどこですか？
   　　　　　　　　　　　　　　　　　　　　　ある　い　　　しゅりじょう

10. 金城　　：この道をまっすぐ行って下さい。そして三つ目の角を右に曲がって下さい。する
    きんじょう　　みち　　　　い　　　　　　　　　　　かど　みぎ　ま
    　　　　　と、首里城は左側にあります。
    　　　　　しゅりじょう　ひだりがわ

11. ベン　　：僕達はあさってまで沖縄にいます。首里城の近くに民宿はありますか？
    　　　　　ぼくたち　　　　おきなわ　　　しゅりじょう　ちか　みんしゅく

12. 金城　　：はい、ありますよ。首里城公園の北口を出て、右に曲がって下さい。そし
    きんじょう　　　　　　しゅりじょうこうえん　きたぐち　で　みぎ　ま
    　　　　　て橋を渡ると民宿が見えます。静かで、きれいな民宿です。
    　　　　　はし　わた　みんしゅく　み　しず　　　　　みんしゅく

13. 皆　　　：ありがとう。じゃあ、さようなら。
    みんな

* 水牛車 – water buffalo cart
　すいぎゅうしゃ

単語 New Words
たん

あさって 明後日 (n) – the day after tomorrow
おととい 一昨日 (n) – day before yesterday
うえ 上 (n) – above, up
した 下 (n) – below, down
ひだり 左 (n) – left
みぎ 右 (n) – right
とおり 通り (n) – avenue, street, way
つぎ 次 (n) – next
すぐ (adv.) – directly, immediately, nearby

こうさてん 交差点 (n) – intersection, crossing
かいだん 階段 (n) – stairs, staircase
かど 角 (n) – corner
しんごう 信号 (n) – traffic light, signal
たてもの 建物 (n) – building
となり 隣 (n) – neighboring
なは 那覇 (pn) – prefectural capital of Okinawa
はし 橋 (n) – bridge
みち 道 (n) – road, path, street

ろうか (n) – corridor, hallway

ドア (n) – door

かんじ　感じ (n) – sense, feeling, sensation

まっすぐ　真っ直ぐ な (adj.) – straight (ahead)

ごちそうさまでした (exp) – (lit.) It was a feast. Said at the end of a meal.

おりる　降りる (v) – disembark (to), get off (a vehicle)

さがる　下がる (v) – descend (to), go back (to), hang down (to)

のぼる　上ぼる (v) – ascend (to), rise (to), climb (to)

まがる　曲がる (v) – turn (to)

わたる　渡る (v) – cross over (to), to go across

いっこ　一個 (counter) – 1 piece/smallish object

にこ　二個 (counter) – 2 pieces/smallish objects

さんこ　三個 (counter) – 3 pieces/smallish objects

よんこ　四個 (counter) – 4 pieces/smallish objects

ごこ　五個 (counter) – 5 pieces/smallish objects

ろっこ　六個 (counter) – 6 pieces/smallish objects

ななこ/しちこ　七個 (counter) – 7 pieces/smallish objects

はちこ　八個 (counter) – 8 pieces/smallish objects

きゅうこ　九個 (counter) – 9 pieces/smallish objects

じゅっこ/じっこ　十個 (counter) – 10 pieces/smallish objects

じゅういちこ(いっこ)　十一個 (counter) – 11 pieces/smallish objects

じゅうにこ　十二個 (counter) – 12 pieces/smallish objects

漢字 Kanji

右 2 1 3 4 5 **5 strokes**	ウ, ユウ, みぎ – right	ノ ナ オ 右 右
	右手 – right hand(ed); 左右 – left and right; みぎて　　　　　　　　　　さゆう 右側 – right side; 右下 – lower right (corner) みぎがわ　　　　　みぎした	
	The katakana ナ is resting on a mouth (ロ), which speaks heavily on the RIGHT side.	

左 1 2 3 4 5 **5 strokes**	サ, シャ, ひだり – left	一 ナ ナ ナ 左
	左手 – left hand(ed) ひだりて	
	The katakana ナ on the LEFT side of the katakana エ, making the "e" sound as in LEFT.	

乗 1 2 3 4 5 **9 strokes**	ジョウ, ショウ, の(る), ～の(り), の(せる) – ride, power, board, multiplication	一 二 三 千 手 乗
	乗る – to get on, to ride in; 乗せる – to place on の　　　　　　　　　　　　　　　　　　　の (something); 相乗 – multiplication そうじょう	乗 乗 乗
	The slash (first stroke) on the top GET(s) ON BOARD a series of strokes that resemble 東. When you BOARD this kanji, you can RIDE even farther on the extra lines.	

降	コウ, ゴ, お(りる), くだ(る), ふ(る) – descend, precipitate, fall	⁷	⁷	阝	阝	阝	阵
10 strokes	降る – to precipitate; 降りる – to get down/descend from (mountain, car, train, etc.)	阵	降	降	降		
	The left three strokes mean place or mound (阝). The right (夂) looks like the top part of 冬. Snow and rain both FALL or DESCEND from the skies, piling up into mounds and filling up ponds.						

首	シュ, くび – neck, counter for songs and poems	丶	⧄	丷	䒑	产	产
9 strokes	首 – neck; 首都 – capital city; 首になる – to be fired; 手首 – wrist	芐	首	首			
	The radical for head (首) has two fingers spinning a record on a needle which is on top of self (自). Musicians and poets put their NECKS on the line when they compose.						

道	ドウ, トウ, みち – road-way, street, journey, teachings	丶	⧄	丷	䒑	产	产
12 strokes	神道 – Shinto religion; 花道 – passage through audience to stage (as in kabuki)	首	首	首	首	道	道
	The upper part is "neck" (首). The lower/left side is the "stop-and-go" radical (辶) indicating motion. Think of two runners, neck and neck, running a tight race down a ROAD or PATH.						

言葉の探索 Language Detection
こ と ば た ん さ く

1. **Basics for giving directions to a location**

   The ability to give and interpret directions for locations is especially important in Japan, where few cities or neighborhoods are laid out in orderly grids. Correct particle usage is crucial to giving, understanding, and responding to directions clearly. In the following examples, study the particle usage closely.

   - を is used after the bridge/street/river/corner to be crossed (the bridge/street/river, etc. functions as the direct object that is the recipient of an action)
   - の is used in sequences of numbers, when speaking, to replace a dash (for instance, in phone numbers or addresses that list the block/building/room number)
   - で comes after the place where one should turn (place of action)
   - に comes after the direction to which one should turn or where something exists
   - へ or に are used after the destination with a verb of motion

A) 橋を渡って = cross the bridge

B) 三番目の交差点で曲がって = turn at the third intersection

C) 左に曲がって = turn left

D) この廊下をまっすぐ行って左の三番目のドアに入って下さい。
= Go straight down this hallway and enter the third door on the left.

E) 右側にあります。 = It's on the right side.

F) 四番目の廊下を左に曲がる*と、山本先生の教室はすぐ右にあります。
= Turn left at the fourth hallway. Mr. Yamamoto's classroom is right there on the right.

G) まっすぐ行って、二番目の角を右に曲がると、右側にあります。
= Go straight ahead, turn right at the second intersection, and it will be on the right.

H) 橋を渡って、四番目の交差点で (or を) 左に曲がる*と左側にあります。
= Cross the bridge, at the fourth intersection turn left, and it will be on the left.

I) 次の角を左に曲がって下さい。 = Please turn left at the next corner.

*Note that と here means "when," NOT "and". This usage of と follows the dictionary form of the verb and precedes another independent clause. と cannot be used to connect て-form verbs.

2. Using multiple adjectives to describe nouns

To describe a noun using several different adjectives, you must change the ending of each adjective in the string except for the last one. For い adjectives, all (except the final adjective) are conjugated by dropping the final い and adding くて. な adjectives have no final ending change. They are simply followed by で (except the final adjective).

- い adjectives – drop the final い and add ~くて (青い ⇨⇨ 青くて)
- な adjectives – add で after the adjective (静か ⇨⇨ 静かで)

The tense of the last adjective in the string of adjectives sets the tense or positive/negative status for the entire sentence.

A) 青くて、新しくて、良くて、小さいです。
= That is blue, new, good, and small.

B) 先生は元気で、優しくて、格好良くて、好きです。
= The teacher is energetic, kind, and has a good appearance, and I like him/her.

C) その映画は怖くて長かったです。
= That movie was scary and long.

D) このTシャツはもう古くて汚いけど、まだ好きです。
= This T-shirt is old and dirty, but I still like it.

自習 Self Check

1. How would you say the following in Japanese?

   A) At the third intersection, turn left.

   B) Cross the street.

   C) Go forward.

   D) It's the third store on the left side.

   E) Cross the bridge and go straight ahead.

2. Match the following directions.

   A) 次の角を 左 に曲がると右側にあります。
   つぎ　かど　ひだり　ま　　　みぎがわ

   B) 二番目 の角を右に曲がって下さい。
   ばんめ　かど　みぎ　ま

   C) まっすぐ 行って、橋を渡ると、 右側にあり
   い　　　はし　わた　　　みぎがわ
   ます。

   D) この道をまっすぐ行って、次の角の 左 側に
   みち　　　　　　　つぎ　かど　ひだりがわ
   あります。

   E) 二番目 の交差点の 後 に橋があります。そ
   ばんめ　こうさてん　うしろ　はし
   のちょっと前に西公園があります。
   まえ　にしこうえん

   ① Go straight ahead, cross the bridge and it's on the right hand side.

   ② At the next corner, turn left and it's on the right hand side.

   ③ Just after the second intersection there is a bridge. Just before that is West Park.

   ④ At the second corner, turn right please.

   ⑤ Go straight ahead on this street and at the second corner, it's on the left hand side.

3. How would you say the following in Japanese?

   A) The candy is red and delicious.

   B) The car is black, new, and stylish.

   C) The picture is interesting, bright, and large.

   D) (describe your pencil [length/color/newness])

   E) (describe an article of clothing you are wearing)

練習時間 Practice Time
れん しゅう

1. Small Group Practice

Use or download a map of your school, a school in Japan, or a neighborhood. Plan out a route to get to another space from where you are now. Tell a partner directions on how to get to where you are going and see if they can follow your directions and end up at the same place.

2. Pair Practice

With your partner, talk about things you see in the room, describing them with more than one adjective. You might talk about something on your desk, what you have in your backpack, posters or pictures on the wall, or objects on the classroom bookshelves. (Note that colors are usually the first in a list of adjectives.)

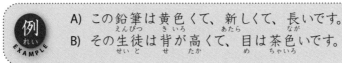

A) この鉛筆は黄色くて、新しくて、長いです。
B) その生徒は背が高くて、目は茶色いです。

文化箱 Culture Chest

Finding addresses in Japan

When you are invited to an event or party in Japan, you will often receive a map rather than simply an address. Finding locations in Japan can be complicated, even with the assistance of a GPS device. Streets and buildings are not necessarily laid out in a linear or sequential order. In large cities, addresses are made up of 区 (wards or boroughs), then 丁 (block or street; several 丁 make up a 区), and the specific block of a particular street (丁 目). The directions will also include the exact block, building, and unit number. If you take a taxi, the driver will input the address into his or her car's navigation system and deliver you directly there. However, even the taxi driver may stop local passersby on the street to ask for directions! Locations are often given in terms of the closest subway station, and even station exit number. For example, here is the address for the Tokyo Tower, which is owned by Nippon Television. Look for directions from 六本木駅 to 東京タワー and write down directions in Japanese for the specifics on how to get where you are going.

NIPPON TELEVISION CITY CORPORATION

東京都 港区芝公園4−2−8（＝4丁目2番8号）

 メール

The following is another letter from Ben's friend Shunichi, with directions for getting to Shuri Castle in Naha, Okinawa.

Points to consider as you read:

❶ Shunichi suggests riding a monorail. What is the name of the monorail?
❷ At what stop should Ben get on? Where should he get off?
❸ Is the Shuri Castle the original building?
❹ What school club does Shunichi belong to?

ベン君。沖縄はどう？僕は他の所に住んだ事がないから、よく分からないけれど、物も安いし、料理も美味しいし、人も*親切だし、いい所だと思うよ。それに、歴史もあるしね！

那覇にいる間に首里城を見に行ってね！何度行ってもすごいなあと思う。首里城への行きかたを書いておくから、がんばって行ってみて。

沖縄県庁の近くに泊まっているんだよね。*沖縄県庁から、一番便利なのは、『ゆいレール』というモノレールだよ。『県庁前』という駅から乗って、『首里』駅で降りて。15分くらいで着くよ。首里城までは、駅から歩いて15分ぐらい。バスもあるけどね。

『首里』駅を降りたら、駅前の広い道をまっすぐ行って、最初の大きい交差点を曲がらないで、まっすぐ歩いてね。そして次の交差点を左に曲がって。守礼門という首里城の正門が左側にあるはず。首里城公園の中は広いから、さっさと回っても一時間半くらいかかるよ。残念だけど、首里城の建物は本物じゃない。アメリカ軍と沖縄で戦争をした時に全部*焼けてしまったんだ。それでも昔の琉球王国の*感じがすると思うよ。君もきっと首里城が好きになると思う。

今日はバスケ部の先輩が厳しくて、ちょっと体が痛い。学校の周りを20周も走ったんだ。僕達はまだ一年生だから、二年生や三年生の先輩に言われた事をしなければならないんだ。時々頭にくるけど、*仕方がないよ。

じゃ、ね。(＾－＾) 玉城俊一

---

* 親切 – gentleness, kindness; 沖縄県庁 – Okinawa Prefectural offices; 焼けてしまった – completely burned down; 感じがする – feel like, give a sense of; 仕方がない – there is no use, futile

左側のドアを引いて下さい。

Please pull open the door on the left side.

1) 首里城は赤くて大きいですね。古いお城ですね。

2) あれ？音楽が聞こえますね。あそこへ行ってみませんか？

3) あれは三味線ですか？

4) はい。でも、沖縄では「三線」と言います。とても古い楽器です。

5) いらっしゃい。三線のコンサートとエイサー踊りを見ませんか？切符は一枚二百円ですよ。切符はお弁当付きです。

6) 嬉しい！

7) じゃあ、四枚下さい。

8) すみません、お手洗いはどこですか？

9) この廊下をまっすぐ行って次の角を右に曲がって下さい。左側のドアを引いて下さい。

10) ああ、踊りが始まりました。沖縄の着物はきれいですね。

11) でも、日本の着物と少し違いますね。

12) 沖縄は暑いから、太い帯をしません。大きい袖の中に風が入って涼しいです。

13) なるほど。

会話 Dialog
かい

(Setting: Naha, Okinawa: Standing near Shuri Castle, waiting to see a musical performance)

1. じゅん　：首里 城 は赤くて大きいですね。 古いお城 ですね。
　　　　　　しゅり じょう　あか　　　　　　　　　　ふる　　しろ

2. キアラ　：あれ？音楽が聞き こえますね。あそこへ行ってみませんか？
　　　　　　　　　　おんがく

3. ベン　　：あれは三味線ですか？
　　　　　　　　　しゃ み せん

4. 友　　　：はい。でも、沖縄では「*三線」と言います。とても古い楽器です。
　　　　　　　　　　　　おきなわ　　　　さんしん　　　　　　　　ふる　がっき

5. 女 の 人：いらっしゃい。 三線のコンサートとエイサー踊りを見ませんか？
　 おんな ひと　　　　　　　　　さんしん　　　　　　　　　　　おど

　　　　　　切符は一枚二百円ですよ。 切符はお弁当付きです。
　　　　　　きっぷ　まい　　　　　　　　きっぷ　　べんとう つ

6. 友　　　：嬉しい！
　　　　　　うれ

7. キアラ　：じゃあ、四枚下さい。
　　　　　　　　　まい

8. ベン　　：すみません、お手洗いはどこですか？
　　　　　　　　　　　て あら

9. 女の人　：この廊下をまっすぐ行って次の角を右に曲がって下さい。 左 側のドアを引い
　　　　　　　　ろうか　　　　　　　　つぎ　かど　みぎ　ま　　　　　　　ひだりがわ　　　　　　　ひ
　　　　　　て下さい。

10. じゅん　：ああ、 踊りが始まりました。 沖縄の着物はきれいですね。
　　　　　　　　　おど　はじ　　　　　　　おきなわ　きもの

11. キアラ　：でも、日本の着物と少し違いますね。
　　　　　　　　　　　きもの　すこ　ちが

12. 友　　　：沖縄は暑いから、太い*帯をしません。大きい*袖の中に風が入って涼しい
　　　　　　おきなわ　あつ　　　　ふと　おび　　　　　　　　　　そで　なか　かぜ　はい　　すず
　　　　　　です。

13. じゅん　：なるほど。

*三線 – three stringed instrument from Okinawa; 帯 – belt of a kimono; 袖 – sleeve
　さんしん　　　　　　　　　　　　　　　　　　　おび　　　　　　　　　　　そで

単語 New Words
たん

あいだ 間 (n) – interval, space [between]

うしろ 後ろ (n) – behind

そと 外 (n) – outside

よこ 横 (n) – side (beside), sideways

えんそう 演奏 (n) – musical performance

ライブ (n) – "live" performance (concert, show, etc.)

こと 琴 (n) – koto (musical instrument/zither)

こと 事 (n) – an intangible thing

しゃみせん 三味線 (n) – shamisen (musical stringed instrument)

たいこ 太鼓 (n) – drum

しょうたい 招待 (n) – invitation

でんとう 伝統 (n) – tradition, convention

ふつう 普通 (n) – general, ordinary; (adv.) – normally, generally

ほか 他 (n) – other, another

はやい 速い (い adj.) – fast, quick

おそい 遅い (い *adj.*) – slow, late

でんとうてき 伝統的 (な *adj.*) – traditional

にほんてき 日本的 (な *adj.*) – Japanese (typically)

わくわく(する) (*v*) – tremble (to), get nervous (to)

かならず 必ず (*adv.*) – always, without exception

かな (*part.*) – I wonder (sentence ending particle); should I? / is it? (question particle); I wish that… (with a negative)

さて (*interj.*) – well, now then

まぜる 混ぜる (*v*) – mix (to), stir (to)

ひく 弾く (*v*) – play (a stringed instrument) (to)

いちばんめ 一番目 (*counter*) – the first

にばんめ 二番目 (*counter*) – the second

さんばんめ 三番目 (*counter*) – the third

よんばんめ 四番目 (*counter*) – the fourth

ごばんめ 五番目 (*counter*) – the fifth

ろくばんめ 六番目 (*counter*) – the sixth

なな/しちばんめ 七番目 (*counter*) – the seventh

はちばんめ 八番目 (*counter*) – the eighth

きゅうばんめ 九番目 (*counter*) – the ninth

じゅうばんめ 十番目 (*counter*) – the tenth

漢字 Kanji

枚 8 strokes	マイ – sheet of… 一枚 – one sheet; 何枚 – how many sheets? いちまい / なんまい	一 十 オ 木 朾 枚 枚 枚

Here is a tree (木), which is used to make paper and a folding chair (攵). You would want to sit if you had to count out all of the SHEETS of paper you could get from one tree.

的 8 strokes	テキ, まと – bull's eye, goal, ending for adjectives 目的 – purpose, goal; 一般的 – popular, typical, もくてき / いっぱんてき 伝統的 – traditional でんとうてき	' 亻 冃 白 白 的 的 的

To see the whites (白) of their eyes is a GOAL for military leaders. The ladle on the right (勹) is to serve the celebratory punch after you achieve your GOAL.

新 13 strokes	シン, あたら(しい) – new 新しい – new; 新車 – a new car; あたら / しんしゃ 新聞 – newspaper; 新年 – New Year しんぶん / しんねん	' 亠 亠 立 立 辛 辛 辛 新 新 新 新

If you stand (立) on a tree (木) holding an ax (斤), you can get a NEW view of your surroundings.

古 5 strokes	コ, ふる(い) – old (things), ancient, aged, outdated 古い – old (things); 古典 – old book, classics; ふる / こてん 中古車 – used car ちゅうこしゃ	一 十 十 古 古

Ten (十) on top of a mouth (口) means OLD. It looks like a very OLD bonsai tree in a pot, waiting patiently for new leaves.

線 15 strokes	セン – line, track, string	く	幺	幺	糸	糸	糸
	二番線 – track/platform 2; 山手線 – Yamanote にばんせん　　　　　　　やまのてせん line; データ回線 – data-circuit; 三味線 – shamisen 　　　　かいせん　　　　　　　しゃみせん	糸'	糸'	糽	紵	紵	緽
		綧	線	線			
	On the left is piece of thread or silk (糸). The right is a spring or a fountain (泉). The LINE(s) of the train TRACK(s) often follow the LINE made by a stream of water.						

横 15 strokes	よこ, オウ – sideways, side, horizontal, width	一	十	オ	木	杙	杙
	横 – sideways, side, horizontal, width; 横浜 – (city よこ　　　　　　　　　　　　　　　　　よこはま of) Yokohama; 横文字 – European-style writing, 　　　　　よこもじ cross-wise writing	栫	栫	栫	栈	横	横
		横	横	横			
	The tree (木) on the left sits to the SIDE of yellow (黄) on the right. Yellow is the color of caution, so remember to look from SIDE to SIDE when you see it.						

個 10 strokes	コ, カ – individual, counter for pieces, smallish objects	ノ	イ	仃	们	佀	佀
	一個 – one piece/smallish object; 個人 – an いっこ　　　　　　　　　　　　　　こじん individual	佀	佀	個	個		
	A person (イ) is holding a box (口) containing several old (古) SMALL OBJECT(s).						

後 9 strokes	コウ, ゴ, のち, うし(ろ), うしろ, あと – behind, back, later	ノ	ラ	彳	祒	衫	衫
	後 – after, later; 後ろ – behind; この後 – after this; あと　　　　　　　　うし　　　　　　　　　　あと 午後 – p.m. ごご	移	後	後			
	This was introduced in *Beginning Japanese*. New pronunciations are noted here.						

自習 Self Check
じしゅう

Match the following.

(ア) Go straight on that street please.

(イ) Turn right at the traffic light please.

(ウ) Turn right at the second street please.

(エ) Go straight to the school please.

A) 二番目の道で曲がって下さい。
　　　　　　みち　ま

B) 信号で右に曲がって下さい。
　しんごう　みぎ　ま

C) 学校へまっすぐ行って下さい。
　がっこう

D) その道をまっすぐ行って下さい。
　　　みち

練習時間 Practice Time
れん しゅう

1. Pair Practice

Practice saying the directions in Part A with your partner in Japanese. Next, use the 町の道 map and cards for Chapter 2 Section 3 on **TimeForJapanese.com** to play the board game in part B.

A) 1. Go straight on this street please.

2. Turn right after the corner.

3. Turn left at the second signal light.

4. Cross the bridge and turn left.

5. Go straight to the second corner and turn right. It's the third store on the right side.

B) Write the stores/places from the game board on a set of cards. Turn the cards face down. Take turns drawing a card (don't show your partner). Give your partner directions on how to get to the location on the card. Take turns, starting from your last location on the board.

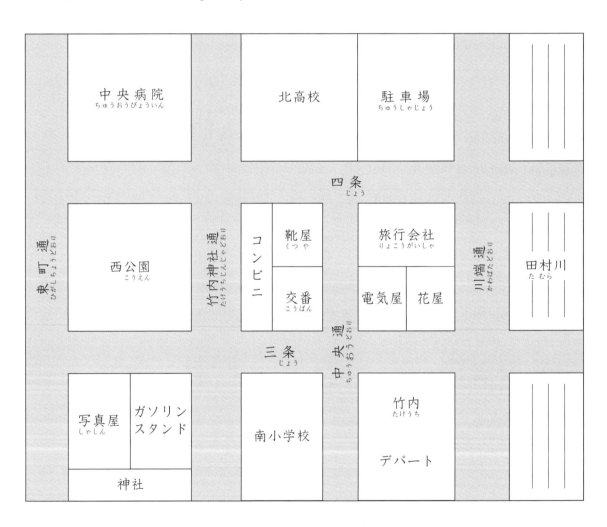

文化箱 Culture Chest
ぶん か ばこ

沖縄の音楽と踊り (Okinawan Performing Arts)
おきなわ　おんがく　おど

Traditional Okinawan, or Ryukyuan, music comes in both 古典 (classical) and 民謡 (folk) styles. Classical
こてん　　　　　　　　　　　　みんよう
music of the Ryukyu Islands, enjoyed by the king, his court, and various dignitaries, developed for the enjoyment of the Ryukyuan nobility. Folk songs (such as "Kaisare") developed at a more grass-roots level, on
the separate islands, and were passed down through the generations. Okinawan folk songs, like those in
other cultures, changed over time to meet contemporary needs and tastes. For instance, the popular song
"Haisai Ojisan," written by a young Shoukichi Kina and sung by his band Champloose in 1972, was based
on traditional Okinawan melodies and instrumentation, but with a reggae beat. It is still popular today.

Dance in Okinawa has a similarly ancient tradition. Court dancing, which developed when the Ryukyu
Islands were an independent kingdom, was influenced by Chinese and Japanese classical music and incorporated elements of Noh and Kabuki, as well as aspects of Southeast Asian dance. A dance called 組踊 ,
くみおどり
dating to the early 1700s, is a blend of traditional Okinawan court dance and Japanese noh and kabuki
traditions. It is designated a "National Treasure" by the Japanese government and is also enjoying a resurgence in popularity. Eisa, a 盆踊り performed in late summer to show respect for ancestors whose spirits
ぼんおど
are said to return to the family altars then, is considered the most famous traditional Okinawan dance. It
has a long history and is accompanied by traditional instruments such as the sanshin or drums. カチャー
シー is an energetic 盆踊り, a type of folk dance, where the audience enthusiastically joins in. Conduct
ぼんおど
an online search to find other traditional dances in Japan from different regions. Do you notice any similarities? What are the differences?

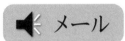 メール

This letter from Ben's friend Shunichi is about Shunichi's love of music.
Points to consider as you read:

❶ How does Shunichi describe the musical sound of his band?

❷ What instruments does Shunichi himself play?

❸ Shunichi compares the musical scale used by Okinawan music with what other country's scale?

❹ Does Shunichi himself compose songs? Which kanji answer this question?

❺ What does Shunichi say he must go do, at the end of his letter?

ベン君。毎日、色々な所に行って疲れたんじゃない？沖縄は暑いから、たくさん休まないとだめだよ。おじいちゃんたちは毎日昼寝をしてる。スペインのシエスタみたいかな。外に出る時は必ず帽子をかぶって、水をたくさん飲んだ方がいい。僕は疲れたらいつも音楽を聞くよ。学校にはアイポッドを持って行ってはいけないから、家でしか聞けないけど。

さて、実は昨日は僕のバンドのライブだったんだ！そう、僕は友達とバンドを*組んでるんだよ。友達のうちが喫茶店をやっていて、時々そこで音楽の演奏を*させてくれるんだ。僕達のバンドは、沖縄の音楽と今の音楽を混ぜて、新しい音楽を作って演奏してる。もともとの沖縄の音楽と、日本のJ-POPと、アメリカのロックを全部ぐちゃぐちゃに混ぜたような感じ。僕は三線という、日本の三味線に似たギターも弾くし、普通のエレキギターも弾く。他の皆も普通にベースやドラムもやるけど、時々笛を吹いたり、締太鼓や他のパーカッションなどをたたいたりしてる。

沖縄の音楽は、ドレミファソラシドではなく、レとラがなくて、ドミファソシド。これは、インドネシアとか、ほかのアジアの国にもある*音階*らしいよ。J-POPのミュージシャン達は、必ず一*曲は沖縄風の音楽をアルバムに入れているから、ベン君も聞いたことがあるんじゃない？もっともっと沖縄の音楽が世界中に*影響していけばいいなあと思っている。僕も作曲をするので、いつかアメリカのミュージシャンが僕の曲を演奏してくれて、君達がそれを聞いてくれたらと思うと、わくわくするよ！

じゃ、これからバンドの練習に行ってくるから、この辺で。

また。玉城 俊一

* 組んでる – assemble, put together; させてくれるんだ – do us the favor of allowing us to (play); 音階 – musical scale; らしい – seemingly; 曲 –tune, melody; 影響 – influence, effect

えーっと、二泊お願いします。
Uhmm, two nights please.

1) いらっしゃいませ。民宿「都」へようこそ。

2) あのー。今晩、泊まりたいんですが、部屋はありますか?

3) ご予約は?

4) 予約はしていません。

5) 少々お待ち下さい。今調べます。何泊でしょうか?

6) えーっと、二泊お願いします。

7) かしこまりました。何名様でしょうか?

8) 四人です。

9) はい、空いている部屋がございます。皆さん一緒の部屋ですね。二泊・夕食付きでお一人様四千円です。

10) 安くて良かった!

11) はい、こちらがお部屋のかぎです。お部屋は二階の二〇三号室です。この廊下をまっすぐ行って、右側の階段を上がって下さい。二〇三号室は左側の三番目です。

12) 晩ご飯は何時からですか?

13) 午後七時に沖縄料理をお部屋に持って行きます。大きいお風呂は南館一階の「デイゴの間」です。朝六時から夜十二時まで開いています。

14) 沖縄料理と一緒にお寿司を注文出来ますか?

15) はい。かしこまりました。ごゆっくりどうぞ。

16) ありがとう。

会話 Dialog

(Setting: The group enters a minshuku guesthouse to see if there are rooms available for the night.)

1. フロント ：いらっしゃいませ。民宿「都」へようこそ。

2. じゅん ：あのー。今晩、泊まりたいんですが、部屋はありますか？

3. フロント ：ご予約は？

4. ベン ：予約はしていません。

5. フロント ：少々お待ち下さい。今調べます。何泊でしょうか？

6. ベン ：えーっと、二泊お願いします。

7. フロント ：かしこまりました。何名様でしょうか？

8. キアラ ：四人です。

9. フロント ：はい、空いている部屋がございます。皆さん一緒の部屋ですね。二泊・夕食付きでお一人様四千円です。

10. じゅん ：安くて良かった！

11. フロント ：はい、こちらがお部屋のかぎです。お部屋は二階の二〇三号室です。この廊下を真っ直ぐ行って、右側の階段を上がって下さい。二〇三号室は左側の三番目です。

12. 友 ：晩ご飯は何時からですか？

13. フロント ：午後七時に沖縄料理をお部屋に持って行きます。大きいお風呂は南館一階の「デイゴの間」です。朝六時から夜十二時まで開いています。

14. 友 ：沖縄料理と一緒にお寿司を注文出来ますか？

15. フロント ：はい。かしこまりました。ごゆっくりどうぞ。

16. 皆 ：ありがとう。

単語 New Words

りょこうがいしゃ 旅行会社 (n) – travel agency/company
かいしゃ 会社 (n) – company
(ご)ちゅうもん (ご)注文 (n) – order, request
よやく 予約 (n) – reservation
おうふく 往復 (n) – round trip, return ticket
かたみち 片道 (n) – one-way (trip)

きんえん 禁煙 (n) – non-smoking
せき 席 (n) – seat, place
のりかえる 乗り換える (v) – transfer (to)
ゆき/いき 行き (n) – bound for
みんしゅく 民宿 (n) – guest house
ようふう 洋風 (n) – Western style

ようしつ　洋室 (*n*) – Western-style room
ようしょく　洋食 (*n*) – Western-style meal
わふう　和風 (*n*) – Japanese style
わしつ　和室 (*n*) – Japanese-style room
わしょく　和食 (*n*) – Japanese-style meal
コンビニ/コンビニエンスストア (*n*) – convenience store
なんめい　何名 (*inter.*) – how many people
なんめいさま　何名様 (*inter.*) – how many people (polite)
しょくじつき　食事付き (*exp.*) – with meals (included)
にしょくつき　二食付き (*exp.*) – with 2 meals included
あう　会う (*v*) – meet (to)
ちゅうもんする　注文する (*v*) – order (to)
とまる　泊まる (*v*) – stay at [e.g., hotel] (to)
よやくする　予約する (*v*) – reserve (to)
いっぱく　一泊 (*counter*) – stopping one night
にはく　二泊 (*counter*) – stopping two nights
さんぱく　三泊 (*counter*) – stopping three nights
よんぱく/はく　四泊 (*counter*) – stopping four nights
ごはく　五泊 (*counter*) – stopping five nights

ろっぱく　六泊 (*counter*) – stopping six nights
ななはく　七泊 (*counter*) – stopping seven nights
はっぱく　八泊 (*counter*) – stopping eight nights
きゅうはく　九泊 (*counter*) – stopping nine nights
じゅっぱく　十泊 (*counter*) – stopping ten nights
なんぱく　何泊 (*inter.*) – stopping how many nights?
いっかい　一階 (*counter*) – first floor
にかい　二階 (*counter*) – second floor
さんかい/がい　三階 (*counter*) – third floor
よんかい　四階 (*counter*) – fourth floor
ごかい　五階 (*counter*) – fifth floor
ろっかい　六階 (*counter*) – sixth floor
ななかい　七階 (*counter*) – seventh floor
はっかい or はちかい　八階 (*counter*) – eighth floor
きゅうかい　九階 (*counter*) – ninth floor
じゅっかい　十階 (*counter*) – tenth floor
なんかい/がい　何階 (*inter.*) – what floor?

漢字 Kanji

注	チュウ, そそ(ぐ), つ(ぐ) – pour, irrigate, focus on	丶	丶	氵	泛	泞	汁
1 2 6 7 4 5 8 9 3	注意 – caution, being careful; 注文 – order, request ちゅうい　ちゅうもん	汁	注				
8 strokes	If water (氵) is POUR(ed) drop by drop on top of the master (王), he won't be able to FOCUS ON running his domain.						

文	ブン, モン, ふみ, あや – sentence, literature, art, script	丶	一	ナ	文		
1 2 4 3	文字 – letter (of alphabet), character; 文化 – culture, もじ　ぶんか civilization; 文学 – literature; 文書 – document, ぶんがく　ぶんしょ writing, archives						
4 strokes	This kanji is itself a radical. It looks like a stack of books on LITERATURE or ART sitting in the middle of a table, just waiting to be appreciated.						

晩	バン – nightfall, night		丨	冂	日	日	日'	日゛
	今晩 – tonight; 一晩 – one evening, overnight; こんばん　　　　　ひとばん 晩ご飯 – dinner ばん　はん		日〃	昭	晘	晚	晚	晩
12 strokes	The sun (日) sits waiting to be excused (免) when NIGHT comes.							

宿	シュク, やど, やど(る) – inn, lodging, dwell(ing)		`	ン	宀	宀	宀	宀
	宿る – to lodge, to dwell; 宿題 – homework; やど　　　　　　　　　　しゅくだい 民宿 – guest house; 安宿 – cheap hotel みんしゅく　　　　　　やすやど		宀	宿	宿	宿	宿	
11 strokes	Under a roof (宀) is a person (亻) who leads 100 (百) men. These people need to be LODGE(d) in an INN or DWELL(ing).							

少	ショウ, すく(ない), すこ(し) – few, small		亅	小	小	少		
	少ない – few, a little; 少し – small quantity, little, すく　　　　　　　　　　すこ few; 少女 – girls; 少年 – boys しょうじょ　　　　しょうねん							
4 strokes	The top radical means small (小). Imagine the fourth stroke cutting what you have into SMALL(er) and SMALL(er) bits, leaving you just a FEW.							

多	夕, おお(い) – many, frequent, much		ノ	夕	夕	夕	多	多
	多い – many, numerous; 多数 – countless, majority; おお　　　　　　　　　　たすう 多角 – many-sided, versatile たかく							
6 strokes	夕 means night. Two nights can lead to MANY more.							

調	チョウ, しら(べる), しら(べ), ととの(う) – tune, meter, prepare, investigate		`	二	言	言	言	言
	調べる–to investigate, to inspect; 調子 – tune, しら　　　　　　　　　　　　　　ちょうし tone, key, rhythm; 協調 – cooperation, harmony きょうちょう		言	訁	訊	訊	誷	調
			調	調	調			
15 strokes	The left radical means to say (言), the right is circumference or circuit (周). When you have fully circled something, you've PREPARE(d) or INVESTIGATE(d) it.							

皆	カイ, みな, みんな – all, everything		一	ヒ	比	比	比	比
	皆さん – everyone; 皆様 – everyone (polite) みな　　　　　　　　みなさま		皆	皆	皆			
9 strokes	The top left radical here means to compare (比) while the bottom radical is white (白). Think of comparing ALL white things, or EVERYTHING that is white.							

		７	３	阝	阝¯	阝￪	阝ˊ
階 12 strokes	カイ – story, stair	阝比	阝比	阝￪	階	階	階
	一階 – first floor; 階段 – staircase; 音階 – musical scale <small>いっかい</small> <small>かいだん</small> <small>おんかい</small>						
	The left radical means a small village (阝) while the right means all or everything (皆). Every small village can build a multi-storied hall.						

		ノ	人	𠆢	会	会	会
会 6 strokes	カイ, エ, あ(う) – meet(ing), association, join						
	会う – to meet; 会わせる – to make/let (someone) meet; 会社 – company, workplace; 社会 – social studies; 教会 – church <small>あ</small> <small>あ</small> <small>かいしゃ</small> <small>しゃかい</small> <small>きょうかい</small>						
	The top radical here is person (人), the bottom is another kanji for "to say" (云). People often MEET in ASSOCIATION(s) and say things to each other.						

言葉の探索 Language Detection
<small>こ と ば たん さく</small>

1. **Counting days and nights (length of a stay/trip)**

To talk about the duration of a trip (e.g., a one night, two day trip), use the counters 泊 and 日. For <small>はく</small> <small>にち</small>

instance, a one night, two day trip would be 一泊二日; a two night, three day trip would be 二泊三 <small>いっぱくふつか</small> <small>にはくみっ</small>

日. Other ways to talk about the duration of a trip are 二日間 (two days' time) or 二泊 (two nights). <small>か</small> <small>ふつかかん</small> <small>にはく</small>

2. **Making reservations**

When traveling in Japan, you might have to get a table at a coffee shop or restaurant, reserve lodging, or reserve seats for train/plane travel. Some specialized vocabulary words are often required. However, the questions asked are generally universal. Knowing what to expect from the person assisting you, as well as a few common words and phrases, will smooth your trip planning. Here are some examples of expressions and questions you might hear.

A) Restaurant

(ア) いらっしゃいませ。 = Welcome

(イ) 何名様ですか。 = How many (people)?
<small>めいさま</small>

(ウ) ご注文は・・・ = What would you like (to order)?
<small>ちゅうもん</small>

(エ) それだけです。 = That's all.

(オ) 少々お待ち下さい。 = Wait just one moment please.
<small>しょうしょう</small>

(カ) 以上ですか。 = Is that all? (Are you finished?)
<small>い じょう</small>

B) Lodging

(ア) 何泊お泊まりですか。 = How many nights would you like to stay?

(イ) 洋室と和室と両方ありますが。 = We have both Western and Japanese style rooms.

(ウ) お食事付き = including meals

C) Here are some useful expressions that relate specifically to travel by train or plane.

(ア) 予約をしたいんです。 = I would like to make a reservation.

(イ) 席を予約したいんです。 = I would like to make (take) a seat reservation.

(ウ) 席は… = (your) seat… (What kind of seat would you like?)

(エ) 禁煙席 = non-smoking seat

(オ) 自由席/指定席/窓側/通路側の席 = non reserved/reserved/window/aisle seat

(カ) 席がバラバラです。 = The seats are not together.

(キ) 乗り換え = connection/transfer

(ク) コインロッカー = coin (operated storage) locker

(ケ) 次の＿＿＿＿行きの電車は何時 = When is the next train to ＿＿＿＿?
ですか。

(コ) ＿＿＿＿までいくらですか。 = How much is the fare to ＿＿＿＿?

(サ) ＿＿＿＿行きの電車は何番線から = From what platform does the train for ＿＿＿＿
出ますか。 leave?

(シ) この電車は＿＿＿＿行きですか。 = Is this train going to ＿＿＿＿?

(ス) 片道 = one-way

(セ) 往復 = round-trip/return

(ソ) 何時に着きますか。 = What time does it arrive?

3. More about time expressions and adverbs

One group of time expressions includes words such as 朝, 今日, 来年, etc., that indicate a specific time. Time words can be used as either adverbs or nouns. When used as adverbs, they indicate the degree or extent of time that has passed. These words can be followed by the particle に.

Another group of adverbs includes words that could be termed as "degree" words. These include とても, 良く, まあまあ, ちょっと, 少し, 速く, etc. Some typical adverbs indicate a positive degree while others, such as あまり and 全然, indicate a negative degree. An adverb that indicates a negative degree must be followed by a negative adjective or a negative verb. Read the following examples carefully. Be able to provide a reason for each sentence ending. This group of words is not followed by the particle に.

A) ベン君はいつも眠いです。 = Ben is always sleepy.

B) 私は少し疲れています。 = I am a little tired.

C) けん君はあまり眠くないです。 = Ken is not very sleepy.

D) 愛子ちゃんは全然疲れていません。 = Aiko is not at all tired.

E) ベン君はいつも朝ご飯を食べます。 = Ben always eats breakfast.

F) 私は朝ご飯を少し食べます。 = I eat a little breakfast.

G) けん君は朝ご飯をあまり食べません。 = Ken doesn't eat much breakfast. (OR, Ken doesn't eat breakfast very often.)

H) 愛子ちゃんは朝ご飯を全然食べません。 = Aiko doesn't eat breakfast at all.

自習 Self Check

1. How would you state the following?

   (ア) 2 days, 1 night (ウ) 5 days, 4 nights

   (イ) 4 days, 3 nights (エ) 7 days, 6 nights

2. Here are the replies to four questions. What are the questions which would be asked?

   (ア) 二泊、泊まりたいです。 (ウ) 月曜日から水曜日まです。

   (イ) 和食がいいです。 (エ) 二枚お願いします。

3. Look at the pictures below. Describe some aspect of each, using at least one adjective and one adverb in your description.

練習時間 Practice Time

1. Pair Practice

Take turns with a partner playing the roles of customer and travel agent. Find an itinerary using Japan Rail (JR) or a Japanese bus service and talk each other though the booking process. Record your conversation so that you can listen to it later to see how you did and consider how to improve. Include dates of departure/return, how many days and nights, what level of travel (comfort), etc.

2. Pair Practice

Explore a visit to Okinawa. Use a mapping site to explore options and menus for the tasks below. Have conversations with a partner to "make reservations," have conversations, etc. to accomplish the tasks below. With your partner, choose one of the following situations to create a dialog of at least 10-12 lines. Practice your dialog at least twice, switching between the roles of お客さん and the 社員. Your teacher may ask you to present your dialog to the class.

1) make reservations at a restaurant for dinner, and find out what is on the menu
2) purchase a long-distance Green Car (グリーン車) train ticket from Tokyo to Kita Kyushu
3) make hotel or inn reservations for three days and two nights
4) telephone a souvenir shop to find out if they have a certain item
5) contact a travel agent to get details on a week-long package trip to Guam
6) ask your doctor if you can safely travel, even though you are sick

3. Pair Practice

Think about a variety of people you know pretty well. Have a conversation with a partner or yourself through which you ask and answer questions about the skill levels of 花子 and 真一. Your goal is to fill in all the information gaps on your activity on the sheet. Use the appropriate verb conjugation.

  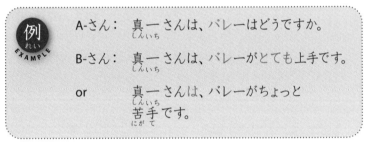

例

A-さん： 真一さんは、バレーはどうですか。

B-さん： 真一さんは、バレーがとても上手です。

or　真一さんは、バレーがちょっと苦手です。

文化箱 Culture Chest

Traditional Music of Okinawa Today

The traditional music of Okinawa was rarely heard beyond its shores until 1993, when the rock band The Boom released their huge hit single, 島唄. The band's leader Kazufumi Miyazawa was inspired by the music of this island chain and spread its distinct sounds to mainland Japan. More recently, りんけんバンド, a group of Okinawan folk musicians, made waves in the international music scene with their fusion of traditional Okinawan-style and 20th c. pop sounds. Do you know any other bands that combine traditional music with pop, J-pop, or other modern sounds?

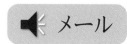 **メール**

This email was sent to Ben from Shunichi, with suggestions on how to get tickets to a concert.
Points to consider as you read:

❶ In Japan, to buy tickets to well-known shows, how far in advance does Shunichi suggest you reserve them?

❷ What price range does Shunichi think one ticket will probably sell for?

❸ Why is Shunichi talking about "Family Mart" in his message?

❹ Why hasn't Shunichi bought tickets for himself yet?

❺ Have you heard of this band? What sort of concert tickets do you buy?

ベン君。メールありがとう。コンサートに行ってみたいって?日本では、有名なミュージシャンのコンサートのチケットは1ヶ月以上前に予約しないとだめだよ。君の友達はMONGOL800 (モンパチ) のコンサートに行きたいんでしょ?モンパチは沖縄出身のバンドだし、僕も大ファンだよ。『小さな恋の物語』は良かったよね。新垣結衣も歌っているけど、彼女も沖縄の出身。聞いた事がなかったら、インターネットで聴いてみてね。

とにかく、モンパチのコンサートが今年の年末にあると聞いて、僕も行けたらいいなと思ってる。12月27日だったかな。場所は沖縄市民会館。*ググってみて。

チケットの料りょう金きんは、もう少したったら、沖縄市民会館に電話するか、『*ぴあ』というチケットサイトに行けば書いてあるはず。多分、一枚5000円から10000円くらいだろうと思う。とても人気があるから、*なるべく早く予約した方がいいよ。予約は*デパ地下や駅ビルの中にある『ぴあ』のお店でも出来るし、近くのコンビニでも出来るよ。僕の場合は、近くに『ファミマ』(ファミリーマートという名前のコンビニ) があるので、そこの*機械を使って予約したり、買ったりしてる。予約する場合も一応クレジットカードの番号を入れないと予約出来ないから、忘れないでカードを持っていかないとだめだよ。

じゃあ、また。予約する時に問題があったらいつでもメールしてね。僕も次の*お小遣いが入ったらすぐ予約するつもり。

玉城 俊一
たまき しゅんいち

---

* ググって – to Google (to search for on the Internet); ぴあ – entertainment ticket sales venue; なるべく – as much as possible; デパ地下 or デパートの地下 – department store basement; 機械 – machine; お小遣い – allowance

沖縄の料理は健康に良いです。
おきなわ　りょうり　けんこう

Okinawan cooking is healthy.

(Setting: The characters are in their room, wearing yukata and relaxing, having just returned from their onsen bath.)

1. 民宿の人 ： 失礼します。お食事を持って来ました。
   みんしゅく　　　しつれい　　　しょくじ
   どうぞ！

2. 友 ： うわあ。美味しそう。いただきます。これは豚肉
   ですか？それとも牛肉か鶏肉ですか？甘くて
   ぎゅうにく　とりにく　　あま
   美味しいです。でも、ちょっと辛いです。
   おい　　　　　　　　　　　　　から

3. 民宿の人 ： はい。これは豚肉の料理で、「*ラフテー」です。
   みんしゅく　　　　　　ぶたにく　りょうり

4. 友 ： この魚はしんせんで美味しいです。
   さかな　　　　　　おい

"Rafute in Waikiki" (photo by: takaokun)

5. 民宿の人 ： はい、今日の朝釣りました。
   みんしゅく　　　　　あさつ

6. ベン ： このお茶はちょっと苦いです。
   にが

7. 民宿の人 ： それは紅花茶です。ハイビスカスから作ります。
   みんしゅく　　　べにばな

8. キアラ ： これはお酒ですか？私達はまだお酒は飲めません。
   さけ　　　　　　　　　　さけ

9. 民宿の人 ： いいえ。それは黒酢です。酸っぱいですよ。気を付けて下さい。
   みんしゅく　　　　　　くろず　　す　　　　　　　き　つ

10. 友 ： 沖縄の料理は健康に良いです。だから、沖縄の人は長生きします。
    おきなわ　りょうり　けんこう　　　　　　　　　おきなわ　　　ながい

* ラフテー – chunks of pork stewed in awamori (rice wine), soy sauce and miso; 黒酢 – black vinegar
　　　　　　　　　　　　　　　　　　　　　　　　　　　　　　　　　　　くろず

しゃくはち 尺八 (n) – shakuhachi, end-blown bamboo flute

ふえ 笛 (n) – flute

あまい 甘い (い adj.) – sweet

からい 辛い (い adj.) – spicy

すっぱい 酸っぱい (い adj.) – sour

にがい 苦い (い adj.) – bitter

しあわせ 幸せ (な adj.) – happiness, good fortune

きをつける 気を付ける (exp.) – take care, be careful

つる 釣る (v) – fish (to)

漢字 Kanji

付 **5 strokes**	つ(ける), つ(く) – attach, include	ノ	イ	仁	付	付
	付く – to be attached; 食事付き – including meals つ　　　　　しょく じ　つ					
	The left radical is the kanji for person; the right is a measurement.					

肉 **6 strokes**	ニク – meat	丨	冂	内	内	肉	肉
	筋肉 – muscle; 焼き肉 – yakiniku (Japanese dish きんにく　　　　　や　にく with grilled meat), Korean barbecue					
	This kanji is made up of the downward box radical (冂) with two people (人) inside; it looks similar to beef rib MEAT in a package.					

酒 **10 strokes**	シュ, さけ – Japanese sake, alcohol	丶	冫	氵	汀	汀	沔
	日本酒 – Japanese sake; 甘酒 – sweet sake; 　　しゅ　　　　　　　あまざけ 地酒 – local sake じ ざけ	沔	沔	酒	酒	
	Water (氵) is next to west (西) with an extra stroke. A liquid that came from the west of Japan (i.e., China) is SAKE.					

言葉の探索 Language Detection
ことば　たんさく

Record yourself talking about the type of foods that you eat, which you consider are more healthy than what others are eating. Give yourself some advice on what you should do to improve your health.

文化箱 Culture Chest
ぶん か ばこ

Okinawan Food

Like other aspects of Okinawan culture, and just like one of its most famous dishes チャンプルー, this cuisine is a mixture of influences from China, Southeast Asia, Japan, and, more recently, the West. The staples in the traditional diet are sweet potatoes, goya (bitter melon), luffa (towel gourd), pork and goat meat, and many more herbs and spices than those commonly found in foods of the Japanese mainland. Okinawan people tend to eat very healthy diets and have the highest longevity rates in all of Japan—and the world.

Do some research for the dishes below to see which you would like to sample, and make and enjoy tasting one of them if you can!

- 島豆腐（地豆腐） – tofu with a soft creamy pudding-like texture
  - しまとうふ　　じまめとうふ
- 豆腐よう – red, fermented tofu
  - とうふ
- サーターアンダーギー – deep-fried balls of dough
- ゴーヤチャンプルー– Okinawa style stir-fry made with goya—a long, bumpy green vegetable sometimes called bitter melon
- フーチバージューシー – rice porridge with a bitter leaf vegetable (ヤモギ)
- タコライス – taco rice, topped with a fried egg (introduced by the U.S. Military forces stationed in Okinawa)

🔊 メール

This is an email to Ben from his friend Shunichi, talking about Okinawan food in general, and school lunches in particular.

Points to consider as you read:

❶ Who makes Shunichi's lunch bento and why must he take it to school?

❷ What do Shunichi's little brothers do for lunch?

❸ Shunichi talks about "pork egg set meal (定食)." What does this contain?
　　ていしょく

❹ What does Shunichi think about the lunches eaten by the girls at his school?

❺ At the end of the letter, what does say he will do?

ベン君。沖縄の食べ物はどうですか。沖縄の料理は豚（ポーク）中心だから、ポークが食べられない人は大変だと思うけど、僕は豚肉が大好きだから、沖縄人でラッキーです。毎日、お弁当を開けて豚肉のおかずが入っているとすごく幸せになります。僕の今の学校はカフェテリアがないので、毎日叔母さんに頼んでお弁当を作ってもらいます。クラブがある日はすごくお腹が空くので、結構大きなお弁当を持って行くけど、それでも夕食までもちません。育ちざかりだからね！

僕の弟の学校にはカフェテリアがあるから、僕がお弁当をもらってかばんに入れていると、とてもうらやましそうです。でもカフェテリアもなかなか良さそうで、僕は*うらやましいと思う時もあります。一食300円で、ご飯と*おかずが付いて来るそうです。飲み物は別売りですが、お茶とお水はただですから、別に買う必要もありません。特に人気があるのは、ポーク玉子定食だそうです。ポーク玉子は、スパムというアメリカのハムを焼いたものとスクランブルエッグで、沖縄では人気のある定食です。他にもラフテー定食や牛丼やカレーライスも人気があるそうです。ご飯はお代わり自由だから、お腹いっぱい食べられて、弟達男の子

には人気があります。女の子達はカフェテリアではなくて、学校の中にある売店で、サンドイッチとか菓子パンを買って食べているそうです。よくお腹が空かないなあと思うけど。ダイエットしているのかもしれないな。僕の学校でも、女の子達はいつも「また太った」とか、そんな話ばかりしているから。お弁当の大きさも、僕の三分の一くらいです。

　こんなことを書いていたら、お腹が空いてきたので、下に行って叔母さんに今日の夕食は何か聞いて来ます。

　じゃあまた！

　玉城　俊一

* うらやましい – jealous; おかず – accompaniment for rice dishes, main dish or side dish

江戸 1830年
えど

Visual Aesthetics of Edo and Beyond

The characters arrive in Edo in 1830. A newly-expanded middle class was ready and willing to enjoy a range of cultural experiences, previously only appreciated by the very wealthy elite. Many citizens viewed Kabuki and other dramatic performances for the first time, and for the first time, members of the growing middle class could afford to buy artwork.

In this chapter, various artists from Japan and Europe are discussed and compared. Creative license has been taken by the authors regarding time travel in that the works of the Impressionist artists mentioned were not actually completed until the last half of the 19th century when prints and other works from Japan began flowing into European markets.

Learning and Performance Goals

This chapter will enable you to:
- review particles used with location words
- make comparisons using もっと
- talk about the locations of people and objects within a room or place
- use 〜の方が…〜より as a method of comparison
- use ほど for a comparison in the negative (not as…)
- use から to mean "because"
- use ですから and the less formal だから meaning "so" or "therefore"
- use new adverbs なかなか, けっこう, 逆に
  ぎゃく
- use the potential form of verbs
- learn about some aspects of the visual arts during the Edo period
- use 20 additional kanji

絵の真ん中に大きい橋がありますね。

In the middle of the picture is a large bridge.

1) 上野公園の池の中に弁天堂がありますね。

2) はい。春に桜の下でお弁当を食べます。

3) こんにちは。水芸を見ませんか？

4) すごい！刀と扇子から水が出ます。扇子の上で紙のちょうちょ；が飛んでいます。

5) 後ろにカーテンがありますね。カーテンの後ろに何がありますか？

6) 絵の国です。世界の絵が五百枚あります。絵の国に入っても良いですよ。

7) 私達の前に浮世絵があります。

8) 絵の真ん中に大きい橋がありますね。そして橋の上を人が歩いています。

9) 橋の後ろに何がありますか？

10) 橋の後ろに富士山があります。橋の下に船があります。

11) 北斎は三十六枚富士山の絵を描きました。歌川広重も「東海道五十三次」で五十三枚絵を描きました。

(Situation: Walking on a path around the Lake Shinobazu in Ueno Park, the characters stumble across a water magic show.)

1. キアラ ：上野公園の池の中に*弁天堂がありますね。
2. じゅん ：はい。春に桜の下でお弁当を食べます。
3. *芸人 ：こんにちは。*水芸を見ませんか?
4. じゅん ：すごい! 刀と扇子から水が出ます。扇子の上で紙のちょうちょ；が飛んでいます。
5. キアラ ：後ろにカーテンがありますね。カーテンの後ろに何がありますか?
6. 芸人 ：絵の国です。世界の絵が五百枚あります。
　　　　　絵の国に入っても良いですよ。

(The characters walk into the picture world.)

7. キアラ ：私達の前に浮世絵があります。
8. じゅん ：絵の真ん中に大きい橋がありますね。そして橋の上を人が歩いています。
9. 芸人 ：橋の後ろに何がありますか?
10. キアラ ：橋の後ろに富士山があります。橋の下に船があります。
11. 芸人 ：北斎は三十六枚富士山の絵を描か きました。
　　　　　歌川広重も「東海道五十三次」で五十三枚絵を描きました。

* 弁天堂 – Buddhist temple on Shinobazu Pond in Ueno Park dedicated to 弁天, goddess of the arts, knowledge and wisdom; 芸人 – performer; 水芸 – water magic performance

単語 New Words

いし 石 (*n*) – stone
え 絵 (*n*) – painting, picture
かたな 刀 (*n*) – sword, saber
せんす 扇子 (*n*) – folding fan
タヒチ (*pn*) – Tahiti
ちょうちょう 蝶々 (*n*) – butterfly
ベッド (*n*) – bed

そば 傍 (*n*) – nearby, side
てまえ 手前 (*n*) – before, this side (of)
まんなか 真ん中 (*n*) – middle, center, mid-way
むこう 向こう (*n*) – across, opposite, over there
おおい 多い (い *adj.*) – many, numerous

すくない 少ない (い *adj.*) – few, a little
いつも (*adv.*) – always, every time
たいてい (*adv.*) – usually, generally
よく (*adv.*) – well, often
とぶ 飛ぶ (*v*) – fly (to), jump (to), leap (to)

Previously introduced: いす – chair; 机 – desk; 窓 – window; ドア – door

漢字 Kanji

公 4 strokes	コウ – public, official, governmental	ノ	八	公	公		
	公園 – (public) park; 公開 – open to the public; こうえん　　　　　　　　　　こうかい 公立学校 – public school こうりつがっこう						
	The top radical, 八 sits above katakana ム, which stands for "myself" or "private". If the private side of ム is viewed at least eight times, it would be OFFICIALLY PUBLIC.						

園 13 strokes	エン, その – park, garden, farm	丨	冂	冂	圓	周	周	周
	公園 – (public) park; 祇園 – entertainment こうえん　　　　　　　ぎおん district in Kyoto; 動物園 – zoo 　　　　　　　　　どうぶつえん	周	周	周	園	園	園
	The inner part of this kanji resembles capital (京) with one extra mark to the right as a signpost showing that within this enclosure (囗) is one of the famous GARDENS of the capital.						

前 9 strokes	ゼン, まえ – in front, before	丶	丷	丷	产	并	首
	午前 – morning; 名前 – name ごぜん　　　　　　なまえ	首	前	前			
	The top of this kanji looks like two seeds popping up above the ground, while the bottom includes a moon and a knife, both objects important to have BEFORE planting any seeds.						

NOTE▶ The kanji 前 was introduced in chapter 1 of *Beginning Japanese*.

紙 10 strokes	シ, かみ – paper	く	纟	纟	纟	糸	糸
	紙 – paper; 和紙 – Japanese (rice) paper; 原稿用紙 かみ　　　わし　　　　　　　　　　　げんこうようし – Japanese writing paper; 手紙 – letter 　　　　　　　　　　　てがみ	紅	紅	紙	紙		
	The thread (糸) has been looped over on itself as if to sew the family crest of a clan or 氏, onto うじ the intermingled fibers of PAPER.						

刀 2 strokes	トウ, かたな – sword, saber	フ	刀				
	刀 – sword; 太刀 – long sword かたな　　　　たち						
	The two sharp strokes of this kanji are a radical meaning SWORD.						

飛 9 strokes	ヒ, と(ぶ), ～と(ばす) – fly, skip (pages), scatter	乀	乁	飞	飞	飛	飛
	飛行機 – airplane; 飛ばす – to fly, to fire; 飛球 – fly ひこうき　　　　　　　と　　　　　　　　　ひきゅう (ball)	飛	飛	飛			
	This kanji is itself one of the more complicated radicals. Imagine it as a series of stacked cliffs with some supports underneath. Two sets of wings flap in an attempt to FLY after they JUMP.						

絵	カイ、エ – picture, drawing, painting, sketch	く	幺	幺	幺	糸	糸
	絵 – picture, drawing; 浮世絵 – (colored) wood block print from Edo pd.; 絵の具 – paints, colors; 絵本 – picture book	糸	糸	糸	給	絵	絵
12 strokes	A thread (糸) loops around and around, woven to meet (会) many other fibers to form the canvas of a PICTURE or PAINTING.						

言葉の探索 Language Detection

Stating location

In Chapter 2 of this volume, you were introduced to the basics of giving directions. Here, you will learn in more detail how to state precisely "where" something is.

Object A は object B の 右 にあります。= A is on B's right.

This pattern indicates that something is on/under/to the left/to the right, etc. "of" something else.

A)	犬はドアの前にいます。	= The dog is in front of the door.
B)	プレゼントはテーブルの下にあります。	= The present is below the table.
C)	机の上にあります。	= It is on top of the desk.
D)	箱の隣にあります。	= It is next to the box.

自習 Self Check

How would you state the following locations in Japanese?

(ア) It is on top of that table.

(イ) It is to the left of this desk.

(ウ) It is inside the box.

(エ) It is under that chair over there.

(オ) It is behind the science teacher.

練習時間 Practice Time

1. Whole Class Practice

For this exercise, you will need a blank sheet of paper and colored drawing materials. Listen to audio file found on the **TimeForJapanese.com** website for Chapter 3 section 1 and draw what you hear. Play the file twice only. After you have finished, click on the link below the audio to unveil the image to check the accuracy of your drawing

2. Pair Practice

First, download the two images for the Chapter 3, section 1 練習の時間. A-さん looks at image A while B-さん looks at image B. Take turns describing the room to your partner. Be as specific as you can about the relative locations of objects in the room. When you have finished describing all of the items in the rooms, compare images to check your accuracy!

文化箱 Culture Chest

上野公園 was designated as 東京の first public park in 1873. It now includes many museums as well as the 上野動物園 (Ueno Zoo). Popular sites in the park include the tranquil 不忍の池, a large statue of 西郷隆盛—"the last samurai"—and more than 1,000 cherry trees. Use the map to answer these questions.

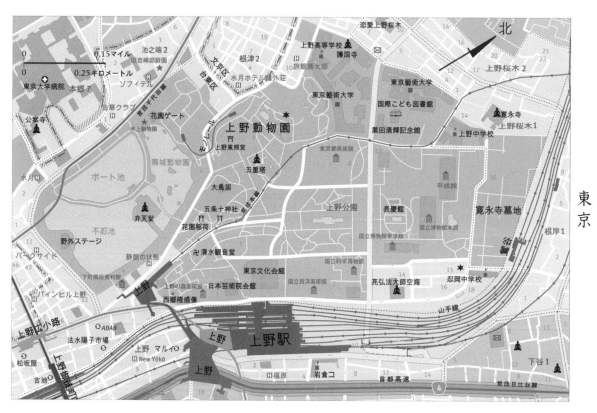

❶ From Ueno station 上野駅, which direction is the 動物園?

❷ From the zoo, how would you walk to 不忍の池?

❸ Now go take a look at the statue of 西郷隆盛. Which direction is it from the 池 (pond)?

❹ Pick another destination in the park. How would you direct a visitor who wanted to walk from the 西郷隆盛 statue near the station to another destination in the park? Write the directions and the final destination in parentheses

Here is a message from Kiara's art teacher in Japan, in response to her request for more information about 浮世絵.

Points to consider as you read:

❶ When does Miyazaki 先生 say that 浮世絵 prints first developed?

❷ According to Miyazaki 先生, during what period did the technical qualities of 版画 reach their peak?

❸ What are a few of the popular subjects for 浮世絵 prints?

キアラさん

　日本での*暮らしはどうですか？　不思議 なこともあるかと思いますが、楽しんでくれると嬉しいです。もし 助けて欲しい事があれば、いつでも私のいる 教員室に話に来ていいですよ。家族と離れて暮らすのは、なかなか 大変 ですからね。

　日本の芸術 に*興味を持ってくれてありがとう。浮世絵のことについてもっと知りたいと言ってたね。キアラさんの美術 の先生としてはとても嬉しいです。もう知っているかも知れないけれど、浮世絵は、*浮世絵 という 意味です。浮世絵の版画は*数百 年前のものです。

　版画の技術 は、長い間かけて日本で発達したんですよ。西洋では、*印刷機 はこれよりもっと早くに開発されたよね。でも日本では、漢字やカナを使うので、なかなか同じ印刷*技術 を使うことが出来なかったんだ。だから版木に文字を彫って*印刷する、版画の技術を使い続けたんだ。この芸術に近い技術は徳川時代に一番高い*水準 に達したんだよ。世界に、この印刷技術ほど優れた印刷はなかったから、海外の国の切手も印刷していたのを知っているかな？

　浮世絵の版画は、様々で、*風景だったり、街や地域の暮らしの様子だったり、有名な歌舞伎役者だったり、芸者さんだったり、鶏や虎、龍や牛、犬等の動物だったりね。

　次の機会にもっと浮世絵や浮世絵師し のことを書きますね。

宮崎先生

---

*　暮らし – living, livelihood; 興味 – interest (in something); 数百 – several hundreds; 印刷機 – printing press; 水準 – standard; 技術 – art, craft, technique; 風景 – scenery

どちらの方が好きですか？

Whose do you like better?

1) 北斎と広重は日本の色々な所に行って絵を描きました。青い空と青い海がきれいですね。

2) この絵は日本の絵ではありません。誰が描きましたか？

3) ゴッホです。ゴッホは浮世絵を３００枚以上、本を５０冊ぐらい持っていました。

4) 男の人の後ろにたくさん日本の絵がありますね。

5) これはモネが描きました。女の子は着物を着て扇子を持っています。

6) ゴッホの絵はモネの絵より明るいです。そして黄色をたくさん使っています。

7) これはゴーギャンの絵ですね。ゴーギャンの絵は広重の絵より明るいです。

8) キアラさんは北斎と広重と、どちらの方が好きですか？

9) 私は富士山が大好きです。だから北斎の方が好きです。

10) 広重の絵の中に面白い人々がたくさんいます。だから広重の方が好きです。

11) 私はきれいな女の人が大好きです。だから歌麿がもっと好きです。

会話 Dialog
かい

KEEP IN MIND!
As mentioned earlier, the European artists and works shown here are actually from the latter half of the 1800s.

(Setting: The group and others are having a discussion about popular artists of the 19th c., in both Japan and Europe.)

1. 田中　：北斎と広重は日本の色々な所に行って絵を描ました。
　　たなか　　　ほくさい　ひろしげ　　　　　　　　　　ところ　　　　　　　　か
　　　　　　　青い空と青い海がきれいですね。
　　　　　　　　　そら

2. ベン　：この絵は日本の絵ではありません。誰が描きましたか?
　　　　　　　　　え　　　　　　　　　　　　　　　　だれ　か

3. 芸人　：ゴッホです。ゴッホは浮世絵を300枚以上、本を50冊ぐらい持っていました。
　　げいにん　　　　　　　　　　うきよえ　　　　　　　　　　　　さつ

4. キアラ　：男の人の後ろにたくさん日本の絵がありますね。

5. 芸人　：これはモネが描きました。女の子は着物を着て扇子を持っています。
　　げいにん　　　　　　か　　　　　　　　　　　　　　　せんす

6. ベン　：ゴッホの絵はモネの絵より明るいです。そして黄色をたくさん使っています。
　　　　　　　　　　　　　　　　　あか　　　　　　　きいろ

7. キアラ　：これはゴーギャンの絵ですね。ゴーギャンの絵は広重の絵より明るいです。
　　　　　　　　　　　　　　　　　　　　　　　　　ひろしげ　　　　あか

8. 芸人　：キアラさんは北斎と広重とどちらの方が好きですか?
　　げいにん　　　　　　ほくさい　ひろしげ

9. キアラ　：私は富士山が大好きです。だから北斎の方が好きです。
　　　　　　　　ふじさん　　　　　　　　　ほくさい

10. ベン　：広重の絵の中に面白い人々がたくさんいます。だから広重の方が好きです。
　　　　ひろしげ　　　　　　　　　　　　　　　　　　　　ひろしげ

11. 芸人　：私はきれいな女の人が大好きです。だから歌麿がもっと好きです。
　　げいにん　　　　　　　　　　　　　　　　うたまろ

単語 New Words
たん

インプレッショニズム (n) – Impressionism

くうかん　空間 (n) – space

シンメトリックデザイン (n) – symmetric design

アシンメトリックデザイン (n) – asymmetric design

せん　線 (n) – line

そら　空 (n) – sky

たけ　竹 (n) – bamboo

ちきゅう　地球 (n) – earth, globe

ちず　地図 (n) – map

じしん　地震 (n) – earthquake

ヨーロッパ (pn) – Europe

ゴーギャン (pn) – Gauguin, Paul

ゴッホ (pn) – Van Gogh, Vincent

たいら　厚い (い adj.) – thick, heavy (coating), deep (color)

たいら　平 (な adj.) – flat

うすい　薄い (い adj.) – thin, pale/light, weak (taste)

でこぼこ　凸凹 (な adj.) – unevenness, ruggedness

から (part.) – because

より (part.) – than ~

だから (conj.) – so, therefore (plain form of ですから)

ですから (conj.) – so, therefore

ほう　方 (n) – direction (prev. learned as かた for person as in この方)

漢字 Kanji

方 4 strokes	かた, ～かた, ～がた, ホウ – direction, person, alternative	丶	宀	方	方		
	この方; ～の方が ・・・・ – ~ is more... かた　　　ほう						
	A PERSON can use the lid on top of this two-pronged fork to determine the best DIRECTION						

空 8 strokes	クウ, そら, あ(き) – empty, sky, void	丶	ハ	宀	宀	空	空
	空港 – airport; 空 – sky; 空き – space, emptiness; くうこう　　　　そら　　　　あ 空気 – air, atmosphere くうき	空	空				
	A hole (穴) on top of craft (工), represents the VOID that exists before construction begins to fill the SKY with new structures.						

地 6 strokes	チ, ジ – ground, earth	一	十	土	坦	坤	地
	地震 – earthquake; 地方 – area, locality; 地下 – じしん　　　　　　ちほう　　　　　　　ちか basement; 地球 – the earth ちきゅう						
	The left side of this kanji (土) is soil or ground, while the right (也) means "to be". GROUND is still just EARTH.						

竹 6 strokes	チク, たけ – bamboo	ノ	ト	个	竹	竹	竹
	竹 – bamboo; 青竹 – green (young) bamboo; たけ　　　　　あおだけ 竹の子 – baby bamboo shoots たけ　こ						
	This kanji is the radical for BAMBOO.						

所 8 strokes	ショ, ところ, ～ところ, どころ – place	一	丆	戸	戸	戸	所
	所 – place; 台所 – kitchen; 場所 – place, location ところ　　　だいどころ　　　　　　ばしょ	所	所				
	The PLACE where grandfather kept the axe (斤) to cut firewood was to the right of the door (戸).						

速 10 strokes	ソク, はや(い), はや～, はや(める), すみ(やか) – quick, fast	一	一	三	中	申	束
	速い – quick, fast; 速やか – speedy, prompt; はや　　　　　　　　　　すみ 高速 – high speed こうそく	束	涑	速	速		
	Here a large, FAST moving (辶) mouth (口) scuttles up a tree (木) trying to eat QUICKly.						

言葉の探索 こと ば たん さく Language Detection

1. _____is more _____ than _____ – ～の方が・・・・～より。
　　　A　　　　　　　　　　　　　B　　　　　ほう

There are several ways to make comparative statements in Japanese. One basic method is to use the ～の方が・・・より pattern. Remember that one of the definitions of 方 is "direction." The word preceding 方 indicates which direction is bigger, smarter, taller, etc. The pattern is:

例１：　_____ ＋ より ＋ _____ ＋ の方が ＋ _____ です。
　　　　　　object A　　　　　　　　object B　　　　　　　　　adjective

　　　　そばよりうどんの方が好きです。　= More than soba, I like udon.

　　　or

例２：　_____ ＋ の方が ＋ _____ ＋ より ＋ adjective です。
　　　　　　object A　　　　　　　object B

　　　　うどんの方がそばより好きです。　= I like udon more than soba.

NOTE Notice that the word order can be rearranged to have a slightly different emphasis.

A) 京の方が東京より歴史があります。
　　と　　　とうきょう　れき し
　　= Kyoto has more history than Tokyo.
B) お寿司の方がカレーライスより値段が高いです。
　　す し　　　　　　　　　　　ね だん
　　= The price of sushi is more expensive than curry and rice.
C) 赤より、青の方が好きです。　= More than red, I like blue.
D) 鈴木先生より、山本先生の方が優しいです。
　　すず き　　　　　　もと　　　　やさ
　　= More than Mrs. Suzuki, Mr. Yamamoto is kinder.

2. Because or since (cause or reason) – から/ですから/だから
The particle から can be used as "because" or "since". The particle から appears after the cause/reason and before the effect/result.

　　This usage of から differs from the meaning "from," introduced in *Beginning Japanese*. Here it shows a cause-and-effect relationship. The first clause provides the reason or cause; this is followed by から or ですから/だから. The second clause is the result or effect. The sentence-ending verb usually determines the formality of the sentence. The use of a comma after から is optional.

　　_____ (dictionary form of verb) から、 _____.
　　　　reason　　　　　　　　　　　　　　　　　　　result

or　　_____ ですから、 _____.
　　　　reason　　　　　　　　　　　result

Read the following examples carefully, noting the various verb endings that precede から.

A) because/since – から

(ア) じゅん君のいとこ二人が仙台に住んでいるから、時々会いに行きます。
= Because/Since Jun's two cousins live in Sendai (city), he sometimes goes to meet them.

(イ) 弟はいっぱい食べるから、いつもお腹が痛くなります。
= Because/Since my younger brother eats a lot, his stomach always starts to hurt.

(ウ) たくさん勉強するから、いい成績をもらいます。
= Because/Since I study a lot I get good grades.

B) "so," "therefore" – ですから (more formal) or だから (less formal)

As a conjunction, から can be combined with the copula です (or its plain form of だ) to create ですから (or だから). This expression can also be used after a reason to imply "so…" or "therefore…".

(ア) 僕はバスケが大好きですから、毎日練習します。
= I love basketball so I practice every day.

(イ) リサさんはのりが好きだから、いつもおにぎりと一緒に食べます。
= Lisa likes nori so she always eats it with onigiri.

(ウ) 土曜日は忙しいから、日曜日に来て下さい。
= Saturday is busy, so please come on Sunday.

NOTE ▶ Note that while から alone can only be used as a conjunction, both ですから and だから can also be used at the beginning of a sentence, to mean "therefore" or "consequently."

明日は夏休みの初めの日です。だから、学校はありません。
= Tomorrow is the first day of summer break. Therefore, there is no school.

3. **Rather than red, I like blue more. – 赤より、青がもっと好きです。**

This pattern combines より (from Language Detection point #1 above) and もっと (taught in *Beginning Japanese*). To say one object is more of a particular adjective than the other, use this comparative pattern.

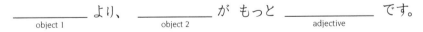
より、 _____ が もっと _____ です。
object 1   object 2   adjective

Aより、Bがもっと ＋ 早い ＋ です/います/あります。
Rather than A, B is (much) earlier.

A) スーツより、Tシャツがもっと好きです。   = Rather than a suit, I like T-shirts more.

B) Tシャツより、スーツがもっと高いです。   = Rather than T-shirts, suits are more expensive.

C) 電車より、新幹線がもっと速いです。   = Rather than electric trains, the Shinkansen is faster
                                           (more fast).

自習 Self Check
じ しゅう

1. How would you say these in Japanese? First, decide whether to use the ~の方が/より pattern or the より/もっと pattern. Use the examples as models.

> 例
> REI
> EXAMPLE
>
> （ア）　イタリアの食べ物の方が、イギリスの食べ物より、美味しいと思います。
> 　　　= I think that Italian food is more delicious than English food.
> （イ）　イギリスの食べ物より、イタリアの食べ物がもっと美味しいと思います。
> 　　　= Italian food is more delicious than English food, I think.

A)　I like black better than yellow.

B)　My mother likes cats better than dogs.

C)　There is a prettier dress over there. Wouldn't you like to try it on?

D)　Tom likes American football better than baseball.

E)　Do you have any larger shoes?

2. Match the "reason/cause" with the best choice "result/effect."

A)　足が痛いですから、　　　　　　　1. お腹が空きました。

B)　朝ご飯を食べなかったから、　　　2. 電車で学校へ来ます。

C)　車の運転が出来ませんから、　　　3. 今日、あまり歩きたくないです。

D)　絵を描くのはあまり上手じゃないから、　4. 先生に悪い成績をもらいました。

練習時間 Practice Time
れん しゅう じ かん

1. Pair Practice

With a partner, take turns making comparative statements about the following. Use the example as a model sentence.

> 例
> れい
> EXAMPLE
>
> hamburgers and hotdogs → 私はハンバーガーよりホットドッグの方が好きです。

A)　horses and cows

B)　sushi and spaghetti (スパゲッティ)

C)　winter and summer

D)　jazz and rock

E)　soccer and sumo

2. Small Group Practice

Cause and effect: Talk to yourself or your partner about making choices, based on the comparative practice targets in this section. Use choices about where to have dinner, see a movie, hang out, etc.

文化箱 Culture Chest
ぶん か ばこ

Japonisme

Admiral Perry's "Black Ships" first landed in Japan in 1853. Returning to Japan a year later, Perry's ships were important in "opening" the country to the West. For the first time, silks, art, and artifacts began flowing from Japan to new markets around the world. Japanese artists and their work were very important influences on the art of the Impressionist movement in Europe. The French term "Japonisme" was coined in 1872 by a Parisian art critic to describe the infatuation for all things Japanese. Several Impressionist artists of the time, most notably Van Gogh, Gauguin, Lautrec, and Degas, amassed large collections of 浮世絵 (うきよえ) prints and were strongly influenced by their style. Japanese influence is evident in the strong use of line, lighting, and point of view in many Impressionist works. Shortly after this time, Japanese artists in turn began experimenting with Western-style Impressionist art. They were greatly influenced by Western-style perspective drawing and the Impressionists' use of light and shadow.

Three 浮世絵 (うきよえ) artists favored by the collectors were 喜多川歌麿 (きたがわうたまろ) (1753-1806), 葛飾北斎 (かつしかほくさい) (1760-1849), and 歌川 広重 (うたがわ ひろしげ) (1797-1858). The fame of 歌麿 (うたまろ) came from his portraits of women known as 美人画 (びじんが), while some of the most famous images of Japan today are the views of Mt. Fuji and the Great Waves prints of 北斎 (ほくさい). Their contemporary, 広重 (ひろしげ), was best known for his detailed landscape series, including his "53 Stations of the Tokaido" (東海道五十三次 (とうかいどう つぎ)), which depict images from various parts of Japan and contemporary life of the 1830s.

The 浮世絵 (うきよえ) pieces collected by these Western Impressionist artists clearly affected the development of the unique Impressionist style. For example, the 漫画 (まんが) in Section 3-1 shows how some European works were direct copies of works by Japanese counterparts. Notice the use of strong black outline and flatness of color in the backgrounds. Also, notice the point of view that the artist forces the viewer to adopt.

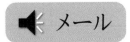

Another message from Kiara's art teacher, Miyazaki.

Points to consider as you read:

❶ Which two artists are being compared here?

❷ What does the teacher think are the two most famous images of Japanese scenery in the West?

❸ What does the teacher think Hiroshige was good at selling?

キアラさん

　キアラさんの言う通り1830年代に一番有名だった浮世絵師は、安藤広重と葛飾北斎だよ。二人とも日本中を旅行して回り、*記録に残したんだ。芸術家や詩人が、*田舎に行って見た事や聞いた事を*記録に残すことをよくしたんだよ。詩人の芭蕉も一生のうち何度も長い旅に出たんだ。

　北斎は70年間ずっと絵描きでした。最初は有名な歌舞伎役者の版画を描いていましたが、後になって日常生活を記録し始めたんだ。東海道を京都から江戸まで旅してスケッチしたものが、後に様々な版画になったんだ。北斎は北斎漫画や富士山と*波を題材にした『*富嶽三十六景』で有名だよ。この二つの*風景が西洋では日本のイメージとして一番有名ですね。

　北斎より若手の広重も東海道を旅して版画を作ったんだ。風景に関しては北斎より広重の方が上手だと言う人が多いけれど、キアラさんはどう思う？私は広重の鳥と花の作品が風景よりもっと優れていると思います。広重は北斎よりも自分の作品を売るのが上手だったんだ。だからても成功したんだよ。逆に北斎は変わっていて、何度も*引っ越しをを繰り返したんだ。描けるものは何でも絵や版画にして、90才になるまで描き続けたんだよ。

　この二人の浮世絵師はとても素晴らしい芸術家だと思います。また次のメールでお話しますすね。

宮崎先生

---

* 記録に残す – to leave a record, or an image; 田舎 – rural area, countryside; 波 – wave; 富嶽 三十六景 – 36 views of Mt. Fuji; 風景 – scenery; 引っ越し – moving (home/office), changing residence

それに北斎の有名なテーマはほとんどが景色でした。

On top of that, Hokusai's famous themes were mostly scenic landscapes.

1) 歌麿はたくさん美人の絵を描きました。

2) えーっ？全然きれいじゃないです。きれいな人は目と口が大きいです。そして鼻があまり大きくないですよ。

3) 江戸時代は違いました。美人は顔と鼻が長くて目が切れ長です。そして口は小さいです。顔の色が白くて髪の毛は黒くて長いです。歌麿は北斎よりたくさん女の人を描きました。

4) 広重と北斎の年は、同じぐらいですか。

5) 広重は1797年生まれで、北斎より37才下です。それに北斎さんの有名なテーマはほとんどが景色でした。

6) そうそうそう。北斎は七十才で『富嶽三十六景けい』を描いて九十才で死にました。九十三回*引っ越しをしたそうです。そして名前を三十回変えました。お金が嫌いで貧乏でした。

7) 北斎はちょっと変わった人でしたね。でも北斎の絵はデザインが面白くてダイナミックで素晴らしいです。

8) 広重は北斎よりもっとたくさん青を使いましたね。それをヒロシゲ・ブルーと言います。広重は人々の生活や風景を細かく描きました。

会話 Dialog

(Setting: The group is having a discussion about artists of the time and the subject matters of their prints.)

1. 友　　：歌麿はたくさん美人の絵を描きました。

2. ベン　：えーっ？全然きれいじゃないです。きれいな人は目と口が大きいです。そして鼻があまり大きくないですよ。

3. 友　　：江戸時代は違いました。美人は顔と鼻が長くて目が切れ長です。そして口は小さいです。顔の色が白くて髪の毛は黒くて長いです。歌麿は北斎よりたくさん女の人を描きました。

4. ベン　：広重と北斎の年は、同じぐらいですか。

5. 友　　：広重は1797年生まれで、北斎より37才下です。それに北斎さんの有名なテーマはほとんどが景色でした。

6. 芸人　：そうそうそう。北斎は七十才で『*富嶽三十六景けい』を描いて九十才で死にました。九十三回*引っ越しをしたそうです。そして名前を三十回変えました。お金が嫌いで貧乏でした。

7. 友　　：北斎はちょっと変わった人でしたね。でも北斎の絵はデザインが面白くてダイナミックで素晴らしいです。

8. ベン　：広重は北斎よりもっとたくさん青を使いましたね。それをヒロシゲ・ブルーと言います。広重は人々の生活や風景を細かく描きました。

*富嶽三十六景 – 36 Views of Mt. Fuji by Hokusai; 引っ越しをした – moved

単語 New Words

けしき　景色 (n) – scenery, landscape

けっこう (n) – splendid, nice; (な adj.) – sufficient, I'm) fine, no thank you; (adv.) – reasonably, fairly

しぜん　自然 (な adj.) – nature; (adv.) – naturally

かなり (adv.) – considerably, quite

ぎゃくに　逆に (adv.) – conversely, on the contrary

なかなか (adv.) – very, considerably, easily, by no means (with neg. verb)

しかし (conj.) – however, but

すぎる　過ぎる (v) – pass (to), exceed (to), above (to be)

漢字 Kanji

		ノ	ク	タ	タ	夕	外
然	ゼン, ネン – sort of thing, so, if so	夕犬	夕犬	夕犬	然	然	然
12 strokes	自然 – natural; 全然 – not at all しぜん　　　　ぜんぜん						

The main radical for this kanji is fire (火, 灬) on the bottom. Imagine a warm fireplace in the evening (夕) with a dog (犬) sitting by the fire as the SORT OF THING memories are made of. IF SO, it is a good thought.

言葉の探索 Language Detection
ことば たんさく

Adverbs that show degree: なかなか, けっこう, 逆に
　　　　　　　　　　　　　　　　　　　　　　　　　　　ぎゃく

A)　なかなか – very, considerably, or by no means (with a negative verb)

(ア) 私の友達は成績を良くしたいけど、なかなか勉強しない。
　　　　　　　　せいせき
= My friend wants to get better grades, but he doesn't study. (by no means does he study)

(イ) 時間がなかなかありませんね。　　　　　　= There just really isn't enough time.

B)　けっこう – reasonably, fairly

(ア) 柔道はけっこう難しいです。　　　　　= Judo is fairly difficult.
　　じゅうどう　　　　むずか

(イ) あの友達は背がけっこう高いです。　　= That friend over there is fairly tall.
　　　　　　　せ

C)　逆に – conversely, on the other hand (can be used to show contrast)
　　ぎゃく

(ア) ベン君は外国語が本当に上手です。 逆に数学が苦手です。
　　　　　　　　　　　　　　　　　　ぎゃく　すう　にが
= Ben is really good at foreign languages. On the other hand, he is not very good at math.

(イ) 北斎の浮世絵はたいてい色が明るいです。 逆に国芳の浮世絵はちょっと暗いです。
　　ほくさい　うきよえ　　　　　　　　　　ぎゃく　くによし　うきよえ
= Hokusai's ukiyoe are generally bright. Conversely, Kuniyoshi's ukiyoe are a little dark.

自習 Self Check
じしゅう

Adverb practice

Insert the words in parentheses into each sentence. Then restate each sentence in English.

(ア) あの浮世絵の色は明るいです。(なかなか)
　　　うきよえ　　　あか

(イ) 歌麿の絵の人はきれいですね。(けっこう)
　　うたまろ　　ひと

(ウ) 朝ご飯をたくさん食べました。 昼ご飯に何も食べませんでした。(逆に)
　　あさ　はん　　　　　　　　　ひる　はん　　　　　　　　　　　　　ぎゃく

(エ) (free choice sentence and adverb)

Tic-tac-toe: pair practice

Make tic-tac-toe boards. Then, with your partner, take turns writing the descriptive words below in the boxes. じゃんけん to see who goes first. Player A chooses a box, creates a Japanese sentence using a word from below, and then restate it in English. If no one disputes it, that box belongs to Player A. If Player B challenges and proves that the sentence is incorrect, Player B begins his/her turn. Continue playing until someone wins, or until the game is tied. Use the list of words below to fill in your chart.

ちょっと	けっこう	大変 たいへん	なかなか	良く	少し すこ
まあまあ	時々	あまり	とても	毎日	全然 ぜんぜん
逆に ぎゃく	いつも	全く まった	たくさん	次 つぎ	後で
今	速く はや	遅く おそ	たいてい	明日 あした	昨日 きのう

文化箱 **Culture Chest**
ぶん か ばこ

Eastern and Western Ideals of Beauty

During the relatively peaceful Edo period (1600–1868), city dwellers flocked to the theatre to see the kabuki plays and their actors whose images they had seen adorning shop windows and walls. This excitement and the massive increase in popularity spurred the art scene in Edo. One particular genre of 浮世 うき よ 絵 え prints was 美人画 びじん が (images of beautiful women). These images set the standards for beauty in their day, and were the equivalent to our modern fashion magazines. Compare the prints below. What can you conclude about ideals of beauty in Japan and in the West during the 1700s and 1800s? How would you compare these standards of beauty to those of the West today?

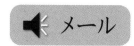 **メール**

Here is a letter to Kiara from Miyazaki-sensei, her art teacher, about the influence of ukiyo-e prints on European Impressionist artists like Lautrec and Degas.

Points to consider as you read:

❶ What did Miyazaki sensei invite Kiara to do with his family?

❷ What were some items from Japan first seen by Westerners in the late 19c?

❸ Miyazaki sensei finds similarities between Van Gogh and Hokusai. What are they?

キアラさん

　元気にやってますか。日本にいる間雨が降る事もなくて、なかなかお天気で何よりです。私は2週間後に家族と富士山に良い景色を見に行くつもりですが、キアラさんも私の家族と一緒に行きませんか?良かったらじゅん君の家族に話してみます。

　1800年代後半に、北斎や他の浮世絵師がフランスの印象画家達に*影響を及ぼしたというのは、その通りだよ。ペリーの*黒船が日本へ来て、ヨーロッパに(浮世絵を持って)帰った時に、初めてロートレックやドガやモネ、ゴッホやゴーギャンなどの芸術家達は浮世絵を見ました。ちょうど江戸時代が終って1868年に明治時代が始まった時です。西洋の人達はその時日本の美術品や*衣装、食器などを初めて見たんだ。

　ゴッホと兄弟のテオは数百点の浮世絵を集めて、どんなに素晴らしいかを話し合ったそうだ。ゴッホは日本の芸術家が明るい色に黒い線を引くという事にとても驚きを覚えたそうだよ。ゴッホが*変わった人だったというのは聞いたことがあるかな。北斎も同じように変わり者ものだと思われているんだよ。北斎も広重もヨーロッパの芸術家によって勉強され、模倣された程なんです。

　キアラさん、じゅん君の家族にもよろしくお伝え下さい。ではまた書きますね。

宮崎先生
みやざき

---

* 影響を及ぼす – to influence; 黒船 – Black Ships (specifically, American steam-powered ships that arrived on the Japanese coast for the first time in 1853); 変わった人 – unusual/different person

馬は泳げません。
うま　およ

Horses can't swim.

1) 広重は北斎ほどたくさん漫画を描きませんでした。北斎は、漫画を十五冊も描きました。

2) えっ！本当ですか？

3) これは北斎の漫画です。あ、「金太郎」の絵本がありますね。

4) 金太郎は相撲が強くて優しい人です。絵が簡単でユーモラスです。見えますか？水の中に馬がいます。馬は泳げません。

5) でも、今の漫画と違いますね。話がとても短くて簡単です。

6) 相撲の漫画はおかしいですね。この力士は弱いですね。ベン君、力士の話が読めますか？

7) うーん。漢字も難しくて読めません。もっと勉強しなければ！

8) 上から下、右から左に読んで下さい。

9) ああ、分かった。読み方は分かりました。

会話 Dialog
かい

(Setting: the characters are in an art shop, talking with a shop owner and an artist about comparative styles of ukiyo-e artists.)

1. 芸人　：広重は北斎ほどたくさん漫画を描きませんでした。北斎は、漫画を十五冊も
   げいにん　　ひろしげ　ほくさい　　　　　まんが　か　　　　　ほくさい　　まんが　　じゅうごさつ
   描きました。
   か

2. ベン　：えっ！本当ですか？

3. 芸人　：これは北斎の漫画です。あ、「金太郎」の絵本がありますね。
   げいにん　　　　ほくさい　まんが　　　　　　きんたろう　　えほん

4. ベン　：金太郎は相撲が強くて優しい人です。絵が簡単でユーモラスです。見えます
   　　　　きんたろう　すもう　　　　やさ　　　　　　　かんたん
   か？水の中に馬がいます。馬は泳げません。
   　うま　　　　うま　およ

5. キアラ　：でも、今の漫画と違いますね。話がとても短くて簡単です。
   　　　　　　　まんが　ちが　　　　　　　　　みじか　かんたん

6. じゅん　：相撲の漫画はおかしいですね。この力士は弱いですね。ベン君、力士の話が読
   　　　　　すもう　まんが　　　　　　　　　りきし　よわ
   めますか？

7. ベン　：うーん。漢字も難しくて読めません。もっと勉強しなければ！
   　　　　　　　　むずか　　　　　　　　　　べんきょう

8. 芸人　：上から下、右から左に読んで下さい。
   げいにん　　　　　みぎ　　ひだり

9. ベン　：ああ、分かった。読み方は分かりました。

単語 New Words
たん

わかい　若い (い adj.) – young　　｜　としをとる　年を取る (v) – grow old (to); age (to)

漢字 Kanji

簡	カン – simplicity	ノ	⺅	⺓	⺮	竹	竹	竹	竹	笁
18 strokes	簡単 – simple かんたん	笁	笁	笁	笁	箚	箚	簡	簡	簡

The top radical of this kanji is bamboo (竹), while the bottom (間) is an interval of time. Bamboo growth is an example of SIMPLICITY, each section is one simple cylinder atop another.

	タン – simple, one, single	丶	ソ	ソ	ツ	ヅ	肖
	簡単 – simple; 単語 – word, vocabulary かんたん ／ たんご	肖	単	単			
9 strokes	Here is a SIMPLE equation of three SINGLE grains placed above a field (田). Add water to get a ten-fold (十) harvest.						

	ジャク, よわ(い) – weak, frail; よわ(まる) – to weaken	フ	コ	弓	弓	弓	弱
弱	弱気 – timid, faint-hearted よわき	弱	弱	弱	弱		
10 strokes	These two bows (弓), without any arrows, each have two dots of ice crystals that make them very WEAK.						

	ナン, かた(い), むずか(しい) – difficult, impossible, trouble	一	十	廾	艹	芇	芇	莒	莫
難	難しい – hard, difficult; 難民 – refugees むずか ／ なんみん	莫	菓	蓳	蓳	鄭	鄭	難	難	難
18 strokes	This kanji seems more DIFFICULT than it is. The grass radical (卄) is on top of a mouth (口) trying to get through a lid (一) covering a big (大) prize, making it DIFFICULT for the bird (隹) on the right side to get out.								

言葉の探索 Language Detection
ことば　たんさく

1. **Potential verbs: お箸が使える？ = Can you use chopsticks?**
はし

   To say that you can, or cannot, do something, use the potential form of a verb. This pattern is created as follows:

   - Type 1 or う Verbs – change the "い" ending sound of the (〜ます) verb stem to an "え" ending. For example, み changes to め, に changes to ね, び changes to べ, etc.

   - Type 2 or る Verbs – add 〜られる to the verb stem of the plain form. (Use 〜られます to the verb stem of the 〜ます form.)

   - Irregular Verbs – する/します becomes 出来る/出来ます and 来る/来ます become 来られる /来られます.
   でき　でき　　　　く　き　　　　こ
   こ

Below are some verbs and their potential forms. Refer to the Verb Chart Appendix for more examples.

Type 1 (う) Verbs

		English	dictionary form/ます form	Potential form (can...)	Potential negative form (cannot...)
み		to drink	飲む/飲みます	飲める/飲めます	飲めない/飲めません
に		to die	死ぬ/死にます	死ねる/死ねます	死ねない/死ねません
び		to play	遊ぶ/遊びます	遊べる/遊べます	遊べない/遊べません
い		to meet	会う/会います	会える/会えます	会えない/会えません
ち		to wait	待つ/待ちます	待てる/待てます	待てない/待てません
り		to return (home)	帰る/帰ります	帰れる/帰れます	帰れない/帰れません
き		to write	書く/書きます	書ける/書けます	書けない/書けません
*		to go	行く/*行きます	行ける/行けます	行けない/行けません
ぎ		to swim	泳ぐ/泳ぎます	泳げる/泳げます	泳げない/泳げません
し		to speak	話す/話します	話せる/話せます	話せない/話せません

Type 2 (る) Verbs

English	dictionary form/ ます form	Potential form (can...)	Potential negative form (cannot...)
can eat	食べる/食べます	食べられる/食べられます	食べられない/食べられません
to look/see	見る/見ます	見られる/見られます	見られない/見られません
to open	開ける/開けます	開けられる/開けられます	開けられない/開けられません
to begin	始める/始めます	始められる/始められます	始められない/始められません

Irregular Verbs

English	dictionary form/ ます form	Potential form	Potential negative form
can do	する します	出来る 出来ます	出来ない 出来ません
can come	来る 来ます	来られる 来られます	来られない/ 来られません

2. Comparison in the negative using ほど

Use the particle ほど with a negative predicate ending to say that something is NOT as old, new, bright, etc. as something else. Used alone, ほど indicates an approximate extent or degree. When using ほど, the ending must be negative.

_____ は _____ ほど _____。
　 noun A 　　　　 noun B 　　　　 negative adj conjugation

or

_____ ほど _____ は _____。
　 noun B 　　　　 noun A 　　　　 negative adj conjugation

例
れい
EXAMPLE

（ア）パリの人口は東京の人口ほど多くありません。
　　　　 じんこう　　　　 　じんこう　　 おお
　　　= The population of Paris is not as large as that of Tokyo.

（イ）新幹線ほど普通の電車は速くありません。
　　　 しんかんせん　 ふつう　 でんしゃ　 はや
　　　= Regular trains are not as fast as shinkansen (bullet trains).

（ウ）オーストラリアほど日本は広くありません。= Japan is not as spacious as Australia.

（エ）私には、美術ほど英語は面白くありません。= For me, English is not as interesting as art.
　　　　　　 びじゅつ

自習 Self Check
　 じ しゅう

1. Practice restating the following in the potential form.

A) 飲みます (drink)　　　E) 聞きます (listen)　　　I) 見ます (see)

B) 読みます (read)　　　F) 泳ぎます (swim)　　　J) 来ます (come)
　　　　　　　　　　　　　　 およ

C) 待ちます (wait)　　　G) 話します (speak)

D) 帰ります (return)　　　H) 食べます (eat)

2. Use ほど to compare the sets of images below. Use these guidelines to help with your sentence patterns.

例
れい
EXAMPLE
AはBほど新しくありません。
or
AはBほど新しくないです。

A　　　　　　　B　　　　　　　C　　　　　　　D　　　　　　　E　　　　　　　F

練習時間 **Practice Time**
れん しゅう

1. Pair Practice

Use the potential verb form to ask your partner if he/she can do various actions. Use the images below for ideas if you need them.

例
REI
EXAMPLE

A-さん： この漢字が書けますか。　= Can you write this kanji?

B-さん： ええ、 書けます。　= Yes I can write it.

(teach)

(use chopsticks)

(eat)

(dance)

2. Pair Practice

With your partner, take turns describing differences among the people pictured here. Give them names, and consider their ages, height, eye color, hearing, weight, or hair when making your sentences. Use ほど in each of your descriptions.

例
れい
EXAMPLE

大輔君ほど太郎さんは若くありません。　= Taro is not as young as Daisuke.
だいすけ　　たろう　　わか

A

B

1. 漫画
まん が

Have you ever wondered how the first 漫画 was created? Some say that the first 漫画, literally translated
まん が   まん が

as "whimsical sketches," date back to the scrolls drawn in the 12th century. We know that the first sets

of drawings to be called 漫画 were produced in the late 1700s. Although this style of drawing has been

around for a long time, the first modern 漫画 are considered to have been created during the U.S. occu-

pation of Japan, immediately following WWII. At that time, artists such as 手塚冶虫 (1928–1989) popu-
て づかおさむ

larized Japanese manga. 手塚先生 created the 漫画 character 鉄腕アト
て づか   てつわん

ム, known as Astro Boy in the West, to try to express his ideas about the

rapid social and scientific changes brought about by new technologies.

手塚先生の漫画 arrived on American shores soon after and immedi-
て づか

ately gained popularity.

    In this chapter, Kiara is quite surprised to see a famous 漫画 drawn

by 北斎in the early 1800s, since its style closely resembles a later form
ほくさい

of 漫画. Hokusai's drawings and sketches consisted of imaginary crea-
まん が

tures, ghosts, and goblins. There were also images of frogs and other

animals in human poses. Look for examples of these and other 浮世絵
うきよえ

done in 漫画 style online. See if you can discover ways that historical art

has influenced modern 漫画.

2. 金太郎の昔話
きん た ろう むかしばなし

Many popular 昔話 tell stories about 金太郎. The boy 金太郎 is usually depicted wearing a tradi-
むかしばなし   きん た ろう   きん た ろう

tional apron with the character 金きん in the middle. As with any folk hero, stories of his origin vary,

some saying he was the child of a wealthy villager and others holding that his mother had abandoned him

in the forests. 金太郎 was an incredibly strong child and many tales revolve around his super-human
きん た ろう

strength, which eventually helped him become a retainer (assistant) to the samurai 源頼光 (944–
みなもとのよりみつ

1021年). 金太郎's image appears often in Japan's folk traditions and popular culture. He can be found
きん た ろう

everywhere in popular culture, from Edo-period 浮世絵 prints to modern-day candy, Children's Day dolls,
うきよえ

and 21st century アニメ and video games.

🔊 メール

Here is a letter from Kiara's art teacher about the history of manga in Japan.

Points to consider as you read:

❶ What traditional food is eaten on very hot days in Japan?

❷ What were early manga like? Did they have dialogue?

❸ What sorts of pictures were included in early manga?

❹ What differences do you see between Japanese manga and American comics?

キアラさんへ

　今日は本当に暑い日だったね。東京のこの時期の暑さに慣れてないのではないかと心配でした。うちの家族はこんな暑い日は鰻を食べに行きます。日本人は暑い日に鰻を食べると元気が出ると信しんじているんだ。

　漫画がどうやって出来たか興味があるんだね。初めのころの漫画は、あるテーマについて描かれた一連の絵だったんだよ。北斎は10冊以上の漫画を版画にしたんだ。それぞれ2、3ページの長さでした。こうした初期の漫画には言葉はなかったんだ。相撲取りや踊り子、悪魔などの絵だけだった。インターネットで調べてみると色々な漫画の例が出て来るよ。*第二次世界大戦の終わり頃から*アメリカ軍の駐留時代にかけて、言葉と一緒に印刷されるようになったのが現代の漫画だ。日本人の描く漫画はアメリカ人の描くのとかなり違うよね。キアラさんはどんなところが違うと思うかな?

　そろそろ終わりにします。明日の授業の準備をしなければならないからね。ではまたね。

宮崎先生
みやざき

---

* 第二次世界大戦 – WW II; アメリカ軍の駐留時代 – the American Occupation

狸の歴史の方がもっと長いですよ。
たぬき　れきし　ほう

Tanuki history is longer!

1) 絵の国の旅行は楽しかったですね。

2) そうですね。アメリカで浮世絵について少し勉強しましたが、その歴史はあまり知りませんでした。これからもっと日本史を勉強します。

3) 日本史はアメリカ史よりもっと長いです。

4) アメリカ史はオーストラリアの歴史ほど短くないですよ。

5) 狸の歴史の方がもっと長いですよ。

6) 北斎の漫画は今の漫画ほど面白くないです。でも、北斎の絵は素晴らしいです。

7) はい。北斎の「赤富士」は一番美しくて、すごい浮世絵です。

8) 富士山と津波の絵は「赤富士」より力があります。

9) 私は店に行って浮世絵のポスターを買います。

10) 浮世絵は印刷出来ます。私は浮世絵のTシャツを三枚持っています。

 会話 Dialog
かい

(Setting: The group compares various things.)

1. じゅん ： 絵の国の旅行は楽しかったですね。
　　　　　　　　　　　りょこう

2. キアラ ： そうですね。アメリカで浮世絵について少し勉強しましたが、その歴史はあまり
　　　　　　　　　　　　　うきよえ　　　　　すこ　べんきょう　　　　　　　　れきし
　　　　　　　知りませんでした。これからもっと日本史を勉強します。
　　　　　　　し　　　　　　　　　　　　　　　　　　　し　べんきょう

3. ベン ： 日本史はアメリカ史よりもっと長いです。
　　　　　　　　　し　　　　　　し

4. キアラ ： アメリカ史はオーストラリアの歴史ほど短くないですよ。
　　　　　　　　　　し　　　　　　　　　　れきし　みじか

5. 友 ： 狸の歴史の方ほうがもっと長いですよ。
　　　　　たぬき　れきし

6. ベン ： 北斎の漫画は今の漫画ほど面白くないです。でも、北斎の絵は素晴らしいです。
　　　　　　ほくさい　まんが　　　まんが　　　　　　　　　　　ほくさい　　　すば

7. じゅん ： はい。北斎の「赤富士」は一番美しくて、すごい浮世絵です。
　　　　　　　　ほくさい　あかふじ　　　　　　　　　　　うきよえ

8. 友 ： 富士山と津波の絵は「赤富士」より力があります。
　　　　　ふじさん　つなみ　　　あかふじ　　　ちから

9. キアラ ： 私は店に行って浮世絵のポスターを買います。
　　　　　　　　みせ　　　うきよえ

10. 友 ： 浮世絵は*印刷出来ます。私は浮世絵のTシャツを三枚持っています。
　　　　　うきよえ　いんさつ　　　　　　うきよえ

* 印刷 – printing
　いんさつ

 単語 New Words
たん

ちから 力 (n) – power

はやい 早い (い adj.) – early

おそく 遅く (adv.) – slowly

はやく 早く (adv.) – early (in the day)

漢字 Kanji

早 6 strokes	はや(い), はや, はや〜 – early	丨	口	卩	日	旦	早
	早い – early; 早く – early, soon; 早起 – early rising はや　　　　　　はや　　　　　　はやおき						
	The sun is high in the sky by ten (十) o'clock since it comes up very EARLY in the morning.						

 力 2 strokes	リョク, リキ, ちから – power, strong, exert	フ 力				
	力 – power, strength; 力づける – to encourage (someone); 入力 – input, (data) entry, にゅうりょく 力強い – powerful, strong ちからづよ					
	This kanji is also a radical. The two strokes form a very STRONG right angle.					

言葉の探索 Language Detection
こと ば たん さく

1. Review of comparisons: ～より～の方が、～ほど、逆に
ぎゃく

Each of these patterns has a slightly different implication when making a comparison. Review these examples.

A) ～の方が～より

東京の方が平泉より大きいです。　= Tokyo is larger than Hiraizumi.
ひらいずみ

B) ～ほど

東京ほど平泉は大きくありません。　= Hiraizumi is not as large as Tokyo.
ひらいずみ

C) 逆に – conversely, on the contrary (can be used to show contrast)
ぎゃく

東京の人口は本当に多いです。逆に平泉は全然多くありません。
ぎゃく　　ひらいずみ

= Tokyo's population is really large. On the contrary, Hiraizumi's is not big at all.

2. Review of new elaborative words

なかなか – very, considerably (with a positive verb), or by no means/can hardly... (with a negative verb)

なかなか難しいです。　　　　= It is (becoming) considerably more difficult.
むずか

そのクラスはなかなか面白いです。　= That class is (becoming) considerably more interesting.

なかなか時間がありませんね。　= There is less and less time.

けっこう – reasonably, fairly

柔道はけっこう難しいです。　　= Judo is fairly difficult.
じゅう　　　　むずか

あの友達は背がけっこう高いです。　= That friend over there is fairly tall.
せ

自習 Self Check
じ しゅう

1. Use at least six of the following adjectives with nouns of your choice to practice the three comparison patterns taught in this chapter.

① ～より・・・・の方が　　② ～ほど + negative adj. conjugation　　③ 逆に・・・
ぎゃく

明るい	大きい	うるさい	背が高い	かわいい	元気
			せ		
危ない	難しい	美味しい	嫌い	速い	早い
あぶ	むずか	お　い	きら	はや	はや

2. On a separate sheet of paper, use your favorite graphic organizer to group the following words into two or three different categories (for instance, words related to time, words indicating extremes, etc.).

ちょっと	けっこう	大変 <small>たいへん</small>	なかなか	良く	少し <small>すこ</small>
まあまあ	時々	あまり	とても	毎日	全然 <small>ぜんぜん</small>
逆に <small>ぎゃく</small>	いつも	全く <small>まった</small>	たくさん	次 <small>つぎ</small>	後で
今	速く <small>はや</small>	遅く <small>おそ</small>	たいてい	明日 <small>あした</small>	昨日 <small>きのう</small>

練習時間 Practice Time
<small>れん しゅう</small>

Class Interview Practice

Use a piece of paper for an interview sheet. Write some questions that you would like to ask or that you think you should prepare for. First write your own statements of comparison for each situation. Next, ask a classmate what he/she thinks about the comparisons you created. Your classmate should write his/her name in Japanese in the "正しい" box if he/she thinks that your statement is true. If he/she does not agree with your statement, say 失礼しました and move on to another student. You may only make two statements to each student.

Vocabulary you might use include 好き, 嫌い, 美味しい, 優しい, etc.

Use each of the following methods of comparison at least twice:

〜の方が　　　　〜より　　　　〜もっと　　　　〜ほど + negative　　　　〜。逆に〜
<small>ぎゃく</small>

 パーソンズ先生の方がスミス先生より背が高いと思いますか。
<small>せ</small>
(Do you think Mr. Parsons is taller than Mr. Smith?)

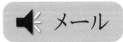 メール

Miyazaki sensei is writing Kiara about the possibility of her giving a presentation to the class.
Points to consider as you read:

❶ Miyazaki sensei is asking Kiara to make a class presentation on what topic?
❷ How long would he like Kiara's presentation to be?
❸ He suggests two teachers who could help her with this. Who are they and what do they teach?

キアラさんへ

　色々な日本の芸術と同時に、漫画と浮世絵にもとても興味があるんだね。来月、京都で研究会に行かなくてはならないんだ。私のグループは、中国の、平安時代以前の日本の*彫刻への*影響を研究しているんだ。来春にはこのテーマで教師の雑誌に記事を書くつもりだよ。

　私が京都に行っている間に、1時間だけこのテーマについて授業で発表をしてくれませんか？キアラさんが習った日本の芸術と芸術家のことを聞くのは、皆にとって本当に勉強になると思うよ。日本の芸術と印象派の芸術家について話してもらえたら、とても嬉しいです。

*準備はもちろん手伝うよ。キアラさんの歴史の先生の山本先生もきっと、喜んで手伝ってくれるはずです。発表に必要だと思う*資料は何でも使っていいですよ。20分程話してくれたら、残りの時間は*質疑応答にするといいと思う。もう一人の美術の先生の森口先生に、キアラさんを手伝ってくれるように頼んでおくよ。

　2、3日考えて、それから話しに来て下さい。きっと面白い授業になると思いますよ。

宮崎先生
みやざき

---

*　彫刻 – carving, sculpture; 影響 – influence; 研究する – to research; 準備 – preparation; 資料 – materials, resources; 質疑応答 – question-and-answer (period)

江戸　1815年
えど

Traditions of Performing Arts

第4課
か

Our group continues their exploration of Edo in 1815. They are strolling through the city, winding through the streets and alleyways of Asakusa, a center of nightlife and drama throughout much of the Edo period. The main kabuki theatre in Tokyo today is in the Ginza area.

Learning and Performance Goals

This chapter will enable you to:
- review 持って行く and 連れて行く, etc.
- review verbs of giving and receiving
- use the particle の to replace a noun and to nominalize adjectives and a review using verbs as gerunds
- use a variation of どんな〜 – 何の… (what kind of)
- say that you "can do ~" or it is possible "to do ~" (〜が出来る)
- say someone is expected to do something (つもり) and that "I" intend to do something (はず)
- show cause and effect by using the conjunction それで
- use the particle ので – since/given that…/because of…
- talk about kabuki and other popular dramatic arts in 19th c. Edo
- use some informal speech as well as some elements of 敬語 (polite Japanese)
  けいご
- use 11 additional kanji

第4課の1

今日は何の話をするの?

What sort of story will you tell today?

1) あっ、紙芝居の おじさんが来るよ。

2) さあ、皆、紙芝居をするよ! 私の前に座って。

3) 今日は何の 話をするの?

6) ああ、そう?じゃあ「桃太郎」に するか。紙芝居の後でおかしを 売るよ。皆お金を持ってる?

4) 「浦島太郎」をやるよ。

5) えーっ。「浦島太郎」は前に聞いたよ。

7) うん、持ってる。私はあめを買うの。

8) 私は餅と 煎餅と。。。。

9) シーッ!静かに。紙芝居が始まるよ。

10) 昔々、あるところに、おじいさんと おばあさんが住んでいました。。。。

会話 Dialog
かい

(Setting: Our group spots dozens of children, gathered in a clearing around an older gentleman travele[r]
in a clearing.)

1. 供達　　　　：あっ、紙芝居のおじさんが来るよ。
   こどもたち　　　　　　かみしばい

2. 紙芝居屋　：さあ、皆、紙芝居をするよ！私の前に座すわって。
   かみしばいや　　　　　　かみしばい

3. 男の子1　：今日は何の話をするの？

4. 紙芝居屋　：「浦島太郎」をやるよ。
   かみしばいや　　　　うらしまたろう

5. 男の子2　：えーっ。「浦島太郎」は前に聞いたよ。
   　　　　　　　　　うらしまたろう

6. 紙芝居屋　：ああ、そう？じゃあ「桃太郎」にするか。紙芝居の後でおかしを売るよ。みんな
   かみしばいや　　　　　　　　ももたろう　　　　　かみしばい　　あと
   お金を*持ってる？

7. 女の子3　：うん、持ってる。私はあめを買うの。

8. 友　　　　：私は餅と煎餅と…
   　　　　　　　もち　せんべい

9. 男の子4　：シーッ！静かに。紙芝居が始まるよ。
   　　　　　　　　しず　　　かみしばい

10. 紙芝居屋　：昔々、あるところにおじいさんとおばあさんが住んでいました…
    かみしばいや　むかし　　　　　　　　　　　　　　　　　　す

*持ってる – informal for 持っている

単語 New Words
たん

かみしばい 紙芝居 (n) – picture
story show

しゅっぱつ 出発 (n) – departure

さあ (interj.) – Well..., Well, let's ~

それとも (conj.) – or, or else

なんの 何の (exp.) – what kind of?

しゅっぱつする 出発する
(v) – depart (to)

つく 着く (v) – arrive at (to)

とうちゃく 到着 (n) – arrival

はじまる 始まる (v) – begin (to)

漢字 Kanji

連	レン, つれ(る) – take along/escort, lead, connect	一	厂	戸	戸	亘	亘
	国連 – United Nations; 連れる – to take along/escort こくれん　　　　　　　　　つ	車	車	連	連		
10 strokes	A cart (車), next to the stop-and-go radical (辶), stops to pick up/escort passengers and TAKE them ALONG to another location.						

1. Informal speech

Most Japanese people, when speaking casually, do not use what is often referred to as the です/ます form (the standard polite form). Beginning learners, however, usually learn this speech pattern first, because it is important to use a more polite form of Japanese language when first meeting people. Once you become closer to your Japanese friends and colleagues, the level of speech used in daily conversation is usually more casual.

What is the difference between formal (polite) and informal (plain) speech? One of the biggest audible differences is found in the sentence endings. In informal/plain speech, verbs in their present and future tense use the dictionary form; the plain past tense is the 〜た form. To conjugate most verbs in the plain form, here are a few key points to keep in mind:

- the present and future tense uses the dictionary form of the verb. The dictionary form is created by dropping the 〜ます ending and changing the final remaining hiragana from an い ending sound to an う ending sound for Type 1 (う) verbs (e.g.: 飲みます ➡ 飲む). For Type 2 (る) verbs, simply drop the 〜ます and add る (e.g.: 食べます ➡ 食べる). Note special changes in the irregular verbs.

- the past tense for Type 1 (う) verbs is conjugated like the 〜て-form, except that た replaces て (e.g.: 飲んで ➡ 飲んだ). For Type 2 (る) verbs, simply replace the る with た (e.g.: 食べる ➡ 食べた)

- to create the plain negative form for Type 1 (う) verbs, change the い sound to あ (い ➡ わ, み ➡ ま, り ➡ ら, etc.) and then add ない (e.g.: 飲みません ➡ 飲まない); for Type 2 verbs, simply add ない to the stem (e.g.: 見る ➡ 見ない)

- to create the negative past form, use the plain negative stem (that is, the あ stem for Type 1 verbs, and the verb stem for Type 2 verbs), and add なかった (e.g.: 飲まなかった)

Refer to the following charts for examples. Note that verb stems ending in い (without a consonant) change to わ in the negative and negative past forms.

Informal Verb Conjugation Chart

Type 1 – う verbs

〜ます **stem form**	**Present/future**	**Past**	**Negative**	**Negative Past**
飲み	飲む	飲んだ	飲まない	飲まなかった
読み	読む	読んだ	読まない	読まなかった
言い	言う	言った	言わない	言わなかった
手伝い つだ	手伝う	手伝った	手伝わない	手伝わなかった
待ち	待つ	待った	待たない	待たなかった

～ます stem form	Present/future	Past	Negative	Negative Past
知り	知る	知った	知らない	知らなかった
帰り	帰る	帰った	帰らない	帰らなかった
買い	買う	買った	買わない	買わなかった
分かり	分かる	分かった	分からない	分からなかった
聞き	聞く	聞いた	聞かない	聞かなかった
行き	行く	行った	行かない	行かなかった
泳ぎ	泳ぐ	泳いだ	泳がない	泳がなかった
話し	話す	話した	話さない	話さなかった

Type 2 – る verbs

～ます stem form	Present/future	Past	Negative	Negative Past
開け	開ける	開けた	開けない	開けなかった
食べ	食べる	食べた	食べない	食べなかった
始め	始める	始めた	始めない	始めなかった

Irregular Verbs and the Copula – です

The exceptions are the copula です and the verbs 来る and する which conjugate in the plain form differently.

～ます stem form	Present/future	Past	Negative	Negative Past
来ます	来る	来た	来ない	来なかった
します	する	した	しない	しなかった
です	だ	だった	ではない じゃない	ではなかった じゃなかった

2. Basic questioning in the plain form

There are several aspects of the language which change when using plain speech, however two basic considerations can be thought of when asking questions in the plain form:

① The particle か is dropped and the intonation of the final sound questions rises. (新しい車を買う。= Are you going to buy a new car?)

② The pitch at the end of sentences rises if the example is a question, and falls if it is a statement. This is similar to the difference between でしょう statements and questions.

Statement: 東京へ行きます。 ⇨ 東京へ行く。 = I am going to Tokyo.
Question: 東京へ行きますか。 ⇨ 東京へ行く。 = Are you going to Tokyo?

3. 何の・・・ = **what kind/sort of...**

何の is used when specifically asking what kind or what sort of thing. どんな, though similar, only refers to "what kind of" in a more general sense. Both 何の and どんな are normally followed by a noun unless the topic is understood.

A) 何の事 = What kind of thing?
B) 何の話 = What kind of speech/talk?
はなし
C) 何の車 = What kind of car?

自習 Self Check
じしゅう

1. Restate each of the following as plain form verb. State each out loud to yourself as you do so.

    ア）買いません   → ＿＿＿＿＿＿＿＿＿＿＿

    イ）紹介しました   → ＿＿＿＿＿＿＿＿＿＿＿
    しょうかい

    ウ）起きませんでした   → ＿＿＿＿＿＿＿＿＿＿＿
    お

    エ）言います   → ＿＿＿＿＿＿＿＿＿＿＿

    オ）疲れていきます   → ＿＿＿＿＿＿＿＿＿＿＿
    つか

2. Plain form questions: put these polite questions into plain form question format.

    ア）昨日、友達と買い物に行きましたか。
    きのう

    イ）明日、おばあさんは家に*親戚を連れて来ますか。
    あした   しんせき   つ

    ウ）毎日、犬に食べ物をやりますか。

    エ）あの木の上に鳥がいますよ。聞こえますか。
              とり

    オ）橋を渡って、右側にありますか。
      わた   がわ

*親戚 – relative
しんせき

練習時間 Practice Time
れんしゅう

康祐君の一日
こうすけくん　　いちにち

午前6:00	起きる お	午後12:00	友達と話す
午前6:30	シャワーを浴びる あ 歯をみがく (brush teeth) は	午後3:10	学校の*掃除をする そうじ
午前6:45	朝ご飯を食べる あさ　はん	午後3:15	自転車で塾に行く じてんしゃ　じゅく コンビニで*おやつを買う
午前7:00	家を出る	午後6:20	家へ帰る
午前7:35	学校に行く	午後9:35	宿題をする しゅくだい
午前8:55〜	授業が始まる じゅぎょう　はじ	午後11:00	寝る ね

*掃除 – cleaning; おやつ – snack(s)
そうじ

1. Pair Practice

Take turns with your partner. Use informal speech to ask and answer questions about Kosuke's daily schedule, based on the chart on page 135.

based on the chart on page 135.

例
れい
EXAMPLE

A-さん： 康祐君は六時半に起きる。
　　　　こうすけくん　　　　　　お

B-さん： うん、六時に起きる。
　　　　　　　　　　お

or 　　ううん、六時半に起きない。
　　　　　　　　はん　　お

2. Small Group Activity

Form groups of 3-4 students. Read the cards your teacher gives you or use those found on **TimeForJapanese.com** for this chapter. The bottom half is for reading, the top half is for listening. Do じゃんけん to see who goes first. When your teacher says はい、始めましょう!, Person A restates the line on the bottom
はじ
of his/her card in Japanese. The person whose top line matches, then repeats what was said, but changes the verb ending into the て-form, and then adds the line on the bottom of his/her card (making compound sentences) to continue the story. Continue until time is up, or you have reached the first line again.

For example:

Person A: (I will go to Hokkaido) 私は北海道へ行きます。
　　　　　　　　　　　　　　　　　ほっかいどう

Person B: 私は北海道へ行って、ラーメンを食べます。
　　　　　　ほっかいどう

Person C: ラーメンを食べて、電車で広島へ行きます。
　　　　　　　　　　　　　　　ひろしま

Person D: 電車で広島へ行って、それから、飛行機で大阪へ帰ります。
　　　　　　ひろしま　　　　　　　　　ひこうき　　おおさか

Continue until all of the cards have been used, including the first line on the first card. Then switch cards and repeat, restating them in English

文化箱 Culture Chest
ぶん　か　ばこ

紙芝居
かみ　し　ばい

The Japanese tradition of 紙芝居, sometimes called "paper theatre", had its origins in the Buddhist story-
かみ　し　ばい
telling of the 12th century. Priests and others used 絵巻 (picture scrolls) to tell stories detailing Buddhist
　　　　　　　　　　　　　　　　　　　え　まき
moral ideals, historical tales, and legends. The tradition continued, in various fashions, into the Meiji peri-

od, and was revived in its modern form in the early 20th century. The storyteller rode into town on his bicycle, a small wooden stage fastened to the back. The "clap! clap!" of the 拍子木 (two hard wooden sticks) being
ひょうし　き
knocked together signaled the beginning of the show. As excited children gathered around, the storyteller placed an illustrated card into the "stage". To tell the tale, the storyteller dramatically read the story lines printed on the back of each card. Selling candy to the audience was the primary source of income for these itinerant bards.

Kamishibai storytelling about Basho's life and travels (photo by P. Valentine)

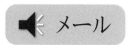

This message is from Ben's friend Misao Tayama, who is replying to Ben's previous note to her about kamishibai.

Points to consider as you read:

❶ When does Misao say kamishibai began?

❷ What two reasons can you give for the kamishibai man being so popular among children?

❸ What was television first called in Japanese?

❹ Does Misao think the kamishibai tradition continues today?

❺ If you were to write and perform a kamishibai, what story would you choose?

　ベン君へ

　紙芝居について知りたいようで嬉しいわ。絵を使ったお話は平安時代の終わり頃に生まれたの。もともと、絵巻と言って絵と一緒に書かれた物語は、お坊さんが*仏教の中のお話を語るときに使われていたのよ。

　ベン君が見た紙芝居は、1930年代に紙芝居のおじさんが街頭で子供達に話して聞かせる街頭芝居というものよ。紙芝居屋は、話を聞きに来る子供達に*駄菓子を売って生計を立てていたの。だから、*小銭を持った子供達が集まるところで盛んだったのよ。テレビの登場で、紙芝居は殆どなくなってしまったの。テレビが最初登場した時は「電気紙芝居」とも呼ばれたそうよ！　60年代になるとお母さん達が自分の子供のために手作りの紙芝居を作るようになって、紙芝居の文化は今だに*続いています。

　紙芝居は「絵」と紙芝居を読む人の「語り」が中心だけど、漫画はこの「語り」を「絵」の中に書き込んだものと見ることも出来るわね。アニメは「絵」と「*セリフ」が主体で紙芝居にかなり近いわね。

　インターネット（Youtubeなど）でも当時の紙芝居を楽しむ事が出来るわ。ベン君も自分でお話を作って、絵を描いて、手作り紙芝居を作ってみたら？

　じゃ、気を付けて旅行を続けてね！

田山　美沙緒

* 仏教 – Buddhism; 駄菓子 – traditional Japanese sweets; 小銭 – small change (money); 続いている – continuing; セリフ – script

踊る事が出来ます。
おど

I can dance.

1) すみません。
あなたは市川團十郎さんの甥御さんですか。

2) はい、そうたが。

3) 初めまして。僕はベンです。歌舞伎を見るのは初めてです。僕も歌舞伎を勉強して、舞台に立ちたいです。

4) 歌舞伎座の中はとても暗いから、明るい色の着物を着るけど、いいかな？

6) 目と口を上手に動かす事は出来るかな？

5) はい、出来ますよ。自分でメイクも出来ます。

7) はい、出来ます。僕は目が大きいから目立ちますよ。

8) 大きい声で歌ったり、踊ったりする事が出来るかな？

10) 女形はどうだろう？

9) 踊る事は出来ます。でも、歌うのは苦手です。

12) そうか。今日、歌舞伎を見に来る事が出来るかな？「義経千本桜」をやるよ。

11) 女形はちょっと出来ません。でも動物は出来ますよ。馬と犬と狸が得意です。

13) はい！もちろん見に行きます。

会話 Dialog

(Setting: Yoshikazu has escorted the group to Ishikawa's classroom.)

1. べん : すみません。あなたは市川團十郎さんの*甥御さんですか。

2. 市川の甥 : はい、そうだが。

3. ベン : 初めまして。僕はベンです。歌舞伎を見るのは初めてです。僕も歌舞伎を勉強して、舞台に立ちたいです。

4. 市川の甥 : 歌舞伎座の中はとても暗いから、明るい色の着物を着るけど、いいかな？

5. ベン : はい、出来ますよ。自分でメイクも出来ます。

6. 市川の甥 : 目と口を上手に動かす事は出来るかな？

7. ベン : はい、出来ます。僕は目が大きいから目立ちますよ。

8. 市川の甥 : 大きい声で歌ったり、踊ったりする事が出来るかな？

9. ベン : 踊る事は出来ます。でも、歌うのは苦手です。

10. 市川の甥 : 女形はどうだろう？

11. ベン : 女形はちょっと出来ません。でも動物は出来ますよ。馬と犬と狸が得意です。

12. 市川の甥 : そうか。今日、歌舞伎を見に来る事が出来るかな？「義経千本桜」をやるよ。

13. ベン : はい！ もちろん見に行きます。

* 甥御 (or 甥) – nephew

単語 New Words

おんながた 女形 (n) – male actor in female Kabuki role

あう 合う (v) – come together (to), fit (to), match (to)

あわせる 合わせる (v) – match (to), mix (to)

うごく 動く (v) – move (to), operate (to)

うごかす 動かす (v) – move (to), set in motion (to)

おどる 踊る (v) – dance (to)

できる 出来る (v) – able to do (to be)

漢字 Kanji

形 (7 strokes)	ギョウ, ケイ, かた, かたち – shape, form	一	二	开	开	开	形
	人形 (にんぎょう) – doll; 女形 (おんながた) – male actor in female Kabuki role; 形 – shape or form	形					
	The left radical of this kanji means to open or begin; the right three strokes look like three strikes from a sculptor's chisel that is changing the SHAPE or the FORM into something new.						

合 (6 strokes)	ゴウ, あう, 〜あ(う), あ(い), あ(わす), あ(わせる) – fit, suit, join	ノ	人	스	合	合	合
	合わす (あ) – to match (rhythm, speed, etc.), to add up, to combine; 合う (あ) – to fit, to match, to suit, to agree with						
	The top of this kanji is a person (人). Below it is one (一) mouth (口). The test is to see if the one thing the person will eat will MATCH or FIT his/her taste.						

言葉の探索 (ことばのたんさく) Language Detection

1. **Using the particle の to make adjectives into nouns; and a review of gerunds (making verbs into nouns) = 〜の**

   ① With adjectives: 安いの = the cheap one

   の may be used after the adjective or descriptor to replace an understood noun.

   A) 背が高いのは秀之 (ひでゆき) さんだ。 = The tall one is Hideyuki. (Here, の replaces 人)
   B) 緑 (みどり) のを下さい。 = Please give me the green one.
   C) かわいいのが好きだ。 = I like the cute one.
   D) 妹はいつも小さいのがほしい。 = My younger sister always wants the small one.

   ② With verbs: 食べる事 or 食べるの = eating (the act of)

   Make the gerund (nominative or -ing) form of a verb by adding 事 to the dictionary form of the verb (食べる事). A second way to make a gerund phrase is to use the particle の after the dictionary form of the verb (食べるの). It cannot be used immediately before the copula です.

   A) 食べる事 ⇒ 食べるの = eating (the act of) 食べるのが好きです。
   B) 歩く事 ⇒ 歩くの = walking (the act of) 歩くのが楽しいです。
   C) する事 ⇒ するの = doing (the act of) 剣けん道をするのは難しいです。

2. can do ~ or it is possible to do ~ = ～が出来る

This pattern is used to refer to something that can be done or is possible. It can be preceded by nouns or gerunds (verbs used as nouns; see Language Detection Point 1, above). Note that this pattern uses the particle が.

A) 日本語で新聞を読む事が出来る。 = I can read a newspaper in Japanese.
B) お寿司を食べる事が出来る。 = It is possible to eat sushi.
C) 外で食べる事が出来る。 = It is possible to eat outside.
D) 遅くまで寝る事が出来る。 = It is possible to sleep late.

自習 Self Check

1. Read each of the following aloud to yourself. Then match each with the English equivalent.

ア) もっと大きいのをくれ。 　　　　1. The cheap one, please.
イ) 先生が言っている事は、何？ 　　2. The one on the left is good.
ウ) 電車で行くのは簡単だ。 　　　　3. Please give me a bigger one.
エ) 安いのをちょうだい。 　　　　　4. It's easy to go by train.
オ) 左側にあるのはいいんだよ。 　　5. What is it that the teacher is saying?

2. Restate each expression in Japanese using the ～事が出来る pattern.

ア) Tom can introduce himself (give a self introduction).
イ) I can come to school by (means of) subway.
ウ) My grandfather can cross that bridge.
エ) My little sister can dance.

 I can swim. ⇨ 泳ぐ事が出来ます。

練習時間 Practice Time

Pair Practice

Use the interview form from **TimeForJapanese.com** for this Pair Practice. Take turns interviewing your partner about things he/she can, or cannot, do using ～事が出来る. Record the results in your notebook. If you don't know, answer 知りません. Be prepared to report some of your results to the class.

お寿司を食べる事が出来ますか。
はい、お寿司を食べる事が出来ます。
or いいえ、お寿司を食べる事は出来ません。

歌舞伎
か ぶ き

歌舞伎 is a highly-stylized traditional form of dramatic performance, supposedly begun by the 神道
か ぶ き   しんとう
Priestess Okuni of Izumo in 1603. The all-female actors helped to raise money for the repairs to 出雲大
いづもたい
社 (Grand Shrine), one of the oldest in Japan. Their 歌舞伎 performances immediately earned popularity
しゃ   か ぶ き
with the growing merchant class and other patrons in the entertainment areas of 京都 and eventually 江
と   え
戸. The Tokugawa government began to worry about lax morality and banned women from performing in
ど
1629. Thus the 女形 tradition, where men take on all roles, was born. The stories used in 歌舞伎 plays
おんながた   か ぶ き
are drawn from 狂言 (comedy), 浄瑠璃 (puppet theatre), and other aspects of the rich dramatic his-
きょうげん   じょうるり
tory of Japan, including historical tales, family legends, and dances. The architecture of the Kabuki theatre
is also unique. A long, stage-level walkway called the 花道 juts from the stage, out into the audience for
はなみち
dramatic entrances and exits. It also serves to quickly draw the audience into the story by placing them
within reach of the action. In a traditional theatre, there would be an open space instead of a roof. Kabuki
is still quite popular in Japan today and is performed regularly in theatres around the country.

Though there are many popular Kabuki plays, 義経千本桜 is one of the most famous. It revolves
よしつねせんぼんざくら
around the exploits of Minamoto no Yoshitsune and his faithful retainer, Benkei. Yoshitsune's mistress
Shizuka, palace courtiers, priests, a white fox, and a drum with magical powers are just some of the characters woven into the drama.

🔊 メール

This is message to Ben from a Japanese friend of Ben's mother. The friend had previously worked at the Kabukiza, so Ben asked her for information on how to purchase kabuki tickets and for directions to the theatre.
Points to consider as you read:

❶ What is the easiest, and cheapest way for Ben to go to the Kabuki theatre?

❷ Can you purchase tickets for that day's show at the Kabuki theatre?

❸ How can tickets be reserved in advance?

❹ Is there any way to see a shorter version of Kabuki plays?

❺ What do you think an イヤホンガイド is? Would you use one, if you went to go see a kabuki play? Why
or why not?

ベン君へ

こんにちは、ベン君。久しぶりですね。お手紙をありがとう。
ひさ
歌舞伎を見に行くんですね。
か ぶ き

歌舞伎座は、東銀座にあります。ベン君は*広尾から行きますよね？バスに乗ったら何度も乗り換えなければなりません。バスより地下鉄の方が*便利です。160円で行くことが出来ます。広尾駅から地下鉄の日比谷線で東銀座駅まで14分です。乗り換えはありません。歌舞伎座は、東銀座駅の出口のすぐ前にあります。

*公演は、昼の部と夜の部になっています。昼の部はたいてい午前11時に始まり、夜の部は4時半頃に始まります。歌舞伎座で*当日券を買うことが出来ます。人気のある公演は早く売り切れます。勧進帳や、義経千本桜は、とても人気があります。だから、混みます。切符は先にインターネットや電話で予約することも出来ます。

切符は座席によって値段が違います。1階と2階の1等席は15,000円で、一番いい席です。舞台のそばで、よく見る事が出来ます。2等席なら11,000円です。3階のA席は4,200円、B席は2,500円ですが、あまり*お勧めしません。舞台から遠くてよく見ることが出来ません。

昼の部と夜の部は、それぞれ4時間位の間に三幕あります。幕の間に10分から30分の幕間と呼ばれる休憩時間があります。歌舞伎座の中でお弁当を売っていますので、この時間に席やロビーで食事が出来ます。レストランもありますが、混み合いますので予約を入れておいた方がいいです。

もし4時間が長ければ、幕見席という座席があります。一幕だけ800円〜1200円という値段で、少しだけ歌舞伎を楽しむことも出来ますよ。

昭和50年に、おばさんが歌舞伎座で働いていた時「イヤホンガイド」が始まりました。イヤホンガイドは、お芝居に合わせて、色々な説明をしてくれます。日本人も歌舞伎は「難しい」、「分からない」と思っていました。でも、「イヤホンガイド」のお陰で、多くの人が歌舞伎を見に来ました。そして、外国人には英語の「イヤホンガイド」があります。ベン君もこのイヤホンガイドを借りて下さい。きっと歌舞伎がもっと楽しくなりますよ。

それから、お母さんにお土産を買ってあげて下さいね。歌舞伎座の1階に売店があります。ベン君のお母さんはそこの羊羹が大好きです。

*広尾 – part of Tokyo; 便利 – convenient; 公演 – public performance; 当日券 – day ticket; お勧 – recommendation

花道に花を三本持って行ってもいいですか？
（はなみち）

May I take three flowers to the hanamichi?

1）歌舞伎に友達を三人連れて来てもいいですか？

2）ああ、いいよ。私の弟子の三郎が入り口に切符を四枚持って行くから。

3）ありがとうございます。お弁当とお茶を持って来てもいいですか

4）ああ、いいよ。たばこも持って来ていいよ。

5）えっ！たばこは持って行きません。花道に花を三本ぼん持って来てもいいですか？赤と白はラッキーカラーですね。

6）花？またの花を持って来るのは変かな。ふつう、お金やお土産を持って来るものだよ。

7）そうですか。知りませんでした。

8）歌舞伎の色は黒と緑と赤だ。でも赤と白もよく使うよ。

会話 Dialog
かい

(Setting: Ben is still talking to Kabuki actor Ichikawa Danjuro's nephew.)

1. ベン	:	歌舞伎に友達を三人連れて来てもいいですか？
2. 市川の*甥	:	ああ、いいよ。私の*弟子の三郎が入り口に切符を四枚持って行くから。
3. ベン	:	ありがとうございます。お弁当とお茶を持って来てもいいですか？
4. 市川の甥	:	ああ、いいよ。たばこも持って来ていいよ。
5. ベン	:	えっ！たばこは持って行きません。花道に花を三本持って来てもいいですか？赤と白はラッキーカラーですね。
6. 市川の甥	:	花？またの花を持って来るのは変かな。ふつう、お金やお土産を持って来るものだよ。
7. ベン	:	そうですか。知りませんでした。
8. 市川の甥	:	歌舞伎の色は黒と緑と赤だ。でも赤と白もよく使うよ。

* 甥 – nephew; 弟子 – apprentice, trainee
おい

単語 New Words
たん

うなぎ (n) – eel

きゅうけい 休憩 (n) – rest, break

こうえん 公演 (n) – performance

こうえん 公園 (n) – park

コスチューム (n) – costume

ことば 言葉 (n) – language, dialect, word

こんど 今度 (n) – now, this time, next time

さき(に) 先(に) (n) – before, ahead, future

ジェスチャー (n) – gesture

じっさい 実際 (n) – practically, practical, reality

しょくひん 食品 (n) – food supplies, foodstuff

つもり (n) – intention, plan

はず (n) – expectation that something has taken or will take place, expected to be まわり

まわり 周り (n) – circumference, edge

やきとり 焼き鳥 (n) – grilled chicken (kebab)

ようひん 用品 (n) – articles, supplies, parts

よけい 余計 (n) – too much, unnecessary, excess

おかしい (い adj.) – strange, funny, ridiculous

めずらしい 珍しい (い adj.) – unusual, rare

へん 変 (な adj.) – unusual, strange

きっと (adv.) – surely, undoubtedly

ので (part.) – that being the case, because of …

～くらい (part.) – about ~

そうそう (interj.) – Oh, yes!, that's right

えんじる 演じる (v) – perform (to)

きゅうけい(を)する 休憩(を)する (v) – take a break (to)

さく 咲く (v) – bloom (to)

まいる 参る (v) – go (to), come (to), visit (to) a grave or shrine (humble for 行きます・来ます)

みせる 見せる (v) – show (to)

漢字 Kanji

			一	十	艹	艻	苂	苂
茶	サ, チャ – tea; brown							
	お茶 – green tea; 茶道 or 茶道 – tea ceremony; ちゃ　　　　　ちゃどう　　さどう 茶色 – brown color ちゃいろ		苶	荼	茶			
9 strokes	The grass (艹) radical is stretched out over a person (人) in a tree. He is picking the leaves to make TEA.							

			'	亠	ナ	亣	亦	亦
変	ヘン; か(える) – to change; かわ(る) – to alter, move, be different							
	変な – strange; 変化 – a change or alteration; へん　　　　　へん　か 変わる – to change, to be different か		亦	変	変			
9 strokes	A lid (亠) is sitting precariously over four lines that are about to go their own DIFFERENT ways. The lid looks STRANGE, perched on top like that.							

			`	口	口	口	口	
品	ヒン, しな – goods, articles							
	用品 – parts, supplies; 食品 – food supplies, foodstuff; ようひん　　　　　　　しょくひん 作品 – written work (ex. book, composition, etc.); さくひん 上品 – elegant, refined じょうひん		品	品	品	品		
9 strokes	Three mouths (口) are stacked up like boxes of SUPPLIES, GOODS and ARTICLES waiting to be distributed.							

言葉の探索 Language Detection
こ　ば　　たん　さく

1. **Review of 持って行く and 連れて行く**

    Chapter 10 in *Beginning Japanese* explained the terms for taking, bringing, and returning things or people. Remember that while the verb 連れる is used when referring to escorting people, the verb 持つ is used when talking about bringing or taking things. The verbs 行く, 来る, and 帰る are attached to the て-form of either 連れる or 持つ to determine direction of motion. Particle を is used to indicate the person or thing being taken or brought.

	take	bring	return with
People:	連れて行く	連れて来る	連れて帰る
Things:	持って行く	持って来る	持って帰る

A) 日曜日に犬を公園に連れて行きました。
= On Sunday, I took the dog to the park.

B) 明日、図書館へ本を二冊さつ持って行きます。
= Tomorrow, I will take two books to the library.

C) 来週のピクニックにおにぎりを持って来て下さい。
= Please bring onigiri to next week's picnic.

D) サム君は車で妹さんを学校に連れて来ます。
= Sam will bring his little sister to school by car.

2. **Using はず and つもり**

A. はず – "he/she" is expected to do something (expresses the speaker's expectation about others)

B. つもり – "I" intend to do something (expresses the speaker's intention about his/her own actions).

These words follow the plain/dictionary forms of the verb. Both はず and つもり are followed by だ or です. They are both dependent nouns and must be preceded by a sentence or a pronoun such as その or あの.

_____ + はずだ/です。 or _____ + つもりだ/です。
<small>verb dictionary form</small> <small>verb dictionary form</small>

A) 東京へ行くはずだ。 = He/She/They are expected to go to Tokyo.

B) 東京へ妹を連れて行くつもりだ。 = I intend to take my little sister to Tokyo.

C) 弟は母の手伝いをするはずだ。 = My younger brother is expected to help our mother.

D) 僕は母を手伝うつもりだ。 = I intend to help my mother.

自習 Self Check

1. Choose the appropriate verb to restate each sentence below in Japanese.

A) He took homework back home.

B) I will bring two friends to see kabuki.

C) I will take a souvenir to my teacher.

D) Please bring that new one.

E) Emiko brought three yellow umbrellas (傘).

2. Restate these sentences in English.

A) マイクさんは、今日の午後、病院に行くはずですよ。

B) 明日は数学のテストがあるので、今日勉強するつもりです。

練習時間 Practice Time

1. Pair Practice

Take turns asking and giving (or denying) permission to bring/take the following objects. Use the 〜ても いいですか pattern to ask permission. Use the verb 〜て form + は + いいです to grant permission, or verb て form + は + だめです (or 〜て form + は + いけません) to deny permission. The first one has been done for you.

> A-さん：コンサートへお弁当を持って行ってもいいですか。
> B-さん：いいえ、コンサートへお弁当を持って行ってはだめです。

to take/bring	to (a place)	yes/no
(例) bentou	concert	no
2 flowers	Kabuki performance (歌舞伎の公演)	
money	karaoke party	
notes (ノート)	school test	
my mother	here	
5 dogs	home	
swimsuit (水着)	bath (おふろ)	
(my) little brother	mall (モール)	
girlfriend/boyfriend	movie theatre (映画館)	
grandfather	inn (旅館)	

2. Small Group Practice

You will need two six-sided dice, and a copy of the chart from **TimeForJapanese.com** for this section. Roll the dice separately. The first die is designated for the verbs in Column "A", the second for the patterns in Column "B." Do じゃんけん to decide who goes first. The first player rolls the dice and, according to the numbers, creates a sentence using a verb from Column "A" and a pattern from Column "B". Add other words as needed and write the sentences down. Your sentence may be somewhat silly, but must be grammatically correct to earn a point. Quickly pass the dice to the next player, who rolls and writes, and so on. Continue until everyone has written six sentences. Share your sentences when everyone is done or when your teacher says 終わりましょう.

If a 1 and 2 are rolled:

　　Verb 1, Pattern B 私は六月にフランスへ行くつもりです。 (I intend to go to France in June.)

If a 3 and 4 are rolled:

　　Verb 4, Pattern C 何の魚を持って来る？ (What sort of fish will you bring?)

Column A (verb)	Column B (pattern)
1. 行きます	A. はず
2. 泳ぎます およ	B. つもり
3. 見せます	C. plain present
4. 持って来ます	D. plain negative
5. 出来ます	E. plain past
6. 紹介します しょうかい	F. て form

文化箱 Culture Chest
ぶん か ばこ

1. Lucky and unlucky colors

Various cultures view the symbolism of colors differently. In the West, children usually draw a yellow sun, but Japanese children draw it as red. The Japanese flag, 日の丸, signifies the sun on a white field. The combination of
ひ まる
red and white 紅白 is considered auspicious in Japan; streamers of red and
こうはく
white hang at wedding receptions and other celebrations. For instance, 紅白
こうはく
饅頭 are red and white rice cakes filled with a mixture of sweetened あんこ
まんじゅう

(red bean paste made from red 小豆 beans), 赤飯 is pinkish colored rice colored by 小豆. These are typi-
あずき せきはん
cal foods that appear at happy and auspicious occasions such as weddings or graduations.

2. 歌舞伎 – elements and exaggeration
かぶき

歌舞伎 theatre costumes are colorful and elaborate. Exaggerated and of-
かぶき
ten ritualized gestures and facial movements are important elements of 歌
か
舞伎 theatre too. Actors speak in formalized phrases, exaggerating their
ぶき
voices and tones as they enunciate their lines while accentuating emotions
through highly stylized movements and vivid expressions. Each movement
is part of a series of 型, or forms, and is accompanied by complimentary
かた
musical beats and notes. One of the most famous of these forms is the 見
み
得 (or 見え), in which the actor momentarily freezes, in an expression of in-
え
tense emotional conflict. This is a pose that has been well captured in many
浮世絵 prints.
うきよえ

🔊 メール

This is another message from the same Japanese friend of Ben's mother.

Points to consider as you read:

❶ When is this friend planning on taking Ben's mother to see kabuki?

❷ What kabuki-related items does the writer ask Ben to buy for his mother?

❸ After the kabuki performance, what do the two women plan to do, and why?

❹ Near the end of the letter, the writer warns Ben not to do what during the performance?

ベン君へ

こんにちは、ベン君、またおばさんです。

おばさんもベン君のお母さんを春休みに歌舞伎に連れて行くつもりです。ベン君のお母さんにも「義経千本桜」を見せたいからです。市川海老蔵が演じていると思います

ベン君、お願いがあります。今度歌舞伎座へ行った時にお金を少し*余計に持って行ってくれませんか?そして、お母さんに義経千本桜のポスターとDVDを買って帰って下さい。DVDは多分5千円くらいです。お母さんは歌舞伎を全然見た事がないので、義経千本桜をDVDで先に見て欲しいのです。歌舞伎は昔の言葉や敬語を使うので、話が全然分からないとあまり楽しめません。でも*あらすじが分かっていると、歌舞伎座での実際の公演がもっと楽しめます。それに、ベン君もDVDでもう一度見ると話がよく分かって、面白いかも知れませんよ!

歌舞伎を見た後は、上野公園に花見に連れて行きます。桜がまだあまり咲いていなければ、不忍池の方へ行ってみます。不忍池は、春は桜、夏は蓮の花がとてもきれいです。きっと池の周りで骨董品や盆栽を売っていると思います。お茶を飲んで、少し休憩して、その後、上野公園の中の*うなぎ屋さんで食事をして、お母さんを家に連れて帰ります。

上野公園の近くにはアメ横というショッピング街があります。安いスポーツ用品屋さんや、魚屋さんや、アジア食品店など色々なお店が並んでいます。アメ横には、焼き鳥屋やお寿司屋もあるのでここで食事をしてもいいかも知れませんね。

*何だか今から楽しみです。それではお母さんによろしくね。ベン君、歌舞伎の*感想を楽しみにしています。そうそう、歌舞伎の公演中は写真を撮ってはいけません。*覚えておいてね!それではまた。

おばさんより

---

* 余計 – too much, unnecessary; あらすじ – outline, summary; うなぎ – eel; 何だか – somehow, somewhat; 感想 – impressions, thoughts; 覚えておいて – be sure to remember

今日のお話は「義経千本桜」でございます。

よしつねせんぼんざくら

Today's story is "Yoshitsune and the 1,000 Cherry Trees."

1) さあ、皆様こちらにお座り下さい。座布団が四枚ございます。

2) ありがとうございます。

3) 始めに司会が話を致します。お聞き下さい。お弁当とお茶は休み時間にお召し上がり下さい。

4) あ、司会が参りました。

5) あのう、これはつまらない物ですが。。。。

6) ありがとうございます。いただきます。

7) 皆様、歌舞伎座によようこそいらっしゃいました。今日のお話は「義経千本桜」でございます。義経と弁慶と静御前は京都から奈良の吉野山まで逃げます。お話の中に有名な侍、寿司屋、狐など、色々出て参ります。ごゆっくりお楽しみ下さい。

8) 歌舞伎の日本語は難しくて全然分かりません。

9) 歌舞伎は古い言葉をたくさん使います。コスチュームとジェスチャーをよく見て。そうすれば分かりますよ。

会話 Dialog

(Setting: Inside the Kabukiza, Ichikawa's apprentice Saburou leads the group to their seats before the performance.) Notice where polite speech, or 敬語, is used.

1. 三郎　　：さあ、皆様こちらにお座すわり下さい。座布団が四枚ございます。

2. 皆　　　：ありがとうございます。

3. 三郎　　：始めに*司会が話を致します。お聞き下さい。お弁当とお茶は休み時間に*お召し上がり下さい。

4. 三郎　　　あ、司会が参りました。

5. ベン　　：あのう、これはつまらない物ですが… (gives gifts and money in envelope)

6. 三郎　　：ありがとうございます。いただきます。

7. 司会　　：皆様、歌舞伎座にようこそいらっしゃいました。今日のお話は「義経千本桜」でございます。義経と弁慶と静御前は京都から奈良の吉野山まで逃げます。お話の中に有名な侍、寿司屋、狐など、色々出て参ります。ごゆっくりお楽しみ下さい。

(Kabuki performance starts.)

8. ベン　　：歌舞伎の日本語は難しくて全然分かりません。

9. 友　　　：歌舞伎は古い言葉をたくさん使います。コスチュームとジェスチャーをよく見て。そうすれば分かりますよ。

*司会 – master of ceremonies; 召し上が – to eat (formal)

単語 New Words

きつね 狐 (n) – fox

けいご 敬語 (n) – polite speech

げんかん 玄関 (n) – entranceway, foyer

ごらん ご覧 (n) – seeing, watching, perusing; honorific for 見る

ざせき 座席 (n) – seat (formal)

ざぶとん 座布団 (n) – lat cushion (used when sitting or kneeling on the floor)

しばい 芝居 (n) – play, drama

ストーリー (n) – story

ばいてん 売店 (n) – shop, stand

ばんぐみ 番組 (n) – program (e.g., a TV program)

ブザー (n) – buzzer

かなしい 悲しい (い adj.) – sad

よろしい (い adj.) – good, OK, fine

それで (conj.) – and, because of that (at beginning of sentence)

ので (conj.) – since, given that…, because of…

(ご)ゆっくり (exp.) – slowly, at ease, restful

ぎりぎり (*adv./ono.*) – just barely, at the last moment / grinding sound

まず (*adv.*) – first (of all), anyway, well then

かりる　借りる (*v*) – borrow (to), rent (to)

ござる　御座る (*v*) – be (to), exist (to), (formal)

いたす　致す (*v*) – do (to), humble for します

いらっしゃる (*v*) – come (to), go (to), somewhere (to be), honorific for 行きます or います

でかける　出掛ける (*v*) – depart (to), set out [on an excursion] (to)

わすれる　忘れる (*v*) – forget (to)

漢字 Kanji

葉　12 strokes	ヨウ, は – leaf, foliage	一 十 艹 芋 芋 芊
	言葉 – words; 葉書 – postcard ことば　　　　　はがき	芊 笹 莋 莘 葉 葉
	The grass radical (艹) lies atop the world (世) which is situated on top of a tree. If you are a bird, you see the world through the LEAVES of the tree.	

忘　7 strokes	ボウ, わす(れる) – to forget	、 亠 亡 亡 忘 忘
	忘れ物 – a forgotten item; 忘年会 – end-of-the-year party わす　もの　　　　ぼうねんかい	忘
	The radical for deceased, or dying (亡) sits heavily over a heart (心), making it difficult to FORGET.	

度　9 strokes	ド, たび – degree; time, repetition	、 亠 广 庐 庐 庐
	一度 – one time; 32度 – 32 degrees いちど　　　　　　　ど	庐 庹 度
	A dotted cliff (广) has two underlined tens (十) beside each other, which makes twenty (廿). This is being counted on top of a table. If you were on a cliff at a picnic table, you would want it to be at least 20 DEGREES Celsius.	

非　8 strokes	ヒ, あら(ず) – un-, mistake, negative, injustice	丿 ナ ヲ ヲ 刲 非
	非ず – is not so, never mind; 非常 – emergency, あら　　　　　　　　　ひじょう extraordinary, unusual	非 非
	This kanji is also the radical for WRONG or MISTAKE. It almost mirrors itself from side to side, but it has a few MISTAKES.	

悲　12 strokes	ヒ, かな(しい) – sad; 悲(しむ) – to be sad, grieve, regret 　　　　　　　　　　かな	丿 ナ ヲ ヲ 刲 非
	悲しい – sad, to be sad かな	非 非 非 悲 悲 悲
	The top radical (非) means mistake or injustice. An injustice of the heart (心) is SAD and REGRETFUL.	

言葉の探索 Language Detection

1. Respectful speech = 敬語

Within 敬語, there are three levels of respectful speech.

    ① 丁寧語 (polite speech)

    ② 尊敬語 (respectful speech)

    ③ 謙譲語 (humble speech)

The ます form (丁寧語) is a standard polite verb form. There are other ways to show "respect." One is to use 尊敬語 to raise the status of the other person; another method is to use 謙譲語 to lower your own status. By raising another's status and lowering your own when appropriate, you are showing respect and also gaining it at the same time. Below are a few common 敬語 terms, distinguished by their humble and honorific forms.

plain/dictionary	丁寧語 (polite)	尊敬語 (honorific)	謙譲語 (humble)
する	します	なさいます	いたします
だ	です	~でございます	
行く/来る	行きます/来ます	いらっしゃいます	参ります
いる	います	いらっしゃいます	おります
食べる/飲む	食べます/飲みます	召し上がります	いただきます
皆	皆さん/皆様		

A) いらっしゃいませ。 = Welcome. (used by a store employees to customers)

B) これは本でございます。 = This is a book. (used by a store employees to customers)

C) 行って参ります。 = I'm off but I'll be back. (a variation of 行って来ます, which is said, informally, by the person leaving)

2. Review verbs of giving and receiving

In Chapter 9 of *Beginning Japanese*, you were introduced to verbs of giving and receiving. Review this chart and the examples here to refresh your memory.

Plain (dictionary) form	意味	例
あげる	to give (to an equal)	ともさんはキアラさんに良い漢字の名前をあげました。
やる	to give (to an inferior or pet)	弟は毎日ねこにミルクをやります。

Plain (dictionary) form	意味	例 れい
さしあげる	to give (to a superior)	先生にこの手紙をさしあげます。 がみ
もらう	to receive (from an equal)	僕はおじさんにニンテンドーの一番高い ぼく ビデオゲームをもらいました。
いただく	to receive (from a superior)	私は先生にかわいいえんぴつをいただき ました。嬉しい! うれ
くれる	to receive (someone gives some-thing to you or your family)	父は私に 新 しい車をくれました。 あたら

3. and/because of that = それで

それで is a conjunction used at the beginning of a sentence. It indicates that the preceding sentence (the cause) is the reason for the second sentence (the effect/result).

cause + それで effect/result.

私はアニメが大好きです。それで日本語を勉強したかったです。

　　　Cause　　　　　　　　　　　　　　　　　　Effect/Result

(I love anime. Because of that, I wanted to study Japanese.)

A) 昨日、具合が悪かったです。それで、学校に来ませんでした。

　　　ぐあい

= Yesterday, I felt bad. Consequently, I didn't come to school.

B) 今日は忙しかったです。それで、宿題は出来ませんでした。

　　　いそが　　　　　　　　しゅくだい

= Today was busy. So, I couldn't do my homework.

C) 僕の英語はあまり上手ではありません。それで、アメリカの*交換留学生と話があまり出来

　ぼく　　　　　　　　　　　　　　　　　こうかんりゅうがくせい　　はなし

ませんでした。

= My English is not very good. That's why I couldn't talk much with the American exchange

　 student.

D) 先生のプレゼントを家に忘れました。それで、さしあげる事が出来ませんでした。

　　　　　　　　　　わす

= I forgot the present for my teacher at home. Therefore, I couldn't give it to him.

4. since/given that.../because of... = ので

The conjunction ので expresses a reason or cause. ので is similar to, but more formal than から (previously introduced). Unlike それで, which is used at the beginning of a sentence, ので is used to combine two sentences into one. ので is preceded by the plain form of the verb, adjective, or noun and is often followed by a comma. When ので follows a な adjective or a noun, なので is used.

Clause I (reason, plain form) ので、Clause 2 (result)

Verb 　アニメを見るので、時々勉強しません。　= I watch anime, so given that, sometimes

　　　　　　　　　べんきょう　　　　　　　　　　　 I don't study.

Adj. 　アニメは楽しいので、もっと見たい。　　= Since anime is fun, I want to watch it a lot.

Noun 　大好きなアニメなので、また見たい。　　= Since I love this anime, I want to see it again.

A) この部屋へやは明るいので、良く見えます。　= Since this room is bright, I can see well.

B) マイケル君は切符がないので、バスに乗る事は出来ません。
= Because Michael does not have a ticket, he can't ride the bus.

C) 今日は寒いので、必ずセーターを着て下さい。
= Because the weather today is cold, please be sure to wear a sweater.

D) 母に、ダイヤモンドのネックレスを買ってあげたので、今、お金が全然ありません。
= Since I gave my mother a diamond necklace, I have absolutely no money now.

自習 Self Check

1. For each scenario, create a statement that is appropriately polite.

(ア) You receive something from your teacher.

(イ) On the phone, you ask if the school principal is there.

(ウ) You address your classmates.

(エ) The store clerk indicates really cheap shoes on the table.

(オ) Your new boss asks what time you arrived.

2. Fill in the blanks with either それで or ので, then restate each in English.

(ア) 東京に住んでいます。＿＿＿＿＿＿大阪には、あまり行きません。

(イ) 歌舞伎座は銀座駅から近い＿＿＿＿＿＿、そこまで歩いて行って下さい。

(ウ) 高かった＿＿＿＿＿＿、買いませんでした。

(エ) あのレストランの食べ物は安くて、美味しいです。＿＿＿＿＿＿よく食べに行きます。

(オ) 先週、けんたろう君と喧嘩しました。＿＿＿＿＿＿今度の土曜日、デートはしません。

練習時間 Practice Time

1. Small Group Practice

Form groups of 2-3. Each person copies the grid below onto a piece of scrap paper, putting his/her initial in Box 1, and randomly filling in each box with a plain speech word for which there is a 敬語 equivalen (either honorific or humble). For example, if you write 水, the honorific equivalent would be お水. Be sur to use all the verbs listed in the chart in number 1 of the 言葉の探索 section above.

To play, roll a pair of dice, then change the word on that space to its 敬語 equivalent. State the cor rect 敬語, out loud. If your group agrees that you are correct, write your initials in that box. If you ro the same number again, you may play that number on your partners' grids. Continue playing until all th boxes are initialed. The winner is the person whose initials appear in the most boxes.

1	2	3	4	5	6
7	8	9	10	11	12

2. Pair Practice

Several "causes" are listed below. Take turns making sentences that include the "results/effects." First, use それで to connect two sentences. Then use ので to connect the cause/effect in one sentence.

(ア) Because my stomach hurt...

(イ) Because the test was hard...

(ウ) Because my little sister is 6 years old...

(エ) Because Todd ate a lot of pizza...

Because my hat is yellow...
私の帽子は黄色です。それで、よく見えます。
私の帽子は黄色なので、よく見えます。

文化箱 Culture Chest
ぶん か ばこ

いたします (humble) and いらっしゃいます (honorific)

In Japanese, you know that different verbs can be substituted to create either the humble or honorific form of a polite verb. You already know several such humble terms, even though you might not realize it. For example, いただきます is a humble expression that puts you, the speaker, in a position to help or honor your listener. いただきます is the humble form of 貰う, to receive. Another example is the phrase どういたしまして. いたす, the plain/dictionary form of the verb, is the humble form of the verb する. Remember to only use the humble form when speaking about yourself. Can you guess the meaning of お持ちします and in what situation it might be used?

Honorific terms are used when speaking to a superior, or a customer. A store clerk will always say いらっしゃいませ, never 来て下さい. Similarly, if you are asked to sit down, the clerk will use the longer and more respectful term おかけになって下さい or お座りになって下さい, rather than 座って下さい.

You may also use the prefixes お or ご (御) to show respect. お茶 is one example. Can you think of more?

🔊 メール

Jun's uncle works at NHK (the Japanese national television station). On this occasion, he's moderating a TV special on kabuki.

Points to consider as you read:

❶ How would you describe the politeness level of this speech?

❷ Summarize this speech. What is the main objective?

❸ The word 幕間 is used in the last paragraph. From the context, what do you think it means?

皆様、ようこそNHKの歌舞伎スペシャルへいらっしゃいました。

この番組は、初めて歌舞伎を見に行かれる皆様に歌舞伎のマナーをお教えする番組です。歌舞伎座にお出掛けになったと思ってご覧下さい。

今日のお話は「義経千本桜」でございます。あまり公演時間ぎりぎりに行くのはよしましょう。まず、チケットにある座席番号を*確認して下さい。そして、正しい席にお座り下さい。

イヤホンガイドがあると歌舞伎の楽しさが全然違います。イヤホンガイドは、歌舞伎座1階*正面玄関を入って左手にイヤホンガイドセンターがございます。そちらでお借り下さい。*使用料は600円でございます。

幕間の売店はとても込みます。時間がありましたら、お弁当を売店で買うのがよろしいでしょう。

携帯電話をマナーモードにして下さい。もしくは電源をお切り下さい。途中で音が鳴るのは、役者さんにも他の観客の人達にもとても迷惑です。

開演5分前になりますと、ブザーがなります。時間が来ますと、柝という拍子木が打たれます。すると幕が開いてお芝居が始まります。

それでは「義経千本桜」の始まりです。ゆっくりとお楽しみ下さい…。

(The play starts and in a while, a curtain comes down with the sound of 「チョンチョン、チョンチョン」 拍子木の音)

(アナウンサー小さな声で) あ、まだお立ちにならない (立たない) で下さい。これは「つなぎ」の音でございます。すぐに次の幕が開きますよという意味でございます。

(The play continues and a long sound of 『チョーン』拍子木の音)

これが幕間の合図でございます。舞台正面の端に休憩時間が出ます。次の幕まで何分あるかご確認下さい。お手洗いへ行かれたり、お弁当を召し上がったりして下さい。

---

* 正面 – front, main; マナーモード – silent mode; 拍子木 – wooden clappers; 確認 – confirmation; 端 – edge, border

狐は狸ほどすごくないですよ。
きつね　たぬき

Foxes are not as incredible as tanuki, you know.

1) 歌舞伎を良い席で見る事が出来ましたね。

2) 女形はとてもきれいでした。でも、僕は白い狐が一番すごかったと思います。

3) 狐は全然すごくなかったです。狐は狸ほどすごくないですよ。音楽とコスチュームが一番良かったです。

5) でも、「千本桜」のストーリーは悲しかったですね。

4) すみません、天ぷらそばをもう一杯下さい。

7) でも、「時の門」に持って行く事は出来ませんよ。

6) 私は市川さんの浮世絵と手ぬぐいをもらいました。お土産です。

8) ああ、忘れていました。残念ですね。お母さんにあげたかったです。

9) 大丈夫です。家に帰った後で皆をまた歌舞伎に連れて行きます。そして市川さんの曾孫さんに会います。その時にお土産を買えますよ。

会話 Dialog
(かい)

(Setting: After the performance, the group sits in a street stall (屋台), discussing the performance, drinking tea, and eating tempura.)

1. じゅん　：歌舞伎を良い席で見る事が出来ましたね。
　　　　　　（かぶき）　　（せき）

2. ベン　　：女形はとてもきれいでした。でも、僕は白い狐が一番すごかったと思います。
　　　　　　（おんながた）　　　　　　　（ぼく）　　　（きつね）

3. 友　　　：狐は全然すごくなかったです。狐は狸ほどすごくないですよ。
　　　　　　（きつね）　　　　　　　　（きつね）（たぬき）
　　　　　　音楽とコスチュームが一番良かったです。

4. 友　　　：[turns to shop owner]

　　　　　　すみません、天ぷらそばをもう一杯下さい。
　　　　　　　　　　　　（てん）　　　　　　（いっぱい）

5. じゅん　：でも、「千本桜」のストーリーは悲しかったですね。
　　　　　　　　　　　　　　　　　　　（かな）

6. キアラ　：私は市川さんの浮世絵と*手ぬぐいをもらいました。お土産です。
　　　　　　　（いちかわ）（うきよえ）　　　　　　　　　　　（みやげ）

7. 友　　　：でも、「時の門」に持って行く事は出来ませんよ。

8. キアラ　：ああ、忘れていました。残念ですね。お母さんにあげたかったです。
　　　　　　　　　（わす）　　　　（ざんねん）

9. じゅん　：大丈夫です。家に帰った後で皆をまた歌舞伎に連れて行きます。
　　　　　　（だいじょうぶ）　　　　　　（みんな）　　（かぶき）
　　　　　　そして市川さんの*曾孫さんに会います。その時にお土産を買えますよ。
　　　　　　　　（いちかわ）　　（ひまご）　（あ）　　　　　　（みやげ）

*手ぬぐい – hand towel; 曾孫 – great-grandchild
　　　　　　　　（ひまご）

単語 New Words
(たん)

おきゃくさん　お客さん (n) – customer, guest
さいご　最後 (n) – last, conclusion
さいしょ　最初 (n) – first, beginning

どうろ　道路 (n) – road, highway
はらう　払う (v) – pay (to)
もとめる　求める (v) – seek (to), request (to)

言葉の探索 Language Detection
(こと)（ば）（たん）（さく）

Pair Practice

Take turns with your partner creating sentences using the cues below. First create a より sentence; ther with the same information, create a ほど sentence. Follow the example.

例 れい EXAMPLE

Hiroshige's woodblock prints, Hokusai's woodblock prints, bright colors

広重の浮世絵より北斎の浮世絵の方が色が明るいです。
ひろしげ うきよえ ほくさい うきよえ

or

広重の浮世絵は北斎の浮世絵ほど色が明るくないです。
ひろしげ うきよえ ほくさい うきよえ

A) spaghetti, pizza, delicious

B) kabuki, noh, noisy (loud)

C) kamishibai, folk tales, interesting

D) meat, vegetables, healthy (健康的)
けんこうてき

E) dogs, cats, gentle/kind

F) go by plane, go by train, fast

文化箱 Culture Chest
ぶん か ばこ

相槌
あいづち

Utterances that many English speakers make, such as "uh-huh" and "hmmm," etc. are sounds called 相
あい
槌 in Japanese. 相槌 often include gestures, such as nodding the head in agreement, but more often the
づち あいづち
term 相槌 refers to spoken utterances such as そうですか or "本当?". These expressions are common
あいづち
and expected. If you do not respond to a comment with some form of 相槌, your conversational partner
あいづち
might pause and ask if something is wrong.

As with other aspects of Japanese, 相槌 can vary according to the levels of politeness. For example,
あいづち
as you listen to your friend talk, you might use one of these expressions:

へえ = indicates surprise or being impressed with something

うん = indicates that the listener is following what is being said

ええ！ or うそ！ = indicates surprise

When in conversation with a superior, you might say:

はいはい or そうですか = indicates agreement

本当ですか or 知りませんでした = indicates surprise

Can you think of more examples of 相槌 you use or have heard used?
あいづち

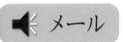

This message, from Ben's friend Akiko, is about street food vendors.

Points to consider as you read:

❶ The yakitori shops Akiko is recommending are so small that the customers have to do what?

❷ Akiko describes yakitori as Japanese ファストフード. What does she mean by that?

❸ How does Akiko suggest that Ben get to her favorite yakitori restaurant?

ベン君へ

　こんにちは、亜希子です。
歌舞伎はどうだった？
歌舞伎座の近くに面白い所があるよ。焼き鳥屋さんがたくさん並んでるんだ。電車のガードの下にあるから、店は小さくて、道路にもテーブルが出てる。だから、店の外でも食べる事が出来るよ。外のテーブルで食べるのは、となりの店のお客さんとも話す事が出来て楽しいよ。

　焼き鳥屋さんは、日本のファストフード。でも、普通のファストフードやカフェテリアと違うのは、テーブルで注文するところよ。お店の人が注文したものを持って来る時にお金を払う店もあれば、逆に、最後にまとめてお金を払う店もあるの。それに焼き鳥は、その場所で料理して持って来てくれるから、ハンバーガーとかのファストフードよりヘルシーよ！

　今度ベン君を連れて行ってあげるよ。いつがいいか教えて！歌舞伎座から歩いて15分程で行く事が出来るの。だから、ベン君のお母さんにも教えてあげてね。

　そうそう、来週は漢字のテストがあるはず。私も今日から勉強するつもり。ベン君も忘れないでね！

　じゃーね。

亜希子

伊豆　1922年
いず

Ryokan and Onsen in Izu

The group of travelers has just exited Edo in 1815 and traveled more than 100 years into the future to land on the Izu Peninsula in 1922. Here, they wander into a small town and come across the beginnings of a novel by a soon-to-be famous author, Yasunari Kawabata.

Learning and Performance Goals

This chapter will enable you to:

- review personal pronouns
- review requesting, giving, and denying permission
- review counters and verb forms
- hone presentation skills in Japanese
- refer to the way something is done using the verb stem ＋ 方
  かた
- create modifying noun clauses to expand a sentence
- use 〜から to mean so, since, or because
- learn about the author 川端康成 and his short story 伊豆の踊り子
  かわばたやすなり　　　　　　　　　　　　いず　おど　こ
- learn about onsen culture and more about ryokan
- learn about regional dialects
- learn about the Izu Peninsula and Shizuoka Prefecture
- talk about air and object temperatures
- use 20 additional kanji

全部書いたら読んでも良いです。

After it is all written, it is all right to read.

会話 Dialog
かい

(Our characters arrive in the Izu Peninsula on a very rainy day. After they stumble through a large puddle by the gate, they want to get warm and wash their clothes.)

1. ベン ：うわあ！ズボンが 汚 くなりました。
きたな

2. じゅん ：ここはどこ？

3. 友 ：えーっと、伊豆だと思います。あ、 男 の人が散歩しています。
いず　　　　　　　　　　　おとこ　　　　　さんぽ

4. 川端 ：ああ、どうも。うわっ、ズボンがどろどろですね。大丈夫ですか？
かわばた　　　　　　　　　　　　　　　　　　　　　　　　　　　　じょうぶ

5. ベン ：はい。前はきれいでしたが、今は本当に 汚 くなりました。すぐに 洗 いたいです。
きたな　　　　　　　　　　あら

6. 川端 ：トンネルの 向こうに天城湯ケ島温泉があります。私は湯本館に泊まっています。
かわばた　　　　　　む　　　　　あまぎゆがしま　おんせん　　　　　　　ゆもとかん　と
　　　　　　 そこでズボンを 洗 ってもいいですよ。
あら

7. ベン ：雨は冷たいですから、 温泉に入りたいですね。
つめ　　　　　　　おんせん　はい

8. 友 ：温泉の後でいせえびが食べたいです。
おんせん

(In Kawabata's room at the inn, the group sees many books, journals, and papers.)

9. 川端 ：大雨ですね。あ、 窓 が開いています。早く閉めて下さい！
かわばた　　　　　　　　　まど　あ　　　　　　　はや　し

10. じゅん ：あれ？このノートは川端さんのですか？タイトル…「伊豆の踊り子」？
かわばた　　　　　　　　　いず　おど　こ

11. 川端 ：そのノートを閉じて下さい。全部書いた後なら読んでも良いです。
かわばた　　　　　　と

単語 New Words
たん

ホテル (*n*) – hotel

りょかん 旅館 (*n*) – ryokan, traditional Japanese inn

つめたい 冷たい (い *adj.*) – cold (to the touch)

あたたかい 暖かい (い *adj.*) – warm (usu. refers to air temp.)

に ついて (*exp.*) – concerning, about

あっ (*interj.*) – A! (exp. of surprise)

びしょびしょ (*ono.*) – sopping wet; drenched

どろどろ (*ono.*) – muddy, sloppy

あらう 洗う (*v*) – wash (to)

かわく 乾く (*v*) – dry (to)

漢字 Kanji

洗	セン, あら(う) – wash	丶	⺀	⺡	⺡	汼	汼
	洗う – to wash; 洗濯 – laundry, washing あら せんたく	汼	汼	洗			
9 strokes	The left is water (⺡), the right is (先) prior, first. WASHing yourself and WASHing your clothes takes priority!						

散	サン, ち(る), ち(らす) – scatter, disperse, squander	一	十	卄	丗	井	昔
	散らす – to scatter, to distribute; 散る – to fall ち ち (leaves/blossoms); 散歩する – to take a walk さんぽ	昔	昔	昔	昔	散	散
12 strokes	This is made up of a well (井) over the radical for month (月). Sit on a folding chair (夂) and watch the full moon as stars SCATTER and DISPERSE across the night sky.						

浴	ヨク; あ(びる) – (to) bathe/shower, (to) bask in the sun	丶	⺀	⺡	汷	汷	汷
	浴びる – to bathe, to sunbathe, to shower; 浴衣 – あ ゆかた light cotton kimono	浴	浴	浴	浴		
10 strokes	The water radical (⺡) is on the left side of a "valley" (谷). The perfect place to BATHE or SHOWER would be in a valley stream.						

湯	トウ, ゆ – hot water, bath, hot spring	丶	⺀	⺡	汨	沺	湂
	お湯 – hot water; 茶の湯 – tea ceremony; 湯花 – hot ゆ ちゃ ゆ ゆばな spring mineral deposits (crystal-like deposits)	湂	湯	湯	湯	湯	湯
12 strokes	Water (⺡) heated by the sun (日) produces HOT WATER that, when poured over your hair, makes your HOT SPRING BATH even better.						

氷	ヒョウ, こおり, ひ, こお(る) – icicle, ice, hail, freeze	丁	刁	氺	氺	氷	
	氷 – shaved ice desert; 氷 – hail; 氷点 – こおり ひょう ひょうてん freezing point; 氷る – to freeze こお						
5 strokes	This is water (水) with a dot of ICE beginning to form.						

泳	エイ, およ(ぐ) – swim	丶	⺀	⺡	泛	汀	泂
	泳ぐ – to swim; 水泳 – swimming およ すいえい	泳	泳				
8 strokes	Water (⺡) with two splashes on the surface lets you know something is SWIM(ming) near the surface.						

1. Presentational Skills in Japanese

Below are some key elements to making successful presentations in Japanese. Keep in mind that precise terminology may vary, but the appropriate level of polite language is very important.

Components of a presentation in Japanese:

① Greeting – こんにちは。〜について話します。

② Introduction – 始めに･･･
はじ

③ Body – main points, with supporting evidence and/or examples

    I. To vary your sentence structure, use conjunctions such as それから, そして, それに, それで, 〜て, でも, たとえば, ところで, ですから (だから), or それとも.

    II. Include comparisons when appropriate: 〜ほど、〜より、 逆 に、もう一つの例は、〜の方が･･･
ぎゃく れい

    方が･･･

    III. Note which points are opinion: 〜と思います

    IV. Note quotations from others with: 〜と言いました

④ Closing – 最後に〜, 終わりです, 以上 です
さいご お いじょう

The following paragraph offers an example of a short presentation for your sister school on a family member, with a supporting graphic.

皆さん、こんにちは。これから祖父について話します。
そふ

  これは僕の祖父の写真です。日本人で、十年前に大学の学長になりました。頭がとても良くて、たくさん本も書きました。書き方が上手で、生徒達にも分かりやすいです。でも、時々面白い事もします。例えば、昨日は雨でした。でも、おじいさんは、傘の代わりに、紙の帽子を被って、家を出ました。学校まで十分かかりますので、学校まで歩いて行くと、頭もジャケットもびしょびしょになりました。その後、風邪を引きました。それで、今日は大学を休んで、薬を飲んで、寝ています。僕は大学生になったら、祖父の大学で勉強したいです。

  終わりです。
お

2. How something is done (verb stem + 方 ex: 歩き方、洗い方、書き方)

Adding 〜方 to the stem of an action verb indicates the manner in which something is done.

話します ⇨ 話し方 = the way of speaking/how to speak
日本語の話し方を勉強しています。 = I am studying how to speak Japanese.
A) 食べます ⇨ 食べ方 = the manner in which she/he eats
　かにの食べ方はちょっと難しい。 = The way of eating crab is a little difficult.
B) 作ります ⇨ 作り方 = the manner in which it is made
　母は美味しいお寿司の作り方を知っています。 = Mom is good at making sushi.
C) 行きます ⇨ 行き方 = the manner of going
　駅への行き方を教えて下さい。 = Please teach/tell me how to get to the train station.

自習 Self Check

1. Take a position on one of the following issues, then write out a brief outline of an argument you can make during a 2–3 minute oral presentation in Japanese. Brainstorm quickly and finish your outline within three minutes.

   Which is better:
   (ア) watching movies at home or at the cinema
   (イ) studying science or studying math
   (ウ) writing on a computer or writing with paper and pencil

2. How would you say the following in Japanese? Use the verbs provided. Use the verb stem + 方 pattern.

Please teach me how to read this word. （読みます）
この単語の読み方を教えて下さい。

(ア) This is how to make a hamburger. (作ります)

(イ) I know how to reserve airplane tickets. (予約します)

(ウ) Teach me how to make a hotel reservation. (予約します)

(エ) Tell (teach) me how to go to North High School. (行きます)

(オ) I don't know how to ride the bus in Tokyo. But I do know how to ride the subway. (乗ります)

(カ) Please teach me how to write that kanji. (書きます)

(キ) Do you know how to play piano? (弾きます)

練習時間 Practice Time
かん しゅう

1. Small Group Practice

As a group, choose a photograph of an animal or person from a magazine, newspaper or the Internet. Take turns creating statements for a presentation on your subject. Give the subject a name and make up a story about where it resides, its work or education, favorite and disliked foods, hobbies, etc. Tell what your subject knows/doesn't know how to do. Be creative and have fun, but make your story plausible. The presentation should last between 1½ to 3 minutes. Be prepared to give your presentation to the class.

2. Pair Practice

Draw three tic-tac-toe boards on a piece of scrap paper. Use your verb chart (or verb flash cards) to fill in the boxes with a different verb in each box, in the dictionary form. Then, take turns playing tic-tac-toe by creating the ～方 (or ～たい) form for your square when it is your turn. In the second round, create the ～て form for each verb.

文化箱 Culture Chest
ぶん か ばこ

川端康成 and 伊豆の踊子
かわばたやすなり　　い ず　おどりこ

Author 川端康成 (1899–1972) became the first Japanese writer to be awarded the Nobel Prize for Litera-
かわばたやすなり
ture, in 1968. Born into a doctor's family in Osaka, 川端 had a wonderful life until, at the age of 15, he
かわばた
became an orphan. He moved into a rooming house to complete his studies and eventually graduated from the prestigious Tokyo Imperial University in 1924. By 1926, 川端 had published his semi-autobio-
かわばた
graphical short story, 伊豆の踊り子, about a traveling college student meeting a young itinerant dancer
い ず　おど　こ
at a hot spring. The concise and lyrical writing style of 川端 has been called poetic, and was influenced
かわばた
by European schools of art such as Expressionism and Modernism. He was part of a group of authors who founded the 新感覚派, a literary group that created art for art's sake. Western artists of the same period
しんかんかく は
who fell into this category include T.S. Eliot and Ezra Pound, Franz Kafka, and Virginia Woolf. Other famous works by 川端 are 雪国 (his first full-length novel), 千羽鶴 (a story continuing earlier themes of
かわばた　ゆきぐに　　　　　　　　　せん ば づる
ill-fated love), and 山の音, a story about aging, from the perspective of the family patriarch Ogata Shingo.
おと

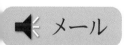

Below is a message from a travel agent to Kiara about lodging choices in the Izu area.

Points to consider as you read:

❶ According to the travel agent, what are the three different types of lodging options in the Izu region?

❷ Once a guest arrives at the ryokan, what is brought to the room?

❸ What are some special advantages to each type of accommodation?

❹ If you were travelling to Izu, which lodging option would you choose? Why?

伊豆トラベルの伊東です。ご宿泊の*お問い合わせをありがとうございました。

伊豆地方のご宿泊には3種類ございます。旅館とホテルと民宿です。

旅館には、全て温泉があり食事付きです。たいてい畳の和室ですが、中にはベッドの洋室もあります。旅館によっては*露天風呂があります。トイレの他に、内風呂が付いているお部屋もあります。お部屋のお布団は、夕食後に旅館のスタッフが敷いてくれ、朝食の前にあげてくれます。

お食事は、お部屋で召しあがるのがいいですか?それとも、旅館内の別のお部屋で他のお客様とご一緒に食べるのがいいですか?お食事のご*希望と露天風呂や内風呂のご希望をお知らせ下さい。いい旅館をご紹介致します。また、夕食をご用意する時間がありますので、*到着*予定時間を前もって旅館に伝える必要があります。旅館に着いたら、仲居さん(旅館の人)がお部屋にお茶とお菓子を持って来てくれますよ。

ベッドの方が*よろしければ、洋式のホテルもあります。ホテルの部屋は全て洋室です。旅館と違って、食事はお部屋で取ることが出来ません。朝食も夕食もホテル内のレストランになります。お部屋にはシャワーとトイレが付いています。ホテルの中には、露天風呂があるところもございます。

もう少し安い所をご*希望であれば、民宿がいいと思います。民宿はすべて和室です。お部屋のお布団は自分で敷いて下さい。民宿の部屋は、トイレとお風呂が*共同のところがほとんどです。食事付きですが、朝食も夕食も他のお客様と一緒に同じ部屋で食べます。民宿も夕食をご用意する時間がありますので、到着*予定時間を前もって伝える必要があります。

宿泊方法がお決まりになりましたら、ご連絡下さい。お待ちしております。

伊豆トラベル
伊東

---

* 問い合わせ – inquiry, interrogation; 到着 – arrival; 予定 – plan, expectation; 露天風呂 – open air (outdoor) bath
敷いてくれ – (敷く) to spread/lay out (please do it); よろしければ – (よろしい) if it's good, if it's OK; 希望 – hope, aspiration; 共同 – co-ed, shared/common (facilities)

そして温泉の中にタオルと石鹸を入れてはいけないよ。

Also, do not put towels or soap into the hot springs.

1) ここでは、男の人と女の人が一緒に温泉に入るんだよ

2) え？それは恥ずかしいです。一緒に入りたくないです。

3) 僕達もキアラさんとは一緒に温泉に入りませんよ。キアラさんと僕達は別々に入ります。

4) じゃ、大丈夫だと思います。水着を着て行っても良いですか？

5) だめだめ！そして温泉の中にタオルと石鹸を入れてはいけないよ。

6) じゃあ、僕とベン君は後で行きます。キアラさんと友さんは先にどうぞ。川端さんは？

7) 私は部屋で本を書きたいな。

8) 皆さん、温泉に入る前に体を洗って下さい。

9) ところで、友さんは今晩の食事のことについて、何も言わないね。

10) いいえ。頭の中は温泉の後の食事の事でいっぱいです。早く入りましょう。

11) 皆さん、温泉の入り方を間違えないで下さいよ！

会話 Dialog

(Setting: at the ryokan)

1. 川端　：ここでは、男の人と女の人が一緒に温泉に入るんだよ。

2. キアラ　：え?それは恥ずかしいです。一緒に入りたくないです。

3. ベン　：僕達もキアラさんとは一緒に温泉に入りませんよ。キアラさんと僕達は別々に入ります。

4. キアラ　：じゃ、大丈夫だと思います。水着を着て行っても良いですか?

5. 川端　：だめだめ!そして温泉の中にタオルと石鹸を入れてはいけないよ。

6. じゅん　：じゃあ、僕とベン君は後で行きます。キアラさんと友さんは先にどうぞ。川端さんは?

7. 川端　：私は部屋で本を書きたいな。

8. 友　：皆さん、温泉に入る前に体を洗って下さい。

9. 川端　：(pointing at 友) ところで、友さんは今晩の食事のことについて、何も言わないね。

10. 友　：いいえ。頭の中は温泉の後の食事の事でいっぱいです。早く入りましょう。

11. 友　：(Then turns to everyone) 皆さん、温泉の入り方を間違えないで下さいよ!

単語 New Words

せっけん　石鹸 (n) – soap

はだし　裸足 (n) – barefoot

みずぎ　水着 (n) – swimming suit

ゆかた　浴衣 (n) – yukata (light cotton) kimono worn in summer or in the evenings in ryokan or homes

*かのじょ　彼女 (pr) – she, girlfriend

*かれ　彼 (pr) – he, boyfriend

はずかしい　恥ずかしい (い adj.) – shy

ぬるい (い adj.) – lukewarm

あびる　浴びる (v) – shower (to), bask in the sun (to), bathe (to)

*previously introduced

漢字 Kanji

女	ジョ, おんな, め – female	く	夂	女			
3 strokes	女 – woman, female; 女性 – woman, feminine gender; 女子 – woman, girl; 少女 – young lady, little girl						
	Imagine this kanji as a WOMAN sitting cross-legged with arms outstretched relaxing.						

男	ナン, ダン, おとこ, お – male	丨	冂	冂	甲	田	罒
7 strokes	男性 – man, male; 男の人 – man; 男の子 – boy; 男女 – men and women	男					
	The MAN is the power (力) working in the field (田).						

温	オン, あたた(かい) – warm; あたた(める) – to warm	丶	冫	氵	汀	汀	沪
12 strokes	温める – to warm/heat (usually liquids); 温度 – temperature	沪	沪	浭	涓	温	温
	The sun (日) is WARM(ing) dishes (皿) with WARM water (氵).						

泉	セン, いずみ – spring, fountain	′	亻	冖	白	白	皀
9 strokes	平泉 – town where Benkei died in Iwate Prefecture; 温泉 – hot spring, spa	臮	泉	泉			
	White (白) water (水) water flows from a natural HOT SPRING.						

若	ジャク, ニャク, わ(かい) – young	一	十	艹	艹	艼	芢
8 strokes	若い – young; 若年 – youth; 若さ – youth; 若く見える – to look (seem) young	若	若				
	The grass (艹) on the right (右) is YOUNG and still short.						

冷	レイ, さ(める), さ(ます), つめ(たい), ひ(やす) – cool, cold (liquid or person), chill	丶	冫	冫	八	伶	冷
7 strokes	冷たい – cool, cold (liquid or aloof person); 冷や – cool water, cold sake	冷					
	Ancient laws or commands (令) were often as CHILL(ingly) COLD as ice (冫) for the people who had to live under them.						

5.2 Also, do not put towels or soap into the hot springs. 173

1. Review of personal pronouns

In Japanese, personal pronouns are used sparingly. And, as you have already learned, あなた (you) is used only rarely. When addressing someone, a more preferable alternative is to use the person's name (川崎さん) or title (ブラウン先生, or simply 先生) if you know it. If you must use pronouns, here are a few possibilities:

彼　　– he/him　　　　　　　あなた – you
彼女 – she/her　　　　　　　君* 　– you (informal)

* You have already seen this kanji many times, pronounced くん, as a suffix to male names.

彼 はあなたの友達ですか？ = Is he your friend?

ALT: あの方はあなたの友達ですか。= Is that person over there your friend?

明日、彼女と一緒に買い物に行くつもりです。= Tomorrow, I intend to go shopping with her.

ALT: 明日、真理子さんと一緒に買い物に行くつもりです。
= Tomorrow, I intend to go shopping with Mariko.

2. Review of requesting and giving permission – 〜てもいいです(か)。

You were introduced to this pattern in Chapter 1 of *Beginning Japanese*, with useful classroom expressions such as:

A) お手洗いへ行ってもいいですか。　　　　= May I go to the washroom?

B) お水を飲んでもいいですか。　　　　　　= May I get a drink of water?

C) ロッカーへ行ってもいいですか。　　　　= May I go to my locker?

You then used your expanded vocabulary to make such requests as:

A) 煎餅を食べてもいいですか。　　　　　– May I eat that senbei?

B) 紙を二枚借りてもいいですか。　　　　= May I borrow two sheets of paper?

C) 明日寿司を持って来てもいいですか。　= Tomorrow, may I bring sushi?

D) 鉛筆で書いてもいいですか。　　　　　= May I write with pencil?

E) 友達のとなりに座ってもいいですか。　= May I sit beside my friend?

F) 宿題をしなくてもいいですか。　　　　= Is it OK if I don't do the homework?

3. Denying permission – 〜てはいけません（〜てはいけない）or 〜てはだめです

When denying permission, use the て-form followed by either 〜はいけません（〜はいけない）or 〜はだめです。The ending 〜てはいけない is slightly less polite, 〜てはだめです is the least formal.

① 立ってはいけません。	= You may not stand. (more formal)
② 立ってはだめです。	= No standing. (less formal)

A) 教科書を開いてはだめです。 = Do not open your textbooks.

B) ここに座ってはだめです。 = Do not sit here.

C) 鉛筆で書いてはいけません。 = You may not write with a pencil.

D) タクシーに乗ってはいけません。 = You may not ride in a taxi.

E) その新しいドレスを洗ってはいけません。 = You may not wash that new dress.

F) 石鹸を使ってはだめです。 = Do not use soap.

G) 高い切符を買ってはだめです。 = Do not buy expensive tickets.

自習 Self Check

1. Using pronouns. Use the information below to make two questions, one question with a pronoun and one question using an alternative. Then put each question into English. The first one is done for you.

彼　川村さん：
彼はどこで生まれましたか。 = Where was he born?
川村さんはどこで生まれましたか。 = Where was Mr. Kawamura born?

（ア）あなた（大輔）　　　　　　　（ウ）君（トム）

（イ）彼（あの男の人）　　　　　　（エ）彼女（その女の人）

2. Make the following requests in Japanese, then grant or deny each request.

　（ア）　May I borrow 4 sheets of paper?

　（イ）　May I open my textbook?

　（ウ）　May I start (begin) the test?

　（エ）　It's raining. May I close the window?

　（オ）　May I bring a friend to the party?

練習時間 Practice Time

Pair Practice

Take turns requesting permission to do the following actions at the locations indicated. Download and use the action cards for this chapter and section on **TimeForJapanese.com** to practice asking, and granting or denying permission with your partner.

文化箱 Culture Chest
ぶん か ばこ

1. 温泉
おんせん

The volcanically-active terrain of Japan abounds in natural geothermal hot springs called 温泉, originally
おんせん

based around outdoor springs called 露天風呂. Modern advertising signs and billboards for 温泉 can be
ろてんぶろ   おんせん

found in many tourist destinations. Look for the symbol ♨ to easily locate them on maps. Many ホテル,

旅館, and 民宿 are built on or near natural hot springs, and their elaborate bathing areas are often local
りょかん   みんしゅく

attractions. The fancier 温泉 contain numerous baths, regulated to different temperatures or containing
おんせん

different minerals. Some 温泉 have waterfalls, scented baths, or scenic vistas. Men and women bathe in
おんせん

separate areas. Determining which area is yours is simple once you can read these two kanji: 男 and 女 .
おとこ   おんな

Here is how to enjoy an 温泉: pay your fee at the entrance, enter the appropriate bathing area, sit on
おんせん

a small stool to thoroughly wash and rinse yourself off at the tap or shower. After carefully testing the wa-

ter temperature with your hand, slip into the tub. Remember to enter slowly, as the water might be quite

hot. Enjoy a soak in the bath, relax, and chat with the other bathers, who may be friends, neighbors, or a

group of company workers on a weekend retreat, all there for the soothing waters.

Neighborhood 銭湯, or public bathhouses, are still found in many cities and towns. They are different
せんとう

from natural hot springs, or 温泉. 銭湯 are public baths often filled only with hot tap water, no minerals
おんせん せんとう

added. The days of homes or apartments without baths or showers are disappearing, but families and local

residents who do not have home bathing facilities visit their local 銭湯 to bathe, soak, and socialize.
せんとう

2. Expressing Temperatures
Written Japanese uses different kanji and sometimes words for hot and cold, depending on what is being
described. Generally, these differences distinguish between surface and air temperatures.

room/air temperature	"to the touch" surface/water
暖 かい (hot/warm) あたた	温 かい (hot/warm) あたた
暑 い (hot) あつ	熱 い (hot), ぬるい (warm) あつ
涼 しい (cool) すず	冷 たい (cool) つめ
寒 い (cold) さむ	

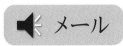

This is another letter from Mr. Ito, the same travel agent, to Kiara, informing her of bathing customs.
Points to consider as you read:

① At the bath, are towels larger or smaller than a hand towel?

② List three things you might find in the dressing room (changing room) outside the bath.

③ Is it all right to get into the bath right away?

④ Who should you ask before adding cool water to the bath?

⑤ Why do you think such strict rules as to what is permitted in the bath exist?

　　旅館にあるタオルは、*手ぬぐいで、ハンドタオル位の大きさです。もっと大きいのはありません。この手ぬぐいで体を洗って下さい。帰る時、お土産に持って帰ってもいいですよ。

　　旅館のお風呂は、男湯と女湯があります。女の人は男湯へ入ってはいけません。間違えないようにして下さい。お風呂の外には、脱衣所があります。そこには、洗面所や、トイレや、服を入れるかごやロッカーがあります。それから、体重を計るのもありますよ。脱衣所で服を脱いだ後、手ぬぐいで体の前を覆って*浴室に入って下さい。

　　すぐに浴槽に入ってはダメですよ。まず、シャワーがなければ*洗面器でお湯を浴びて、石鹸と手ぬぐいで体を洗って下さい。石鹸とシャンプーはたいてい置いてあります。お湯は、湯船（浴槽）の中のを使ってもいいし、蛇口から出るのを使ってもいいです。体から石鹸やシャンプーを完全に洗い流してから湯船に入って下さい。飛び込んではダメです。

　　湯船のお湯はとても熱い時がありますから、手で温度を確認してから入った方がいいです。お湯が熱過ぎる時は、*周りの人に聞いてから、水を入れて下さい。でも、次の人の為にあまりぬるくしてはダメですよ。

伊豆トラベル
伊東

---

* 手ぬぐい – hand towel; 浴槽 – bathtub; 洗面器 – wash basin; 周りの人 – surrounding people

第5課の3

温泉が熱かったから静かに座る事が出来ませんでした。

The hot springs were hot, so sitting quietly wasn't possible.

1）温泉はお湯が温かくて窓からの緑も
きれいで気持ち良かったです。
僕は冷たい水が飲みたいです。

2）私は温泉に
入りたくなかったです。
シャワーを浴びて体を
洗いたかったです。
でも、シャワーは
ありませんでした。
友さんが温泉の中で
泳いだから、私は
恥ずかしかったです。

3）私は泳ぎたくなかったです。でも、
温泉が熱かったから静かに座る事が
出来ませんでした。ところで、
川端さんはよく伊豆に来るんですか。

4）はい。伊豆は歴史が古くて料理が美味しいから、よく
来るよ。それに、鎌倉から遠くないし。

5）僕も伊豆に来てきれいな町を
見てみたかったんです。

6）私はずっと温泉卵が
食べたかったので、
嬉しいです。

会話 Dialog
かい

(Kawabata is in his room at the ryokan, writing. The others have just returned from the onsen.)

1. ベン ： 温泉 は お湯 が 温 かくて 窓 からの 緑 もきれいで 気持ち良かったです。僕は 冷
　　　　　おんせん　ゆ　あたた　まど　　　みどり　　　きも　　　　　　　　　　　つめ
　　　　　たい水が飲みたいです。

2. キアラ ： 私は温泉に入りたくなかったです。シャワーを浴びて体を洗いたかったです。で
　　　　　　　　　おんせん　　　　　　　　　　あ　　あら
　　　　　も、シャワーはありませんでした。友さんが温泉の中で泳いだから、私は恥ずか
　　　　　　　　　　　　　　　　　　　　　　　おんせん　　およ
　　　　　しかったです。

3. 友 ： 私は泳ぎたくなかったです。でも、 温泉 が熱かったから静かに座る事が出来ま
　　　　　およ　　　　　　　　　おんせん　あつ　　　しず　　すわ
　　　　　せんでした。ところで、 川端 さんはよく伊豆に来るんですか。
　　　　　　　　　　　　　　かわばた　　　　い　ず

4. 川端 ： はい。 伊豆は歴史が古くて 料理 が美味しいから、よく来るよ。それに、 鎌
　かわばた　　　い　ず　れきし　ふる　　りょうり　お　い　　　　　　　　　　　　　かま
　　　　　倉から遠くないし。
　　　　　くら　　とお

5. じゅん ： 僕も伊豆に来てきれいな町が見てみたかったんです。
　　　　　　　　い　ず

6. 友 ： 私はずっと*温泉 卵 が食べたかったので、 嬉しいです。
　　　　　　　　　おんせんたまご　　　　　　　　　うれ

*温泉 卵 – egg boiled in a natural hot spring
　おんせんたまご

単語 New Words
たん

きもち 気持ち (n) – mood, feelings
あたたかい 温かい (い adj.) – warm
はずかしい 恥ずかしい (い adj.) – shy, embarrassed, ashamed

きらく 気楽 (な adj.) – relaxing
*から (conj.) – because
だから (conj.) – so, therefore

*Previously introduced

漢字 Kanji

近 5 2 1 / 6 / 3 7 4	キン, ちか(い) – near, close	ノ	ノ	斤	斤	斤	近
	近い – near, close; 近所 – neighborhood; 最近 – recently　ちか　　　きんじょ　　　さいきん	近					
7 strokes	The ax radical (斤), sits atop the stop-and-go radical (辶). You want to be careful when striking something CLOSE to or NEAR your foot with an ax!						

遠 13 strokes	エン, オン, とお(い) – far, distant	一	十	土	吉	吉	吉	吉
	遠い – far, distant; 遠く – far away, at a distance; 遠回り – detour	吉	吉	袁	袁	遠	遠	
	The radical for soil (土), mouth (口), and garments (衣) all combine to stop-and-go (辶) a FAR distance.							

暖 13 strokes	ダン, あたた(かい), あたた(める) – warmth	丨	冂	日	日	日	日	日
	暖かい – warm, mild; 温暖 – warmth; 暖冬 – warm/mild winter	日	日	暖	暖	暖	暖	
	The sun (日) sits next to a base line over three WARM flames. These are on a platform above a friend (友). Between the sun and friends, one feels WARM and content.							

比 4 strokes	ヒ, くら(べる) – compare	一	上	比	比			
	比べる – to compare, to make a comparison; 比較 – comparison							
	This kanji is the "COMPAR(ing)" radical. COMPARE how one side is written correctly as ヒ and the other is not.							

忙 6 strokes	ボウ, モウ, いそ(がしい), せわ(しい) – busy, occupied, restless	、	、	忄	忄	忙	忙	
	忙しい – busy; 大忙し – very busy (person or thing)							
	A heart (忄) being too BUSY and worked to death (亡) is no good.							

言葉の探索 Language Detection

1. **"the person who is …ing something" = 電車に乗っている人**

   Here, a modifying clause is used as a descriptor for a noun. Use this pattern to create longer and more descriptive sentences, such as "The person who is writing is Mr. Kawabata." In Japanese, the clause describing the main noun (Mr. Kawabata) precedes that noun. Use this pattern:

   verb + て form + いる + noun は + _____ です
         <u>main clause</u>   <u>main noun</u>

   書いている + 人は + 川端さんです。
   <u>main clause</u>   <u>main noun</u>

A) 温泉で泳いでいる人はだれですか。 = Who is the person swimming in the hot springs?

B) 寝ている人は弟です。 = The person (who is) sleeping is my younger brother.

C) お風呂に入っている人は祖父です。 = The person in the bath is my grandfather.

D) その車を運転している人は高校生ですよ。危ない！
= The person driving that car is a high school student, you know. Be careful!

2. Tongue twisters = 早口言葉

The Japanese enjoy tongue twisters and have many of them. Not only are they a challenge to say quickly (the name literally means "quick mouth"), they almost always include puns. Try to say this one fast, five times:

隣の客はよく*柿食う客だ

Can you guess the meaning?

*柿 – persimmon

自習 Self Check

1. Modifying clauses.

Restate these in Japanese using the verb + て form + いる + noun は + _____です pattern.
    main clause   main noun
The first one is done for you.

The person who is singing is Mayumi. = 歌っている人は真弓さんです。

(ア)　The person who is singing is Mayumi. = 歌っている人は真弓さんです。

(イ)　The person who is studying is Toshiaki.

(ウ)　The person who lives in Izu is Emi.

(エ)　The person who is talking is the teacher.

(オ)　The person who is taking a walk is my aunt.

(カ)　The person who is riding the bicycle is not Mr. Suzuki.

(キ)　The person who is paying is Tom's father.

(ク)　The person who gave me these rice balls is my friend's mother.

2. 早口言葉

Practice saying the following out loud. Challenge a classmate to see who can repeat each one five times the fastest.

（ア）赤パジャマ青パジャマ黄パジャマ

（イ）生むぎ生ごめ生卵
　　　　なま　　　　なま　　　なまたまご

（ウ）坊主が屏風に上手に坊主の絵を描いた。
　　　ぼうず　　びょうぶ　　　　　ぼうず　　　　　か

translations: （ア）red pajamas, blue pajamas, yellow pajamas

（イ）raw wheat, raw rice, raw egg

（ウ）The monk skillfully drew a picture of another monk on the folding screen.

練習時間 Practice Time
　れん　しゅう

1. Small Group Activity

Use the location and action cards that can be found on **TimeFor Japanese.com**. Player 1 picks one location card. The other players take turns asking questions, in 日本語, to try to guess the location. Player 1 can only answer はい、出来ます –or– いいえ、出来ません. Use either 〜事が出来ますか. –or– the potential form in your questions. The player who guesses correctly thinks of the next location, and play continues.

例
れい
EXAMPLE

Player 2: そこで本が読めますか。
Player 1: はい、本を読めます。
Player 3: そこで食べられますか。
Player 1: いいえ、食べられません。
Player 4: 図書館ですか。
　　　　　　としょかん
Player 1: はい、そうです。図書館です。

2. Pair Practice

The following sentences have adjective errors in them. Take turns rewriting them correctly in your notebook.

A）　この本のテーマは暗いと面白いです。　(This book's theme is interesting and dark.)

B）　友達は頭が良いと背が高いと楽しいです。 (My friend is smart, tall, and fun.)
　　　　　　あたま

C）　私の部屋は青いと狭いとちょっと汚いです。　(My room is blue, small, and a little dirty.)
　　　　　　　　　　　　せま　　　　　　　きたな

D）　あの会社は忙しい、大きい、近いです。
　　　かいしゃ　いそが　　　　　　ちか
　　(That company is busy, big, and close.)

E）　韓国の十二月の天気は寒くて、皆はお正月の準備で忙しかったです。
　　　　　　　　　　　　　　　　　　　しょう　じゅんび　いそが
　　(Korea's December's weather was cold, and everyone was busy with the New Year's Day preparations.)

F）　(free choice)

3. Class Activity

Here are a few more 早口言葉 for you to try. Say each five times, as fast as you can:
　　　　　　　　はやくちことば

右耳右目右目右耳 (right ear, right eye, right eye, right ear)

新幹線　シュルシュル　シュルシュル、線路に沿って走る。
しんかんせん　　　　　　　　　　　　　　　せんろ　そ　　はし
(The Shinkansen (bullet train) goes along the tracks saying "shurushuru.")

蛙　ピョコピョコ　三ピョコピョコ　合わせてピョコピョコ　六ピョコピョコ
かえる　　　　　　み　　　　　　　あ　　　　　　　　　　む
(Take two sets of three frog croaks, add them together and they make six frog croaks.)

4. Class Activity

Put enough chairs in a circle to seat all students except one.
Player 1 (the 鬼) stands in the middle of the circle. The 鬼
makes a sentence using the 〜ている人 pattern (or simply
a descriptive phrase) about another student in the circle. All
students to whom that sentence applies must quickly get up
and find another chair to sit in and the current 鬼 quickly
finds a seat as well. The student left standing is the next 鬼.

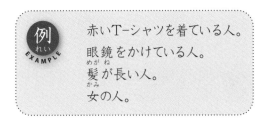

例
EXAMPLE

赤いTーシャツを着ている人。
眼鏡をかけている人。
髪が長い人。
女の人。

文化箱 Culture Chest

伊豆半島と静岡県 (Izu Peninsula and Shizuoka Prefecture)

The setting of the short story 伊豆の踊り子, "The Dancing Girl of Izu," is the town of 天城湯ケ島温泉,
located in the middle of the 伊豆半島 (Izu Peninsula), a mountainous peninsula stretching out to the
west of 東京, just beyond the 関東地方 (Kantou Region) in 中部地方's (Chubu Region's) 静岡県. It
is also almost directly south of 富士山.

This peninsula has other attractions, one of which is the
town of 下田. Here is where the American Navy Commodore
Matthew Perry negotiated America's first port in Japan after
the signing of the Treaty of Kanagawa in 1854. 伊豆半島 also
boasts many 温泉 and is close enough to the capital that it is
a popular day trip. Take the JR express train called the 踊り子,
after the famous dancer. It travels from 東京 at speeds of up
to 120 km/hour on the way to this relaxing destination.

The image above is an ukiyo-e print of
Commodore Perry (center) and other high-
ranking American seamen.

While there, be sure to sample fresh わさび, a specialty of
the area. Visit the resort cities of 熱海, at the northeast end
of the peninsula on your way to 下田, where you can walk along the peaceful streets, or take a taxi to the
little beach just south of town for a hike and a swim. Horror movie fans will know 伊豆 as the setting for
the 1998 Japanese thriller, リング.

地図 Map Skills

伊豆半島

Do some research in both English and in Japanese to see what tour options are available in 伊豆半島 and
choose the most interesting tour you could take to the Mt. Fuji/Izu area from Tokyo. You have a total of

¥50,000 to spend on food, transportation, and lodging. While you are there, be sure to enjoy a dip or two in an 温泉 or 露天風呂 (open-air hot springs).

🔊 メール

The following is a note to Kiara from another travel agent, with information about food at ryokan and at onsen.

Points to consider as you read:

❶ List three items that might appear on a breakfast tray in a ryokan.

❷ On which side of the tray is the rice bowl placed?

❸ According to the message, what are three foods that can be included as the protein portion of the meal?

❹ Compare a Japanese breakfast to a Western-style breakfast.

キアラ様、

　日本の一般的な朝食は、洋風の朝ご飯に比べると少し違います。でもとても健康的で、体には良いんです。

　旅館での食事は、時間に朝食を取る部屋に行くと用意されています。部屋に行くと、旅館の人が温かいご飯と味噌汁をお客様の席まで持って来てくれます。おかずは、テーブルに*置かれています。焼き魚や*生卵、サラダやのりや漬け物が一般的な朝食の*おかずです。おかずの手前に、ご飯の入った*茶碗は左側に、お味噌汁の入ったお椀は右側に置かれます。

　生卵が苦手な人は、そう言うと*目玉焼きにしてくれる事もあります。食べ方は自由ですが、食べる前に「いただきます」と言い、箸を使っておいしく召し上がって下さい。

東山旅行会社
山本　道夫

---

* 健康的 – healthy; 置く – to place, to set down; 生卵 – raw egg; おかず – side dishes; 茶碗 – rice bowl; 置かれる – to be placed, to be put (in a location); 目玉焼き – sunny-side-up fried egg

二階がドンドンうるさいですね。

The second floor is really banging and making a lot of noise, isn't it?

1) 二階がドンドンうるさいですね。一階まで聞こえます。何の音ですか？

2) 旅芸人達が二階の三室に泊まっていて、宴会をしているようだね。一緒に行かないかい？

3) うわあ、この部屋はめちゃくちゃですね。皆ワイワイパーティをしています。

6) 今晩は。私達は箱根から来ました。箱根はとても近いですよ。伊豆はいーずら！

4) 友さんはまた日本料理を食べています。

5) この天ぷらはサクサクで美味しい！ご飯とうどんはあつあつです。

7) ガハハハ。

9) 川端さんは踊り子とぺちゃくちゃ話しています。

8) 私達は遠い国から来ました。あれ？川端さんはどこですか？

会話 Dialog

(Setting: While at the ryokan, our characters hear noises from upstairs.)

1. じゅん ：二階がドンドンうるさいですね。 一階まで聞こえます。何の音ですか?

2. 川端 ：旅芸人達が二階の三室に泊まっていて、宴会をしているようだね。 一緒に行かないかい?

(At the party)

3. ベン ：うわあ、この部屋はめちゃくちゃですね。 皆 ワイワイパーティをしています。

4. じゅん ：友さんはまた日本料理を食べています。

5. 友 ：この天ぷらはサクサクで美味しい!ご飯とうどんはあつあつです。

6. 旅芸人 ：今晩は。私達は箱根から来ました。 箱根はとても近いですよ。 伊豆はいーずら!

7. 旅芸人 ガハハハ。

8. キアラ ：私達は遠い国から来ました。あれ? 川端さんはどこですか?

9. ベン ：川端さんは踊り子とぺちゃくちゃ話しています。

単語 New Words

あつあつ 熱々 (*n/ono.*) – piping hot, passionately in love

おしゃべり (*n*) – chatter, gossip

おと 音 (*n*) – sound

たたみ 畳 (*n*) – tatami mat, rush straw-reed floor mat

たびげいにん 旅芸人 (*n*) – traveling performer

わしつ 和室 (*n*) – Japanese-style room

メチャクチャ (な *adj./ono.*) – messy, disorderly, absurd

ほかほか (*ono.*) – steamy hot food, warm(ly)

わいわい (*ono.*) – noisily, clamorously

〜かい 〜階 (*counter*) – floors, stories

ドンドン (*ono.*) – steadily, drumming (noise), boom boom

サクサク (*ono.*) – crunchy, crisp

〜じょう 〜畳 (*counter*) – tatami mats

〜ま 〜間 (*counter*) – rooms

漢字 Kanji

浜	ヒン、はま – seashore, beach	`	ミ	シ	ジ	ジ	汁
	浜 – beach; 横浜 – city near Tokyo; 白浜 – white sandy beach	汀	汀	浜	浜		
10 strokes	Water (氵) is next to a soldier (兵). Think of an army of little sea-crabs on the BEACH.						

言葉の探索 Language Detection

Counters overview

When travelling, in addition to the generic counters (一つ、二つ、三つ、etc.), there are several other useful counters you should know. What patterns do you notice?

A) 一泊 – stopping (over) one night

B) 二泊三日 – two nights, three days

C) 三日間 – three-day period

D) 一階 – first floor *(that is, the ground floor)

E) 二間 – two rooms

F) 四畳半 – four and one-half tatami mat room (the standard size of a small Japanese-style room)

G) 一番 – No. 1, the first, the best (ordinal counter)

自習 Self Check

Read each Japanese sentence aloud, and then say it in English. Pay close attention to the counters.

(ア) 伊豆への旅行は二泊三日でした。

(イ) 東京から富士山までの切符を三枚お願いします。

(ウ) 一番大きい和室に三泊泊まりました。

(エ) 去年、オーストラリアに行って、十日間シドニーにいました。

練習時間 Practice Time

1. Pair Practice

You are given several scenarios below. Take turns with your partner role-playing the customer and the clerk. Be creative. Be prepared to present your best dialogue to the class.

A) You want to reserve a tatami room at a ryokan for three nights, with dinner. You do not want to include breakfast.

B) You want to buy two train tickets for the green car (グリーン車), from Tokyo to Atami. You inquire the price and the latest possible departure time of the train.

C) You want to spend two nights, for two people, at a minshuku. Inquire about the bath, and whether meals are included (食事付き).

D) You have just decided to fly from Tokyo to Sapporo. Call the airlines to see when the next plane is, and how much a ticket costs.

2. Pair Practice

Consider the 擬態語/擬声語 (mimetic words/onomatopoetic words) samples with each situation below. Take turns with your partner creating a sentence for each situation using the counter and the mimetic/onomatopoetic expression cue.

A) You are staying in the room of the younger brother at your host family. Once you see it, it turns out to be quite messy. (一階, めちゃくちゃ)

B) At the 駅, you try to buy two tickets from Shimoda to Tokyo Station. The clerk speaks too quickly and you become confused. (二枚, ごたごたする)

C) You are going to visit your friend, who lives in a Japanese style 4½ tatami mat room. You knock on his door. (四畳半, とんとん)

D) You are hot and thirsty after walking about sightseeing in Shimoda. You buy a cold drink. (歩いている, ガブガブ飲む)

E) You are trying to find a specific 旅館 that your friend recommended as the best place in town, but you keep getting lost. You are getting frustrated. (一番良い, イライラする)

F) Your room in the 旅館 comes with Japanese-style breakfast. You are doing your best trying to eat the dried fish that came with your rice and soup as a side dish, but they are too crunchy. (和食, さくさく)

G) You meet a new friend, who helps you find a cheap お土産 shop. The new friend turns out to be very chatty and doesn't stop talking. (店, ぺちゃくちゃ)

文化箱 Culture Chest

1. 方言 – Regional Dialects

Despite its relatively small size, the country of Japan is home to many regional and local dialects. Standard Japanese, or 標準語, was originally based on the dialect spoken in Tokyo, but over the years, even the Tokyo language has evolved. Regional dialects (方言) are also called 〜弁, as in 秋田弁 or 博多弁. One of the more well known dialects is 関西弁, which is spoken in the region around Osaka called Kansai, and sometimes is compared to a Southern dialect in the U.S., or a Cockney dialect in Great Britain. In 伊豆, it is common to add a "~ya" sound to words. For example, 危ない → 危にゃ; だいこん → でゃあーこん; 寝たい → 寝てゃあ; and いいでしょう → いーずら. These are the sorts o words that Kiara, Ben, Jun, and Kawabata would be hearing as they spend time with the travelling musicians in the 温泉 of 伊豆. Can you find other examples online of regional 方言 in Japan?

2. 擬態語 • 擬声語 – mimetic words and onomatopoetic expressions

As you know, Japanese often use these words and expressions to add color and interest to their speech. In addition to the words from the manga and dialog for this section, more examples can be seen below. Some of these are associated with certain verbs, such as ガブガブ飲みます (drink in gulps) or イライラしている (irritable). Many of these are reduplicated words, or かさね言葉. You will often see these words written in either katakana or hiragana. Try to make your own sentences using the examples below.

A) 桜がぽつぽつ咲き始めた。 = The cherry blossoms started to pop into bloom.
B) 犬は水をがぶがぶ飲んだ。 = The dog gulped down the water.
C) ぺちゃくちゃしゃべる人。 = That is a gossipy person.
D) 太郎さんはグーグー寝た。 = Tarou slept soundly.

1.	イライラ	irritated; angry	6.	トントン	knocking; rapping
2.	ガブガブ	to drink noisily, to guzzle	7.	ポタポタ	dribble; trickle
3.	ぐらぐら	unsteady; shaky; wobbly	8.	ポツポツ	in small drops or bits
4.	グーグー	snore; rumble; soundly	9.	ぺちゃくちゃ	chatter, babble
5.	ごたごた	confusion, trouble	10.	べたべた	sticky; clinging

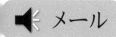

The following message is from Jun's friend Akira, who was born in Shimoda and who is familiar with Izu and Shizuoka dialects. He gives several examples of how that local dialect differs from standard Japanese. Points to consider as you read:

❶ How would someone from Izu say "to begin"?

❷ What is one distinguishing characteristic that someone from Shizuoka might add to the end of words?

❸ What does Akira suggest that Jun do if he has any more questions about the local dialect?

❹ Are there any local dialects in your area? Can you cite any examples?

じゅん君へ

　お手紙ありがとう。僕の家族は下田市の出身です。だから静岡の*方言の中でも、伊豆弁をよく使います。「ようこらんしょ」は伊豆弁で「ようこそ」という意味です。だから、旅館の人はじゅん君達に「いらっしゃいませ」と言ったんだよ。

　伊豆弁には他にも色々あって、標準語とはちょっと違うから難しいかも知れないね。

　例えば、「あかす」は「教える」という意味。だから、伊豆の人が「電車の時間をあかせてくりょー」と言ったときは、「電車の時間を教えて」という意味なんだ。

　「はなる」は「始まる」という意味。だから、「朝食のはなる時間は7時です。」というのは「朝食の始まる時間は7時です。」ということ。

　「たんと食うら」と言われたら「（たんと＝）沢山（食うら＝）食べる」と言う意味だよ。

　静岡では、文章の終わりに、「〜ら」とか「〜だら」という言葉が付く事がとっても多いんだ。また分からない言葉があったらメールしてね。

あきら

*方言 – dialect

それでも、私は帰りたくないです。

Still, I don't want to go home.

1) グラグラ。。。。

2) うわあ、地震だ。危ないから、テーブルの下に入って！

3) 日本は火山が多いから、たくさん地震があってこわいですね。

4) 私は死ぬ前にいせえびが食べたいです。

5) それでも、私は帰りたくないです。私は日本が本当に大好きです。

6) あれ？これは今日の新聞ですね。アインシュタインが日本に来る！

7) すまない、それを持って来て。これはすごいね。東京に行って彼の話を聞きたいよ。彼は頭が良いから地震を止める事が出来るかもしれない。

8) 僕達も連れて行って下さい。

9) 来年、関東に大きい地震が来て142,800人が亡くなりますよ。僕はもう家に帰りたいです。

会話 Dialog

(Our characters are still in Izu with Kawabata-san when they feel a strong earthquake.)

1. グラグラ…

2. 川端　：うわあ、地震だ。危ないから、テーブルの下に入って！
   （かわばた）（じしん）（あぶ）

3. じゅん　：日本は火山が多いから、たくさん地震があってこわいですね。
   （かざん）（じしん）

   (After the tremors cease…)

4. 友　：私は死ぬ前にいせえびが食べたいです。
   （し）

5. キアラ　：それでも、私は帰りたくないです。私は日本が本当に大好きです。

6. キアラ　　あれ？これは今日の新聞ですね。アインシュタインが日本に来る！
   （しんぶん）

7. 川端　：すまない、それを持って来て。これはすごいね。東京に行って彼の話を聞きたいよ。
   （かわばた）（かれ）
   彼は頭が良いから地震を止める事が出来るかもしれない。
   （かれ）（あたま）（じしん）（と）

8. じゅん　：僕達も連れて行って下さい。
   （つ）

9. ベン　：(whispers)来年、関東に大きい地震が来て142,800人が亡くなりますよ。僕はもう
   （かんとう）（じしん）（な）
   家に帰りたいです。

単語 New Words
（たん）

かざん　火山 (n) – volcano

かんとう　関東 (pn) – Kantou (region of Japan including Tokyo and the surrounding area)

なくなる　亡くなる (v) – pass away (to), formal for 死ぬ (cannot be used for one's own death)

漢字 Kanji

止	シ, と(まる), と(める), や(める) – stop, halt	一	ト	止	止		
4 strokes	止まる – to stop; 禁止 – prohibition, ban（と）（きんし）						
	A short person on the left STOPS as his taller friend on the right stretches out a hand and shouts HALT.						

		ノ	ｸ	夕	产	彑	危
危 6 strokes	キ, あぶ(ない) – dangerous, fear						
	危ない – dangerous; 危険 – danger, hazard						
	The top two strokes look like a shield defending against the sharp ends below that could be DANGEROUS.						

自習 Self Check

Conjugate or restate each of these verbs in the designated tense.

ア) 歩く – たい form

イ) 降りる – plain negative form

ウ) もらう – potential form

エ) 渡る – plain past form

オ) 弾く – ～ましょう form

カ) 注文する – て form

練習時間 Practice Time

Small Group Practice

For this activity, you will need one six-sided die or six cards numbered from 1 to 6. Print out the verb cards and game board for this chapter on **TimeFor Japanese.com**. Place the cards face down on the game board and do じゃんけん to see who goes first. Player 1 rolls the die and moves that number of spaces forward. The other players move forward in the same manner. On the second turn, Player 1 draws a card and conjugates the verb on the space where she/he landed. If correct, Player 1 may move forward. If incorrect, Player 1 must follow the instructions on the bottom of the card. Take turns. If one player disagrees with another, say 違います！ If the challenger is correct, that player gets to move forward one space. If the challenger is wrong, they must follow the same instructions on the card. The winner is the first to reach 上がり.

文化箱 Culture Chest

和室 – Japanese style room

The doors and windows in 和室 generally have 障子, sliding wooden frames covered with lightweight white paper that can be closed for privacy. The floor of the 和室 is covered in 畳, woven layered straw mats that are several inches thick and of a standard size that varies according to region. The long sides are usually trimmed in a decorative brocade trim. 和室 often include a 床の間, a shallow alcove, on one wall to display seasonal 生け花, sculptures, dolls, or a hanging scroll. In a private home, many 和室 contain a family 仏壇 (Buddhist altar) and/or 神棚 (Shinto altar) as well as photos of deceased ancestors.

Guests in Japanese homes will often stay in 和室. At bedtime, a 布団 (ふとん) will be taken from a large closet in the room and placed on top of the tatami for sleeping. During the day, the 布団 (ふとん) is quickly folded up and put away, allowing the room to be used as a living room or sitting room. In the middle of the room, there is often a こたつ (table with a heater on the underside) and 座布団 (ざぶとん) cushions to sit on while drinking tea, eating meals, or socializing. Even today, although most Japanese houses and apartments are built in Western style, many Japanese homes still include one 和室.

Modern 床の間 (とこ ま), Akita

地図 (ち ず) Map Skills

You will often see maps like this in hotels and ryokan. What information can you glean from this image?

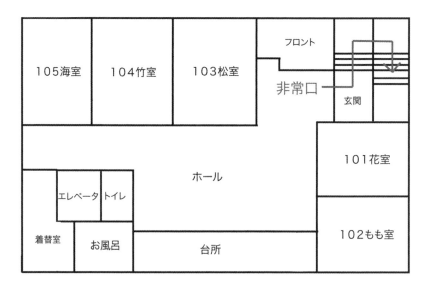

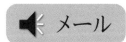 メール

The following is from a poster announcing Albert Einstein's visit to Japan in 1922.
Points to consider as you read:

❶ What will be the location of Einstein's talk?

❷ What is the date and time of the talk?

❸ Is there an entrance fee?

❹ Why do you think Einstein's visit to Japan was such big news?

アルベルト・アインシュタイン博士
はかせ
来日初講演
らいにちはつこうえん

ノーベル物理学賞受賞のアルベルト・アインシュタイン
ぶつり　しょうじゅしょう
博士が来日し、当慶応義塾大学にて初講演が開催されます。
はかせ　　　　　とうけいおうぎじゅく　　　はつこうえん　かいさい

場所　　　：慶応義塾大学　三田キャンパス大講堂
ばしょ　　　　けいおうぎじゅく　　み た　　　　　こうどう

日時　　　：大正11年11月19日午後1時半開始
にちじ　　　　たいしょう　　　　　　　　　　　はんかいし

入場料　：3円
にゅうじょうりょう

講演通訳　：石原純先生
こうえんつうやく　　いしはらじゅん

注意　　　：同講演は、アインシュタイン博士の希望に依り、
ちゅうい　　　　どうこうえん　　　　　　　　　　　　はかせ　きぼう　よ

　　　　　　長時間に渡る場合は、パンの用意あり
　　　　　　　　わた　ばあい　　　　　よう い

男鹿半島 1951年
おがはんとう

Positive Connections Out of a Troubled Past

Kiara, Ben, Jun, and Tomo travel through a torii gate from 1922 Izu and exit through another torii gate at a small jinja in Oga Village on the Oga Peninsula, Akita Prefecture, in 1951. Here, Kiara and the others begin to see positive outcomes growing from a tragic past.

Learning Goals

This chapter will enable you to:
- use the く + なる form of い adjectives (to become)
- use basic greetings and salutations in letters and begin to write informal and introductory letters
- use 以上 and 以下 to say "more than ~" or "less than~"
- use ばかり (only, just, and just that (nothing else))
- use the 〜ないで下さい pattern as a prohibitive command
- ask if it is OK "not" to do something (〜なくてもいいですか)
- use それでは/それじゃ (if it is so~; then; well then)
- say that you or someone else has had the experience of doing something (〜した事がある)
- use the 〜たら verb ending for cause and effect
- learn about お正月 (New Year's)
- learn about Akita Prefecture, some local lore from Oga Peninsula, and a little about the American Occupation after WWII
- use 13 additional kanji

味噌を入れたから美味しくなりましたよ。

I added miso, so it's become even more delicious, you know!

会話 Dialog

(Setting: The group crosses through the torii of a jinja onto a beach on the Oga Peninsula, in the cold climate of northern Japan, December 1951)

1. じゅん　　　　：寒い！冬の風は冷たいですね。頭が痛くなります。

2. 小野太郎　　　：おーい！浜はもっと寒くなって雪が多くなるよ。家に来ないか？家にも
　　　　　　　　　高校生の女の子がいるよ。

3. キアラ　　　　：ありがとう。連れて行って下さい。

　　(Inside the house of Mr. Ono, a local farmer, and his family.)

4. 小野　　　　　：ただいま！これがうちの子供と家内です。

5. 礼子　　　　　：お帰りなさい。皆さん、いらっしゃい。

6. ベン　　　　　：家の中は暖かくて良いですね。じゅん君は顔が赤くなっています。

7. 小野の娘　　　：皆さん、いらっしゃい。きりたんぽを食べてみませんか。食べれば元気に
　　　　　　　　　なりますよ。味噌を入れたから美味しくなりましたよ。

8. 友　　　　　　：秋田の米は美味しくてたくさん食べたくなります。お代わりお願いします。

9. じゅん　　　　：(Looking at a pile of 年賀状) あれは年賀状ですか？

10. 小野　　　　　：そうだよ。後六日でお正月になる。来年は昭和二十八年、巳年だよ。

11. キアラ　　　　：あ！じゃあ、今日はクリスマスですね。皆さん、メリークリスマス！

単語 New Words

あきた　秋田 (pn) – Akita (prefecture)

うち　内 (n) – inside, within, (of the) home

うちのこども　うちの子供 (n) – children (my/our)

うちのひと　うちの人 (n) – one's family, family member

おいれい　お祝い (n) – congratulations

おおみそか　大晦日 (n) – New Year's Eve

おかわり　お代わり (n) – second helping, substitute, alternate

おしょうがつ　お正月 (n) – New Year, New Year's Day

おせちりょうり　お節料理 (n) – food served during New Year's Holidays

かない　家内 (n) – wife (my)

がんたん　元旦 (n) – New Year's Day

クリスマス (n) – Christmas

クワンザ (n) – Kwanzaa

しょうわ　昭和 pn reign period of Emperor Hirohito (1926–1989)

しゅじん　主人 (n) – head (of household), one's husband

(お)としだま　(お)年玉 (n) – New Year's gift (usually money)

ねんがじょう　年賀状 (n) – New Year's card

ハヌカ (n) – Hanukkah

へびどし/みどし　巳年 (n) – year of the snake

198　Intermediate Japanese

むすこ 息子 (n) – son

むすめ 娘 (n) – daughter

ただしい 正しい (い adj.) – correct, right, proper

ほとんど (adv.) – mostly, almost

いわう 祝う (v) – celebrate (to)

しんじる 信じる (v) – believe (to)

かんしゃ 感謝 (n) – thanks, gratitude

かんしゃ(を)する 感謝(を)する (v) – give thanks (to)

かんしゃさい 感謝祭 (n) – Thanksgiving

漢字 Kanji

夕 3 strokes	セキ, ゆう – evening	ノ	ク	夕			
	七夕 – Star Festival; 夕食 – evening meal, dinner; 夕方 – evening; 一夕 – one evening, some evenings						
	In addition to being the katakana for た, this kanji is a radical itself.						

内 4 strokes	ナイ, ダイ, うち – inside, within, among, home	丨	冂	内	内		
	内 – inside, 内部 – inside, internal; 内金 – deposit (to bank account)						
	A downward facing box (冂) encompasses a person INSIDE of a HOME.						

朝 12 strokes	チョウ, あさ – morning, dynasty	一	十	古	吉	吉	吉
	朝ご飯 – breakfast; 北朝鮮 – North Korea; 朝日 – morning sun, name of a popular newspaper	直	卓	軡	朝	朝	朝
	As MORNING breaks, and the sun (日) rises and the moon (月) sets, tens (十) of courtiers come to the court of the emperor.						

昼 9 strokes	チュウ, ひる – daytime, noon	フ	コ	尸	尺	尺	昼
	昼ご飯 – lunch; 昼寝 – nap (noontime sleep); 昼休み – noon break/lunch	昼	昼	昼			
	A flag (尸) with an extra flap on the right side flies above the NOON sun (日). NOON only happens once (一) a day.						

夜 8 strokes	ヤ, よ, よる – night, evening	丶	亠	广	夊	夜	夜
	夜 – night, evening; 一夜 – one night, all night; 昼夜 – day and night	夜	夜				
	A kettle lid (亠) closes a person (亻) next to a folding chair (夊), making it dark like NIGHT or EVENING.						

正	だだ(しい), まさ, セイ, ショウ – correct, justice	一	丁	下	正	正
	正しい – right, correct; 正す – to correct, to amend; 不正 – injustice; 正子 – female given name; 正月 – New Year's Day					
5 strokes	One (一) check after stopping (止) makes everything CORRECT.					

言葉の探索 Language Detection

to become = く-form of い adjectives + なる

The adverbial form, or く-form of い-adjectives plus なる, is used to mean that something will become, or become more, of that particular adjective (e.g., 寒くなる/寒くなります = it will become cold). To use this pattern with い adjectives, drop the final "い" and add "く + なる. To use this pattern with な adjectives, add the particle に + なる to the adjective stem. Below are several examples of this conjugation pattern.

い adjective

A) 大きいです。　　　= It is big.　　　C) 大きくなっています。　= It is becoming big.

B) 大きくなります。　= It will become big.　D) 大きくなりました。　= It became big.

な adjective

A) 静かです。　　　　= It is quiet.　　　C) 静かになっています。　= It is becoming quiet.

B) 静かになります。= It will become quiet.　D) 静かになりました。　= It became quiet.

NOTE A related pattern is the (noun) + になる structure. Use this pattern to say things like 友達になる (to become friends) or いい人になる (to become a good person).

自習 Self Check

Change the following adjectives to the adverbial form according to the given prompts. Say each statement quietly out loud to yourself.

A) ぬるい　　– The tea became lukewarm.　　　E) 静か　　– The park is tranquil/peaceful, isn't it?

B) 遅い　　– I will be late for class.　　　F) 簡単　　– The problem (問題) became simpler.

C) 暖かい – It became warm outside (外).　　G) 変　　– That student has become even stranger.

D) 明るい　– This shirt is becoming lighter (in color).

Pair Practice

Use the cues to create questions and answers with your partner.

(cool)

A-さん：外は 涼 くなりましたか。 = Has it become cooler out?
　　　　　　 すずし

B-さん：ええ、 涼 しくなりました。 = Yes, it's become cooler.
　　　　　　　　 すずし

| 1. (hungry) | 2. (friends) | 3. (skillful) | 4. (busy) |
| 5. interesting | 6. (happy) | 7. (dark) | 8. (delicious) |

文化箱 Culture Chest
ぶん か ばこ

お正月
　 しょうがつ

Pine, bamboo, and plum blossoms (松、 竹、 梅) are symbols used in New Year's decorations. During
　　　　　　　　　　　　　　　　　　　 まつ たけ うめ

this holiday, families visit shrines and temples, and everyone consumes special foods and drinks. All of

these, and more, are part of the New Year's celebration in Japan, one of the most important celebrations

on the Japanese calendar. January 1 (お正月) and the weeks before and after that day are full of rituals

and activities. Here are some things you might experience or see during お 正 月 in Japan:
　　　　　　　　　　　　　　　　　　　　　　　　　　　　　　　　　　しょうがつ

大掃除	house cleaning prior to お正月
門松 （かどまつ）	special お正月 decorations meant to bring good luck and fortune. These are placed at the entrance way to the house (門) and are usually constructed of pieces of bamboo, pine branches, and pine cones
年賀状 （ねんがじょう）	New Year cards to send good wishes for the coming year
大晦日 （おおみそか）	New Year's Eve, the evening of December 31, when many families visit their local shrine and maybe watch singing competitions on TV
おせち料理 （りょうり）	special お正月 foods whose colors and other attributes have positive symbolic meaning. These foods (fish, beans, seaweed, etc.) are served in beautiful tiered lacquered boxes.
年越しそば （としこ）	special noodles eaten for long life
初詣 （はつもうで）	the first visit of the year to a shrine or temple
除夜の鐘 （じょや　かね）	the ringing of bells in Buddhist temples around the country at midnight on Dec. 31
お年玉 （としだま）	colorful envelopes containing New Year's gift money for children
福笑い （ふくわら）	a New Year's game similar to pin-the-tail-on-the-donkey
羽根突き （はねつ）	a badminton-like game played at New Year's

Conduct some research to find out more information about the New Year Celebration in Japan.

地図（ちず） Map Skills

　本州（ほくせい）の北西に秋田県（あきたけん）という所があります。秋田県（あきたけん）は「田舎の県（いなか　けん）」とよく言われますが、さまざまな事で有名です。

　県（けん）の中心付近（ちゅうしんふきん）に、一番大きな市、秋田市（人口　320万）があります。西に、なまはげ祭（まつ）りや美しい岩石（がんせき）の海岸線（かいがんせん）で有名な男鹿半島（おがはんとう）があります。県（けん）の北東（ほくとう）と東には、火山の噴火でできた、二つの大きな湖（みずうみ）があります。十和田湖（とわだこ）と田沢湖（たざわこ）です。十和田湖は十和田八幡平国立公園（とわだはちまんたいこくりつこうえん）の中にあります。田沢湖（たざわこ）は日本で一番深い湖です。一番深い所で水深（すいしん）423メートルもあります。北にある大きな市は、能代市（のしろし）（人口（じんこう）　60万人以上）、南には、二つの大きな市、大仙市（だいせんし）と横手市（よこてし）があります。それぞれの人口は、100万人くらいです。

　秋田県はさまざまな事で有名です。例（たと）えば、「あきたこまち」という名前の美味しいお米（こめ）、漁業（ぎょぎょう）、温泉（おんせん）、祭（まつ）り、郷土料理（きょうどりょうり）、そして冬の大雪です。秋田県の方言はとても面白いです。時々、他（ほか）の県から来た人には分からない事もあります。秋田弁（あきたべん）と呼ばれ、「そうですね」を「んたすな！」と言います。

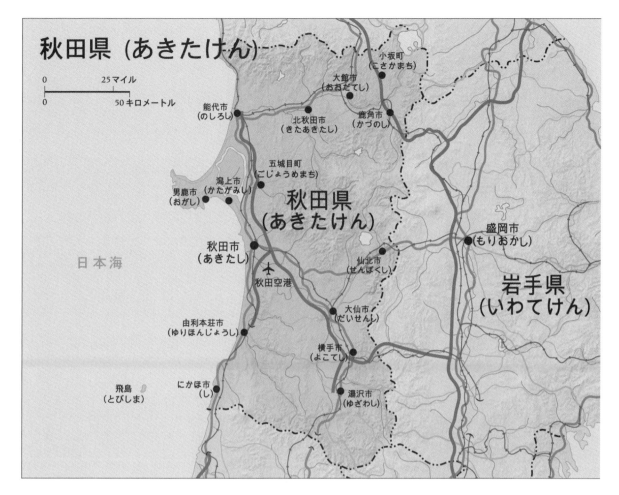

Using the map and the passage above, answer the following questions in Japanese.

❶ 秋田県の一番人口が多い市は何ですか。

❷ 秋田県の一番北にある大きな市は何ですか。

❸ 十和田湖より田沢湖の方が深い(deep)ですか。

❹ 秋田県は何で有名ですか。

❺ 秋田の方言の例を一つ書いて下さい。

🔊 メール

This message is a letter from Kiara's grandfather Watson to Ben, replying to a Christmas card Ben had sent from Akita.

Points to consider as you read:

❶ What is Mr. Watson's connection to Akita?

❷ When did Mr. Watson's ancestors come to America?

❸ What was the weather like the day Mr. Watson visited his relatives in Oga?

❹ How did Mr. Watson feel about meeting his Japanese relatives?

ベンへ、

元気ですか。こちらは皆元気です。

　ベンのクリスマス・カードが昨日秋田から届きました。ありがとう。今年のクリスマスはキアラの両親の家に家族が皆で集まって、とても楽しかったです。

　ところで、このカードを秋田からもらって、とても*びっくりしました。すごく*偶然ですが、私もずっと前に秋田へ行った事があります。それは1952年で、私はそのころ青森の*アメリカ軍基地の兵隊でしたから、アメリカ軍基地のクリスマスの後で秋田の男鹿半島を訪ねました。

　実は私の*曾祖父は百年ぐらい前に日本からアメリカに来ました。秋田の男鹿半島の出身だったと祖父から聞いていました。それで私は十二月三十日に男鹿半島の先祖の親戚の家に訪ねて行ったんです。朝早い電車に乗って、電車の窓から青くて冷たい日本海を眺めながら行きました。

　夕方になって男鹿半島に着きました。その日は朝から雪がたくさん降ったので、辺りは真っ白になっていました。家々の屋根の下には長いつららが垂れ下がっていました。そして、冷たい風がピューピューと日本海から吹いてきて、とても寒かったのを覚えています。

　日本の親戚に会うのは初めてなので、私は胸がどきどきしていました。でも、曾祖父の親戚のおじいさんは私を見て、「よぐ（＝よく）来た。よぐ来た。そど（＝そと）はさびがら（＝寒いから）、まんず（＝まず）上がれ。」と嬉しそうな声で言いました。そして、すぐ家の中に私を*案内してくれました。

　土間で靴を脱いで、おじいさんの家族と暖かい*いろりのそばに座りました。いろりの真ん中にはきりたんぽなべが煮立っていました。「きりたんぽでも食べで（＝食べて）、早ぐ（＝早く）暖がぐ（＝暖かく）なれ。」とおじいさんは言いました。曾祖父の家族と一緒にいろりを囲んできりたんぽを食べて、その時私は心も体も暖かくなりました。

　ベンたちも男鹿で親切な人たちにお世話になって、よかったですね。いつまで男鹿半島にいますか。キアラにも宜しく。

十二月二十七日
キアラのおじいさんより

*びっくりする – to be surprised; 偶然 – coincidentally; アメリカ軍基地の兵隊 – soldier on an American military base; 曾祖父 – great- grandfather; 案内 – information, guidance; いろり – an open, central fire pit used for cooking and heat in houses in northern Japan

第6課の2

悪い子と怠け者の子ばかりを探す。
They search only for bad children and lazy children.

1) アメリカでは、子供達はサンタに手紙を書くんですよ。

2) そうですか？どんな事を書きますか？

3) 例えば、「サンタさんへ、お元気ですか？私は一年間良い子だったから、プレゼントを下さい。新しい本が欲しいです。キアラより。」

4) 秋田では、クリスマスにサンタは来ないけど、大晦日になまはげが来ますよ。なまはげは怖い鬼で、悪い子と怠け者の子ばかりを探します。大人はなまはげに酒と餅をあげますよ。

5) 日本では大晦日に年越しそばを食べて除夜のかねを聞きます。お正月に、初詣をして子供達はお年玉をもらいます。

6) そうですよ！お年玉の中身を毎年楽しみにしています。でも、なまはげはとても怖いから、逃げたくなります。

会話 Dialog

(Setting: Oga Peninsula, at the house of Mr. Ono and his daughter.)

1. キアラ　　：アメリカでは、子供達はサンタに手紙を書くんですよ。

2. じゅん　　：そうですか?どんな事を書きますか?

3. キアラ　　：例えば、「サンタさんへ、お元気ですか?私は一年間良い子だったから、プレゼント
　　　　　　　を下さい。新しい本が欲しいです。キアラより。」

4. 小野の娘　：秋田では、クリスマスにサンタは来ないけど、大晦日になまはげが来ますよ。なま
　　　　　　　はげは怖い鬼で、悪い子と怠け者の子ばかりを探します。大人はなまはげに酒と
　　　　　　　餅をあげますよ。

5. 友　　　　：日本では大晦日に年越しそばを食べて除夜の鐘を聞きます。お正月に、
　　　　　　　初詣をして子供達はお年玉をもらいます。

6. 小野の娘　：そうですよ!お年玉の中身を毎年楽しみにしています。でも、なまはげはとても怖い
　　　　　　　から、逃げたくなります。

単語 New Words

おとな　大人 (*n*) – adult

おに　鬼 (*n*) – ghost, devil

きりたんぽ (*n*) – regional (Akita) dish of cooked
and pounded rice, grilled on skewers

きょうかい　教会 (*n*) – church

ぶっきょう　仏教 (*n*) – Buddhism

キリストきょう　キリスト教 (*n*) – Christianity

ユダヤきょう　ユダヤ教 (*n*) – Judaism

イスラムきょう　イスラム教 (*n*) – Islam

ヒンズーきょう　ヒンズー教 (*n*) – Hinduism

しんとう　神道 (*n*) – Shinto religion

さいじつ　祭日 (*n*) – holiday

としこしそば　年越しそば (*n*) – special New Year's soba

なかみ　中身 (*n*) – contents, interior

なまけもの　怠け者 (*n*) – lazy person

なまはげ (*n*) – folklore demon of Oga Peninsula, seen
on New Year's Eve

だけ (*part.*) – only, just, as

など (*part.*) – et cetera, and the like

より (*part.*) – from (when writing a letter)

ばかり (*part.*) – only, just

にげる　逃げる (*v*) – escape (to), run away (to)

漢字 Kanji

 14 strokes	ヨウ,さま – way, manner, suffix		一	十	オ	木	木゙	杉゙	栏゙
	本田 様 – Mr. Honda; この 様 – this way _{さま} _{よう}		栏	样	样	样	様	様	様
	This kanji is made up of three radicals, tree (木), sheep (羊), and water (水). A respectful shepherd keeps his flock in the MANNER that provides shade and water.								

 11 strokes	ダイ, テイ – number (#)		ノ	ト	午	㐅	竹	竹	
	第一 – first, foremost; 第一課 – Chapter 1 _{だい} _{だい} _か		竻	笋	笋	第	第		
	The top of this kanji is bamboo (竹), the bottom is similar to 弟. Your own little brother is always Number 1!								

 10 strokes	キ, おに – devil, demon, ghost		ノ	イ	冖	币	由	白	
	鬼 – devil, demon, ghost _{おに}		甶	鬼	鬼	鬼			
	A spot of a GHOST appears above a rice field (田) with legs that resemble ハ and ム. The ghost walks around the field screaming a scary ムーハハハ.								

言葉の探索 Language Detection
_{こと ば たん さく}

1. Register

In Chapter 4, you learned about informal speech in Japanese. Whether you are interacting with a friend, or with someone older than you, it is important to maintain consistency in level of politeness in both spoken and written Japanese. This means that if your speech is informal or humble, all of your language should reflect that style using the plain/dictionary forms of verbs; informal speech omits particles when appropriate. If you are using the more polite です/ます form (with the 〜ます forms of verbs and full and complete sentences), continue using that form for consistency.

2. Only, just and just that (nothing else) = ばかり

A. verb 〜た form + ばかり

The particle ばかり has two main uses. One is to show that an action has just taken place. For this pattern, ばかり immediately follows the past plain form (the 〜た form) of the verb.

1) 私達は昼ご飯はんを食べたばかりです。 = We have just finished eating lunch.

2) 友子さんは日本から帰ったばかりです。 = Tomoko has just returned from Japan.

3) マークさんは試験が終わったばかりです。 = Mark has just finished his exam.

B. noun + ばかり

A second use of ばかり is immediately after a noun. Here, ばかり indicates that only that particular noun exists (in this situation; it can also connote a sense of excess).

1) 先生は肉を食べないで、野菜ばかり食べていました。
= The teacher doesn't eat meat, so he only ate vegetables.

2) このクラスには、いい生徒ばかりいます。
= In this class, there are only good students.

3) 家で友弘君はビデオゲームばかりしています。
= At home, Tomohiro only plays video games.

C. 〜て form + ばかり

Placing ばかり immediately after the て form of a verb means "is doing nothing but" the action that is currently stated. For this use of ばかり, the sentence ends with either います or しています (is doing).

1) 毎日山田君はテレビを見てばかりいます。
= Every day, the only thing Yamada is doing is watching TV.

2) 今晩、明子さんは絵を描いてばかりいます。
= This evening, the only thing Akiko is doing is drawing pictures.

3) その猫は寝てばかりいます。
= The only thing that that cat is doing is sleeping.

自習 Self Check

1. Practice making sentences in the register indicated.

(ア) Tell your mother good morning and tell her that you are going to go to the convenience stor later.

(イ) Tell your boss, Mr. Suzuki, good morning and that you are writing a memo (メモ).

2. Say the following in Japanese. Use ばかり.

(ア) I have just finished my homework.

(イ) Yasuhiro and Emi just became friends.

(ウ) This school only has high school students (no other students).

(エ)　My friend only drives old cars.

(オ)　On Saturday, Mr. Tanaka is only running.

(カ)　Keiko only wears jeans.

練習時間 Practice Time
れんしゅう

1. Small Group Practice

Form groups of two or three. Each person has just returned from a different trip to Akita. You are very excited about the things you have done and seen and want to tell your friends everything. Take turns telling each other where you went and other information about your trip. Each listener needs to take notes about what happened and makes any necessary corrections.

Destination	Transportation	Activities	Foods	Time
The town of Oga (男鹿町) おがまち	airplane and bus	hiking, なまはげ 博物館 (museum) はくぶつ	すし, きりたんぽ	New Year's Day
Lake Tazawa (田沢湖) たざわこ	train and bus	skiing, onsen	おでん, 焼きそば や	December 20
Yokote City (横手市) よこてし	train	鎌倉祭り, かまくらまつ カラオケ	インド料理, りょうり すき焼き や	February 15 and 16

2. Pair Practice

Look at the pictures below. Take turns stating what each person is always <u>only</u> doing.

例
れい
EXAMPLE
いつも、明子さんは泳いでばかりいます。　= Akiko is always only swimming.
あき

真理子（絵を描く）　　伊東先生(漢字を書く)　　おばあさん（料理する)
まりこ　　か　　　　　いとう　　　　　　　　　　りょうり

太郎（遊ぶ） たろう あそ	お父さん（写真/撮る） しゃしん と	友子（三味線/弾く） しゃ み せん ひ

文化箱 Culture Chest
ぶん か ばこ

秋田美人と祭り – Beauties and Festivals of Akita
あき た び じん まつ

Akita is not only well known for its delicious rice, sake, and its cold winters, but it is also noted for 秋田美人 and a wide variety of 祭り. The women of 秋田 are said to have beautiful skin because of the delicious rice grown in the region. Akita also boasts some of the most interesting festivals in the country.

When you visit, try to catch the 秋田竿燈祭り in early August, to see performers balance poles adorned with tiers of lanterns. The performers move the poles around, balancing them on hip, hand, and shoulder as they travel up and down the main boulevard of 秋田市. The poles and their lights wave high in the air like golden stalks of rice, ready for harvest. The 竿燈 are 12 m tall and weigh over 50 kg; it is quite a sight to see over 200 of them parading along the streets!

In mid-February, you can visit 横手市, in the 秋田県 の南の方, to see the 鎌倉祭り. 鎌倉 are snow domes or houses, similar to igloos, built along the winding streets and the riverbank to provide temporary havens for deities.

秋田県, like other locales, boasts its own specialty foods. Some tasty treats you might want to try include しょっつる (fish and vegetable stew) and がっこ (pickles).

🔊 メール

Here is a 年賀状 from Kiara's grandfather in the United States to Ben, and below is the letter to Ben that accompanied Mr. Watson's New Year's card.

Points to consider as you read:

❶ In what animal year was Mr. Watson born?

❷ What are the "three friends" (三友)? Where else would you find these "three friends" used?

❸ What is the significance of the daruma doll at New Year's?

❹ Have you ever made your own holiday cards? What designs did you/would you put on them?

　日本で見た年賀状を思い出して，この年賀状に絵を描いてみました。

　新しい年、1953年は確か、巳年だったと思います。だから、年賀状にヘビをまず描きました。男鹿のおじいさんが十二支の動物を教えてくれました。「ね（ねずみ）・うし・とら・う（うさぎ）・たつ・み（へび）・うま・ひつじ・さる・とり・いぬ・い（いのしし）」の*順番です。その年私は24才だったから、私は巳年生まれだと知りました。キアラのお母さんは　その12年後の1965年に生まれたから、やっぱり巳年生まれです。ベン君は今年何才になりますか。ベン君は何年でしょうね。

　年賀状に松と竹と梅の絵も描きました。この三つの木は三友と言って、年賀状や新年の*飾りによくあります。ベン君も町の飾りを見てもう*気が付いていたでしょう。この三つの木にはそれぞれすばらしい意味があります。

　松は根が強くていつも緑。竹は風が吹いても*折れない。そして、幹に節があって、毎年の*成長が分かる。梅の木は寒い冬に一番最初に花が咲く。だから、三友はいつでも強くて美しいから、そういう人になりましょう、という意味です。

　三友はきれいな木のイメージと意味とで、他にも色々な時に使います。例えば、寿司は松寿司、竹寿司、梅寿司などと言います。それから、日本の旅館でもよく部屋に松の間、竹の間、梅の間などの名前を付けます。

　最後に赤くて丸い人形を描きました。何だか分かりますか。達磨の絵です。達磨は*禅仏教を始めた人です。九年間ずっと座って、座禅をしました。そしてやっと悟りを開きました。その達磨さんのように*諦めない、という願いが達磨さんの絵の意味です。日本人は新年に達磨人形を買って、願いをかけた*印に目を一つだけ塗ります。その願いがかなった時、もう一つの目も*塗ります。

　ベン君も自分の年賀状を描いてみませんか。面白いと思いますよ。

ワトソンおじいさんより

* 順番 – order; 飾り – decoration; 気が付く – to notice; 折れない – will not break; 禅仏教 – Zen Buddhism;
諦める – to give up; 諦めない – do not give up; 印 – a sign; 塗る – to paint

友さん、きりたんぽを五本以上食べないで下さい。

(い じょう)

Tomo, please do not eat more than five sticks of kiritanpo.

1) 友さん、きりたんぽを五本以上食べないで下さい。そして、台所で寝ないで下さい。

2) 私はホストファミリーに手紙を書きました。見てくれませんか？

3) いいですよ。あ、この漢字は違います。正しい漢字はこれです。

4) あっ、ペンで書かないで下さい。鉛筆で書いて下さい。

5) じゃあ、僕が読みましょう。

6) でも、恥ずかしいから大きい声で読まないで下さい。それから、じゅん君のお父さんとお母さんにはまだ言わないで下さい。

7)「ホストファミリーのお父様、お母様へ。お元気ですか？ こちらは朝晩ととても寒くなりましたが、昼は少し暖かいです。早いもので、私が日本に来てもう四ヶ月になります。もうすぐお正月になります。秋田では大みそかの夜に「なまはげ」という鬼が来ます。でも東京は遠いから来ないでしょう。私はホストファミリーの皆様のおかげで楽しくホームステイをする事が出来て、日本が大好きになりました。ありがとうございます。これからも日本語と日本文化をもっと勉強したいです。これからもお世話になりますが，よろしくお願いします。お体に気を付けて、風邪を引かないで下さい。良いお年を。2009年12月25日、キアラより。」

会話 Dialog

(Setting: The group is in the living area of Mr. Ono's home.)

1. ベン　　　：友さん、*きりたんぽを五本以上食べないで下さい。そして、台所で寝ないで下さい。

2. キアラ　　：私はホストファミリーに手紙を書きました。見てくれませんか?

3. 友　　　　：いいですよ。あ、この漢字は違います。正しい漢字はこれです。

4. キアラ　　：あっ、ペンで書かないで下さい。鉛筆で書いて下さい。

5. じゅん　　：じゃあ、僕が読みましょう。

6. キアラ　　：でも、恥ずかしいから大きい声で読まないで下さい。それから、じゅん君のお父さんとお母さんにはまだ言わないで下さい。

7. じゅん　　：「ホストファミリーのお父様、お母様へ。お元気ですか? こちらは朝晩とても寒くなりましたが、昼は少し暖かいです。早いもので、私が日本に来てもう四ヶ月になります。もうすぐお正月になります。秋田では大みそかの夜に「なまはげ」という鬼が来ます。でも東京は遠いから来ないでしょう。私はホストファミリーの皆様のおかげで楽しくホームステイをする事が出来て、日本が大好きになりました。ありがとうございます。これからも日本語と日本文化をもっと勉強したいです。これからもお世話になりますが、よろしくお願いします。お体に気を付けて、風邪を引かないで下さい。良いお年を。2009年12月25日、キアラより。」

単語 New Words

いか 以下 (n) – not more than; ... and less than/below

いじょう 以上 (n) – not less than; ... and more than, above

おかげ お陰 (n) – thanks to or owing to, assistance

おせわ お世話 (n) – help, assistance

だいどころ 台所 (n) – kitchen

ぶんか 文化 (n) – culture

ホームステイ (n) – homestay

ホストファミリー (n) – host family

ゆうがた 夕方 (n) – evening

もうすぐ (exp.) – very soon

よいおとしを よいお年を (exp.) – have a good New Year

にぎやか 賑やか (な adj.) – bustling, busy

さそう 誘う (v) – invite (to)

漢字 Kanji

怖	フ, こわ(い), こわ(がる) – scary, be frightened	㇒	㇒	忄	忄	忄	忄	
	怖い – dreadful, scary; 恐怖 – fear, dread	怖	怖					
8 strokes	Putting a white cloth (布) over a live heart (忄) makes a very SCARY ghost.							

以	イ, も(って) – by means of, because, compared with	㇀	㇀	㇀	以	以	
	以上 – not less than, beyond; 以下 – not exceeding, below; 以外 – with the exception of						
5 strokes	The two strokes on the left look like a foot, the MEANS OF kicking the ball (the middle stroke) over the person (人) on the right. The foot on the left, COMPARED WITH the person on the right, is much larger.						

言葉の探索 Language Detection

1. **Letter Writing Part A: Informal letter writing**

   As noted earlier, letter writing in Japanese may range from formal requests for information to an in formal note to a friend or host family. For an informal letter, such as the one Kiara writes to her host family in the 会話 above, here are some standard expressions you might use:

   Greetings/openings

お元気ですか。	= How are you?
おかげさまで、元気です。	= Thanks to you, I am doing well.
手紙ありがとう。	= Thank you for the letter.

   Weather-related expressions

   最近、秋になって、涼しい日が続きます。
   = Recently, fall has arrived, and cool days are continuing.

   寒い冬ですので、風邪を引かないようにして下さい。
   = In the midst of this cold winter, please do not catch a cold.

   Endings/closings/final greetings

体に気を付けて下さい。	= Take care of yourself.
お返事を待っています。	= I await your reply.
では、今日はこれで	= Well, that's all for today
じゃ、またね	= See you later

2. **more than 10 and less than 10 = 10 以上 and 10 以下**

A number, immediately followed by 以上 (or 以下), is one way to state that more of (or less of) something exists. For example,

500人以上 = more than 500 people

500人以下 = fewer than 500 people

A) 学校の野球部は半分以上の試合で勝ちました。
= The school's baseball team won by more than half of the games.

B) 秋田では冬にたいてい雪が一メートル以上降ります。
= In winter, in Akita, usually more than one meter of snow falls.

C) 食べ物があまりにもたくさんあって、半分以上残しました。
= There was so much food, we left more than half.

3. **Please don't do ～ = ～ないで下さい**

Prohibitive commands (previously introduced in *Beginning Japanese*) use the ～て form of a verb + は + いけません / だめです. For example, ここに座ってはいけません (You may not sit here). To make a more polite prohibitive request for Type 1 (う) verbs, change the い ending sound to an あ ending sound (the plain negative form). For example, "Please don't drink" becomes 飲まないで下さい. For Type 2 (る) and irregular verbs, simply drop the ます and add ないで下さい.

Type 1 (う) Verbs

飲みます　⇒　飲まないで下さい。
言います　⇒　言わないで下さい。
聞きます　⇒　聞かないで下さい。
行きます　⇒　行かないで下さい。

Type 2 (る) Verbs

食べます　⇒　食べないで下さい。
始めます　⇒　始めないで下さい。
閉めます　⇒　閉めないで下さい。
見ます　⇒　見ないで下さい。

Irregular verbs

します　⇒　しないで下さい。
来ます　⇒　来ないで下さい。

4. **Asking/giving permission NOT to do something**

When politely asking whether it is all right NOT to do something, use the plain negative verb stem as in the prohibitive commands described above. Then add ～なくてもいいです(か).

plain negative verb stem + なくて + も + いいです(か)
歌わない → 歌わな~~い~~ + なくて + も + いいです
　　　verb stem
歌わなくてもいいです。 = It is OK if you don't sing.

A) 飲まないで下さい。　　　　　= Do not drink (it), please.

⇩

飲まなくてもいいですか。　　= Is it OK if I don't drink (it)?

or

飲まなくてもいいです。　　　= It is all right NOT to drink (it).

B) 持って来ないで下さい。　　= Do not bring (it), please.

⇩

持って来なくてもいいですか。 = Is it all right NOT to bring (it)?

or

持って来なくてもいいです。　= It is all right NOT to bring (it).

5. If it is so/then/well then = それでは/それじゃ

A) The formal conjunction それでは and the less formal それじゃ are used to link two related ideas. Place this expression at the beginning of the second sentence. It can be abbreviated, and used less formally, as in それじゃ、それじゃあ、では、or じゃ.

① 皆様、時間になりました。それでは、始めましょう。
= Everyone, it's time. Well then, let us begin. (formal)
② ベン君、お寿司が嫌いですね。それじゃ、ラーメンを食べましょう。
= Ben, you dislike sushi, right? Well then, let's eat ramen.
③ 友子さんも、明日英語の試験がありますね。それじゃ、一緒に勉強しませんか。
= Tomoko, tomorrow you also have an English test, don't you? If so, won't you study with me?

B) A second way to use それでは is to conclude a conversation, leaving open the intention of talking or meeting again in the future.

① それでは、… = Well then…
② それじゃ、… = Well then… (informal)
③ それでは、また来週話しましょう。　= Well then, let's talk again next week.
④ それじゃ、後で焼きそばを食べに行きましょう。　= Well then, let's go and eat yakisoba later.

自習 Self Check

1. Say the following in Japanese using 以上 and 以下.

(ア) More than 50 sheets of paper.　　(ウ) Less than 10 floors.

(イ) More than 5 nights.　　(エ) Fewer than 25 people came to the party.

2. State the following prohibitive commands in Japanese.

    (ア)   Please don't eat that cake now.   (ウ)   Is it OK if I don't do that test?

    (イ)   Please don't stand there.   (エ)   Is it OK if I don't go shopping?

3. Choose one of the levels of formality below to match to each expression.

   ____ それでは、行きませんか。   ① very formal

   ____ それじゃ、…   ② somewhat formal

   ____ じゅん君、数学が得意でしょう。   ③ informal

   ____ それじゃ、これは出来る？   ④ very informal

   ____ それでは、また明日。

   ____ それでは、明日の宿題は第五課です。

練習時間 Practice Time

1. Pair Practice

Think of a Japanese friend or host family to whom you can send an informal letter. With your partner, take turns creating parts of an informal short letter. Remember to use a greeting, make small talk about the weather, and include a closing. This activity is timed, so speak quickly. When your teacher says 時間です, stop speaking and/or writing. Try to make your letter interesting, since you may be asked to share it with your class.

2. Class Activity

You will interview at least three classmates about their habits during the week. Copy the following chart onto a piece of scrap paper. Using the question cues below, choose from number 1 through 6. Your first question will use the pattern 以上 or 以下. On the basis of the answer, create a second question using the pattern ばかり; on the basis of that answer, create a third suggestion, using それでは. Record your classmates' answers on your chart. Be prepared to report your results to the class.

A)   study, more than 2 hours everyday

B)   part time job (アルバイトをする), more than 10 hours every week

C)   listen to music, more than one hour every day

D)   play only computer games, less than one hour every day

E)   every year, in the summer, swimming, less than two times (二回)

F)   free choice

Person A: お名前は何ですか。

Person B: ジョンです。

Person A: 毎日、二時間以上勉強しますか？

Person B: ええ、毎日、二時間以上勉強します。

Person A: じゃ、勉強ばかりしていますか。

Person B: いいえ、本も読んでいます。

Person A: それじゃ、いっしょに勉強しましょう。

Person B: いいですよ。

名前	action	以上 / 以下	ばかり	それでは (suggestion)
John	study	more than 2 hours/day	no, also reads books	study together

3. Small Group Activity

Use the Tsunagaru game board file and location cards for this activity. Begin by making a drawing a card and creating a prohibitive command that would be appropriate for the location on your card. If your fellow players agree that your command is correct, roll the dice and move that many spaces ahead on the game board. If your command is incorrect or inappropriate, stay where you are. To finish, you must roll the exact number on the dice to reach 終わり. If not, try again next round. The first person to reach 終わり is the winner. HINT: use your Verb List or the list in the Appendix as needed to help you create interesting prohibitions.

>   (you land on the spot marked 神社): 神社でうるさい音楽を聞かないで下さい。

文化箱 Culture Chest

なまはげ

On the evening of December 31, all over 男鹿半島, young men don scary masks and straw capes and descend from the mountains to the village houses, asking whether the children have been good or not for the past year. As they march from house to house, these demons shout: なまけもの は いねが。泣く子は いねが。Scared children flee and hide behind their parents. After the children promise to be good and なまはげ have been given food and drink, they reluctantly leave, promising prosperity for the coming year. The origins of this tradition are unclear, but the howling demons, carrying buckets and waving large wooden knives, make quite an impression on the children. This ritual, however, is considered private; sightseers are not encouraged. Fortunately, a local museum, the なまはげ館, offers a なまはげ experience year round, open to the public. On your way out, visit their gift shop to get your own なまはげ mask and pose for photos!

地図 Map Skills
_{ち ず}

You and Jun are going to watch the 竿燈祭り in Akita City in an hour. Jun's host family gave him in-
_{かんとうまつ}
structions on where to meet you and your group on the festival route, but he left the map and location at
home. He is going to call you to ask for directions from 秋田駅 to your location at the 秋田市役所. Use
_{あきた し やくしょ}
a mapping app to study the route and record a message giving directions.

🔊 メール

This letter is from Ben's Japanese teacher in Australia, 鈴木先生, in response to a note that he wrote to
_{すずき}
her from Akita.

Points to consider as you read:

❶ What is the weather like in Australia?

❷ In what season did 鈴木先生 visit Akita and what did she see?
_{すず き}

❸ 鈴木先生 requests that Ben do what when he returns to his Japanese class in Australia?
_{すず き}

ベン君へ

　明けましておめでとう、ベン君。元気ですか。
　あ
　秋田からのお手紙ありがとうございました。こちらはとても元気です。男鹿半島はとても寒
　　　　　　　　　　　　　　　　　　　　　　　　　　　　　　　　おがはんとう
そうですね。こちらは今夏ですから、暑い日が続いています。でも先生はお陰で毎日元気に教
　　　　　　　　　　　　　　　　　　　つづ
えています。ところでベン君は日本語がとても上手になりましたね。お手紙を読んで感心しま
　　　　　　　　　　　　　　　　　　　　　　　　　　　　　　　　　　　　　かんしん
した。嬉しかったです。
　うれ
　先生は学生のころ友達とたくさん日本を旅行しました。秋田市と男鹿半島にも行った事が
　　　　　　　　　　　　　　　りょこう
ありますよ。先生は八月に、秋田に行きました。東北地方の夏は東京より涼しくて気持ちが
　　　　　　　　　　　　　　　　　　　とうほくちほう　　　　　　　　すず
良かったです。そして、東北三大祭の一つ、秋田の竿燈祭りも見ました。秋田のお米は美
　　　　　　　　　さんだいまつり　　　　　かんとう　　　　　　　　　こめ
味しくて有名ですが、竿燈祭りはお米の豊作を神様に願うお祭りです。秋田の人達が浴衣を
　　　　　　　　　　　　　　　ほうさく　　ねが　　　　　　　　　　　　　　　　ゆかた
着て町の大通りに集まって、とても賑やかでした。お祭の笛と太鼓の音が町中に聞こえ
　　　おおどお　　あつ　　　　　　　にぎ　　　　　　　　ふえ　たいこ
て、胸がわくわくしました。
　むね
　秋田市の後で、小さい*遊覧船に乗って、男鹿半島を海から見ました。海岸には大きい岩
　　　　　　　　　　ゆうらんせん　　　　　　　　　　　　　　　　かいがん　　　　　いわ
がたくさんあって、とてもきれいでした。遊覧船を降りて、灯台の下で友達とピクニックをしま
　　　　　　　　　　　　　　　　　　　　　　とうだい
した。その日は空が青く、海が静かで、涼しい風が吹き、人もいなかったので、本当にすばら
　　　　　　　　　　　　しず　　　　　　　ふ
しかったです。東京に帰りたくなかったですよ。

秋田は古くてユニークな伝統がたくさん残っているところです。竿燈祭りの他には、なまは
げ祭りも有名です。それで、先生たちは男鹿のなまはげ館にも行きました。そこでなまはげのコ
スチュームを着てみました。そして「なぐ子はいねがあ?(＝泣く子はいないか。)」と怖い声で
言ってみました。でもベン君は本物のなまはげを見るんですね。先生もいつか冬に日本に帰っ
たら、本物のなまはげを見に男鹿に行きたいです。

　ベン君、オーストラリアに帰った時、日本語のクラスの皆にもなまはげの話をして下さいね。

　それでは、今日はこれで終わります。元気で男鹿半島の毎日を楽しんで下さい。またベン君
に会える日を楽しみにしています。

一月二日

鈴木先生より

* 豊作 – harvest; 遊覧船 – excursion boat, sightseeing boat

皆によろしく。

Please give my regards to everyone.

第6課の4

1) 僕も学校の友達に手紙を書きました。読んで下さい。

2) 「たくやへ。元気?冬休みが始まってほとんど会わないね。僕は冬休みの宿題を全然していないから、一月のテストが心配。また宿題を見せてくれる?一月はテストが多くて、三年生はイライラするね。ところで僕は今秋田県にいるよ。秋田は東京より寒いけど、大晦日とお正月にたくさんイベントがあって面白い。もうすぐ「なまはげ」が来るから子供達はドキドキしているよ。なまはげは怖いけど、素晴らしい文化だね。長い歴史があるから。じゃあ、良いお年を。皆によろしく。　ベンより。」

3) ベン君の日本語は完璧ですね。

4) でも、ベン君の字はミミズに見えます。

5) ひどい!手もボールペンも冷たいから、上手に書けなかったんだよ。

会話 Dialog

(Setting: The group is in the living area of Mr. Ono's home.)

1. ベン ：僕も学校の友達に手紙を書きました。読んで下さい。

2. 友 ：「たくやへ。元気?冬休みが始まってほとんど会わないね。僕は冬休みの宿題を全然していないから、一月のテストが心配。また宿題を見せてくれる?一月はテストが多くて、三年生はイライラするね。ところで僕は今秋田県にいるよ。秋田は東京より寒いけど、大晦日とお正月にたくさんイベントがあって面白い。もうすぐ「なまはげ」が来るから子供達はドキドキしているよ。なまはげは怖いけど、素晴らしい文化だね。長い歴史があるから。じゃあ、良いお年を。皆によろしく。ベンより。」

3. じゅん ：ベン君の日本語は完璧ですね。

4. 友 ：でも、ベン君の字はミミズに見えます。

5. ベン ：ひどい!手もボールペンも冷たいから、上手に書けなかったんだよ。

単語 New Words

けいぐ 敬具 (n) – closing expression for written letters

はいけい 拝啓 (n) – opening expression for written letters

おそろしい 恐ろしい (い adj.) – afraid

こわい 怖い (い adj.) – scary

さびしい 寂しい (い adj.) – lonely, lonesome

すると (conj.) – therefore, then, and (then) [used mainly in written language] イライラ (ono.) – nervous

ドキドキ (ono.) – excited, pitter-patter

漢字 Kanji

配	ハイ、くば(る) – distribute, apportion	一	一	三	西	西	西
	心配 – worry; 配る – distribute, ration しんぱい くば	酉	酉	酉	配		
10 strokes	Part of the kanji for wine (酉) is to the left of oneself (己). One should RATION and DISTRIBUTE things without overindulging.						

言葉の探索 Language Detection
こ と ば た ん さ く

1. More on 擬声語/擬態語 – mimetic/onomatopoetic words
ぎ せい ご ぎ たい ご

As you know, the Japanese language contains many words that mimic manmade or natural sounds
(擬声語 and 擬態語) as well as other words that represent bodily feelings or states of being (擬態
ぎ せい ご   ぎ たい ご   ぎ たい
語). Note that some mimetic or onomatopoetic words may be written in katakana. In addition to the
ご
words you have already learned, here are a few more:

イキイキ	= lively	ヘラヘラ	= act frivolously
きらきら	= glitter/sparkly	ブンブン	= buzz, buzz (bee)
ぐずぐず	= dawdle, meander slowly	ざあざあ	= pouring, streaming (rain)
ケロケロ	= croak, croak (frog)		

2. Letter Writing Part B: Formal Letters

An informal letter-writing style was introduced in the previous section. Remember however, when writing letters to teachers, host parents, or other adults, it is best to use the more polite です/ます style.

For more formal letters, standard opening and closing expressions are used in Japanese letters in a manner similar to the English "Dear so-and-so" and "Sincerely yours." These expressions are always used in fixed pairs since it is important to maintain a consistent level of formality. Here are three common opening/closing sets of expressions:

opening		closing
拝啓 はいけい	and	敬具 (used in many (formal) letters) けい ぐ
謹んで申し上げます つつし もう あ	and	*かしこ (used by women in formal letters)
前略 ぜんりゃく	and	草々 (used in less formal/shorter letters) そうそう
お元気ですか	and	お元気で or ではまた (used only between close friends)

* かしこ is written only in hiragana and is possibly a modern example of 女手, or women's writing, dating back to the Heian Period when hiragana was first developed.

3. Horizontal or Vertical?

Whether the letter is written horizontally or vertically depends on the purpose of the letter. Professional letters are almost always written horizontally, and normally typewritten. Personal letters and letters to superiors can be typewritten or handwritten depending on the relationship. If handwritten, however, black or blue ink should be used. Look for examples of various types of letters on the Japanese Online website. Try to pinpoint similarities in formatting.

自習 Self Check

1. Letter writing. Identify each phrase below as formal or informal and match the pairs.

(ア) 前略
ぜんりゃく

(イ) じゃあ or, また

(ウ) 敬具
けいぐ

(エ) 早々

(オ) お元気ですか

(カ) 拝啓
はいけい

2. Onomatopoetic expressions: match each Japanese expression to the best English equivalent.

(ア) ワンワン

(イ) ドンドン

(ウ) ボロボロ

(エ) スラスラ

a. thud

b. in disrepair, shabby

c. smoothly

d. dog's barking

練習時間 Practice Time
れんしゅう じ かん

枝豆を食べた！
えだまめ

For this activity, download the Edamame game board from **TimeForJapanese.com** and play with a partner

You will be playing a game where you and your opponent try to "eat" each other's 枝豆 pods. As with the game Battleship, on the game board draw a total of 5 枝豆 pods [two 小 size 枝豆 (2 squares each]
しょう
two 中 size 枝豆 [3 squares each]; and one 大 size 枝豆 [4 squares]. Do not show your partner. You
ちゅう
だい
goal is to locate your partner's 枝豆 and "eat" them. Do this by conjugating a verb (Y-axis) according to the pattern listed on the X-axis, and then adding information as necessary to create a complete statemen or question.

例
れい
EXAMPLE

A-さん decides to try for the spot 1, 1. He/she might choose to ask:

(服を) 洗ってはだめです。
ふく　あら

B-さん then states either ミスです (miss) or 当たりです (hit).
あ

Once an 枝豆 is entirely "eaten," the person who just lost an 枝豆 says: もう食べた！

Keep playing until the largest 枝豆 is eaten. The winner says: ごちそう様でした！
えだまめ

文化箱 Culture Chest
ぶん か ばこ

Letter-writing styles 手紙の書き方

Formal Japanese letter writing can be quite complex. Even the Japanese themselves often consult lette writing reference books when they have to write important letters. Formal letters are usually writte by hand, vertically, on Japanese letter writing paper. An eloquent formal letter will open with classical phrases, poetic allusions, or small talk about the weather. The greeting and other sections of the letter are quite structured, and depend on the level of formality. A letter to a host parent would require a different level of politeness and formality than a request for a reference letter to a teacher.

To write to a friend, the format is more fluid and less prescribed. You may open a letter to someone named 明子 with a greeting like "明子さん、お元気ですか," and then mention the weather or the season, before moving into your reason for writing. In closing a letter to a close friend, "お返事を下さい" (please send a reply) or a request to extend your best wishes to their family such as ご家族によろしくお伝え下さい might be used. Notes such as these may be written either vertically or horizontally.

🔊 メール

This message is a letter from Kiara's grandfather to Kiara about namahage he saw in Oga in 1952. Points to consider as you read:

❶ What did Mr. Watson remember the grandmother making for dinner on the night of Dec. 31?

❷ What do the namahage cry out? What does that mean in English?

❸ What refreshments were offered by the grandfather and grandmother? What happens after that?

❹ What is Mr. Watson looking forward to?

キアラへ、

　もうすぐお正月ですね。男鹿半島の年の暮れはどうですか。おじいさんも兵隊の時12月から1月まで男鹿半島にいたのでとても懐かしいです。そしてキアラにもおじいさんと同じように男鹿半島の*思い出ができるのがとても嬉しいです。

　男鹿の冬のいい思い出はたくさんありますが、一番ユニークなのはなまはげ祭りの思い出です。

　12月31日、一年の最後の日の夕方でした。親戚の家ではおばあさんが台所で年越しそばを作っていました。辺りはもう暗くなっていましたから、子供たちも家に入って晩御飯を待っていました。

　その時、私は山の方からとても怖い声を聞きました。その声は「泣ぐ子はいねがあ！怠げ者はいねがあ！」と何度も言っていました。その声はだんだん大きくなって、おじいさんとおばあさんの家の前で止まりました。私はびっくりして何も分からなかったので、静かにしていました。

すると、おじいさんは玄関に行って、家の戸を開けました。家の戸の前には体の大きい赤鬼と青鬼が*わらでできたみのを着て大きい*包丁と桶を持って、立っていました。そして、家の中をじろじろ見回しました。そしてまた、前よりもっと怖い声で「泣ぐごはいねがあ！怠げ者はいねがあ！」と叫びました。その声を聞いて、子供たちは怖くて飛び上がって急いで家の奥に*隠れてしまいました。鬼たちは子供たちを見るとどんどん家の土間から座敷に上がって、「怠げ者は出て来い！」と言って子供たちを捜しました。

子供たちは初めは静かに隠れていましたが、怖くて*泣いてしまいました。鬼たちはその泣き声を聞いて子供たちを見つけると、座敷に引っ張って連れて行きました。そして子供たちに、「来年はいい子になるがあ！（＝来年はいい子になるか。）」と聞きました。でも子供たちは鬼が怖くてもっと泣きます。するとおじいさんがおいしいお酒を持ってきて、鬼たちにあげました。そして「はい、はい。うじのごたちは（＝うちの子たちは）いい子になります。どうぞ、このお酒でも飲んでください。そして、来年もまた来て下さい。今日はわざわざありがどう（＝ありがとう）ございました。」と言って、何回も鬼に*お辞儀をしました。鬼はおいしい秋田のお酒を少し飲むと、いい気分になっておじいさんの家を出て行きました。

鬼の声が家から遠くなって、子供たちはやっと安心して、年越しそばを食べることができました。私も*ほっとしましたよ。それから、真夜中になって、町のお寺からは除夜の鐘の音が聞こえて、新しい年が始まりました。

今でも男鹿半島ではなまはげの鬼が家に来ると聞きました。小野さんの家にも多分来るでしょう。後でキアラのなまはげの話を聞くのが楽しみですよ。じゃ、また。

12月31日
ワトソンおじいさんから

---

*思い出 – memory, remembrance; わらでできたみの – a straw raincoat; 包丁と桶 – knife and bucket; 隠れてしまう – to hide completely; 泣いてしまう – to cry, burst into tears; お辞儀をする – to bow; ほっとする – to be relieved, relaxed

キアラさんのおじいさんは今秋田にいるかも知れません。

Kiara's uncle may be in Akita now.

1) キアラさんはアメリカ人よね。
ちょっと前にアメリカ人兵士に
コーラとチョコレートをもらったのよ。
私のおじはアメリカ人兵士と写真をとったのよ。

2) 今、その写真を
持って来るね。

3) このアメ
リカ人は背が
高くてハンサ
ムですね。

4) あれ？見せて下さい。
私は前にこの写真を
見たことがありますよ。

5) 写真をよく見ると、
裏に名前が書いてありますよ。
「マイケル・オカーナー、
ユージーン・スミス、
クリス・ワトソン、
１９５１年１１月２３日」

6) クリス・
ワトソンは
私の祖父です！

7) すごい！
キアラさんのおじいさんは
今秋田にいるかも知れません。
手紙を書きませんか？

8) はい、今すぐ
書きたいです。
ベン君、早く、
ボールペンを
貸して下さい。

会話 Dialog

(Setting: At the house, our group is chatting with Mr. Ono and his daughter.)

1. 小野の娘 ：キアラさんはアメリカ人よね。ちょっと前にアメリカ人*兵士にコーラと
チョコレートをもらったのよ。私のおじはアメリカ兵士と写真をとったのよ。

2. 小野の娘 　今、その写真を持って来るね。(Brings back a photo.)

3. ベン ：このアメリカ人は背が高くてハンサムですね。

4. キアラ ：あれ?見せて下さい。私は前にこの写真を見たことがありますよ。

5. 友 ：写真をよく見ると、裏に名前が書いてありますよ。「マイケル・オカーナー、ユージ
ーン・スミス、クリス・ワトソン、1951年11月23日。

6. キアラ ：クリス・ワトソンは私の祖父です!

7. じゅん ：すごい!キアラさんのおじいさんは今秋田にいるかも知れません。
手紙を書きませんか?

8. キアラ ：はい、今すぐ書きたいです。ベン君、早く、ボールペンを貸して下さい。

*兵士 – soldier

 単語 New Words

おじ (*n*) – uncle

チョコレート (*n*) – chocolate

うら 裏 (*n*) – back(side), reverse

かもしれません かも知れません (*exp.*) –may, might, perhaps

かもしれない かも知れない (*exp.*) – may, might, perhaps (informal)

いのる 祈る (*v*) – pray (to), wish (to)

たすかる 助かる (*v*) – saved (to be), rescued (to be

たすける 助ける (*v*) – save (to), rescue (to)

漢字 Kanji

知	チ, し(る), し(らせる) – know, wisdom	ノ	㇄	匕	钅	矢	知
	知る – to know; 知恵 – wisdom, sense, intelligence	知	知				
8 strokes	The left is an arrow (矢) with a mouth (口) next to it. If you KNOW an arrow is pointing at you, your mouth would be open shouting "Stop!".						

1. **"have eaten ~", "have had the experience of eating ~"** = 食べた事がある

To say that you or someone else has had the experience of doing something, use the plain past verb tense + 事がある.

In *Beginning Japanese*, the use of the dictionary form of the verb + 事 was introduced. For example, 食べる事が好きです - I like eating or 泳ぐ事が嫌いです – I dislike swimming. The 〜た事がある
　　　　　　　　　　　　　　　　　　　きら
pattern is similar, but the verb here is in the plain past tense, not the dictionary form. To say that you have NOT had the experience of doing something, use the plain past verb tense + 事がありません (or ない). Remember, the plain past tense of a verb is formed by dropping the 〜ます and adding 〜た, for Type 2(る) and irregular verbs. For Type 1(う) verbs, change the 〜て in the て form to た (e.g., 書いた、聞いた、読んだ、etc.).

A) じゅん君は北海道へ行った事があります。	= Jun has been to Hokkaido.
B) 先生と日本語で話した事があります。	= I have had the experience of speaking Japanese to my teacher.
C) 僕はたこ焼きを食べた事がありません。	= I have not eaten takoyaki.
	や	
D) 私は沖縄へ旅行した事がない。	= I have not travelled to Okinawa.
おきなわ	

2. **if~/when~/after~** = 〜たら

たら is attached to the plain past tense of a verb. It connects two clauses and indicates that the action in the first clause takes place before the action in the main (or second) clause. To form this pattern, use the same conjugation pattern learned for making the て form but replace て with たら.

Study the examples below of 〜ます, 〜て, and 〜たら forms of some common verbs.

Type 1 Verbs

飲みます	飲んで	飲んだら
言います	言って	言ったら
知ります	知って	知ったら
聞きます	聞いて	聞いたら
行きます	行って	行ったら

Type 2 Verbs

食べます	食べて	食べたら

Irregular Verbs

します	して	したら
来ます	来て	来たら

例	食べたら嬉しくなります。	= If you eat it, you will become happy.
れい EXAMPLE	A) 食べたら味が分かります。	= If you eat it, you will understand the flavor/taste.
	B) そのケーキを食べたら晩ご飯を食べないでしょう。	= If you eat that cake, you won't eat dinner.
	C) 日本へ行ったら京都に行ってみたいです。	= If I go to Japan, I want to go to see Kyoto.
	D) アルバイトをしたらお金がもらえる。	= If you do a part-time job, you receive money.
	E) 日本へ行ったら友達に会いたいです。	= If I go to Japan, I want to meet my/a friend.
	F) 宿題が早く終わったら、私の家へ来て下さい。	= If you finish your homework early, please come to my house.

3. **May, might, possibly ~ =～かも知れません/～かも知れない**

To say that you or someone else may, might, or possibly will do something, add かも知れません or かも知れない to the dictionary form or the negative dictionary (ない) form of a verb.

例	A) 遅く食べるかも知れません。	= We might possibly eat late.
れい EXAMPLE	B) 天気が良くなるかも知れない。	= The weather may turn nice.
	C) 友達も家に来るかも知れません。	= My friend may also come to my house.

自習 Self Check
じしゅう

Say the following in Japanese, using the ～た事がある/ない pattern.

(ア) I have never eaten yakisoba.

(イ) Have you used chopsticks?

(ウ) Have you been camping? (キャンプをする)

Say the following in Japanese using the ～たら pattern.

(ア) If I go to Japan, I want to see Mt. Fuji.

(イ) If you help your mother, she will take you to Japan.

(ウ) If I study well, I will receive a good grade.

Say the following in Japanese, using the ～かもしれません pattern.

(ア) I will possibly go early.

(イ) We might eat sushi tonight.

(ウ) The store may have a sale. (セール)

練習時間 Practice Time

1. Group Activity: "Two Truths and a Lie"

Using the 〜した事がある pattern, each student should write down three statements in 日本語, two that are true for him/herself, and one that is not. Say your statements to a partner. The partner has to guess which statements are true and which are false. If your partner guesses correctly, sign his/her paper; if not, don't. Switch partners and continue until your 先生 says はい、時間です. See who can get the most signatures.

> **例**
> A-さん： チョコレートクッキーを食べた事があります。そして、オーストラリアへ
>   行った事があります。それから、馬に乗った事があります。
> B-さん： オーストラリアへ行った事がありません。
>   or オーストラリアへ行った事はないでしょう。
> A-さん： はい、そうです。(If B-さん's statement is correct.)
>   or いいえ、本当ですよ。(If B-さん's statement is incorrect.)

2. Pair Activity

For this exercise, A-さん starts with ten cards, each containing the first half of a sentence while B-さん receives ten cards with the second halves. The goal is to create complete and logical sentences using the various halves within the allotted time. For this exercise, use the file from this section on **TimeForJapanese.com**.

文化箱 Culture Chest

American Occupation

When Japan surrendered to the Allied Powers on August 14, 1945 after the atomic bombings of Hiroshima and Nagasaki, the country was subsequently occupied by a foreign power for the first time in its history. This was also the first time for many Japanese citizens to hear the voice of the Emperor, Hirohito, as he announced the surrender over the radio. U.S. President Harry Truman appointed General Douglas MacArthur as Supreme Commander for the Allied Powers (SCAP). MacArthur arrived in Japan on August 30 and immediately set about reforming the government and rebuilding a war-shattered country. MacArthur, sometimes called the 外人将軍, introduced a new constitution, encouraged the Diet to dismantle the 財閥 (corporate monopolies), and instituted other reforms that helped democratize Japan. American soldiers spread out across the country and it was then that most Japanese saw 外国人 for the first time. The Occupation officially ended in 1952, with the implementation of the San Francisco Peace Treaty.

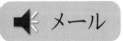 メール

This is a letter from Kiara to her Grandpa Watson.

Points to consider as you read:

❶ How did she get to the shrine and how long did it take?

② What did the grandmother make for her?

③ What did someone take a photo of?

④ What had she seen before?

おじいさんへ

　新年　明けましておめでとうございます。今年もよろしく。

　なまはげの思い出のお手紙をありがとう。読んでびっくりしました。でも12月31日の晩、なまはげが小野さんの家に来た時、おじいさんの手紙のお陰で助かりました。

　元旦の朝は早く起きて、小野さんの家族と一緒に近くの神社にお参りに行きました。その小さい神社は山の森の中にあって、家から歩いて二十分ぐらいでした。雪で白い田んぼに明るい太陽が光って、きれいでしたよ。他の町の人達も来ていました。一人一人神社の鐘をガランガラン鳴らして、新年の*幸運を祈りました。

　また歩いて家に帰るともう昼ご飯でした。おばあさんはお雑煮というお正月の料理を作ってくれました。*お椀の中に*汁とお餅と*野菜が入っていました。お餅はちょっとねばねばしましたが、美味しいと思いました。お腹が空いていたので、二杯も食べました。

　その後、家の前で女の子達と*羽根突きをしました。バドミントンに似ていますが、難しかったです。ベン君は男の子たちと一緒に広くて真っ白い田んぼに行って、*凧揚げをしました。女の子達も凧揚げを見に行きました。でも風がだんだん強くなって、ベン君の凧は木の枝に*引っかかってしまいました。

　そこで困っていた時、偶然*アメリカ軍の*兵士さんたちが近くを通りかかって、ベン君の凧を木の枝から取ってくれました。そして、皆にガムやチョコレートをくれました。その時小野さんの娘さんが写真を一枚持って来ました。その写真には若いアメリカ人の兵士さんたちと日本人の*お百姓さんが一人*写っていました。日本人のお百姓さんは私のお世話になっているおじいさんです。そして、その隣にアメリカの兵士の服を着ている日本人が立っていました。私はその写真を前に見たことがあると思いました。そうです。それは1953年当時のおじいさんの若い時の写真でした。おじいさん、すごい偶然ですね。私も日本の曾祖父さんの親戚の家にお世話になっていたんです！

　早くおじいさんに会ってこの話を一緒にしたいです。写真を見て、すごく*興奮したので、今晩は眠れないかも知れません。

　じゃ、おじいさん、体に気をつけて！

一月一日　　　　　　　　　　　　　　　　　　　　　　　　　　　　キアラより

---

*アメリカ軍 – American army; 兵士 – soldier; お椀 – bowl; 汁 – soup, broth; 野菜 – vegetables; 幸運 – good luck; 羽根突き – Japanese badminton; 凧揚げをする – to fly a kite; 引っかかってしまう – get completely tangled up in; お百姓さん – farmers; 写す – to be photographed, copy; 興奮する – to be excited

東京　1892年

The Identities Behind the Pen Names

The group exits another torii in Oga-machi, in the newly renamed city of Tokyo (formerly Edo), in 1892. Here, they find a coffee shop located near the Haginoya Literary Academy, where they meet the author Ichiyou Higuchi and talk about how Japan has changed since the Meiji Period began in 1868.

Learning and Performance Goals

This chapter will enable you to:

- say that something "must" happen (〜なければなりません/〜なければいけません)
- say that you/someone else want(s) something (〜が欲しい/欲しがっている) or want(s) something to be done (食べて欲しい/欲しがっている)
- use い and な adjectives as pronouns (大きいの〜/静かなの〜)
- use the provisional or hypothetical ば-form meaning "if" (ドーナツをたくさん食べれば、太ります。)
- learn basic information about the Meiji Period
- learn about the comparative geographic layout of Edo and modern Tokyo
- learn more about the history of poetry in Japan
- use Japanese emoticon expressions
- learn about the author Ichiyou Higuchi
- use 11 additional kanji

船に乗れば外国に行く事が出来る。
（ふね）

If I ride a boat, I can go to a foreign country.

1) ちょっと疲れましたね。もう少し歩けば喫茶店に着きますよ。

2) いらっしゃいませ。何にしますか。

3) 私はカレーを食べなくてはならないし、その後、コーヒーを飲まなければなりません。そうすれば、元気になります。

4) 私はレモネードとあんパンをお願いします。あれ、あの女の人を前に見た事があります。

5) あっ！あれは樋口一葉ですよ。五千円さつの中の人です。彼女は東京の有名な作家です。

6) 明治時代になって、色々便利になったね。鹿鳴館に行けばダンスも出来るし。

7) 英語を勉強すれば外国人と話せるね。

会話 Dialog
かい

(Setting: Tokyo, 1892, a coffee shop near Haginoya Academy)

萩の 塾 舎の近くの喫茶店 「ダイヤモンド珈コー琲ヒー店てん」
はぎ　じゅくしゃ　　　　　　きっさてん

1. ベン　　　　：ちょっと 疲れましたね。もう少し 歩けば喫茶店に着きますよ。
　　　　　　　　　　つか　　　　　　　ある　きっさてん

2. マスター　：いらっしゃいませ。何にしますか。

3. 友　　　　：私はカレーを食べなくてはならないし、その後、コーヒーを飲まなければなりません。そうすれば、元気になります。

4. キアラ　　：私はレモネードとあんパンをお願いします。あれ、あの女の人を前に見た事があります。
　　　　　　　　　　　　　　　　　　ねが

5. じゅん　　：あっ！あれは樋口一葉ですよ。五千円さつの中の人です。 彼女は東京の有名な
　　　　　　　　　　　ひぐちいちよう　　　　　　　　　　　　　　　　かの
　　　　　　　＊作家です。
　　　　　　　さっか

6. 樋口　　　：(talking to her friend) 明治時代になって、色々便利になったね。 鹿鳴館に行け
　ひぐち　　　　　　　　　　めいじじだい　　　　　べんり　　　　　ろくめいかん
　　　　　　　ばダンスも出来るし。

7. ＊詩人　　：(Looking at the visitors.) 英語を勉強すれば外国人と話せるね。
　しじん　　　　　　　　　　　　　　　　べん

＊作家 – author; 詩人 – poet
　さっか　　　　　しじん

単語 New Words
たん

あんパン (n) – roll or bun filled with sweet red bean paste (anko)

カステラ (n) – sponge cake

ドーナツ (n) – doughnuts

カレーライス (n) – curry and rice

きっさてん 喫茶店 (n) – coffee house (traditional), coffee lounge

しっぱい 失敗 (n) – failure, mistake

じだい 時代 (n) – period, era

ダンス (n) – dance

めいじじだい 明治時代 (n) – Meiji Period (1868-1912)

はくぶつかん 博物館 (n) – museum

ぶぶん 部分 (n) – portion, section, part

レモネード (n) – lemonade

めいわく 迷惑 (な adj.) – trouble, bother

しかる 叱る (v) – scold (to)

つかれる 疲れる (v) – become tired (to)

まかせる 任せる (v) – entrust (to), leave to a person (to)

漢字 Kanji

治	ジ, おさ(める), おさ(まる), なお(る) – reign, be at peace, calm down	`	⸴	氵	氵	氵	治
8 strokes	明治 – Meiji reign period; popular brand of chocolates; 政治 – politics; 治る – to be cured, to get well	治	治				
	This kanji is made up of a CALMING water radical (氵) next to the kana ム resting PEACEFULLY on top of a mouth (口).						

代	ダイ, よ, か(える), か(わる) – to change, to substitute, period/age, counter for decades	ノ	イ	仁	代	代	
5 strokes	世代 – generation; 時代 – period, era; 三十年代 – 30s						
	A person is standing (イ) next to a ceremony (弋) for AGES and AGES, so long that the ten (十) begins to CHANGE.						

疲	ヒ, つか(れる), つか(れ) – exhausted, tire	`	亠	广	广	广	疒
10 strokes	疲れる – to become tired; 旅行疲れ – fatigue from travel	疒	疓	疲	疲		
	Sickness (疒) surrounds the skin or hide (皮) of a TIRED and EXHAUSTED creature.						

言葉の探索 Language Detection

1. **if (and only if) eaten ~ -or- "when" eaten ~ = 食べれば～**

   The provisional or hypothetical ば form is a conjunction that indicates "if (and only if)". To use this conjugation:

   A) Type 1 (う) verbs – drop the ます ending of the <u>potential</u> form and add ば.

   B) Type 2 (る) verbs – to the verb stem, add れば.

   C) Irregular verbs – する/します becomes すれば, 来る/来ます becomes 来れば.

   The meaning of the ば form differs from the ～たら pattern explained in the previous chapter. The ～たら (conditional) form is conditional, meaning that if X happens, Y will follow. The ば–form on the other hand, is provisional or hypothetical; in other words, if certain conditions exist, Y could happen. Though these are similar patterns, there are subtle differences.

例
EXAMPLE

A) お寿司屋さんへ行ったら、カッパ巻きを食べます。 = When I go to the sushi restaurant, I eat cucumber roll.

B) お寿司屋さんへ行けば、カッパ巻きを食べます。 = If/When (ever) I go to the sushi restaurant, I eat cucumber roll.

Type 1 (う) verbs:

飲む ⇨ 飲めば

手伝う ⇨ 手伝えば

待つ ⇨ 待てば

買う ⇨ 買えば

行く ⇨ 行けば

Type 2 (る) verbs

食べる ⇨ 食べれば

見る ⇨ 見れば

Irregular verbs

する ⇨ すれば

来る ⇨ 来れば

This pattern has a variety of uses.

A) 夏に日本へ行けば、花火が見れます。 = If I go to Japan in summer, I can see fireworks.

B) 一日に試験が三つもあれば、頭が痛くなります。
= If I have three tests in one day, my head will start to hurt.

C) たくさん雪が降れば、車の運転が出来ません = If a lot of snow falls, I cannot drive a car.

D) 時間があれば、家へ来て下さい。 = If you have time, please come to my house.

E) 先生に聞けば、分かるでしょう。 = If you ask the teacher, you'll probably understand.

2. **You must eat this. = 食べなければなりません**

Use the 〜なければなりません pattern to state that something "must" happen. To form this pattern, start with the plain negative form of the verb (e.g.: 食べない, しない, 乗らない, etc.). Replace the ない with 〜なければなりません.

Type 1 (う) Verbs 待たない ⇨ 待た ＋ なければなりません – must wait

行かない ⇨ 行か ＋ なければなりません – must go

Type 2 (る) Verbs 食べない ⇨ 食べ ＋ なければなりません – must eat

Irregular Verbs 来ない ⇨ 来 ＋ なければなりません – must come

しない ⇨ し ＋ なければなりません – must do

This pattern may be shortened to be more informal. Do this by abbreviating 〜なければなりません to 〜なきゃならない or 〜なければならない or the even shorter なきゃ/なくちゃ, as in the examples below.

食べなければなりません ⇨ 食べなきゃならない

or 食べなきゃ

A) この天ぷらを食べなければなりません。

= You must eat this tempura.

B) 来週の日曜日、午前六時に起きなければなりません。

= Next Sunday, I have to get up at 6 a.m.

C) もう遅いから、帰らなければならない。

= It's late, so I have to go home.

D) 明日、期末試験あるから、勉強しなきゃ。

= Tomorrow is the semester final exam, so I have to study.

自習 Self Check

Practice changing verbs into the provisional ～ば form and the ～なければなりません form by filling in the blanks in the chart below. The first one is done for you.

Dictionary form	～ば (conditional)	英語	～なければなりません (must, have to)	英語
見る	見れば	if I see, if I look	見なければなりません	must see, must look
	洗えば			must wash
持って来る			持って来なければなりません	
(free choice)				

練習時間 Practice Time

1. Small Group Activity

Form groups of 3-4 students. The first student makes an "if" (conditional) statement about something he/she would do if he/she had a lot of money. The second student uses the same verb to create another "if" statement, and so on. Continue playing until everyone agrees the idea has been exhausted, then start over with a new verb. Continue playing as long as you can, or until your teacher says 時間です。

A-さん ： お金がたくさんあれば、日本へ行きます。

B-さん ： 日本へ行けば、すしを食べます。

C-さん ： すしを食べれば、喉がカラカラになります。

D-さん ： 喉がカラカラになれば、水を飲みます。

and so on...

2. Pair Work

For each situation below, take turns stating something that your partner must do. Your partner either agrees or disagrees with your recommendation.

> 例
> れい
> EXAMPLE
>
> (Situation: there is a test tomorrow)
> A-さん： 勉強しなければなりませんか。
> B-さん： はい、そうですね。 **or** いいえ、もう勉強しました。

ア) all of your friend's socks are dirty

イ) your friend has not finished his/her homework and it's getting late

ウ) the library is across the bridge and your friend needs to borrow (借りる) a book

エ) your friend will go to Kyoto and spend the night at a ryokan but does not have a reservation

オ) you must go to Roppongi by subway but don't have a ticket

カ) your friend has a Japanese book but the kanji is a little difficult

Useful vocabulary: 洗濯する – to launder/wash (clothes), 借りる – to borrow, 予約する – to reserve
　　　　　　せんたく　　　　　　　　　　　　　　　　か　　　　　　　　　　　よやく

文化箱 Culture Chest
ぶん か ばこ

1. 明治時代 (1868–1912)
めい じ じ だい

The 明治時代, which began in 1868 with the Meiji Restora-
めい じ じ だい
tion, marked a time of intense change and modernization for
Japan. After the 徳川　government capitulated to Commo-
とくがわ
dore Perry's pressure to open the country, the 明治 govern-
めいじ
ment worked to reestablish the importance of the emperor
and undertook the grand task of transitioning Japan from its
feudal system in order to modernize and strengthen it. Under

the 明治 emperor, the government issued a new constitution, established a Diet (parliament) and House
めい じ
of Peers, and standardized currency. The government also invited in many foreign experts to speed along
the reconstruction, and renamed the city of 江戸 – 東京 (Eastern Capital). The emperor's primary resi-
dency was also moved there from Kyoto. The speed at which this modernization (and Westernization) process took place was breathtaking. In just a little over two decades, Japan was able to dominate both China
and Russia in separate wars, proving that it had become a strong regional power.

2. 樋口一葉 and 萩の舎
ひ ぐちいちよう　　　 はぎ や

Born into a middle-class samurai family in Tokyo, 樋口一葉 (born 樋口奈津, 1872–1896) convinced her
ひ ぐちいちよう　　　　 ひぐち な つ
family to let her enter Haginoya, a poetry school, where she was able to polish her literary skills. Despite
her short 24-year life, she wrote over 4,000 tanka and more than twenty stories. One of her most famous

is "Takekurabe," published in 1894. Struggling to earn a livelihood throughout most of her life, Higuchi died of tuberculosis at a young age. Still, she is notable, as an early professional female writer of modern Japan. She has been recognized for her great contributions by having her image placed on the ¥5,000 note. Higuchi was part of a flourishing group of literary writers that included Ishikawa Takuboku, the poet/teacher in Hokkaido that you met in Chapter 1 of this volume.

地図 Map Skills
ちず

Many of Tokyo's neighborhoods have been in existence for a very long time. Many of the neighborhoods that lie along and within JR's 山手線 were part of 江戸, as the city was known until the end of the 徳川 時代. Can you find these locations on a map of 東京?

1. One of the most famous landmarks of 浅草, where Jun and his family live, is 浅草寺. With its large red lantern and ferocious guardian warrior statues at its gate, the area was a center of popular culture during much of the 江戸時代. Even today, 浅草 is filled with small bustling shops and interesting sights.

2. 日本橋 (formerly known as 江戸橋), literally "bridge of Japan," has at its center the bridge crossing the 日本橋川, first built by the 三井 clan in 1603 (owners of Japan's first department store, Mitsukoshi). The bridge was the eastern end of the 東海道, the road between 京都 and 江戸. It was once one of the most prosperous districts of the city.

3. 神田 was home to many of the working class people of 江戸. Still primarily residential, it also contains many educational institutions and bookstores.

4. 上野 is also home to 寛永寺 (a site Kiara and her friends visit), built by the 将軍 in 1624. It was a place mainly "off limits" to others, reserved for the upper class. 上野駅, along with 東京駅, has long been somewhat of a busy entryway to 東京 from 成田空港 and 東北 for northern-bound 新幹線 lines. This area includes a thriving business district and is home to 上野 公園 and its many 美術館 (art museums), 博物館 (museums), and the 動物園 (zoo).

5. 品川 was home to many samurai during the 江戸時代. Once the 徳川 government stabilized the country, many samurai invested their earnings in new business opportunities.

To learn more about how the connections between 江戸 and 東京 overlap, a useful resource is *Old Tokyo, Walks in the City of the Shogun* by Sumiko Enbutsu (Tuttle, 1993). To explore the beginnings of 江戸 and the process of change into the modern city of 東京, visit 江戸東京博物館 near 東京の両国 station when you visit 東京. Complete a search for more information on this museum and others online to see what new things you can discover.

🔊 メール

Jun's friend Masato writes to recommend several interesting 喫茶店, formal cafés or coffee lounges in Tokyo.

Points to consider as you read:

① What two examples of interesting coffee shops does Masato offer?

② Masato says that if you stay at a jazz coffee shop for a long time, you will think that you've done what?

③ What is another reason Masato is writing to Jun?

じゅん君、元気?

　この間話した美味しい喫茶店のことなんだけど。渋谷と新宿に行けば、いくつかいい喫茶店があるよ。僕はよく「ダイアモンド珈琲店」に行くんだ。そこに行けば、たいていアイスティーかアイスコーヒーを飲むよ。喫茶店で、美味しいコーヒーを飲めば、元気がでるよね。日本の面白い喫茶店といえば、漫画喫茶やジャズ喫茶かな。漫画喫茶に行けば、色々な漫画がたくさん読めるよ。漫画を読めば、楽しく日本の文化やユーモアを学べる。面白そうだろう？それから、ジャズ喫茶に行けば、ジャズの音楽が聞けるよ。長い間座れば、コンサートに来たみたいな気分になる。ああ、そういえば、僕の彼女の友達がじゅん君に会いたいみたい。じゅん君のこと、すてきだと思っているらしいよ。彼女の*身長は154センチで、髪が長いんだって。そして、ジャズなんかが好きなんだって。じゅん君もその子に会えば、気に入ると思うよ。コーヒーは僕の*おごりで！どうかな。会ってみたい？

正人より

*身長 – height; おごりで – treat (someone to a meal)

新しいのが欲しいです。

I want a new one.

1) 皆、この新聞読んだ？面白い漫画が載っているわよ。

2) あ、本当ですね。面白い！

3) この漫画の文字はカタカナですね。女の子は洋服を着ています。

4) 私の友達は漫画が大好きだから、この漫画をお土産に欲しいです。

5) いいわよ。じゃあ、昨日の新聞も持って行けばいいわよ。

6) 私も見たいです。

7) すみません！

8) あっ！漫画が汚くなりました。どうしよう。新しいのが欲しいです。

9) 後で新しいのを買いましょう。

10) 大丈夫。私は色々な漫画を持っているから、キアラさんに五冊あげるわよ。

11) 私はコーヒーがもう一杯欲しいです。

12) でも日本の喫茶店はお代わり自由じゃないですよ。

13) ああ、忘れていました！もうコーヒーは欲しくなくなりました！

会話 Dialog

(Setting: Yoshikazu has escorted the group to Ishikawa's classroom.)

1. 樋口 ：皆、この新聞読んだ？面白い漫画が載っているわよ。

2. じゅん ：あ、本当ですね。面白い！

3. ベン ：この漫画の文字はカタカナですね。女の子は洋服を着ています。

4. キアラ ：私の友達は漫画が大好きだから、この漫画をお土産に欲しいです。

5. 樋口 ：いいわよ。じゃあ、昨日の新聞も持って行けばいいわよ。

6. 友 ：私も見たいです。(Knocks over his coffee then a slight pause)

7. 友 ：すみません！

8. キアラ ：あっ！漫画がきたなくなりました。どうしよう。新しいのが欲しいです。

9. ベン ：後で新しいのを買いましょう。

10. 樋口 ：大丈夫。私は色々な漫画を持っているから、キアラさんに五冊あげるわよ。

11. 友 ：私はコーヒーがもう一杯欲しいです。

12. じゅん ：でも日本の喫茶店はお代わり自由じゃないですよ。

13. 友 ：ああ、忘れていました！もうコーヒーは欲しくなくなりました！

漢字 Kanji

漫 14 strokes	マン – cartoon	丶	冫	氵	氵	氵	氵	氵
	漫画 – (Japanese) comic; 漫画喫茶 – manga club	氵	氵	氵	氵	漫	漫	漫
	The sun (日) shines again and again on the reclining (又) eye (目) that drips tears of water (氵) as it reads the sad CARTOON/MANGA.							

画 8 strokes	ガ, カク – brush-stroke, picture	一	厂	厅	帀	雨	面	画
	漫画 – (Japanese) comic; 映画 – film; 計画 – plan, schedule	画						
	When planning a PICTURE, it should be the best one (一) you've drawn, with a good reason (由) to put a frame (凵) around it.							

由 ³ ² ₄ ₅ **5 strokes**	ユ, ユウ, よし – a reason, significance		イ	口	中	由	由
	自由 – free; 由来 – origin, history; 理由 – reason, motive						
	The REASON for a firmly-planted stake (the center vertical stroke) in a rice field (田) is to ensure that new crops grow straight.						

言葉の探索 Language Detection

1. 〜が 欲しいです／〜は 欲しくないです – **(I) want ~ / (I) don't want ~**

   When stating personal preference, that is, when you yourself want/don't want some thing or item, use this construction:

   (object) + が + 欲しいです/欲しくないです.

   This is the same construction as (object) + が + 好きです/嫌いです or

   (object) + は + 好きではありません for the negative.

   A) いい成績が欲しいです。 = I want a good grade.
   B) チーズバーガーが欲しいです。 = I want a cheeseburger.
   C) 速い車が欲しいです。 = I want a fast car.
   D) あの古い帽子は欲しくないです。 = I don't want that old hat.

2. A variation on the above pattern can be used to say that <u>someone else</u> wants an object. To say this use the ending (object) + を + 〜欲しがっている.

   A) キアラさんはコーヒーを欲しがっています。 = Kiara wants coffee.
   B) 豊君は新しい黒ペンを欲しがっています。 = Yutaka wants a new black pen.
   C) 母は休みを欲しがっている。 = Mom wants a break/rest.

   NOTE The 〜が欲しい pattern is used for objects that you want. For actions, use 〜たいです pattern

3. 高いの – **an expensive one**

   Review of creating a pronoun from an adjective; adding の to an adjective creates a pronoun meaning "one" (大きいの = a big one).

When the context is clear, an い or な-adjective can be followed by の, which replaces the noun. For な adjectives, be sure to include the な after the adjective. This use of の may also be preceded by the plain (informal) past form of a verb (持って来たのを… – the one I brought...).

A-さん：	どんな犬が欲しいですか。	= What sort of dog do you want?
B-さん：	小さいのが欲しいです。	= I want a small one.
A-さん：	どんなマーカーを使いますか。	= What kind of marker will you use?
B-さん：	黒いのを使いたいです。	= I want to use a black one.
A-さん：	どんな部屋がいいですか。	= What sort of room is best?
B-さん：	静かなのがいいです。	= A quiet one is best.

 自習 **Self Check**

1. **〜が欲しいです/〜は欲しくないです**
   Make "I want"/"do not want" sentences using the English prompts.

   (ア) sushi
   (イ) black necktie
   (ウ) expensive picture/painting
   (エ) slow boat

   (オ) green pants
   (カ) plane ticket
   (キ) scary pet
   (ク) good grade

2. **adjective + の**
   For the reply in each short dialog below, answer by replacing the noun with an adjective + の according to the English cues.

A-さん：	昨日のパーティの食べ物はどうでしたか。	= How was the food at yesterday's party?
B-さん：	美味しいのがたくさんありましたよ。	= There was a lot of delicious food there!

   (ア) A-さん： どんなTシャツを買うつもりですか。
   B-さん： _____ が買いたいです。(answer using cheap)

   (イ) A-さん： どんなカメラが好きですか。
   B-さん： _____ が好きです。(answer using simple)

練習時間 Practice Time
れん しゅう

Pair Practice

Download and print out the つながる game board found on **TimeForJapanese.com** and have a pair of dice ready. With your partner, take turns filling in the 3-D tsunagaru game board. Use Japanese to fill in every other box with an object that you want, or don't want (ケーキ, 宿題, 赤い車, etc.). Fill in the re-maining boxes with something you want or don't want to do (ソックスを洗う, ビデオを借りる, etc.).

When all boxes have been filled in, exchange with another group. Player 1 rolls the die and makes a sentence stating whether the object/action on that box is desired or not. If you both agree that the sentence is correct, move the marker to that spot. Player 2 takes a turn. The game ends when someone has rolled the exact number of spaces needed to reach 終わり or when your teacher says 時間です.

object:	黒猫 ⇒	黒猫が欲しいです。黒いのを買います。
action:	かわいい人/デートする ⇒	かわいい人がいますね。デートをしたいです。

文化箱 Culture Chest
ぶん か ばこ

明治時代の文学
めい じ じ だい ぶんがく

With the advent of the new 明治 government in 1868, newspapers and other publications became more widespread. The first editorial opinion appeared in the 東京日日新聞 in December 1874; soon, more newspapers began publishing editorials or articles that disagreed with the government. 明治 printmak-ers and artists, now free to express their own opinions, began including political satire and irony in their works, in an attempt to influence public opinion. They often used manga-style illustrations to make their point. Weekly or monthly magazines like 少女界 and 女学雑誌 offered young female readers the op-portunity to learn more about their rapidly changing society.

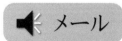

This letter, also from Jun's friend Masato, talks about the coffee shop culture in modern Japan and com-pares it to other countries.

Points to consider as you read:

❶ According to Masato, if you want a quiet place to slowly sip coffee, where should you go?
❷ When and where did a coffee-drinking culture begin in Tokyo?
❸ Masato thinks that coffee shops are most convenient for what sort of people?
❹ What does Masato usually drink at coffee shops?

じゅん君、気づいたかな?

　日本の喫茶店の習慣は他の国とは少し違うんだ。お店に長くいると、飲み物をおかわりしたいけど、おかわりは自由じゃないところが多いよ。これは大きな文化の違いだね。それに喫茶店とコーヒーショップも違うよ。静かにゆっくり座ってコーヒーを楽しむときは、喫茶店に行った方がいいかな。喫茶店は伝統的な古いタイプのお店で、中は落ち着いている。

　喫茶店の歴史は長いんだ。西洋の文化が日本にやってきて、最初の喫茶店が東京の上野に出来たのは1888年なんだよ。日本のコーヒーを飲む習慣の始まりだね。この時(明治時代)から日本人の喫茶店も始まったんだよ。最近は、どんどん喫茶店の数が少なくなっている。コーヒーショップが増えているからね。コーヒーショップは外国からきた新しいタイプのお店だよ。例えば、スタバ(スターバックス)が日本でも有名だね。コーヒーショップは、会社員などの忙しい人にとても便利なお店だよね。注文すれば、すぐに飲み物が飲めるから。だから、ゆっくり飲み物を飲む時間がないなら、コーヒーショップに行った方がいいと思うよ。

　じゅん君は、喫茶店やコーヒーショップでよく何を飲む?僕はあまり高いのは飲みたくないから、エスプレッソやカプチーノは注文しないよ。当たり前だけど、*濃いコーヒーが欲しくないなら、アメリカンコーヒーを注文した方がいいね。味が*薄いからね。

　今度一緒に喫茶店やコーヒーショップに行って、コーヒーを飲んでみない?

正人より

*濃い – thick, dark; 薄 – light, thin

第7課の3

やさしい日本語にして欲しいです。

Please put it into simple Japanese.

1) 僕は樋口さんに新しい短歌を詠んで欲しいです。

2) いいわよ。私は皆さんに俳句を作って欲しいわ。俳句は五七五、短歌は五七五七七で作るの。初めは上手に出来なくてもいいから。

3) えーっと。。。「和の心　西洋の風　明治の美」。

4) いいですね。友さんにも俳句を書いて欲しいです。

5) 私の俳句はすごいですよ。「すし食べてみそ汁欲しい旅の空」

6) 食べ物の俳句は作らなくてもいいです。樋口さん、今度は短歌を詠んでくれませんか。

7) 「うらやまし霜に雪にも色かえでおのれみどりの庭の姫松」

8) この短歌はちょっと難しいですね。やさしい日本語にして欲しいです。

9) これは冬の短歌で、「霜と雪が来ましたが庭の松はずっと緑だからうらやましいです。」「松」は「待つ」と言う意味よ。

会話 Dialog
かい

(Setting: Later that day, still in the coffee shop, talking to the author Higuchi Ichiyou)

1. ベン ：僕は樋口さんに新しい短歌を詠んで欲しいです。
   　　　　　　　ひぐち　　　　　　たんか　よ　　ほ

2. 樋口 ：いいわよ。私は皆さんに俳句を作って欲しいわ。俳句は五七五、短歌は
   ひぐち　　　　　　　　　　　　　はいく　　つく　ほ　　　　はいく　　　　　　　　たんか
   　　　　五七五七七で作るの。初めは上手に出来なくてもいいから。
   　　　　　　　　　　　　　　　はじ

3. じゅん ：えーっと…「和の心　西洋の風　明治の美」。
   　　　　　　　　　　わ　　こころ　せいよう　かぜ　めいじ　び

4. キアラ ：いいですね。友さんにも俳句を書いて欲しいです。
   　　　　　　　　　　　とも　　　　　はいく　か　　ほ

5. 友 ：私の俳句はすごいですよ。「すし食べて　みそ汁欲しい　旅の空」
   　　　　　　わたし　はいく　　　　　　　　　　た　　　しるほ　　　たび　そら

6. キアラ ：食べ物の俳句は作らなくてもいいです。樋口さん、今度は短歌を詠んでくれませ
   　　　　　た　もの　はいく　つく　　　　　　　　　ひぐち　　　　　　たんか　よ
   　　　　んか。

7. 樋口 ：「うらやまし　霜に雪にも　色かえで　おのれみどりの　庭の姫松」
   ひぐち　　　　　　　　　しも　ゆき　　　いろ　　　　　　　　　　　にわ　ひめまつ

8. ベン ：この短歌はちょっと難しいですね。やさしい日本語にして欲しいです。
   　　　　　　たんか　　　　　むずか　　　　　　　　　　　　　　ほ

9. 樋口 ：これは冬の短歌で、「霜と雪が来ましたが庭の松はずっと緑だからうらやましい
   ひぐち　　　　　　　たんか　　しも　ゆき　　　　　にわ　まつ　　　　みどり
   　　　　です。」「松」は「待つ」と言う意味よ。
   　　　　　　まつ　　　ま　　　い　いみ

単語 New Words
たん

へいき　平気 (な adj.) – coolness, calmness, unconcern

さいきん　最近 (n) – nowadays, most recent

びっくりする　ビックリする (v) – surprised (to be), amazed (to be)

おどるく驚 (v) – surprised (to be), amazed

漢字 Kanji

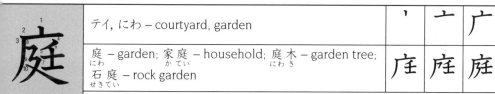

庭	テイ, にわ – courtyard, garden	丶	亠	广	庐	庐	庭
	庭 – garden; 家庭 – household; 庭木 – garden tree; 石庭 – rock garden	庄	庭	庭	庭		
10 strokes	A misshapen king (壬) (not the usual 王) sits high on a cliff (广) overlooking the people zigzagging (廴) through a beautiful GARDEN.						

| 松 | ショウ, まつ – pine tree | 一 | 十 | オ | 木 | 木 | 朴 |
| 8 strokes | 松本 – family name; 赤松 – red pine (tree); 松原 – Japanese city
まつもと　　　あかまつ　　　まつばら | 松 | 松 | | | | |

Under a PINE TREE (木), eight (八) cows are contentedly ム-ing.

言葉の探索 Language Detection
こと　ば　　たん　さく

1. 歌って欲しい = I want you to sing.
   ほ

   When stating that you want someone else (equal or lower in status to you) to do something, use the

   て-form of the verb followed by 欲しいです. The particle に follows the name of the person of whom
   ほ

   an action is requested (think about getting down on your knee [に] to ask a favor).
   ほ

   NOTE Note that it is impolite to directly tell someone of a higher status what you want him/her to do.

   > A) じゅん君にこの歌をカラオケで歌って欲しいです。
   >   ほ
   >   = I want Jun to sing this song in karaoke.
   > B) 友達に夏休みに奈良へ行って欲しいです。
   >   なら　　ほ
   >   = I want my friend to go to Nara over summer break.
   > C) 私は、学校のフットボールチームに勝って欲しいです。
   >   か　　ほ
   >   = I want the school football team to win.
   > D) 鈴木さんにこのチョコケーキを食べて欲しいです。
   >   すず　　　　　　　　　　　　ほ
   >   = I want Mr. Suzuki to eat some of this chocolate cake.
   > E) ユーンワ君に韓国語を教えて欲しいです。
   >   かん　　ほ
   >   = I want Yoonwa to teach me Korean.

2. **In Chapter 3-6, you learned the pattern** ～なくてもいいです = It is ALL RIGHT IF YOU DON'T ...
   Two other simple changes for this pattern are shown here:

   ① ～なくてはだめです = not doing ___ is bad.
   ② ～なくてはいけません = You must ___. (It is prohibited not to ___.)

   Use this pattern to say it is all right if someone else DOES NOT do something, or to ask if it is OK if

   you DO NOT do something. Start with the plain negative form of the verb (食べない, 飲まない, 泊ま
   と

   らない, etc.), change the ない ending to なくて, and add (the particle) も + いいです.

plain negative verb stem + なくて + も + いいです (か)

歌わなくてもいいです。	= It is OK if you don't sing.
歌わなくてはだめです。	= It is bad if you don't sing.
歌わなくてはいけません。	= You must sing. (It is prohibited to NOT sing.)

A)   じゅん君はこの歌をカラオケで歌わなくてはだめです。= Jun, it's NOT all right if you do not sing this song at karaoke.

(This is a double negative, but they're not cancelled out in Japanese. In other words, Jun MUST sing the song.)

B)   クラスへ行かなくてはだめです。 = It is NOT all right to cut class.

(In other words, you MUST go to class.)

C)   試験を受けなくては、いけません。 = It is NOT all right to skip the test.
     (In other words, you MUST take the test.)

This pattern is similar to the prohibitive command pattern you studied in Ch 6-3 (～ないで下さい, e.g., バスで来ないで下さい。= Please do not come by bus). The ～なくてもいい construction, however, is not strictly prohibitive and makes allowances for other possibilities.

A) そのお茶を無理して飲まなくてもいいです。 = It is all right not to drink too much of that tea.
B) 窓を開けなくてもいいです。   = It is OK not to open the window.
C) そのワークシートをしなくてもいいですよ。 = It is all right not to do that worksheet.

自習 Self Check

1. Suggest to a partner that a third friend wants him/her to do each of the following. Use the ～て欲しいです pattern.

先生は皆に宿題をやって欲しいです。= The teacher wants everyone to do the homework.

a. write a letter
b. drive a car
c. buy a book
d. help around the house

e. play (弾く) guitar
f. order coffee (注文する)
g. play soccer

2. State that you don't have to or must not/may not do the following:

a. eat breakfast
b. cross the bridge
c. ride a plane
d. make reservations

e. sit behind your friend
f. speak in Japanese
g. ask questions

練習時間 Practice Time
れん しゅう

Small Group Practice

This is the Complaint Game (It's all right if you don't/It's not all right if you don't). Each player should write down 4–5 complaints or things he/she does NOT like to do (ex.: homework, washing the dog, cleaning the house, washing clothes, etc.). Be sure you can make each statement in Japanese. Do じゃんけん to see who goes first. A-さん makes one complaint to B-さん (the person to his/her left). B-さん listens carefully and responds by either telling A-さん that it's all right if he/she does not do it or that he/she must do it. Continue taking turns until everyone has had a chance to make all his/her complaints. Be generous for some things, strict about others!

A-さん： 数学の宿題をするのが好きじゃないです。　= I don't like to do math homework.
B-さん： 今日、宿題をしなくてもいいです。明日して下さい。

= Today, it's all right not to do the homework. Do it tomorrow please.

B-さん： にんじん(carrots)が好きじゃないです。　= I don't like carrots.
A-さん： 晩ご飯に、にんじんがあるから食べなくてはだめです。

= For dinner, we have carrots so it is not all right for you NOT to eat them.
(That is, you must eat them.)

文化箱 Culture Chest
ぶん か ばこ

1. 俳句, 和歌, and other poetic styles
はい く　わ か

俳句, a short 5 - 7 - 5 syllable poem that has come to symbolize the heart of poetry in Japan, is part of a
はい く
long poetic history. Japanese-style poems, or 和歌, are recorded in some of the earliest Japanese writings, including the 古事記 (early 700s), 日本書紀 (720 C.E.), and the 万葉集 (760 C.E.). 紀貫之 col-
こ じ き　　に ほんしょき　　　まんようしゅう　　きのつらゆき
lected famous 和歌 poems in his 古今和歌集 (early 900s). During the 平安時代, 紫式部 included
わ か　　　　こ きん わ か しゅう　　　　　　へいあん じ だい　むらさきしき ぶ
many 和歌 in her 源氏物語, as you learned in *Beginning Japanese*.
わ か　　　げん じ ものがたり

After the 平安時代, 連歌 (or linked poetry) became popular and 和歌 later fell in and out of favor.
へいあん じ だい　れん が　　　　　　　　　　　　　　　　わ か
俳句 were popularized in the late 19th century. 和歌 enjoyed a revival during the 明治時代 when poets
はい く　　　　　　　　　　　　　　　　わ か　　　　　　　　　　　　　　　　　めい じ じ だい
such as 樋口一葉, 石川啄木, and 与謝野晶子 (a late 明治時代 poet and social activist) began ex
ひ ぐちいちよう いしかわたくぼく　 よ さ の あき こ　　　　　　めい じ じ だい

ploring and stretching the bounds of poetry and literature. 正岡子規 (1867–1902) was an important proponent of 和歌 and encouraged writers to modernize poetry in the same way that Japan had modernized other aspects of society. Here is one 短歌 by 子規 from 1898. He created the term 短歌 to refer to new/modernized 和歌. In this 短歌, he combines classical phrasing, such as 久方の (distant), and 見れど飽かぬかも (won't get bored with even after watching for a very long time), a more modern-style phrasing. Influenced by the newly-arrived Western sport of baseball, this poem incorporates a mix of traditional and modern traditions. This was in step with evolving Japanese cultural trends of the time.

久方の
アメリカ人の
はじめにし
ベースボールは
見れどあかぬかも

2. 顔文字 – Emoticons

When typing, many Westerners use emoticons to represent the eyes, but the primary focus is on the mouth. Some examples include: :-), :-(, :D, and :P.

Japanese 顔文字, on the other hand, focus more on the eyes to express emotions. These Japanese 顔文字 use parentheses to indicate the entire face. Also, the greater number of typewritten Japanese symbols allows for a broader range of 顔文字.

Can you match each of the following 顔文字 with its counterpart?

A)	(^-^)	1) sleeping
B)	(-_-)	2) peace!
C)	(T-T)	3) wink with a star
D)	(^-^)v	4) :/
E)	(..)∅	5) taking a memo (note)
F)	(^_-)-*	6) :-)
G)	(-_-)zzz	7) crying (>へ<) or (>_<): trying to hold back tears)

Answers: A-6, B-4, C-7, D-2, E-5, F-3, G-1

🔊 メール

Taeko, Kiara's Japanese friend from Chicago, is writing to ask for a favor.
Points to consider as you read:

1) Where does Taeko ask Kiara to go?

2) What does Taeko ask Kiara to buy for her? And how many?

3) What do the emoticons that Taeko uses in her note each indicate?

キアラへ

　元気にしてる？私はとても元気だよ(￣ー￣)v　シカゴはだんだん暖かくなってきて、ここ数日は日中65°Fくらいかな。朝と夜は、まだまだ寒いんだけど。日本はどう？蒸し暑いんじゃない？そう言えば、日本に行ってから何をした？もう東京ディズニーランドには行った？色々教えてよ。あー、日本が懐かしいな(:＿;)

　あのさ、ちょっとお願いがあるんだけど、いいかな。こっちにいる友達にいい*下敷きをあげたいの。シカゴにある日本のお店で探したけど、全然いいのが*見つからない(x＿x;)　それでね、時間があったら、キアラに新宿の*高島屋へ行って欲しいんだけど…。高島屋の10階の奥に*文房具屋があって、そこには絶対カッコいいのがあるんだよ。お願いm(.＿.)m

　それでね、もし行く時間があったら、人気がある歌手の下敷きを二枚と、漫画のキャラクターのを二枚と、格好いいのを二枚、全部で六枚買って欲しい(^^ゞもちろん、お金は全部払うよ。だから全部でいくらだったか教えてね☆時間があるときでいいので送ってください。すぐ送らなくてもいいよ、ゆっくりで大丈夫だから。

　ごめんね！ありがとう(*^＿^*)

妙子より

---

* 見つかる – to find; 高島屋 – upscale Japanese department store; 文房具屋 – stationery store

これ以上食べてはいけません。
You may not eat any more than this.

1) 僕はキアラさんに俳句を紹介して欲しいです。

2)「国動き　花鳥同じ　神の道」

3) その俳句はすばらしいね。上手！

4) 私ももう一つ短歌を作って見ました。「白ご飯　すき焼きの海　肉さがす　漬物の花　母の手作り」。私はてりやきチキンが食べたくなりました。

5) 友さん、これ以上食べてはいけません。体に悪いですよ。

6) 私は少し休みたい。タバコを吸ってもいい？

7) 店の中でタバコを吸ってはいけないよ。でも店の外に出ればいいよ。

8) 分かったわよ。じゃあ、吸うのはやめるわ。

会話 Dialog

(Setting: Later that day, still in the coffee shop, talking to the author Ichiyou Higuchi)

1. ベン ： 僕はキアラさんに俳句を 紹 介して欲しいです。

2. キアラ ： 「国動き　花鳥同じ　神の道」

3. 樋口 ： その俳句はすばらしいね。上手！

4. 友 ： 私ももう一つ短歌を作って見ました。
「白ご飯　すきやきの海　肉さがす　漬物の花　母の手作り」。
私はてりやきチキンが食べたくなりました。

5. じゅん ： 友さん、これ以 上 食べてはいけません。体に悪いですよ。

6. 樋口 ： 私は少し休みたい。タバコを吸ってもいい？

7. *詩人 ： 店の中でタバコを吸ってはいけないよ。でも店の外に出ればいいよ。

8. 樋口 ： 分かったわよ。じゃあ、吸うのはやめるわ。

*詩人 – poet

単語 New Words

きそく　規則 (n) – rules, regulations

じゅう　銃 (n) – gun, arms

まやく　麻薬 (n) – drugs, narcotic

めんど(う)くさい　面倒くさい (い adj.) –
bother(some) to do, tiresome

いがい　以外 (adv.) – with the exception of, excepting

ぐうぜん　偶然 (exp.) – chance (by), accident (by)

タバコをすう　タバコを吸う (v) – smoke tobacco (to)

漢字 Kanji

飯	ハン, めし – meal, cooked rice	ノ	八	牛	今	今	今
	ご飯 – meal, cooked rice; 五目飯 – rice dish with fish and vegetables; 握り飯 – rice ball	食	食	飠	飣	飯	飯
12 strokes	Eating (食) COOKED RICE or a MEAL by a cliff on a table (反) is relaxing.						

言葉の探索 Language Detection
こと ば たん さく

More 規則 (rules)
きそく

You already know how to tell someone that they may do (〜てもいいです) or may not do (〜てはいけません or 〜てはだめです) some action. You've also learned how to say it is all right NOT to do something (〜なくてもいいです). Here are more examples of 規則 you might use at school:

A) 教室で食べてはいけません。 = You may not eat in the classroom.
きょうしつ

B) ガムをかんではいけません。 = You may not chew gum

C) タバコを吸ってはいけません。 = You may not smoke cigarettes.
す

D) 喧嘩をしてはだめです。 = You may not fight. (Fighting is bad.)
けん か

E) 学校で携帯電話を使ってはだめです。 = You may not use a cell phone in school. (Using a cell
けいたい　　　　　　　　　　　　　　　 phone in school is bad.)

F) 悪い言葉を使ってはいけません。 = You may not use bad language.
こと ば

G) ドレスを着なくてもいいです。 = It is all right NOT to wear a dress.

H) 質問を書かなくてもいいです。 = It is all right NOT to write the questions.
しつもん
答えだけを書いて下さい。 = Please only write the answers.
こた

自習 Self Check
じ しゅう

Where or in what situations might each of these 規則 apply?
きそく

a. 靴をはかなくてはだめです。　　　e. ネクタイを貸してもいいです。
くつ　　　　　　　　　　　　　　　　　　　　　　 か

b. お酒を飲んではだめです。　　　　f. どこに座ってもいいです。
　　　　　　　　　　　　　　　　　　　　　　　　 すわ

c. 友達と話してはだめです。　　　　g. お昼ご飯を食べなくてもいいです。
　　　　　　　　　　　　　　　　　　　　　　　 ひる はん

d. 大きい声で話してはいけません。
こえ

練習時間 Practice Time
れん しゅう じ かん

Pair Practice

A. My Perfect School: With your partner, come up with two lists of rules (6-8 rules each). One list is for your current classroom and school. The second list is for your ideal school. When you are done, compare your lists with other groups. Be prepared to share part of your list with the class.

B. My Perfect Roommate: You and your classmate are looking for a new roommate. Together, list at least six things you would NOT like your roommate to do and four things your roommate could do. Be prepared to share part of your list with the class.

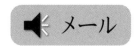 **メール**

Taeko, Kiara's Japanese friend in Chicago, writes about life in Chicago and her experience with Japanese poetry.

Points to consider as you read:

❶ What does Taeko say recently happened to her at school?

❷ Why does Taeko like the two poems by Matsuo Basho that she cites here?

❸ Do you have any modern poets that you enjoy reading?

キアラ、元気? 妙子だよ。

　最近、街でキアラのお母さんに会ったよ。キアラがいないから、シカゴはつまらないよ。でも、日本で楽しんでる? この間、ディテンションになったの。クラスで携帯電話を使ってはいけないのに、テキストしてたの、見つかっちゃった。もう学校で携帯電話は絶対に使わないよ。*居残りは面倒くさいんだもん。日本の学校にはないのになあ。

　あ、そうだ。樋口一葉さんと俳句の勉強してるんだね。難しい? 日本の国語の教科書にはよく、樋口一葉や正岡子規、それから、松尾芭蕉の短歌や俳句があって、私達はたくさん勉強したのよ。私は松尾芭蕉の『古池や 蛙 飛びこむ水の音』や『閑さや岩にしみ入る蝉の声』が好き! この二つはイメージ*しやすい*でしょ?

　他には、与謝野晶子がいるわ。『清水へ祇園をよぎる 桜 月夜 こよひ逢ふ人みな美しき』。素敵ね。

　何かキアラも素敵な短歌や俳句を作ったら教えてね。じゃメール待ってる。

またね!

妙子

---

*居残り – detention; しやすい – easy to make, easy to do; でしょ – an abbreviated and informal form of でしょう

私はもっと皆と話してみたいな。

I want to try to talk more with everyone, you know.

1) すみません、お茶を
もう一杯下さい。それから
ケーキも一つお願いします。

2) ケーキはチョコレートと
いちごとカステラがありますが、
どれにしますか？

3) じゃあ、
カステラに
します。

4) ああ、
甘くて美味しい！
キアラさん、
このカステラを
食べて見て下さい。

5) 本当、いい味です。これほ
ど美味しい物は初めてです。

6) 僕は樋口さんの
俳句や短歌をもっと
読んで見たいです。

7) 私はもっと皆と
話していたいな。

8) はい、でも時間です。
明日、東京で友達と
会わなければなりません。

9) ああ、そう。残念ね。じゃあ、
皆、日本語の勉強がんばって。

10) たくさん素晴らしい本や俳句や短歌
を書いて欲しいです。

11) さようなら。

会話 Dialog

(Setting: Later that day, in the coffee shop, saying farewell to the author Ichiyou Higuchi)

1. じゅん ：すみません、お茶をもう一杯下さい。それからケーキも一つお願いします。

2. マスター ：ケーキはチョコレートといちごとカステラがありますが、どれにしますか?

3. じゅん ：じゃあ、カステラにします。

4. じゅん ああ、甘くて美味しい!キアラさん、このカステラを食べてみて下さい。

5. キアラ ：本当、いい味です。これほど美味しい物は初めてです。

6. ベン ：僕は樋口さんの俳句や短歌をもっと読んで見たいです。

7. 樋口 ：私はもっと皆と話していたいな。

8. 友 ：はい、でも時間です。明日、東京で友達と会わなければなりません。

9. 樋口 ：ああ、そう。残念ね。じゃあ、皆、日本語の勉強がんばって。

10. じゅん ：たくさん素晴らしい本や俳句や短歌を書いて欲しいです。

11. 皆 ：さようなら。

漢字 Kanji

願 19 strokes	ガン, ねが(う), 〜ねがい – request, petition	一	厂	厂	厈	厏	盾	原	原	原
	お願いします – to request, to beg; 願い出る – to apply for	原	原'	原''	願	願	願	願	願	願
	A meadow (原) is made up of a cliff (厂), white (白), and small (小). The right side is a leaf (頁). On the bottom sits a shell (貝), an ancient form of money. Imagine your mother REQUEST(ing) you to clean up the small leaves and white bits of rocks from the cliff before you can get your allowance.									

初 7 strokes	ショ, はじ(め), はつ – first time, beginning	、	ラ	ネ	ネ	ネ		
	初め – start, beginning; 初めまして – How do you do? (lit. I am meeting you for the first time); 初日 – first or opening day; 最初 beginning, outset	初	初					
	A sword (刀) slashes the clothing (ネ) prices on the BEGINNING day of a sale.							

言葉の探索 Language Detection

1. Try and eat this = 食べてみて下さい

To invite someone to try to do something, use the て form of an action verb + みて下さい. This phrase does not use the kanji 見 (to see), but you can think of this meaning "try and see if…".

Direct object を + て-form (action verb) + みて下さい。

A) スノーボードをやってみて下さい。	= Please try snowboarding and see (how it is).
B) 麦茶を飲んでみて下さい。	= Try and drink that mugicha [barley tea] and see (how it is).
C) その寿司を注文して、食べてみて下さい。	= Order that sushi and try it.

2. To state that you WILL try something, use the same pattern but change the ending to the ～ます or dictionary form.

Direct object を + て form + みます(みる)

A) スノーボードをやってみます。	= I will try snowboarding (and see how I like it).
B) 麦茶を飲んでみます。	= I will try to drink some mugicha.
C) その寿司を注文して、食べてみる。	= I will order that sushi and try eating it.

自習 Self Check

How would you suggest someone try these activities?

a. practice flower-arranging (いけばなをする)
b. telephone a friend
c. try to wear these new shoes (はく)
d. read the newspaper
e. speak Chinese
f. have a meal here
g. turn right
h. get off the bicycle (降りる)

練習時間 Practice Time

Small Group Activity

In groups of 3-4, play the game 百万円あったら… As a group, brainstorm ten activities you would do if you had a million yen. Next, each group member should secretly choose five of the activities that he/she would like to try the most (without telling the other players). After all have decided, take turns predicting which activities each of your group members would like to try by asking if they would like to try something. You might be asked to report your findings to the class. Some sample activities are: buying a boat, going to Hawaii, taking a long vacation, travelling to Africa, touring the Metropolitan Museum of Art in New York City, going to the Ghibli Studio (ジブリスタジオ) outside of Tokyo, etc.

例 <ruby>れい<rt></rt></ruby> EXAMPLE

アフリカへ行ってみて

A-さん ： 百万円あったら、アフリカへ行ってみたいですか。

B-さん ： いいえ、行きたくないです。

or いいえ、行ってみたくないです。暑いですから。

A-さん (to class) ： B-さんは、百万円あってもアフリカへ行ってみたくないです。

🔊 メール

Ben's friend Yoshikazu is writing to suggest various Japanese foods that Ben might try.

Points to consider as you read:

❶ What does Yoshikazu consider to be one major difference between restaurants in Japan and restaurants in America?

❷ In a Japanese restaurant, how do you pay the bill?

❸ Name one phrase commonly used by restaurant customers in Japan.

ベン、

　レストランで何を注文するか… ん〜俺はよく枝豆、焼き鳥、からあげ、ぎょうざ、天ぷら、親子どんぶりやカレーライスにする。食べた事がある？枝豆は boiled green soybeans、焼き鳥は grilled skewered chicken、からあげは fried chicken、ぎょうざは pot stickers、天ぷらは deep fried fritters、親子どんぶりは chicken and egg over steamed rice で、最後のカレーライスは curry and rice だよ。どれも美味しいから、ぜひ食べてみて！後で、どれにしたか教えてね。

　ところで、日本のレストランと、アメリカのレストランの大きな違いは何だと思う？アメリカではたいていレストランに行ったら、チップをテーブルの上に置いて帰るよね。晩御飯だと、だいたい15%〜20%くらいかな。けれども、日本にチップの*習慣はないんだよ。「お勘定をお願いします」と言って、ウエイターやウエイトレスから伝票を受け取る。君のテーブルのウエイターやウェイトレスはいないから、誰に言ってもいいよ。それから、レジに行って、お金を払うんだ。ウェイターやウェイトレスにお金は払わないからね。

　もう一つの日本の習慣は、ほら、ご飯を食べる前に「いただきます」、食べた後に「ごちそう様でした」と言うでしょ。僕はいつも帰る時にお店の人が僕に「ありがとうございました」と言ったら、「ごちそう様でした」って返事をするんだ。

　何かまた聞きたいことがあったらメールしてね。

　じゃ、後で。

良和
よしかず

---

* 習慣 <ruby>しゅうかん<rt></rt></ruby> – custom, tradition; 伝票 <ruby>でんぴょう<rt></rt></ruby> – the bill, check

東京　1960年

Effects of Geology and Weather

This chapter is dedicated to the victims and survivors of the To-oku Earthquake and Tsunami of 2011.

The Great Kanto Earthquake occurred on Sept. 1, 1923, shortly after our group said farewell to Kawabata Ya-unari in Izu. From Izu, Kiara and her friends exit a to-ii on the campus of 東京大学 in 1960. The group sees college students receiving Disaster Prevention Day raining. This day was instituted as a national day of bservance after the Great Kanto Earthquake, in order o reduce damage and fatalities in case of disasters. The travelers are inspired by what they see.

In a nearby neighborhood, the travelers come cross a ballroom dance studio. Jun remembers his randmother's stories about teaching dance in a dance tudio when she was young. Entering the studio, they meet the ballroom dancing teacher, who is, they soon ealize, the dancing girl from Izu (伊豆の踊り子).
いず　おど　こ

Learning and Performance Goals

This chapter will enable you to:
- learn about the Pacific Ring of Fire and Disaster Prevention Day in Japan
- review the particle から
- review strategies to enrich language by adding adjectives, adverbs, conjunctions, and other details
- understand the difference between transitive and intransitive verb pairs and to use each correctly
- say that it seems like something has happened or will happen using 〜そうです/だ
- use だけ to say that "only~" or "just~"
- say "when" something happens using 〜の時
- say something is completely finished by using the pattern 〜て form + しまいました
- use an additional 11 kanji

何が始まりますか？
はじ

What is about to begin?

1) 東大の赤門の前に
たくさん大学生がいますね。
何が始まるんですか？

2) 1923年の今日（9月1日）に
関東大地震があったから、
今日を「防災の日」にしました。
それに、9月には台風がよく来ます。
今、東大生達が訓練を始めています。

3) 天災は地震と台風だけじゃない。
火事や津波もある。関東大地震は
昼の十二時二分前に始まったから、
台所から火が出て火事になった。
今からバケツリレーをするから、
皆集まって。バケツに水を入れて、
右側の人に渡して。始め！

4) 次は外でご飯を作る訓練だ。
かばんから米と水を出して、
なべに入れて。それから木を
集めて火を起こす。
今日は風が強くて危ないから、
気を付けて。

5) ご飯？私が
手伝います！

6) 次は壊れた家の下にいる
人を見つけて助ける訓練！
犬を連れて来て。

7) じゃあ、
それは私が
手伝います！

会話 Dialog
かい

(Setting: Outside the main gate of Tokyo University, September 1, 1960)

1. ベン ：東大の赤門の前にたくさん大学生がいますね。何が始まるんですか？
　　　　　　とうだい　あかもん　　　　　　　　　　　　　　　　　　　はじ

2. じゅん ：1923年の今日 (9月1日) に関東大地震があったから、今日を「防災の日」にしまし
　　　　　　　　　　　　　　　　かんとうだいじしん　　　　　　　　　　　ぼうさい　ひ
　　　た。それに、9月には台風がよく来ます。今、東大生達が*訓練を始めています。
　　　　　　　　　　　　　たいふう　　　　　　　　　　　とうだいせいたち　くんれん　はじ

3. 東大生1 ：天災は地震と台風だけじゃない。火事や津波もある。関東大地震は昼の
　　　　　　てんさい　じしん　たいふう　　　　　　　　かじ　つなみ　　　　かんとうだいじしん
　　　十二時二分前に始まったから、台所から火が出て火事になった。今から*バケ
　　　　　　　　　　はじ　　　　　　　　たいどころ　ひ　で　かじ
　　　ツリレーをするから、みんな集まって。バケツに水を入れて、右側の人に渡して。
　　　　　　　　　　　　　　　　あつ　　　　　　　　　　い　　　がわ　　　わた
　　　始め！
　　　はじ

4. 東大生2 ：次は外でご飯を作る訓練だ。かばんから米と水を出して、なべに入れて。
　　　　　　　　　　はん　　くんれん　　　　　こめ　　　だ
　　　それから木を集めて火を起こす。今日は風が強くて危ないから、気を付けて。
　　　　　　き　あつ　ひ　お　　　　　　かぜ　つよ　あぶ

5. 友 ：ご飯？私が手伝います！
　　　　　　はん　　　つだ

6. 東大生3 ：次は壊れた家の下にいる人を見つけて助ける訓練！犬を連れて来て。
　　　　　　つぎ　こわ　　　　　　　　　　　　たす　くんれん

7. キアラ ：じゃあ、それは私が手伝います！

*訓練 – practice, training; バケツリレー – bucket relay (for fighting fires)
くんれん

単語 New Words
たん

こくさい 国際 (n) – international

こくさいこうりゅう 国際交流 (n) – international
exchange

しぜん 自然 (n) – nature

ふこう 不幸 (な adj.) – unhappiness, misfortune

あく 開く (v) – open (to)

あける 開ける (v) – open (to) (eyes, doors, etc.)

しまる 閉まる (v) – close (to)

しめる 閉める (v) – close (to)

あつまる 集まる (v) – meet (to), congregate (to)

あつめる 集める (v) – collect (to), put together (to)

おこす 起こす (v) – wake someone up (to), rise (to)

きょうみをもつ 興味を持つ (v) – have an interest (to)

はじめる 始める (v) – start (to)

わたす 渡す (v) – hand over (to), pass along (to)

漢字 Kanji

関 14 strokes	カン, せき – barrier, gateway, related to		丨	冂	冂	尸	門'	門	門		
	関東 – the Kanto (eastern) region; 関西 – the Kansai (western) region; 一ノ関 – Ichinoseki (city)		門	門	門	閂	関	関	関		
	Below the gate (門) is a tally of two marks, passing on to heaven (天). This is an important GATEWAY.										

開 12 strokes	カイ, ひら(く), ひら(ける), あ(く), あ(ける) – open, unfold		丨	冂	冂	尸	門'	門			
	開ける – to open (a door or window); 開く – to open (a book); 公開 – public exhibit		門	門	閂	閂	開	開			
	Under this gate (門) is something that looks like the kanji for heaven (天), but the center line of this has been pulled OPEN for people to enter.										

閉 11 strokes	ヘイ, と(じる), と(ざす), し(める), し(まる) – closed, shut		丨	冂	尸	尸	門'	門			
	閉じる – to close (books, eyes, meetings, etc.); 閉まる – to be shut, to be closed; 閉める – to close, to shut		門	門	閂	閉	閉				
	Under this gate (門) is a katakana オ, as if saying, "Oh no! The shop is already CLOSED."										

台 5 strokes	タイ, ダイ – pedestal, platform, counter for vehicles and machines		ㄥ	ㄥ	台	台	台				
	台風 – typhoon; 車一台 – one vehicle; 台湾 – Taiwan; 仙台 – Sendai (city); 台所 – kitchen										
	A katakana mu ム sits like a modern sculpture atop the mouth-shaped (口) PEDESTAL or PLATFORM.										

始 8 strokes	シ, はじ(まる), はじ(める) – start, begin		く	女	女	如	如	始			
	始めましょう – let's begin; 開始 – to commence or begin		始	始							
	This woman (女) who is about to START or BEGIN her day, first meditates. She makes the sound "アォム" with her mouth (口).										

次 6 strokes	シ, ジ, つぎ – next, order or sequence		`	冫	冫	汄	次	次			
	次男 – second son; 次に – next, and then										
	The ice radical (冫) is next to miss or lack (欠). After the ice melts, what will come NEXT?										

集	シュウ, あつ(める), あつ(まる) – to collect, to gather	ノ	イ	イ´	仁	什	仹
	集まる – to gather; 集合する – to meet, to assemble	仹	隹	隹	隼	集	集
12 strokes	A short-tailed bird (隹) sits on a tree (木), waiting TO MEET or GATHER TOGETHER with the other birds.						

伝	デン, つた(える), つた(え), つた(わる) – transmit, legend, communicate	ノ	イ	イ	仁	伝	伝
	手伝う – to help; 伝える – to transmit (relay a message); 伝統的 – traditional (style); 伝説 – legend; 伝送 – to transmit, to communicate						
6 strokes	A person (イ) is trying to TELL or TRANSMIT a double (二) message — "ム・ム".						

言葉の探索 Language Detection

1. Review of the uses of から

The particle から has many functions. Here are previously described uses of から with examples:

A) from someone: 祖父から = from my grandfather

B) from one place or time to another: 家から学校までバスで来ました。

　= I came from home to school by bus.

C) because: 友さんが温泉の中で泳いだから、私は恥ずかしかったです。

　= I was embarrassed because Tomo was swimming inside the hot springs pool.

2. Transitive and intransitive verbs

Here is an example of a transitive/intransitive verb pair:

(T) ゲームを始める – (someone) begin(s) the game (transitive)

(I) ゲームが始まる – the game will begin (intransitive)

In English, some verbs can be used as both transitive and intransitive verbs. The word "begin" in the examples above is one. Another example is "grow." "Hiro grows tomatoes" is transitive (active) with a direct object, while "Tomatoes grow over there" is intransitive (passive).

Japanese verb transitive-intransitive pairs, however, generally have the same beginnings and endings, but the middle syllables differ. Here are some essential differences in their usage:

- **transitive (active) verbs** require a direct object (the object of action) that takes the particle を. These verbs usually express an action that happens to the direct object and is caused by someone/something.

- **intransitive (passive) verbs** demonstrate passive movement or changes that occur spontaneously or involve emotion. These events just "happen," with no actor actively causing the action to occur. Intransitive verbs do not require direct objects, therefore the particle を is rarely used with intransitive verbs. The particle が may be used after the subject.

Here are some transitive/intransitive verb pairs and example usages. Look for patterns in this chart.

transitive (active)		intransitive (passive)	
始める はじ	クラスを始めましょう。 はじ = Let's begin class.	そろそろクラスが始まります。 はじ = The class will begin soon.	始まる はじ
閉める し	ドアを閉めましょう。 し = Let's close the door.	ドアが閉まっています。 し = The door is closed.	閉まる し
開ける あ	ドアを開けて下さい。 あ = Please open the door.	ドアが開いています。 あ = The door is open.	開く あ
聞く き	音楽を聞きましょう。 き = Let's listen to music.	音楽が聞こえますか。 き = Can you hear the music?	聞こえる き
見る	映画を見ませんか。 えい が = Won't you watch the movie?	映画が見えますか。 = Can you see the movie? or Are you able to see the movie?	見える

自習 Self Check
じ しゅう

1. **Using から**

   Use から to restate each of the following in Japanese.

   (ア) I studied from 7 a.m. until 10 a.m.

   (イ) My mother traveled from New York to Shanghai last year.

   (ウ) You will receive 15,000 yen from an uncle for your birthday.

   (エ) You have a stomachache because you ate too much sukiyaki.

   (オ) The weather will be cold, so you must buy a coat.

   (カ) Class is finished, so close your textbook.

2. **Transitive/intransitive verbs**

   Make two sentences using each of the objects listed below. Use a transitive (active) verb for one and an intransitive (passive) verb for the other. Use the two examples as models.

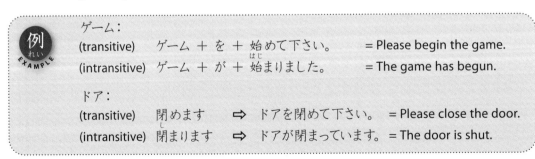

例 EXAMPLE
れい

ゲーム：
(transitive)　ゲーム ＋ を ＋ 始めて下さい。　= Please begin the game.
　　　　　　　　　　　　　　はじ
(intransitive)　ゲーム ＋ が ＋ 始まりました。　= The game has begun.
　　　　　　　　　　　　　　はじ

ドア：
(transitive)　閉めます　⇒　ドアを閉めて下さい。　= Please close the door.
(intransitive)　閉まります　⇒　ドアが閉まっています。　= The door is shut.
　　　　　　し

犬：　　出ます　出します　　地図：　見ます　見えます　　まど：　開けます　開きます
　　　　で　　だ　　　　　　ちず　　　　　　　　　　　　　　　あ
鳥の声：聞きます　聞こえます　　授業：　始めます　始まります
とり こえ　　　　　　　　じゅぎょう　はじ

練習時間 Practice Time
れんしゅうじかん

Small Group Activity

Divide into groups of 3-4. Your teacher will give each group a set of verb cards that include Japanese transitive and intransitive verb pairs. Lay them out on your desk. Choose one person from your group to be the "caller." The "caller" will say a sentence using the verb in English. The other group members try to slap EITHER the transitive or intransitive form of that verb—whichever has just been used—and say it, as quickly as they can, in Japanese.

Option 2: Play "Old Maid" with your set of verb cards. To begin, pull one of the cards (don't look at it, this is the ババ抜き – "old maid" card) and set it aside. Deal out all of the cards. Each player lays out any transitive-intransitive card pairs face up. Next, the player to the left of the dealer draws one card from the dealer's hand and tries to make a transitive-intransitive verb pair. If no pairs can be made, the next player draws a card, and so on. The player with the most verb pairs without the ババ抜き card is the winner.

文化箱 Culture Chest
ぶんかばこ

Geography: The Pacific Ring of Fire – 環太平洋火山帯
かんたいへいようかざんたい

Japan is a nation where four tectonic plates converge, rubbing each other and at times sliding and grinding violently. In fact, these four plates collide just off of the coast of 東京. Up to 1,500 tremors or earthquakes are recorded annually throughout the country. Most of these only shake shelves and cause ceiling lights to gently sway back and forth. But in 1923, the 関東大震災, or Great Kanto Earthquake, was one of the worst in Japan's history. Buildings collapsed and the ensuing fires were devastating, quickly engulfing entire neighborhoods. The 東日本大震災および津波 of 2011 showed how Japan had learned from previous earthquake disasters. Building standards were far superior to those of earlier times and prevented most destruction from this earthquake, which registered 9.0 on the Richter scale. The ensuing 津波, however, proved to be devastating, and was much bigger than anyone had anticipated.

Japan is located on the edge of what is known as the "ring of fire." This "ring" runs from Japan to the Philippines and Indonesia, through the South Pacific to Hawaii. It then extends up the North American Pacific coastline along California and north to Alaska, where it follows the curve of the Aleutian Islands and turns back down toward Japan. The entire ring is lined with volcanoes, and almost 90% of the world's earthquakes occur in the region. Japan alone contains 10% of the world's active volcanoes. 富士山, though currently dormant, is the most famous.

Strong feelings about nature have always been a part of the Japanese psyche. Though a large percentage live in urban areas, most Japanese still feel a connection to nature. One area where this is evident is the Japanese response to natural disasters. Japan is one of the top donor nations for disaster relief around the globe.

Geological circumstances being what they are, residents of Japan must be prepared for many types of emergencies: earthquakes, volcanic eruptions, and tsunami. When in Japan, you can see examples of earthquake preparedness in homes and businesses. Bookcases and shelving are often secured to the wall and buildings are equipped with emergency evacuation materials such as ladders or chutes. Modern buildings have strict construction codes meant to reduce earthquake damage. What types of disaster prevention preparations exist in your area?

This message is from Jun's father, telling Jun about Jun's grandmother and her time as a university student. He also mentions her experience as a dance teacher and her suspicions about the owner of the dance studio.

Points to consider as you read:

❶ Jun's father enclosed two photographs with his letter. What were they of?

❷ What university did Jun's grandmother attend? In what district is it located?

❸ Jun's grandmother loved studying. and what else did she enjoy?

❹ What were his grandmother's suspicions about the owner of the dance studio?

じゅんへ

　じゅん、元気にしているか。父さんは元気だ。今日家族のアルバムを見ていたら、父さんの母親、じゅんのおばあちゃんの若い時の写真が出てきた。写真の中でおばあちゃんは着物を着て、日本舞踊を踊っている。そこで、今日はおばあちゃんのことを書こうと思う。

　おばあちゃんはすごく頭が良くて、小さい時から勉強が大好きだった。だから、大学は日本で一番難しいと言われる東京大学に合格した。東大は本郷という所にある。本郷と言えば、樋口一葉の家があることでも有名な所だ。そして、おばあちゃんは頭がいいだけじゃなく、小さい時から日本舞踊を習っていて、踊りも上手だった。大学に通いながら、大学の近くにあるダンス教室で日本舞踊を教えていた。その教室のオーナーで先生のたま子さんは、十代の時、伊豆半島で旅芸人の踊り子をしていたそうで、あの川端康成の小説の「伊豆の踊り子」に出てくる踊り子に違いない、とおばあちゃんは*ひそかに思っていたが、聞けなかったそうだ。

　そのダンス教室では、伝統的な踊りだけじゃなく、*社交ダンスなどモダンダンスも教えていた。おばあちゃんも、社交ダンスに*興味を持ち、日本舞踊を教えながら、社交ダンスを習い始めたそうだ。ドレスを着てタンゴを踊っている写真の女性もおばあちゃんだ。

　この2枚の写真から分かるように、ダンスをするおばあちゃんはとても美しかった。じゅんにもそのことを覚えていて欲しいので、写真をいっしょに送ることにする。大切に持っていて欲しい。

父さんより

*ひそかに – secretly; 社交ダンス – social dancing

友さんはいつも元気そうですね。

Tomo always seems so energetic.

1) 防災訓練は大変そうでしたね。あれ？ここは樋口さんが住んでいた所ですよ。

2) ああ、ここは浅草の隣の町ですね。僕の家はあそこですよ。それに祖母は、この近くの日本舞踊の教室で、アルバイトをしていました。

3) 本当ですか？じゃあおばあさんに会いに行かなければなりませんね。

4) この町はきれいな家がたくさんありますが、関東大震災のすぐ後はひどかったでしょうね。

5) キアラさんはちょっと悲しそうですね。大丈夫ですか？

6) ええ、地震の事を考えて怖くなりました。今地震が来れば家がめちゃくちゃになりますね。道で寝なければなりません。家族や友達が心配です。

7) 心配しないで。皆で力を合わせて一緒にがんばれば大丈夫ですよ。

8) ほら、浅草の雷おこしは美味しそうだから皆で一緒に食べませんか。

9) 友さんはいつも元気そうですね。私も元気にならなきゃ。

会話 Dialog
（かい）

(Setting: In Hongo-cho, near Tokyo University, September 1, 1960)

1. 友　　：防災訓練は大変そうでしたね。あれ？ここは樋口さんが住んでいた所ですよ。
　　　　　　（ぼうさいくんれん）　　　　　　　　　　　　　（ひぐち）　　　　　　　　　（ところ）

2. じゅん　：ああ、ここは浅草の隣の町ですね。僕の家はあそこですよ。
　　　　　　　　　　　　（あさくさ）（となり）
　　　　　　それに祖母は、この近くの日本舞踊の教室で、アルバイトをしていました。
　　　　　　　　　（そぼ）　　　　　　　　　　　　　（ぶよう）（きょうしつ）

3. ベン　　：本当ですか？じゃあおばあさんに会いに行かなければなりませんね。

4. キアラ　：この町はきれいな家がたくさんありますが、*関東大震災のすぐ後はひどかった
　　　　　　　　　　　　　　　　　　　　　　　　　（かんとうだいしんさい）
　　　　　　でしょうね。

5. じゅん　：キアラさんはちょっと悲しそうですね。大丈夫ですか？
　　　　　　　　　　　　　　　　　（かな）　　　　　　　（だいじょうぶ）

6. キアラ　：ええ、地震の事を考えて怖くなりました。今地震が来れば家がめちゃ
　　　　　　　　　（じしん）（かんが）（こわ）　　　　（じしん）
　　　　　　くちゃになりますね。道で寝なければなりません。家族や友達が心配です。
　　　　　　　　　　　　　　　　　（ね）　　　　　　　　　　　（かぞく）　　　　　（しんぱい）

7. ベン　　：心配しないで。皆で力を合わせて一緒にがんばれば大丈夫ですよ。
　　　　　　　　　　　　　　　（ちから）（あ）　　（いっしょ）　　　　　（だいじょうぶ）

8. 友　　：ほら、浅草の雷おこしは美味しそうだから皆で一緒に食べませんか。
　　　　　　　　（あさくさ）（かみなり）　　　　　　　　　　（いっしょ）

9. キアラ　：友さんはいつも元気そうですね。私も元気にならなきゃ。

* 関東大震災 – Great Kanto Earthquake Disaster
　（かんとうだいしんさい）

単語 New Words
（たん）

きねんび 記念日 (n) – anniversary, memorial	(お)はか (お)墓 (n) – grave, tomb	じゅんび(を)する 準備(を)する (v) – prepare (to)

漢字 Kanji

考	コウ, かんが(える), かんが(え) – consider, think about	一 十 土 耂 考 考
2 4 1 5 3 6 7	考え – thinking, thought, ideas; 思考 – thought, （かんが）　　　　　　　　　　　　（しこう） consideration; 参考 – reference, consultation 　　　　　　　　（さんこう）	
6 strokes	THINK about breaking through the soil/earth (土), then CONSIDER how the two strokes below the soil meander like roots, spreading THOUGHTS and IDEAS.	

言葉の探索 Language Detection

1. 高そうです/だ – It seems that "X" is expensive

To say that "it seems that some aspect of X is something" or "it seems that something has happened," use 〜そうです or 〜そうだ.

A) Adjectives: If you want to say that something seems to be expensive, delicious, healthy, etc., place the adjective stem before そうです or the less formal そうだ.

   1. い adjectives: for い adjectives, drop the final い (高~~い~~そうです/だ = it seems expensive).

   2. な adjectives: for な adjectives, don't change the adjective, but add そうです/だ after it (祖父は元気そうです = my grandfather seems healthy).

B) Verbs: For verbs, use the verb stem + そうです/だ (今日は暑くなり~~ます~~そうですね。= It looks like it's going to become hot today.)

A) そのレストランは安そうだ。	= That restaurant seems cheap (economical).
B) このゲームは難しそうです。	= This game seems difficult.
C) 彼女の部屋はちょっと汚そうです。	= Her room seems a little dirty.
D) あの公園は静かそうだ。	= That park seems quiet.
E) 明日雪が降りそうですね。	= Tomorrow it seems as though it will snow.
F) そのチームは強いから勝ちそうです。	= That team is strong so it seems they will win.

2. だけ – only or just, and だけではありません – is not only or not just

The particle だけ means "only." It implies that the preceding information is exclusive, or that only the specific subject and verb are eaten, wanted, studied, etc. and nothing else. だけ can be followed by the particles は, が, and を. Here are some examples of the difference between だけ and the previously learned ばかり:

　良和君は焼きそばだけ食べました。　= Yoshikazu ate only yakisoba (nothing else from all of the dishes at the table).

Here, it is implied that Yoshikazu ate nothing else from any of the other dishes, however it doesn't necessarily mean that a large quantity was eaten or that this is a pattern for Yoshikazu. In this instance, he ate only yakisoba.

　良和君は焼きそばばかり食べました。　= Yoshikazu only ate yakisoba (all of the time).

Here, it is implied that Yoshikazu eats yakisoba all of the time. In other words, he only eats yakisoba and may indeed eat more than his share.

	A) 日本語だけ勉強しました。	= I only studied Japanese. (though not necessarily a lot)
	B) 日本語ばかり勉強しました。	= I only studied Japanese. (implying that I studied it a lot and did nothing else)
	C) ピザだけ食べました。	= I only ate pizza (but not necessarily much of it).

自習 Self Check

1. そうです/そうだ

Change each statement to mean that it "seems to be…" using the そうです/そうだ pattern.

(ア) その映画は面白いです。　　(ウ) その赤ちゃんは泣きます。(泣く = crying)

(イ) 田中先生が帰ります。　　(エ) 秋田のなまはげは怖こわいです。

2. だけ

Insert だけ into each sentence, then restate it in English. The meaning may change depending c where you place だけ in the sentence.

(ア) 日本語を話す　　(ウ) 犬と一緒に散歩をする

(イ) 友子さんとデートした　　(エ) 豆腐を食べた

練習時間 Practice Time

1. **Pair Practice**

Gather at least 10 photos of famous people to use for this activity. じゃんけん to decide who will be th first interviewer. The interviewee should choose one of the famous people to "be," while the interview asks questions in Japanese and takes notes. Ask questions about what the person appears to do, likes ar dislikes, what he/she seems to be good at, about physical attributes, etc. After time is called, interviewe take turns restating the information collected; the class tries to guess the identity of the famous perso based upon the given clues.

	Clue 1: その人は絵を描くのが好きそうだ。	= That person seems to like painting.
	Clue 2: その人の一番有名な絵は波だそうだ。	= That person's most famous artwork seems to be (of) a wave.
	Clue 3: その人は江戸時代の男の人だそうだ。	= That person seemed to have been an Edo Period man.
	Answer: 広重	

2. Pair Work

In this practice, review using the pattern ですから (cause and effect). Begin by brainstorming several activities you want to do (verb たい form): for example, go horseback-riding, eat kiritanpo, fly to Brazil, go to Okinawa, get an "A" on the next test, date a movie star, etc. Write down 5-6 of your thoughts, in 日本語. Choose one idea and make a statement to your partner. Your partner will tell you something that you "must" do (〜しなければなりません) in order to accomplish your goal.

A-さん： もう暑いから、プールへ行きたいです。(It's already hot, so I want to go to the pool.)

B-さん： じゃ、水着を持って行かなければなりませんね。(Well, you have to take a swimming suit.)

文化箱 Culture Chest

防災の日 - Disaster Prevention Day

The first 防災の日 took place on September 1, 1960, a day chosen in memory of the victims of the Great Kanto Earthquake (関東大震災) of 1923, which struck on September 1 at 11:58 a.m. It happened at lunchtime, when many were cooking their meals. Gas lines broke and cooking stoves toppled, creating massive fires that caused the majority of the fatalities. To prevent similar unnecessary deaths, and to help the public prepare for the typhoons that often hit during this time of year, local governments use Disaster Preparation Day (防災の日) to organize emergency practices for firefighters, office workers, and student groups. For more recent earthquake disasters and how Japan prepared for and learned from them, research the Great Hanshin Earthquake (阪神大震災) of 1995 and the Tohoku Earthquake (東日本大震災) of 2011.

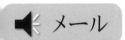

Jun's grandmother hears that Jun is going to visit her former dance teacher, Tamako 先生, so she writes to give Jun more background information and to make some requests.

Points to consider as you read:

❶ What did Jun's grandmother do in her college days?

❷ Why did she like Tamako?

❸ How did Tamako's attitude change on one specific day every year?

❹ What does she ask Jun to do?

じゅんへ

　お元気ですか。おばあちゃんは元気です。

　この前の手紙でお父さんから私が大学時代に*日本舞踊を教えていたこと、そして*社交ダンスを習っていたことを聞いたそうですね。若い時、おばあちゃんはダンスが大好きでした。日本舞踊は小さい時から習っていましたが、社交ダンスは初めてでした。日本の踊りと社交ダンスは音楽も踊りも全然違いますが、私は両方好きでした。

　たま子先生のことも聞いたそうですね。たま子先生の踊りは*上品で美しくて、私はいつかたま子先生のように踊れるようになりたい、と思っていました。たま子先生はいつも明るくて、踊ることも教えることも大好きで、とてもいい先生でした。でも、毎年関東大震災が起こった9月1日になると、とても悲しい顔をしていたのを覚えています。今でも9月1日が近づくと、毎年たま子先生のことを思い出します。たま子先生はあの地震で、ご家族をなくしました。関東大地震の*記念日にはたま子先生はきっと今でも亡くなったご家族のことを思って悲しんでいると思います。

　そこでじゅんにお願いがあります。たま子先生に黄色いお花を持って行ってもらえませんか。たま子先生は黄色が大好きで、いつもご家族の*お墓や仏壇に黄色い花を飾っていました。花を持って、たま子先生に会いに行って、元気づけてあげて下さい。

　それから、本郷に行ったら、ダンススタジオの向かい側のおにぎり屋さんに寄るといいですよ。あそこのおにぎりは本当においしいんですよ。たま子先生とよくあの店のしゃけのおにぎりを買って食べました。*懐かしいです。たま子先生にも買って行ってあげたらどうですか。じゃ、たま子先生によろしく言って下さいね。

おばあちゃんより

---

*日本舞踊 – traditional Japanese dance; 社交ダンス – social dancing; 上品 – elegant, refined; 記念日 – anniversary お墓 – grave; 懐かしい – dear, missed

中学生の時に少し習いました。

I learned a bit when I was a middle school student.

1) あ、じゅん君のおばあさんのダンス教室がありました！音楽が聞こえます。早く入りましょう！

2) ちょっと待って。音楽が止まった時に入りましょう。

3) あ、今音楽が止まったから、入ってもいいですね。

4) あら、皆さん、こんにちは。

5) 初めまして。この黄色い花は友達からの贈り物です。

6) まあ、どうもありがとう。ところで皆さんはタンゴを踊った事がある？

7) 私は中学生の時に少し習いましたが難しそうだからやめました。

8) 僕はタンゴを踊った事はありませんが、ブレイクダンスが出来ます。

9) へえ、それは聞いた事がないけど、面白そうね。

10) ダンゴを食べた事はありますが、タンゴはちょっと。。。。

11) じゅん君のおばあちゃんが嬉しそうで良かったですね。それに、たま子先生は優しそうな先生ですね。

12) 僕達は前にたま子先生に会った事がありませんか。

13) そう？私を見た事がある？

会話 Dialog

(Setting: A dance studio near the Asakusa area of Tokyo, September 1, 1960)

1.	ベン	： あ、じゅん君のおばあさんのダンス教室がありました！音楽が聞こえます。早く入りましょう！
2.	友	： ちょっと待って。音楽が止まった時に入りましょう。
3.	じゅん	： あ、今音楽が止まったから、入ってもいいですね。
4.	先生とじゅんのおばあさん	： あら、皆さん、こんにちは。
5.	じゅん	： 初めまして。この黄色い花は友達からの贈り物です。
6.	たま子	： まあ、どうもありがとう。ところで皆さんは*タンゴを踊った事がある？
7.	キアラ	： 私は中学生の時に少し習いましたが難しそうだからやめました。
8.	じゅん	： 僕はタンゴを踊った事はありませんが、ブレイクダンスが出来ます。
9.	じゅんのおばあさん	： へえ、それは聞いた事がないけど、面白そうね。
10.	友	： ダンゴを食べた事はありますが、タンゴはちょっと…
11.	キアラ	： じゅん君のおばあちゃんが嬉しそうで良かったですね。それに、たま子先生は優しそうな先生ですね。
12.	ベン	： (Staring at たま子)　僕達は前にたま子先生に会った事がありませんか。
13.	たま子	： そう？私を見た事がある？

* タンゴ – tango (dance from Argentina)

単語 New Words

おくりもの　贈り物 (n) – gift

言葉の探索 Language Detection

〜時 – at the time of ~ or when ~

To say "X happened when . . ." or "I did X when . . .," use either a noun + の or the plain/plain-past form of a verb + 時. Because this is used for a specific time, you <u>may</u> use the particle に after 時.

noun:	昼ご飯 ＋ の ＋ 時 (に)	= At lunchtime...
plain verb:	昼ご飯を食べる ＋ 時 (に)	= While eating lunch...
plain-past verb:	昼ご飯を食べた時 (に)〜	= When I ate lunch...
present progressive:	昼ご飯を食べている時に〜	= While eating lunch...

A) パリに行った時にエッフェル塔に上った。
= When I went to Paris, I climbed up the Eiffel Tower.

B) 東京タワーを上った時に、写真をたくさん撮りました。
= When I climbed Tokyo Tower, I took a lot of pictures.

C) 車を運転している時に携帯電話を使わないで下さい。
= When driving a car, please don't use a cellular phone.

自習 Self Check

State something that happens (or happened) when you …

 study Japanese ⇒ 日本語を勉強する時に、よくインターネットを使います。

ア) go to school   (ウ) eat a lot of fish   (オ) ride a subway

イ) help around the house   (エ) see a famous painting   (カ) write a letter

練習時間 Practice Time

Small Group Activity

〜の時に link game

Divide into groups of 3-4 and decide who goes first. The first player makes a statement using the 〜の時に pattern, such as 食べる時に、お箸を使います. The second person must make a 〜の時に statement using the 2nd half of the first statement, such as お箸を使う時(に)は、たくさん食べられません. The third person continues, and so on. See how long your group can continue to link sentences, or until your 先生 calls out 時間です.

文化箱 Culture Chest

Dance-mania

The 1996 Japanese version of "Shall We Dance" was a huge success in Japan, winning 14 Japanese Academy Awards that year. The movie revolves around Shohei Sugiyama, a depressed businessman, whose life takes a turn for the better when he begins ballroom dancing lessons. The movie sparked a resurgence of interest in all forms of dancing in Japan. Ballroom dancing contests aired on television, and children rushed to sign up for ballet classes. Studios that teach Latin dances such as flamenco and tango were fully booked.

The popularity of dancing is just one aspect of the Japanese passion for lifelong learning. Among students, many attend 塾. As for adults, many attend classes to learn traditional Japanese arts, activities that are usually classified as "hobbies": 生け花, 書道, 空手, or 日本舞踊. Some of these grant licenses or certificates. Earning a certificate in your chosen passion is a point of pride for many Japanese.

🔊 メール

This message is from Jun, telling his grandmother about his meeting with Tamako.
Points to consider as you read:

❶ What did Jun learn from his father's letter about his grandmother's past?
❷ State two things Tamako 先生 told Jun about his grandmother.
❸ What did Jun, Kiara, and Ben try to do with Tamako?
❹ What does Jun want to do the next time he sees his grandmother?

おばあちゃんへ

　おばあちゃん、元気ですか。僕は元気で学校に行っています。この前お父さんから手紙をもらうまで、おばあちゃんが昔踊りを教えていたことを知りませんでした。お父さんが送ってくれたおばあちゃんの写真、大切にしますね。この写真のおばあちゃんはとてもきれいです。

　さて、9月1日にたま子先生の教室に行って来ましたよ。おばあちゃんに頼まれた黄色い花を持って行ったら、とても喜んでくれました。そしておばあちゃんのことを色々話してくれました。たま子先生はおばあちゃんの踊りを見たとき、*才能があると思ったそうです。おばあちゃんは教えるのも上手で、生徒さんは皆おばあちゃんのことが大好きだったそうですね。そして、社交ダンスもすぐに上手になったそうです。

　たま子先生は僕達に日本の踊りを教えてくれたんですよ。僕は日本の踊りは小さい時に盆踊りをしただけですし、キアラとベンはもちろん日本の踊りは初めてでした。難しかったけど、皆で踊ったら楽しかったです。たま子先生はとてもいい先生ですね。今まで僕はブレイクダンスしかしたことがなかったけど、色々なダンスを習ってみたくなりました。

　教室を出る時、おじいちゃんと*すれ違った感じがしました。ダンスをするおばあちゃんを見に来ていたんでしょうね。

　今度おばあちゃんに会ったら、僕と一緒にダンスをして下さい。おばあちゃんと一緒に踊ってみたいです。

　では、体に気をつけて。元気でね。

じゅんより

---

*才能がある – have an aptitude for, a genius for; すれ違った感じがしました – felt like something passed by

自然災害を止める事は無理です。
しぜんさいがい　　　　　　　　むり

It is expecting too much to try to stop natural disasters.

1) 世界には色々な災害がありますね。火山の噴火、神戸やハイチの地震、インド洋の津波、ハリケーンカトリーナもひどかったですね。

2) それにアメリカにはトルネードも来ます。自然災害を止める事は無理です。

3) トルネードと台風は地震より早く知る事が出来ますね。テレビやラジオのニュースを聞いたり、ニュースを見たりして、安全な所に行く時間があります。

4) 日本の家の屋根は重いから、台風の時に飛びません。でも地震が来た時は困ります。最近の屋根は強くて軽いそうです。

5) ところで、なまずは地震が来る時を知っているよ。

6) うそ！

7) それ僕も聞いた事がありますよ。

8) 私はおじいさんとよくなまずを釣りに行きました。フライにして食べれば美味しいですよ。

会話 Dialog
かい

(Setting: Tokyo; the group is talking about various types of disasters)

1. じゅん ： 世界には色々な災害がありますね。火山の噴火、神戸や*ハイチの地震、インド
   洋の津波、ハリケーン・カトリーナもひどかったですね。

2. キアラ ： それにアメリカにはトルネードも来ます。自然災害を止める事は無理です。

3. 友 ： トルネードと台風は地震より早く知る事が出来ますね。テレビやラジオのニュースを
   聞いたり、ニュースを見たりして、安全な所に行く時間があります。

4. ベン ： 日本の家の屋根は重いから、台風の時に飛びません。でも地震が来た時は困
   ります。最近の屋根は強くて軽いそうです。

5. 友 ： ところで、*なまずは地震が来る時を知っているよ。

6. キアラ ： うそ！

7. じゅん ： それ僕も聞いた事がありますよ。

8. キアラ ： 私はおじいさんとよくなまずを釣りに行きました。フライにして食べれば美味しいです
   よ。

*ハイチ – Haiti (country of); なまず – freshwater catfish

単語 New Words
たん

あんぜん 安全 (n) – safe
ところ 所 (n) – place, location, spot
やね 屋根 (n) – roof
かるい 軽い (い adj.) – light (weight)

おもい 重い (い adj.) – heavy (weight)
こまる 困る (v) – have trouble (to); be in difficulty
とまる 止まる (v) – stop (to), halt (to)
とめる 止める (v) – stop (something or someone) (to), turn off (to)

漢字 Kanji

困	コン, こま(る) – become distressed, annoyed	一 冂 冂 用 困 困
	困る – to be troubled, worried, or distressed こま	困
7 strokes	This tree (木) has outgrown its container (口) and has the gardener in a state of DISTRESS, WORRIED, and ANNOYED because it's reached its limits.	

言葉の探索 Language Detection

1. Enriching your language

When communicating in Japanese, make every effort to enrich your sentences. You can do this by adding details, such as adjectives and adverbs, and utilizing more complicated sentence patterns. For example, here are two ways to improve and expand the sentence "僕は生徒だ".

⇨ 僕は北高校の三年生です。

⇨ 僕は浅草にある北高校の三年生で、来年、東京大学で数学を勉強するつもりです。

2. Do things like this and that –or– sometimes this and that =〜たり〜たりする

When you want to list two or more two actions in a single sentence, use the _____ + たり (verb stem 1) _____ + たりする (verb stem 2) pattern. The tense of the entire sentence is determined by the final verb ending. This pattern is used when listing several actions, and when presumably several other actions also occur/have occurred. It is possible to make extremely long sentences with this pattern.

お寿司を食べたり、お茶を飲んだり、友達と話したりしました。
dict verb stem + たり　　dict verb stem + たり　　dict verb stem + たり + present/past of します
= I ate sushi, drank green tea, and talked with friends.

EXAMPLE

A) 昨日、ラジオを聞いたり、インターネットで遊んだりしました。
= Yesterday, I did things like listen to the radio and play on the Internet.

B) 友達とパリへ行った時に、私達は美味しい料理を食べたり、セーヌ川を散歩したりしました。
= When my friend and I went to Paris, we did things like eat delicious food and walk along the Seine River.

C) 家に帰ると、妹が宿題をしたり、母が新聞を読んだり、父がテレビを見たりしていました。
= When I returned home, (my family was doing things like) my little sister was doing homework, my mother was reading the newspaper, and my father was watching TV.

自習 Self Check

1. Enriching your language

Make as many statements as you can about this image. Use as many adjectives and adverbs as you can in your descriptions.

EXAMPLE

ちょっと暑いけど、友弘さんは公園できれいな絵を描いています。

(Though it's a little hot, Tomohiro is painting a pretty picture in the park.)

2. Combining actions

「〜たり〜たりする/した」を使って、文書 (sentences) を作って下さい。

例
れい
EXAMPLE
読む, 見る：私は本を読んだり、テレビを見たりします。
(I do things like read books and watch TV.)

（ア）ドアを開けた　　　窓を閉めた
　　　　　あ　　　　　　まど　し
（イ）休んだ　　　　　　テレビを見た
（ウ）バスに乗った　　　見物をした (sightseeing)
　　　　　　　　　　　　けんぶつ

練習時間 Practice Time
れん しゅう

Pair Practice

Prepare, or use prepared images with people doing a variety of activities. Take turns with a partner describing what people are doing and guessing which person the other is talking about.

例
れい
EXAMPLE
A-さん：チェンさんはお母さんを手伝っています。
= Chen is helping his mother.
B-さん：チェンさんは母を手伝ったり、テレビを見たりしています。
= Chen is helping his mother and watching TV.

文化箱 Culture Chest
ぶん か ばこ

地震となまず – Earthquakes and Namazu
じ しん

Many people believe that animals are extraordinarily sensitive to movements deep under the earth'
crust. In Japan, the なまず (catfish) have long been associated with earthquakes. In one myth, a giant な
まず living in the mud below the earth liked to play tricks. When it moved its tail, the earth would shake
Thus, なまず came to symbolize "disorder," in particular, the kind of disorder caused by earthquakes. Af
ter one large earthquake in 1855, なまず絵 flooded the market. So convincing was the theory that catfish
え
and other deep-water fish, were especially sensitive to earth tremors that the Tokyo Metropolitan Govern
ment sponsored a study on that topic that ended inconclusively, in 2004. Nonetheless, the belief contin
ues. After a series of large earthquakes in Haiti and Chile in 2010, nearly two dozen specimens of the rar
giant oarfish called 竜宮の使い washed up on the shores of Northern Japan or were caught in nets
りゅうぐう
This heightened fears that another large quake may strike Japan soon as well. Another catfish connectio
is through the Imperial Family. Prince Akishino, second in line to the Chrysanthemum throne, is a well
known "catfish specialist."

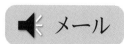 **メール**

Andeica, Ben's friend from Indonesia who is studying earthquake early warning systems at a university near Osaka, writes to Ben about various kinds of disasters.

Points to consider as you read:

❶ What language does the word "tsunami" come from?

❷ What surprised Andeica about the aftermath of the 1995 Kobe earthquake?

❸ Why is Andeica studying disaster early warning systems? What is his long-term dream?

ベンへ

　*久しぶりだね。ベンはまだ東京にいると思うけど、元気かい。今僕は関西外国語大学（関西外大）で地震を*予知するための技術を研究している。僕はこの研究に情熱を持っている。

　僕の国、インドネシアで、2004年に大きい津波があったのを覚えていると思う。あの津波は本当にひどかった。でもあの後、津波を予測し、人々を*避難させるシステムが進んだようだ。日本でも津波は大きな自然災害だよね。ところで、僕は昔、津波という言葉が日本語だということを知らなかった。日本語のクラスで"津"は英語のbayで、波は英語のwaveだと習って、初めて津波の意味を知った。

　日本の自然ん*災害と言えば、火山の噴火もあるね。日本は火山が多いからね。富士山も1707年から1708年まで噴火が続いたそうだね。最近では1991年には雲仙の噴火で大勢が避難したし、今でも鹿児島の桜島は有名な火山だよね。

　日本は火山が多いから地震も多い。1923年の関東大*震災では東京も横浜も*破壊された。1995年の阪神・淡路大震災の時、僕は日本にいたんだ。その時はもう関西外大に留学していた。あの地震の時、現代的な新しいビルが壊れて、伝統的な木造の建物が残っていたのには驚いた。一番記憶に新しいのは、2011年の3月に起こった、東日本大震災だね。地震の直後に大津波に襲われて、三陸海岸は大きな被害を受けた。地震だけじゃなくて、津波で町が飲み込まれ、多くの人が亡くなった。

　日本には台風もよく来るよね。台風のニュースを聞くと、おじから聞いた伊勢湾台風の話を思い出す。1959年に起こった伊勢湾台風では、5000人近くの人がなくなったんだよね。その時、おじは日本に住んでいて、日本からインドネシアに帰って来たおじからその台風の話を聞いたんだ。

毎年世界のどこかで大きな自然災害が起きている。地震予知の研究をして、少しでも自然
災害の被害を小さくすることが僕の夢だ。
　　では、また。

アンディカより

*久しぶり – it's been a while/long time since I saw you; 予知する – to predict, know beforehand; 避難される – to be criti-
cized; 災害 – calamity, disaster; 震災 – earthquake disaster; 破壊された – caused destruction, disruption

災害に対する知識があれば、怖くないよ。

There is no need to be fearful, you know, if you are very familiar with natural disasters.

1)「皆さん、こんにちは！『防災ビデオ』の時間です。NHKの前からの放送です。」

2) さて、僕達が自然災害について学んだ事をお伝えします。

3) 地震が来た時は早くテーブルの下に隠れなければならないよ。テーブルがない時は座布団や大きい本を頭の上に。それからドアや窓を少し開けて下さい。

4) 料理をしている時はすぐに火を消しましょう。

5) 電気が止まった時はけいたいラジオでニュースを聞きましょう。

6) 水、食べ物、懐中電灯、ライター、服をいつも家に用意しておくといいよ。

7) 津波の時は家より遠く高い所へ行こう。

8) 台風が来る前に窓ガラスはフィルムでガードしよう。外に出てはだめ。

9) 災害はよく知ってしまえば、怖くないよ。よく準備をしてね。皆さんも気をつけてね。

会話 Dialog

(Setting: Outside the NHK building in Tokyo, 1960)

1. キアラ ：「皆さん、こんにちは！『防災ビデオ』の時間です。NHKの前からの放送です。」

2. ベン ：さて、僕達が自然災害について学んだ事をお伝えします。

3. じゅん ：地震が来た時は早くテーブルの下に入らなければならないよ。テーブルがない時は座布団や大きい本を頭の上に。それからドアや窓を少し開けて下さい。

4. 友 ：料理をしている時はすぐに火を消しましょう。

5. キアラ ：電気が止まった時はけいたいラジオでニュースを聞きましょう。

6. 友 ：水、食べ物、*懐中電灯、ライター、服をいつも家に用意しておくといいよ。

7. ベン ：津波の時は家より遠く高い所へ行こう。

8. キアラ ：台風が来る前に窓ガラスはフィルムでガードしよう。外に出てはだめ。

9. じゅん ：災害はよく知ってしまえば、怖くないよ。よく準備をしてね。皆さんも気をつけてね。

* 懐中電灯 – flashlight

単語 New Words

NHK (*n*) – Japan Broadcasting Corporation (TV network: 日本放送協会)

ガラス (*n*) – glass

テーブル (*n*) – table

フイルム (*n*) – film (coating)

ぼうさい 防災 (*n*) – disaster prevention

マラソン (*n*) – marathon

ガードする (*v*) – guard (to), protect (to)

はしる 走る (*v*) – run (to)

まなぶ 学ぶ (*v*) – study (in depth) (to), learn (to) or take lessons in

漢字 Kanji

走 7 strokes	ソウ, はし(る) – run	一	十	土	ヰ	ヰ	走
	走る – run; 走り書き – scribbling	走					
	Earth or soil (土) is on top of a leg/foot (足). When RUNNING, you cover a lot of ground with your feet.						

言葉の探索 Language Detection

Finish doing (unexpectedly early or accidentally with some regret) = Verb て-form + しまう/しまった/しまいました

To state that you have completely finished doing something, use the 〜してしまう/しまった pattern. This auxiliary verb pattern follows the て-form of an action verb to show that the action has completely finished.

_____ + しまう/しまった/しまいました
<small>て form of verb</small>

A) 七時十分までに、朝ご飯を食べてしまいました。　= I had eaten breakfast all up by 7:10.

B) アメリカ史の作文は午後11時前に書いてしまいました。
= I completely finished writing my American history essay by 11:00 p.m.

C) 真理子さんは前、スペイン語を勉強したが、今はもう忘れてしまった。
= Mariko had studied Spanish before, but now she's completely forgotten it.

D) 私は二日でその厚い本を読んでしまった。　= I finished reading that thick book in two days.

自習 Self Check

How would you fill in the blanks in the chart below using the 〜しまう/しまった pattern? Write full sentences in the second column.

Dictionary form	〜てしまいました	英語
予約する		
	(昼ご飯を) 食べてしまいました	
		I already introduced myself
歩いて行く		
	(ゲームを) 終えてしまいました	

練習時間 Practice Time

Pair Practice

You will accomplish many things by the time you reach the advanced age of 100. Take turns telling each other what you want to accomplish by that age. Take notes and be prepared to share some of your partner's goals with the class. Continue until your teacher tells you to stop.

百歳になる前に漢字を全部習ってしまいたいんです。

(Before I become 100 years old, I want to learn all of the kanji.)

そうですか。僕は百歳になる前に日本の料理をマスターしてしまいたいんです。
(Before I become 100 years old, I want to master Japanese cooking.)

文化箱 Culture Chest

NHK Broadcasting Corporation

NHK, or 日本放送協会, is called the Japan National Broadcasting Corporation in English. Its first radio broadcast aired in 1925, a year and a half after the Great Kanto Earthquake. NHK began television broadcasting in 1950, and today, NHK is heard and seen around the world in a number of formats (satellite, digital, shortwave, online). In addition to news, weather, sports, music (the annual New Year's Eve singing competition, 紅白歌合戦), dramas (the long-running 大河ドラマ), and educational programming, NHK is required to broadcast emergency warnings. Today's technology allows NHK to broadcast announcements of earthquakes within 2-3 minutes of the first vibration.

🔊 メール

Tomo writes to his children Takehiro and Hanako (who live in the year 2050) about his time-travelling companions.

Points to consider as you read:

❶ According to Tomo, why has time travelling been especially interesting for Ben?

❷ What would Tomo like to do once this trip is finished?

❸ List a few of Tomo's favorite noodle varieties.

竹広と花子へ

　元気か？竹広も花子もいい子にしているか。毎日ちゃんと忘れないで宿題もしているか。

　パパはまだ*過去の旅を続けている。この旅はパパにとって特別な旅だ。過去を旅することができることは、それだけでもドキドキすることがたくさんある。それに、一緒に旅行している*仲間はとてもいい人達なんだ。日本人は高校生のじゅんだけだ。ベンはオーストラリア人で、お母さんが日本のオーストラリア大使館で働いているので、家族と東京に住んでいる。ベンは歴史が大好きだから、このタイムトラベルは彼にとって最高の旅だ。キアラはシカゴ

出身のアフリカ系アメリカ人で日本に留学している。美術が得意で新しい人と会うのが大好きな積極的な女の子だ。毎日一緒にいろいろな*体験をして、僕達はいい仲間になった。この旅が終わっても、この仲間のことは決して忘れないと思う。*将来またいつかみんなで会えるといいと思っている。

さて、パパがヌードルが大好きなことは知っていると思うが、昔の日本の食べ物で食べてみたい麺類がたくさんあった。ラーメン、ざるそば、うどん、そうめん、焼きそばなど日本にはいろいろな麺類がある。冷たいものも温かいものもあるし、スープがあるものもないものもある。この旅行している間にほとんどのヌードルを食べてみることができた。日本のヌードルは最高だよ。

じゃ、パパが帰るまでママの言うことをよく聞いて、いい子にしているんだよ。

パパより

---

*過去 – the past, bygone days; 仲間 – circle of friends, group, partner; 体験 – experience; 将来 – in the future

Rising up from Tragedy and Moving Forward

In Hiroshima, 1958, at the unveiling of the Children's Memorial in the Hiroshima Peace Park, our group of travelers meets a friend of Sadako Sasaki, the young girl whose death from leukemia inspired the creation of the statue.

About this Chapter

Chapters 9 and 10 have been designed to offer practice and review for listening, speaking, reading, and writing skills. Consequently, the focus is on experiencing and producing Japanese. New vocabulary, kanji, and Language Detection points have been deliberately kept to a minimum.

Learning and Performance Goals

This chapter will enable you to:

- learn more about using 〜と言いました; 〜と思います; 〜と聞きました – He/She said…; I think…; I heard…
- have a clearer understanding of women's speech, specifically the use of the sentence-ending particle わ
- review the use of 〜＿＿＿＿＿(verb stem) + 方 = way of doing ~
- use (Aの) 為(に) – for the sake of A -or- because of A
  ため
- learn basic information about Sadako Sasaki, her home, Hiroshima and the surrounding region, as well as regional differences in okonomiyaki
- use 3 additional kanji

第9課の1

禎子さんと千羽鶴の話を聞いた事がある でしょう？

さだこ　　　　　せんばづる

You've heard the story of Sadako and the 1,000 cranes, right?

1) 1958年5月5日の広島市に来ましたよ。皆さん、急いで。式が始まってしまいますよ。

2) 5月5日は子供の日ですね。でも何の式？

3) 早く！

4) 僕達はいつも食べたり寝たりどこかに行ったりしていますね。今日は休日だからゆっくり休めば。。。。

5) あそこは平和公園ですね。人がたくさんいてスピーチをしたり歌を歌ったりしていますね。あっ！あれは「原爆の子」の像ですよ。禎子さんと千鶴子の話を聞いた事があるでしょう？

6) はい、もちろん。千羽鶴は世界平和のシンボルですよ。早く！橋を渡って右に曲がれば式が見られますよ。

7) あれ？あの女の子は橋本千鶴子さんですよ。禎子さんの友達です。千鶴子さんとたくさんの小・中・高生がお金を集めて像を建てました。海外の人達もお金を送ってくれました。

8) 私達はいつまでも禎子さんのことを覚えておかなければなりません。

会話 Dialog

(Setting: The group leaves 1960 Tokyo to travel two years back in time, to Hiroshima in the spring of 1958.)

1. 友　　：1958年5月5日の広島市に来ましたよ。皆さん、急いで。式が始まってしまいますよ。

2. ベン　：5月5日は子供の日ですね。でも何の式？

3. 友　　：早く！

4. じゅん：僕達はいつも食べたり寝たりどこかに行ったりしていますね。今日は休日だからゆっくり休めば…

5. ベン　：あそこは平和公園ですね。人がたくさんいてスピーチをしたり歌を歌ったりしていますね。あっ！あれは「原爆の子」の像ですよ。禎子さんと千鶴子の話を聞いた事があるでしょう？

6. キアラ：はい、もちろん。千羽鶴は世界平和のシンボルですよ。早く！橋を渡って右に曲がれば式が見られますよ。

7. じゅん：あれ？あの女の子は橋本千鶴子さんですよ。禎子さんの友達です。千鶴子さんとたくさんの小・中・高生がお金を集めて像を建てました。海外の人達もお金を送ってくれました。

8. 友　　：私達はいつまでも禎子さんのことを覚えておかなければなりません。

単語 New Words

かいがい　海外 (n) – foreign, overseas
かんがえ　考え (n) – an idea
こどものひ　子供の日 (n) – Children's Day (holiday)
しき　式 (n) – ceremony, rite
へいわ　平和 (n) – peace
ぞう　像 (n) – statue, figure

いそぐ　急ぐ (v) – hurry (to)
おもう　思う (v) – think (to)
おぼえる　覚える (v) – remember (to), memorize (to)
たてる　建てる (v) – build (to)
かんがえる　考える (v) – think (to), consider (to)
きく　聞く (v) – ask (to); listen (to)

漢字 Kanji

覚	カク, おぼ(える), さ(ます), さ(める) – memorize, learn, remember	`	⸏	⸏⸏	⸏⸏⸏	⸏⸏	⸏⸏
	覚え – memory; 覚える – to remember/memorize; 覚ます – to awaken	覚	覚	覚	覚	覚	覚
12 strokes	This kanji has three bits of knowledge pouring again and again into your head, helping you to see (見) more clearly and easily MEMORIZE something.						

式 6 strokes	シキ – style, ceremony, rite	一	二	于	三	式	式
	方式 – form, method; 入学式 – school entrance ceremony; 卒業式 – graduation ceremony						
	This kanji resembles a stage. It takes at least three people (the three strokes of 弋) to construct (工) a stage for a CEREMONY.						

急 9 strokes	キュウ, いそ(ぐ), いそ(ぎ) – hurry, emergency, sudden	ノ	⺈	刍	刍	刍	刍
	急ぐ – to hurry, to rush; 急ぎ – haste, hurry, speed; 救急車 – ambulance; 急行 – express (train)	急	急	急			
	Your heart (心) speeds up when you SUDDENLY have to HURRY and put a cap (the first two strokes) on top of Yo's (ヨ) head.						

文化箱 Culture Chest

広島

The city of 広島 is located in the southwestern end of the main island of 本州 on the 日本海. 広島市 was founded in 1589 by a local warlord who lost control of the castle town to the Asano Clan, supporters of the Tokugawa family. During the 明治時代, 広島's harbor was widened and railroads lines were built to link it to other major cities. This contributed to its rapid industrialization and modernization.

During the first Sino-Japanese War (1894–1895), the Japanese government temporarily moved its headquarters to 広島城 and held peace talks there. During WWII, 広島 was the location of the Second Army and Chugoku Regional Army headquarters as well as a major munitions depot. Due to many factors including its size, location, and the weather events of the day, at 8:15 a.m. on 6 August 1945, the world's first atomic bomb exploded over the city. Some estimates say that 70% of the city was de-

stroyed, and around 30% of the population (80,000 people) were killed immediately; many more died later from various injuries and illnesses related to the radiation. The Prefectural Industrial Promotion Hall, one of the few structures close to the epicenter of the bomb to remain standing, is now known as the 原爆ドーム. It is now part of the 広島平和記念公園. As was the case with other cities after the war, Hiroshima was reconstructed, and today is known internationally as a center for promoting peace.

地図 Map Skills

Do some research to find out what Hiroshima looked like in the early 1940s and what it looks like now. Also look at the 広島平和記念資料館 for more information.

◀ メール

This message is from Kiara's uncle, who teaches Japanese in Seattle. Points to consider as you read:

❶ What did Kiara's uncle say about the statue?

❷ What was the gift to Seattle?

❸ What will Kiara's uncle and aunt do before they next visit Japan?

キアラへ

　キアラ、おじさんだよ。元気にしていますか？「原爆の子の像」の完成式に行ったそうだね。どうだったかい？

　その式があったのは、ちょうどおばさんが日本に住んでいた頃だ。だから、キアラがその頃の日本を見られておばさんはすごく喜んでいるよ。

　「原爆の子の像」は、ここシアトルにとっても、とても大切なものなんだ。禎子さんが亡くなって、平和の為に「原爆の子の像」を建てる運動が始まった。この運動は日本だけでなく、海外へも広がったんだ。禎子さんは病気の*回復を願って千羽鶴を折った。だから、皆も平和を願って千羽鶴を折った。世界中の人が千羽鶴を広島へ送ったんだ。シアトルの人達も沢山の千羽鶴を送ったよ。

　この像が完成したのが1958年。その1年前に、シアトルと神戸市は*姉妹都市になったんだ。その時に、神戸から桜の木がシアトルにプレゼントされたんだ。

　今度おじさんとおばさんは日本に行くつもりだよ。キアラに会ったり、シアトルの姉妹都市の神戸を見たり、広島で「原爆の子の像」や原爆ドームを見学したりする予定だよ。だから、おばさんと一緒に今から鶴を1000羽折っておこうと思ってるよ。

　日本で会う時まで元気で。しっかり勉強するんだぞ。

おじさんより

---

* 回復を願う – to hope for (ask for) recovery (from an illness); 姉妹都市 – sister city

他の人の気持ちを考える事は難しいと思います。
（ほか）

I think it is difficult for us to consider the feelings of others.

1) 私、千鶴子。よろしくね。今日の式をどう思った？

2) 千鶴子さん、初めまして。式は素晴らしいと思いました。

3) でも、ちょっとお腹がすいたね。美味しいお好み焼き屋はこの道をまっすぐ行って右側にあるよ。行こう。

4) やった！広島のお好み焼きは大阪のより美味しいと思います。

5) 私はずっと原爆の事を考えています。どうして原爆を使わなければなかったのでしょう？

6) 外国人は戦争を早く終わらせたかったから、原爆を使ったと思うの。でもはっきりは知らないわ。

7) でも原爆で二十五万人が死んでしまいました。それはひどいと思います。

8) 他の人の気持ちを考える事は難しいと思いますね。

9) そうね。もう戦争で原爆や核兵器を使わないでほしい。「核兵器は作らない、持たない、持ちこませない。」

10) それは広島の友達から聞いた事があります。

11) 世界が早く平和になるといいですね。

会話 Dialog

(Setting: The group meets Sadako's friend Chizuko and goes with her to a restaurant. Along the way, they reflect on the events that occurred at Hiroshima and their hopes for the future.)

1. 千鶴子 ：私、千鶴子。よろしくね。今日の式をどう思った？

2. じゅん ：千鶴子さん、初はじめまして。式は素晴らしいと思いました。

3. 千鶴子 ：でも、ちょっとお腹がすいたね。美味しいお好み焼き屋はこの道をまっすぐ行って右側にあるよ。行こう。

4. 友 ：やった！広島のお好み焼きは大阪のより美味しいと思います。

5. キアラ ：私はずっと原爆の事を考えています。どうして原爆を使わなければなかったのでしょう？

6. 千鶴子 ：外国人は戦争を早く終わらせたかったから、原爆を使ったと思うの。でもはっきりは知らないわ。

7. ベン ：でも原爆で二十五万人が死んでしまいました。それはひどいと思います。

8. 友 ：他の人の気持ちを考える事は難しいと思いますね。

9. 千鶴子 ：そうね。もう戦争で原爆や*核兵器を使わないでほしい。「核兵器は作らない、持たない、持ちこませない。」

10. ベン ：それは広島の友達から聞いた事があります。

11. じゅん ：世界が早く平和になるといいですね。

* 核兵器 – nuclear weapons

単語 New Words

いけん 意見 (n) – opinion, view
せんそう 戦争 (n) – war

たいせつ 大切 (な adj.) – important, valuable
おく 置く (v) – put (to), place (to)

言葉の探索 Language Detection

1. **He/She said...; I think...; I heard... = 〜と言いました; 〜と思います; 〜と聞きました**
   You learned the pattern: ベン君は「…」と、言いました – Ben said "…" in *Beginning Japanese*. This pattern can be expanded to say what one thinks/believes (〜と思う), or what one has heard (〜と聞きました). When using 〜と思います (present or past tense) or 〜と聞きました (past tense only), be sure to use the dictionary form of the verb for the clause that precedes this pattern. When using adjective

with と思う, な adjectives are followed by the plain form of the copula (だ), before the particle と, while い adjectives are not. Verbs preceding the particle と use the plain/dictionary form.

例 EXAMPLE

A) 明日秋葉原で買い物をすると思う。 = Tomorrow I/he/she will go shopping at Akihabara I think.

B) 明日秋葉原で買い物をすると聞きました。 = I heard that tomorrow he/she/they will go shopping at Akihabara.

C) ベン君は歴史が好き*だと思います。 = I think Ben likes history.

D) ベン君は歴史が好き*だと聞きました。 = I hear Ben likes history.

E) そのクラスは本当に楽しいと思います。 = I think that class is really interesting.

F) そのクラスは本当に楽しいと聞いたよ。 = I hear that class is really interesting.

G) その映画はちょっとつまらないと思います。 = I think that movie is a little boring.

H) 広島風のお好み焼きの方が美味しいと聞きました。 = I heard that Hiroshima style okonomi-yaki is more delicious.

NOTE This pattern takes だ after な adjectives and nouns.

2. Woman's speech

Language is constantly changing, reflecting the people and times in which it is spoken. In the dialog above, notice that 千鶴子, a girl in the 1950s, ends her third line with わ. This is an example of this sort of linguistic change. Younger women in contemporary Japan do not use it as much, but the sentence-ending particle わ is still used occasionally by women today to soften the impact of a sentence that might seem too forward for the occasion. In other cases, わ at the end of a sentence might also express a level of intimacy or informality. In the dialog above, 千鶴子 says:

外国人は戦争を早く終わらせたかったから、原爆を使ったと思うの。でも はっきりは知らないわ。

= Foreigners wanted to end the war quickly, so they used the nuclear bomb, I think. But I don't really know.

You will learn more about differences between male and female speech in *Advanced Japanese*.

自習 Self Check

Restate the following in Japanese.

ア) Ben said, "I will go to Hokkaido."

イ) Mom said, "Clean your room."

ウ) I think it will rain tomorrow.

（エ) I think Emiko will come late.

（オ) I heard that we will eat sushi tomorrow.

（カ) I heard that he sings well.

Listening Practice

If you do not know about the story of Sadako and 1,000 Cranes, find a copy of it to read either in printed text or online.

文化箱 Culture Chest
ぶん か ばこ

1. 千羽鶴
せん ば づる

You may have read Sadako's story in the book "Sadako and 1,000 Cranes" by Eleanor Coerr, when you were younger. The book is based on the true story of 佐々木禎子. Only two years old when the atomic bomb was dropped on her home in Hiroshima, 禎子 was 11 when she was diagnosed with leukemia caused by radiation and hospitalized. Her best friend 千鶴子 brought an origami crane into her hospital room and told 禎子 a story. In traditional Japan, it was said that if one folded 1,000 paper cranes, one's wishes would come true. For centuries, Japanese have folded 1,000 paper cranes to wish the recipient good luck (at a wedding) or longevity (to a newborn baby).

禎子 died in 1955, but her story touched the hearts of people around the world, and origami cranes and monetary donations poured in toward building a monument to 禎子 and the other children who suffered. It was at the dedication ceremony for this monument that our travelers met 千鶴子. The 千羽鶴 have become intimately linked to 禎子 and the Peace Memorial in Hiroshima. Visit the Hiroshima Peace Memorial Park to see the monument dedicated to 禎子 and her strength, and to gaze upon the millions of origami cranes sent from all over the world. At the foot of the monument is the inscription:

これは僕らの叫びです　これは私たちの祈りです　世界に平和を築く為の。

How would you translate this phrase into English?*

叫び – cry, call out
さけ
祈り – pray, prayer
いの
築く – to build
きず

*translation: "This is our cry, this is our prayer, that we work to build peace in the world."

2. You might already know how to fold a paper crane. For this exercise, go online and look for an origami shape that you have never tried folding before, and learn how to make it. Do your best origami folding, and be prepared to teach your classmates how to make your new shape.

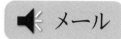 **メール**

This message is again from Kiara's uncle, who teaches Japanese in Seattle.
Points to consider as you read:

❶ Why does Kiara's uncle think it is important to travel with students to Japan?
❷ What does Kiara'a uncle think is one method useful to helping students understand other cultures?
❸ Near the end of this message, what does her uncle ask Kiara to help him with?

キアラへ

　　キアラ、メールをありがとう。世界の国々は違う*意見を持っていると思う。*戦争についての意見もばらばらだと思うよ。でも、皆で*協力したり、*理解し合ったり、どうやって*地球を平和にして行くかを考えたりすることはとても大切だと思うんだ。

　　だから、日本語のクラスの生徒達を日本に連れて行くことは大切な事だと考えているんだよ。違う国や文化を訪ねたり、そこで友達を作ったりすれば、お互いをより理解できるようになるからね。

　　それには、外国語を勉強することがとても重要なことだと思うんだ。そうすれば、自分の国だけでなく、世界の他の国のことを良く理解出来るからね。

　　そうだ、キアラ。今年の夏、おじさんが日本に生徒を連れて行く時、どこに行ったらいいと思う？広島に美味しいお好み焼き屋さんがあると聞いたけど、他にどこか面白いところがあったら教えてくれないか。

じゃ、また。おじさんより

協力する – to cooperate; 理解 – to grasp, understand, comprehend; 地球 – the globe, the earth

お好み焼きの作り方は分かりますか。
Do you know how to make okonomiyaki?

1) お好み焼きの店に着きました。平和公園への戻り方は覚えていますか。

2) はい、覚えています。

3) いらっしゃいませ。お好み焼きの作り方は分かりますか？

4) 私は分かるけど、キアラさんとベン君は？

5) 私は自分で作った事がないから教えて下さい。

6) 始めに豚肉とキャベツを焼きます。次に焼きそばを入れて下さい。それから小麦粉と卵と水のミックスを入れます。そして三分ぐらい待って裏返します。食べる時にソースとかつおぶしをかけて下さい。

7) ご注文は？

8) 私はお腹がペコペコです。

9) 私はイカと豚肉とチーズにします。焼きそばじゃなくうどんを下さい。

10) 美味しそうですね。僕も同じで。あ、でもイカじゃなくてタコにします。

11) キアラさんもベン君も箸の持ち方が上手ですね。

12) 待っている間にお茶を入れておきましょう。

13) 友さん、もうお好み焼き、五枚目ですよ！

会話 Dialog
かい

(Setting: Chizuko and the group enter a popular okonomiyaki restaurant.)

1. 千鶴子　　：お好み焼きの店に着きました。平和公園への戻り方は覚えていますか。
   ちづこ

2. じゅん　　：はい、覚えています。

3. ウエイター：いらっしゃいませ。お好み焼きの作り方は分かりますか?

4. 千鶴子　　：私は分かるけど、キアラさんとベン君は?
   ちづこ

5. キアラ　　：私は自分で作った事がないから教えて下さい。

6. ウェイター：始めに豚肉とキャベツを焼きます。次に焼きそばを入れて下さい。それから小
   麦粉と卵と水のミックスを入れます。そして三分ぐらい待って裏返します。食
   べる時にソースとかつおぶしをかけて下さい。

7. ウェイター：ご注文は?
   ちゅうもん

8. 友　　　　：私はお腹がペコペコです。
   なか

9. 千鶴子　　：私はイカと豚肉と*チーズにします。焼きそばじゃなくうどんを下さい。
   ちづこ

10. ベン　　　：美味しそうですね。僕も同じで。あ、でもイカじゃなくてタコにします。

11. 千鶴子　　：キアラさんもベン君も箸の持ち方が上手ですね。
    ちづこ

12. 友　　　　：待っている間にお茶を入れておきましょう。

13. キアラ　　：友さん、もうお好み焼き、五枚目ですよ!

NOTE Cheese and many other dairy products were not common in rural areas of post-war Japan and were a special treat.

単語 New Words
たん

~かた ~方 (n) – method of "~ing"

だし 出汁 (n) – fish-based soup stock

てっぱん 鉄板 (n) – steel plate

てっぱんやき 鉄板焼き (n) – teppan'yaki (Japanese cooking prepared on a hot steel plate/table)

こしょう コショウ (n) – pepper

しお 塩 (n) – salt

のり (n) – seaweed

言葉の探索 Language Detection
ことば　　たんさく

Review

~____ ＋ 方 = way of doing ~
  verb stem　　かた

Adding 方 to a verb stem is one way to say a "way of doing" or "how to do" something.
かた

A) お寿司の食べ方を教えて下さい　＝ Please show me how to eat sushi
B) 筆の持ち方　　　　　　　　　＝ how to hold a (calligraphy) brush
C) トーストの焼き方　　　　　　＝ how to make toast
D) バスケのやり方は難しくないです。＝ (The way of) playing (doing) basketball is not hard.

自習　Self Check

How would you say the following?

(ア) Please show me how to eat sukiyaki.

(イ) Making yakisoba is not difficult.

(ウ) Please teach me the best way to memorize (覚える) words (単語).

(エ) I learned (習う) how to read that kanji yesterday.

練習時間　Practice Time

Pair Practice

With a partner, write a list of things that you can, or know how to do. Try to use as many action verbs as you can. Be creative and be prepared to share your list with the class.

 難しい漢字の書き方を知っています。ケーキの作り方が分かります。

文化箱　Culture Chest

お好み焼き

On restaurant menus, お好み焼き ("grilled as you like it") is often translated into English as a "Japanese pancake." Don't expect maple syrup and butter to appear on the table, however. These savory pancakes are more for lunch or dinner. They consist of vegetables, meat, and seafood combined in a flour-based batter. Many regional variations of this traditional "fast food" exist. In the Kansai Region, お好み焼き starts with customers receiving a bowl of batter, into which their favorite ingredients are added. The mixture is poured onto a hot griddle on or inset into the table, and cooked. To finish it off, the hungry customer can add toppings of sweet お好み焼き sauce, seaweed bits, and fish flakes.

The Hiroshima version of this meal begins with pouring batter onto the griddle and cooking one side. Once it is sufficiently browned, a thin layer of finely-chopped cabbage is placed on top, followed by layers of other meats and vegetables, fried noodles, and sometimes an egg, before the pancake is flipped over and covered with お好み焼き sauce. Whichever style of お好み焼き you are enjoying, be sure to say "いただきます!" before you eat!

🔊 メール

This message is from Chizuko's mother, describing a recipe for Hiroshima-style okonomiyaki.
Points to consider as you read:

❶ What are the first three steps of this recipe?

❷ What ingredients are needed for this dish?

❸ Describe this dish, first in Japanese then in English.

❹ Have you ever eaten anything like this before and do you think you would like to try it? Why or why not?

千鶴子へ

これが千鶴子が聞いた広島風お好み焼きの作り方よ。

まず、小麦粉にだしを入れて水で*溶きます。鉄板を熱して、油を引いて、その上にお玉で薄く広げます。

ポツポツと穴が開いて来たら、その上にキャベツと*もやしと*天かすをのせます。そして、桜えび、*とろろをのせて、塩とこしょうを少しかけます。広島風お好み焼きと言えば、豚肉です。この上に豚肉を*丁寧に置きます。

この上にまた*さっき小麦粉をだしで溶いたものをかけたら、裏返します。ここで押さえ付けてはいけません！

中のキャベツやもやしを蒸している間に、鉄板の横で焼きそばを焼いて、少しソースで味付けします。

焼きそばが*出来上がったら、その上にお好み焼きを乗せて上から押さえ付けます。

今度はその隣で*目玉焼きを作ります。半熟の目玉焼きの上にお好み焼きと焼きそばをのせます。そして、すぐに*ひっくり返します。そうすると、卵が一番上になりますね。

ここにお好み焼きソースを*塗ります。そして、*青のりを振りかけて食べます。卵が半熟なので、とろりとしてとても美味しいですよ。

よかったらお友達を家に招待したらどうかしら？お母さんが、皆の前で広島風お好み焼きを作ってあげるわよ。

だし – fish-based soup stock; 溶きます – to dissolve; もやし – bean sprouts, 天かす – bits of fried dough; とろろ – grated yam; 丁寧に – carefully, neatly; さっき – some time ago; 押さえ付ける – to press down; 出来上がる – to complete, to finish; 目玉焼き – sunny-side-up fried egg; ひっくり返します – to turn over, flip; 塗ります – to spread or smear; 青のり – green seaweed

それはまずそう！

That sounds disgusting!

1) 関西と広島のお好み焼きはどう違いますか？

2) ちょっと待って。関西風のお好み焼きの作り方があります。

3) 見せて。。。関西風は、まず材料を全部まぜて、それからそれを焼いて肉を上におきます。最後にマヨネーズとソースと青のりをかけます。

5) 東北ではお好み焼きをわりばしに巻いて食べると聞きました。名前は「どんどん焼き」です。

4) その焼き方も美味しそうね。

6) アメリカのコーンドッグみたいですね。

7) 関西では生肉やシーフードをよく使いますが関東では納豆を入れる人もいるそうですよ。

8) 納豆？それはまずそう！

会話 Dialog かい

Setting: The group is relaxing in the okonomiyaki restaurant, talking about regional differences in okonomiyaki recipes.)

1. キアラ ：関西と広島のお好み焼きはどう違いますか?
かんさい このやき ちが

2. 友 ：ちょっと待って。関西風のお好み焼きの作り方があります。
かんさいふう このやき つくかた

3. じゅん ：見せて…関西風は、まず材料を全部まぜて、それからそれを焼いて肉を上におきます。最後にマヨネーズとソースと青のりをかけます。
かんさいふう ざいりょう やき にく
さいご

4. 千鶴子 ：その焼き方も美味しそうね。
ちづこ やき

5. じゅん ：東北ではお好み焼きをわりばしに*巻いて食べると聞きました。名前は「どんどん焼き」です。
このやき ま やき

6. キアラ ：アメリカのコーンドッグみたいですね。

7. ベン ：関西では*生肉やシーフードをよく使いますが、関東では納豆を入れる人もいるそうですよ。
かんさい なま なっとう

8. 友 ：納豆?それはまずそう!
なっとう

生肉 – raw meat; 巻いて食べる – to wrap around (巻き寿司 = rolled sushi)
なま ま まずし

単語 New Words たん

ほうほう 方法 (n) – method	さじ (n) – spoonful
あまい 甘い (い adj.) – sweet	にる 煮る (v) – boil
からい 辛い (い adj.) – spicy	はかる 測る (v) – measure (to)
すっぱい 酸っぱい (い adj.) – sour	まぜる 混ぜる (v) – mix (to)
まず 先ず (adv.) – first (of all), anyway	むす 蒸す (v) – steam (to)
は (interj.) – then, well then, so	やく 焼く (v) – fry (to)

文化箱 Culture Chest ぶんかばこ

round 広島

he western part of 本州, which includes the city of 広島, is known as the 中国 region of Japan, and includes

e city of 広島. Only a 40-minute train and ferry ride from Hiroshima is the sacred shrine of 厳島神社, on
いつくしまじんじゃ

島, an easily accessible day-trip. 厳島神社 has been designated a UNESCO World Heritage Site. The
つくしま いつくしま

社の鳥居 has existed since 1168, although the current structure is only about 150 years old. The island
とりい

(also known as 宮島) is easily recognized as you approach by ferry from the mainland, by the brilliant orange-red 鳥居 set in the shallow waters off the island's shore. It is one of the most photographed sites in Japan.

Nearby, the town of 岩国, home to an American military base, is well-known for its 錦帯橋. This bridge was constructed in 1673 for the use of samurai only. Commoners had to pay to use a boat to cross the river. Today anyone can enjoy this example of traditional barrel-bridge

architecture by crossing its five steep arches to get to the other side. Stopping by 錦帯橋 is a nice addition to a day trip to 宮島 and 厳島神社.

🔊 メール

This message is from Mr. Matsumoto, a travel agent, giving Ben directions on how to best travel from Hiroshima to Miyajima.

Points to consider as you read:

❶ What is Mr. Matsumoto's first question?

❷ If Ben travels directly to Miyajima from the Peace Park, about how long will it take?

❸ What restaurant and dish are recommended by Mr. Matsumoto?

ベン様へ、

　お問い合わせありがとうございます。広島から宮島への行き方ですが、広島のどこからご出発でしょうか？

　広島駅からは、JRで宮島口駅まで行って、フェリーで宮島へ行く方法があります。原爆ドームからは、路面電車で西広島駅に出て、そこからJRで宮島口駅まで行って、船で行きます。

　また、平和公園から直接船で行く方法もあって、40分程度です。船の乗り場は、行けばすぐ分かります。

　宮島で是非行っていただきたいのは『千畳閣』と『大聖院』です。『大聖院』では、*ろうそくにお願いごとをしたり出来ます。

それから『大聖院』に行く途中のお茶屋さんも*お勧めです。是非、ここで休憩して下さい。お茶屋さんは京風の建物なので分かりやすいと思いますよ。

　せっかくの旅行ですので、宮島名物の「あなご飯」を食べてみて下さい。1500円〜2000円程度です。「うえの」のあなご飯はお勧めですが、大変*混み合うと聞いています。下調べしておいて下さい。天気が良ければ宮島口で船に乗る前に「うえの」で「あなご飯」の弁当を買って行くのも良いと思います。

松本　道夫
東山旅行社

ろうそく – candle; お勧め – recommendation; 混み合う – crowded

日本でも平和の為の草の根交流プログラムがありますね。

ため　くさ　ね こうりゅう

In Japan, too, there are grass-roots exchange programs working for peace.

1) ふぅ、美味しかった。私はお好み焼きを六枚も食べてしまいました。外国人もお好み焼きが大好きですね。

2) 最近は外国人が日本に来たり日本人が外国に行ったり出来るようになりました。僕も高校生の間に外国語と文化を経験しておきたいです。今私のおばさんは海外でボランティア活動をしています。

3) 日本でも平和の為の草の根交流プログラムがありますね。日本とアメリカの草の根サミットに二十年間に三万人以上の人が行ったそうです。

4) 草の根交流でどんな事をするの?

5) アジア・ヨーロッパ・中米・オセアニアの人達と交流したり、ホームステイをしたりして彼らの国について勉強します。貧しい人々の為にボランティア活動もします。

6) 私は言語学者になりたいな。その為に色々な国の人と話したり外国語の勉強をしたりしたい。

7) 1990年にフロイドさんと言う人が禎子さんの為にシアトルに記念像を作ったとおじから聞きました。

会話 Dialog
(かい)

(Setting: The group is relaxing after lunch and chatting about volunteering for various grass-roots causes.)

1. 友 ：ふう、美味しかった。私はお好み焼きを六枚も食べてしまいました。外国人もお好み焼きが大好きですね。

2. じゅん ：最近は外国人が日本に来たり日本人が外国に行ったり出来るようになりました。僕も高校生の間に外国語と文化を経験しておきたいです。今私のおばさんは海外でボランティア活動をしています。

3. ベン ：日本でも平和の為の草の根交流プログラムがありますね。日本とアメリカの草の根サミットに二十年間に三万人以上の人が行ったそうです。

4. 千鶴子 ：草の根交流でどんな事をするの?

5. 友 ：アジア・ヨーロッパ・中米・オセアニアの人達と交流したり、ホームステイをしたりして彼らの国について勉強します。貧しい人々の為にボランティア活動もします。

6. 千鶴子 ：私は言語学者になりたいな。その為ために色々な国の人と話したり外国語の勉強をしたりしたい。

7. キアラ ：(whispering to the others in the group) 1990年にフロイドさんと言う人が禎子さんの為にシアトルに記念像を作ったとおじから聞きました。

単語 New Words
(たん)

くさのね 草の根 (n) – grassroots, rank and file
こうりゅう 交流 (n) – exchange (cultural), networking
まずしい 貧しい (い adj.) – poor, needy

ために 為に (conj.) – for, on behalf of
よう 様 (n) – way, manner

言葉の探索 Language Detection
(ことば)(たんさく)

Aの)為(ため[に]) – for the sake of A -or- because of A

This pattern can be used to state a reason why an action is done. It follows nouns or the dictionary form of verbs.

Read these examples closely:

A) 日本でも平和の為の草の根交流プログラムがありますね。
= In Japan, too, there are grass-roots exchange programs working for peace.

B) 貧しい人々の為に、ボランティア活動もします。

= There are also volunteer activities to (for the purpose of) help needy people.

C) その為に色々な国の人と、話したり外国語を勉強したりしたいです。

= To do that, I want to talk with people of many different nationalities, and study many different foreign languages.

D) 1990年にフロイドさんと言う人が、禎子さんの為にシアトルに記念像を作ったと、おじから聞きました。

= I heard from my uncle that in 1990, a person named Floyd built a statue to commemorate Sadako in Seattle.

🔊 メール

This message is from Ben, writing home about his Hiroshima experiences: meeting Chizuko (a friend o Sadako), eating okonomiyaki, traveling by train and ferry to Miyajima, and being chased by deer.

うちの皆は元気?僕は広島に行って来たよ。

広島では、「原爆の子の像」の（完成）式に行ったり、お好み焼きを食べたり、電車と*フェリーで宮島に行って観光したりしたよ。

「原爆の子の像」は、原爆症で亡くなった禎子さんの為に作られたんだ。その禎子さんのお友達の千鶴子さんとお好み焼きを食べに行った。お好み焼きはパンケーキの様だけど、甘くないんだ。広島のお好み焼きの作り方を、千鶴子さんのお母さんが教えてくれた。広島のお好み焼きは、関西のお好み焼きと作り方が違う。今度帰ったら、皆に作ってあげるよ。その時のために、作り方をメモしておいた。

宮島は島なので、*フェリーで行った。海の中に大鳥居があって、とても綺麗なところだった。宮島も皆に見せてあげたいから写真を沢山撮っておいたよ。とても人気があるので、とても混んでいた。人と同じ位、*鹿もいたんだ。*餌をやったら沢山の鹿に追いかけられちゃった！

ではまたメールするね。

ベン

*フェリー – ferry; 鹿 – deer; 餌 – animal food

東京　**Present Day**

Moving Forward and Planning for the Future

The group has departed Hiroshima, only to find themselves in the strangest place they have visited yet. There are more surprises to come.

About this Chapter

This chapter and the previous chapter have been designed to offer practice and review for listening, speaking, reading, and writing skills. Consequently, the focus is on experiencing and producing Japanese. New vocabulary, kanji, and Language Detection points have been deliberately kept to a minimum.

Learning and Performance Goals

This chapter will enable you to:

- say what you want to become: 〜になりたい
- learn about Osamu Tezuka
- talk about plans for college and for the future
- learn how artists and imagery evolved
- learn more ことわざ (proverbs)
- use 5 additional kanji

「漫画の神様」だと思います。

I think he is "the god of manga."

1) あれ？これ、ちょっと変じゃないですか？半分は白黒で、半分は色が付いています。

2) ほら、向こうに男の人がいますよ。大きい眼鏡をかけてベレー帽をかぶっていますね。すみません！僕達は一体どこにいますか。

3) え？ここは「鉄腕アトム」の四十七ページだよ。君達はどうやって漫画の中に入ったの？

4) 「鉄腕アトム？」じゃあ、もしかして、手塚治虫先生じゃないですか。

5) 手塚治虫！手塚先生は「漫画の神様」だと思います。私は「ブラック・ジャック」と「火の鳥」の大ファンです。ああ、でも「メトロポリス」はもっと好きです。手塚先生はウォルト・ディズニーと同じくらい有名ですね。

6) いやいや。ウォルトディズニーの方が世界的に有名だと思うよ。

7) 先生のキャラクターは他の漫画のキャラクターより目が大きくて、キラキラしていますね。

8) 手塚先生、新しい漫画のヒーローは狸にして下さい。狸はジャングルの王様です。

9) うーん、それはちょっと…後で考えておくよ。

会話 Dialog

(Setting: The group exits the torii into a world of half black-and-white, half full-color drawings, and meets someone new.)

1. 友 ：あれ？これ、ちょっと変じゃないですか？半分は白黒で、半分は色が付いています。

2. ベン ：ほら、向こうに男の人がいますよ。大きい眼鏡をかけてベレー帽をかぶっていますね。すみません！僕達は一体どこにいますか。

3. 手塚 ：え？ここは「鉄腕アトム」の四十七ページだよ。君達はどうやって漫画の中に入ったの？

4. じゅん ：「鉄腕アトム?」じゃあ、もしかして、あなたは手塚治虫先生じゃないですか。

5. キアラ ：手塚治虫！手塚先生は「漫画の神様」だと思います。私は「ブラック・ジャック」と「火の鳥」の大ファンです。ああ、でも「メトロポリス」はもっと好きです。手塚先生はウォルト・ディズニーと同じくらい有名ですね。

6. 手塚 ：いやいや。ウォルトディズニーの方が世界的に有名だと思うよ。

7. じゅん ：先生のキャラクターは他の漫画のキャラクターより目が大きくて、キラキラしていますね。

8. 友 ：手塚先生、新しい漫画のヒーローは狸にして下さい。狸たぬきはジャングルの王様です。

9. 手塚 ：うーん、それはちょっと…後で考えておくよ。

単語 New Words

せんこう 専攻 (*n*) – major subject, special study

せんもん 専門 (*n*) – specialty, subject of study

いったい (*n/adv.*) – What the heck?, What on earth?; (*adv.*) – generally, in general

なら/ならば (*conj.*) – if, in case, if it is true that

もしかして (*exp.*) – perhaps, possibly

えらぶ 選ぶ (*v*) – choose (to), select (to)

きめる 決める (*v*) – decide (to)

そつぎょう(を)する 卒業(を)する (*v*) – graduate (to)

文化箱 Culture Chest

手塚治虫 (1928–1989) and 漫画

Manga artist 手塚治虫 was born in Osaka. He always loved drawing and nature. Growing up, his small stature and wavy hair made him the object of teasing by his classmates. His mother was proactive in encouraging his imagination and often took him to see the romantic musicals performed at the nearby Takarazuka Theatre. Here, the costumes and dramatic performances of the all-female cast influenced

Tezuka's drawing style and inspired him to give his characters large sparkling eyes.

Tezuka graduated from Osaka University with a degree in medicine, but decided to follow his dream of becoming a manga artist. One of his most famous characters is 鉄腕アトム, the protagonist in a manga chapter that first appeared in 1951. His stories, such as 鉄腕アトム (known as Astro Boy in the United States), ジャングル大帝 (Jungle Emperor, or Kimba the White Lion), リボンの騎士 (Princess Knight), 火の鳥 (Phoenix), and Black Jack, live on, as does the annual 手塚治虫文化賞 (Tezuka Osamu Culture Prize) for artists who best continue his tradition.

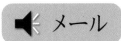 メール

Kiara is writing to her guidance counselor at her high school in Tokyo, asking for advice about colleges and majors. Generally in Japanese schools, the homeroom teacher would answer these questions.

Points to consider as you read:

❶ What level of politeness is Kiara using? How can you tell?

❷ Who at your school would you write to ask for advice about college?

❸ What sort of advice would you give to Kiara?

東高校

進路指導部長　竹中先生

　お元気でいらっしゃいますか。私は、高校三年生になったので、そろそろ大学のことを決めなければなりません。今、色々考えているのですが、高校を卒業したら、アートや美術を勉強したいと思っています。将来、アーティストになりたいからです。それに、せっかく今まで一生懸命日本語を勉強したので、できれば日本の大学か専門学校で勉強したいのです。

　美術を専攻出来る大学が秋田にあるでしょうか。それとも、美術を専攻する*なら、東京や大阪など、大きい町の大学を選んだ方がいいでしょうか。美術の単科大学で勉強した方がいいでしょうか。竹中先生のアドバイスをよろしくお願いいたします。

キアラより

レオの様な白いライオンが一番かっこいいと思います。

I think that a white lion like Leo is the coolest.

会話 Dialog

(Setting: Tezuka Osamu gives Kiara drawing lessons.)

1. キアラ　：手塚先生、漫画の描き方を教えて下さい。

2. 手塚　　：いいよ、じゃあ始めは鉛筆の持ち方。書道で筆を持つ時とは違うよ。こう持って。

3. キアラ　：あ、これは馬ですね。それから次が虎と牛。

4. 手塚　　：そうそう、馬の口の所に「ヒヒーン」と書いて。虎は「ガオー」で牛は穏やかに「モー」と
　　　　　　*鳴くんだよ。

5. じゅん　：キアラさん、すごい！動物を三頭描きましたね。僕も先生の様にジャングルのライオンや
　　　　　　猿や象を描いてみたいです。レオの様な白いライオンが一番かっこいいと思います。

6. キアラ　：レオは英語では、キンバという名前でした。ジャングルの王様になりました。

7. ベン　　：僕は犬が大好きだから犬を二匹描いてみたいです。よろしくお願いします。

* 鳴く – to sing (bird), to bark, purr, etc. (to make animal sounds)

単語 New Words

おなじ 同じ (n) – same, similar, alike

かんきょう 環境 (n) – environment, circumstance

しつもん 質問 (n) – question

ぶっか 物価 (n) – price of commodities, cost of living

りゅうがくせい 留学生 (n) – exchange student, overseas student

えんりょ 遠慮 (n) – tact, thoughtfulness

しらべる 調べる (v) – inquire (to), investigate (to)

とう 頭 (counter) – counter for large animals

わ 羽 (counter) – counter for birds

いっとう 1頭 (counter) – 1 large animal

にとう 2頭 (counter) – 2 large animals

さんとう 3頭 (counter) – 3 large animals

よんとう 4頭 (counter) – 4 large animals

ごとう 5頭 (counter) – 5 large animals

ろくとう 6頭 (counter) – 6 large animals

ななとう 7頭 (counter) – 7 large animals

はちとう 8頭 (counter) – 8 large animals

きゅうとう 9頭 (counter) – 9 large animals

じゅっとう 10頭 (counter) – 10 large animals

なんとう 何頭 (interj.) – How many large animals?

いちわ 1羽 (counter) – 1 bird

にわ 2羽 (counter) – 2 birds

さんわ/ば 3羽 (counter) – 3 birds

よんわ 4羽 (counter) – 4 birds

ごわ 5羽 (counter) – 5 birds

ろくわ 6羽 (counter) – 6 birds

ななわ 7羽 (counter) – 7 birds

はちわ 8羽 (counter) – 8 birds

きゅうわ 9羽 (counter) – 9 birds

じゅうわ/じゅっぱ 10羽 (counter) – 10 birds

なんわ 何羽 (interj.) – How many birds?

漢字 Kanji

牛 4 strokes	ギュウ, うし – cow	ノ	⺧	二	牛		
	牛乳 – (cow's) milk; 牛肉 – beef ぎゅうにゅう　　　　　　　ぎゅうにく						
	This kanji looks like a very abstract head of a COW, poking its head over two strands of wire next to a post.						

匹 4 strokes	ヒツ, ひき	一	丆	兀	匹		
	一匹 – one animal (small) いっぴき						
	In an enclosure (匚) COUNT ONE SMALL ANIMAL with two small legs (儿).						

馬 10 strokes	バ, うま – horse	Ｉ	厂	厂	丐	馬	馬
	馬車 – horse cart/carriage; 乗馬 – horse riding; ばしゃ　　　　　　　　　　じょうば 馬鹿者 – stupid person ばかもの	馬	馬	馬	馬		
	This kanji is a radical. It is similar to island (島) without the feather on top and with the four legs of a HORSE (not a mountain–山) below.						

鳥 11 strokes	チョウ, とり – bird, chicken	′	⼻	冖	户	冎	皀
	鳥居 – Shinto gate; 小鳥 – small bird, songbird; とりい　　　　　　　こ とり 白鳥 – swan; 七面鳥 – turkey はくちょう　　　　しちめんちょう	烏	鳥	鳥	鳥	鳥	
	This kanji is a radical. Similar to island (島), but without the 山, the four marks below look like the BIRD'S beautiful tail feathers.						

虎 8 strokes	コ, とら – tiger	′	⼏	⼴	广	庐	虍
	虎の尾 – tiger's tail とら　お	虏	虎				
	The top of this kanji is the TIGER's spots (虍); as the TIGER lunges forward, its back two legs (儿) leave the ground.						

文化箱 Culture Chest
_{ぶん か ばこ}

Imagery in 漫画 and other illustrated written materials
_{まん が}

漫画 have a long history in Japan. Some trace the use of graphic images back to Buddhist illustrated scrolls (絵巻物) _{え まきもの} depicting parables and other stories, from China. During the Muromachi period (1392–1573), a group of illustrated stories called 御伽草子 were printed in booklets called *なら絵本, and were probably meant to be read aloud. _{お とぎぞうし} Later, in the Tokugawa period, as woodblock printing techniques developed, 浮世絵 prints were often used to depict _{う き よ え} funny or entertaining scenes.

You learned previously that the artist Hokusai was one of the earliest artists to use the term "漫画." Once the military, social, and economic grip of the 徳川 Shogunate (government) was replaced by the relative freedom _{とくがわ} of the 明治時代, Western influences such as the British journal "Punch" and others began arriving in _{めい じ じ だい} Japan. Artists started using 浮世絵 and 漫画 to criticize the political establishment in a way that had not been possible under the strict control of the 徳川 government.

Improved printing technology and rising literacy rates led to mass printings; one magazine, "キング," first published in 1925, sold a million copies of its January 1927 issue. Throughout the 20th century, 漫画 were widely read in Japan and beyond, not only by children and teenagers, but college students, businessmen, housewives, and people from all walks of society. 漫画 are used not only for entertainment, but also for educational purposes and to transmit political, social, historical, and even environmental information.

* short illustrated manuscripts composed during the Muromachi and Edo periods

🔊 メール

Kiara has received a reply from Mr. Takenaka, the guidance counselor at her Japanese high school, with some suggestions about art schools.

Points to consider as you read:

❶ What do one or two students in her class plan to major in, in college?

❷ List four possible specialties within the arts department at Nihon Daigaku.

❸ What are some advantages to studying art in Tokyo?

❹ What are some advantages to studying art in Niigata?

キアラさん

　メールを読みました。色々考えているようですね。私は高校三年生の進路指導をしていますが、みんな、そろそろ受験勉強に忙しくしていますよ。たいていクラスに一人か二人、大学で美術を専攻したい、という生徒がいます。

　ところで、日本の大学に行きたいということですが、日本にはアメリカと同じように、アートを勉強出来る大学や専門学校がたくさんあります。まず、東京に日本大学という大きい大学がありますが、この大学には芸術学部があって、色々なアートを勉強することが出来ます。例えば、デザインや写真、絵画や演劇など、芸術学部の中にも色々な学科があります。海外からの留学生も受け入れています。東京にありますから、生活は便利ですし、色々な美術展を見るチャンスも多いでしょう。

　新潟県にも美術短期大学があります。新潟公立美術工芸短期大学という名前です。こちらは２年間通う大学ですが、日本大学と同じように，色々なアートを勉強することが出来ます。日本大学より小さくて、勉強する期間も短いです。上越市にありますから、キアラさんもご存知の通り、東京より広々としていますし、景色や空気もきれいで、いい環境です。それに、物価は東京よりずっと安いです。

　キアラさんも色々な大学を調べていると思いますが、質問があったら、いつでも遠慮なくメールして下さい。

進路指導部長
竹中　明より

次は友さんに読んでもらいましょう。

Next, let's have Tomo read.

チリン チリン！

1) 今から皆様に僕達の紙芝居を紹介します。では、キアラさんに話を始めてもらいます。

2) お願いします。昔々ある所におじいさんとおばあさんが住んでいました。ある日、おじいさんはラーメンを食べていました。そうするとラーメンの中に小さい男の子がいました。次はじゅん君が読んでくれます。

3) おじいさんとおばあさんは男の子の名前を「ラーメン太郎」にしました。男の子はラーメンの様な髪の毛で、なるとの服を着ています。では次は友さんに読んでもらいましょう。

4) ラーメン太郎は村で一番強い男になりました。そして鬼が島に行ってお姫様を助けてあげました。そして鬼の金・銀・食べ物を村人にあげました。めでたしめでたし。

5) キアラさん、素晴らしいアイディアを教えてくれてありがとう。お土産にアトムとウランの絵をあげるよ。どうぞ。

パチパチ

6) うわあ、先生がお描きになった絵ですね。ありがとうございます。

7) 先生、僕達も先生の絵をいただいてもいいですか？

8) もちろん！お茶の水はかせの絵をあげましょう。

ギューン！

9) あ、鉄腕アトムが飛んで行く！

(Setting: The group presents their picture story of Ramen Tarou to Tezuka sensei.)

リンリン！ (bell rings)

1. ベン ：今から皆様に僕達の紙芝居を 紹 介します。では、キアラさんに話を始めてもらいます。

2. キアラ ：はい。昔々ある所におじいさんとおばあさんが住んでいました。ある日、おじいさんはラーメンを食べていました。そうするとラーメンの中に小さい男の子がいました。次はじゅん君が読んでくれます。

3. じゅん ：おじいさんとおばあさんは男の子の名前を「ラーメン 太郎」にしました。男の子はラーメンの様な髪の毛で、*なるとの 服 を着ています。では次は友さんに読んでもらいましょう。

4. 友 ：ラーメン 太郎は村で一番強い男になりました。そして 鬼が島に行って*お姫様を助けてあげました。そして 鬼の金・銀 ・食べ物を村人にあげました。めでたしめでたし。

パチパチ… (clapping sound)

5. 手塚 ：キアラさん、すばらしいアイデアをくれてありがとう。お 土 産にアトムと*ウランの絵をあげるよ。どうぞ。

6. キアラ ：うわあ、先生がお描きになった絵ですね。ありがとうございます。

7. ベン ：先生、僕達も先生の絵をいただいてもいいですか？

8. 手塚 ：もちろん！*お茶の水はかせの絵をあげましょう。

ギューン！

9. 皆 ：あ、鉄腕アトムが飛んで行く！

なると – the steamed fish-paste cake served on top of ramen as a garnish; お姫様 – princess; ウラン–アトムの妹; お茶の水はかせ – the doctor who adopted アトム

文化箱 Culture Chest
ぶん か ばこ

Post-War conflict and the synthesis of art and intellectuals

The first half of the 20th c. was a time of tremendous technological development that would change the world forever. After WWII, many Japanese artists and writers struggled to find creative ways of analyzing and dealing with a different world and the new technologies that were part of it. For instance, nuclear technology, fueled by war, had become part of a new world reality. Artistic expressions attempting to synthesize these changes produced a range of new creatures who had to deal with an unknown reality. Godzilla is one such product. Tezuka Osamu's character Astro Boy is another example of a creative response to the search for ways to use technology to better the world.

These issues played out in politics and government as well. When the Japanese Self-defense Forces were established in 1954, their status was controversial. Article 9 of the Japanese Constitution states "The Japanese people forever renounce war as a sovereign right of the nation ... land, sea, and air forces, as well as other war potential, will never be maintained." Many Japanese were strongly anti-military in the 1950s and the debate on this issue continues today. That struggle to understand the opposing viewpoints and possible moral implications of military conflicts seems especially poignant in the case of Japan. Japanese stories, whether in 漫画 or アニメ form, whether contemporary or classical, often end in ways that seem unsatisfactory to Westerners. The "good guy" does not always win, and rarely are there simple "happily ever after" endings. Can you think of an example?

アーティストになりたいです。

第10課の4　I want to become an artist.

1) 紙芝居は楽しかったですね。あ、秋葉原駅前でコスプレのイベントをしています。あっちに行ってみましょう。

2) あれ？前にこのアニメコンに来た事がありますよ。

3) あ、友さんは人間と同じ位大きくなっています。狸の様なコスプレですね。

4) じゃあ、友さんは僕達を一番初めに会った時間に連れて帰ってくれたんだね。でも場所は違うね。

5) はい。長い間家族や友達と話す事が出来なくて、寂しいだろうと思ったから。

6) はい、私はホストファミリーの事をよく考える様になりました。

7) 友さん、また僕達を色々な時代や場所に連れて行ってくれますか？僕は友さんの様に日本の生活と歴史を勉強したいです。

8) 私は美術を勉強してアーティストになりたいです。そして未来に連れて行って欲しいです。

9) もちろん、連れて行ってあげますよ。でも今私は四国に帰らなければなりません。

10) 今まで色々教えてくれて本当にありがとう。元気でね。

11) さようなら。

会話 Dialog

(Setting: Back in Tokyo, in Shinjuku station, the group talks about the future.)

1. 友 　　：紙芝居は楽しかったですね。あ、秋葉原駅前でコスプレのイベントをしています。
　　　　　あっちに行ってみましょう。

2. ベン　 ：あれ?前にこのアニメコンに来た事がありますよ。

3. キアラ ：あ、友さんは人間と同じ位大きくなっています。狸の様なコスプレですね。

4. じゅん ：じゃあ、友さんは僕達を番初めに会った時間に連れて帰ってくれたんだね。
　　　　　でも場所は違うね。

5. 友 　　：はい。長い間家族や友達と話す事が出来なくて、寂しいだろうと思ったから。

6. キアラ ：はい、私はホストファミリーの事をよく考える様になりました。

7. ベン　 ：友さん、また僕達を色々な時代や場所に連れて行ってくれますか?僕は友さんの様
　　　　　に日本の生活と歴史を勉強したいです。

8. キアラ ：私は美術を勉強してアーティストになりたいです。そして未来に連れて行って欲しい
　　　　　です。

9. 友 　　：もちろん、連れて行ってあげますよ。でも今私は四国に帰らなければなりません。

10. ベン　：今まで色々教えてくれて本当にありがとう。元気でね。

11. 皆 　　：さようなら。

単語 New Words

うちゅうひこうし　宇宙飛行士 (n) – astronaut
がめん　画面 (n) – screen
しょうらい　将来 (n) – future (near)

みらい　未来 (n) – future (distant)
ばしょ　場所 (n) – place, location, position
タイプ(を)する (v) – type (to)

言葉の探索 Language Detection

日本語の先生になりたい。– I want to become a Japanese teacher.

It is important to know how to talk about your future plans and expectations. Use a dictionary or the I
ternet to add to your vocabulary list at least 10 new words and 3 new kanji that relate to a future in whi
you see yourself. Type these words on a 単語と漢字 list and give a copy to your teacher.

自習 Self Check
<ruby>自習<rt>じ しゅう</rt></ruby> Self Check

Talk about what you would like to be in 10 years (将来の私) and what you would like to be doing then. Be as detailed and descriptive as you can.

練習時間 Practice Time
<ruby>練習時間<rt>れん しゅう じ かん</rt></ruby> Practice Time

Small Group Practice

Interview two people in your group about what they would like to do in the future. Prepare an interview sheet with at least five questions and record your answers. Be prepared to report about your group members to the class. Be sure to change the 〜たい ending to 〜たがっています when talking about what someone else wants to do.

🔊 メール

This message is to Kiara, from a friend at her Japanese school, with directions for filling out a college application.

Points to consider as you read:

1 List the steps Kiara should take, once she has logged on to the website.

2 Have you filled out similar applications on line?

3 What strategies can you think of for filling out an application in Japanese?

キアラさんへ

大学入学の願書のリンクを送り忘れてしまいました。ごめんなさい。パソコンがネットにつながったら、画面の上の方にある、アドレスを記入する欄に、**TimeForJapanese.com**とタイプして、改行のキーを押して下さい。次の画面で入学願書ダウンロードのボタンを探してクリックすると、大学願書のページが出ますから、そこから願書をダウンロードします。分からないことがあったら、メールして下さい。

鈴木より

お帰りなさい。

Welcome home.

1) 秋葉原駅から浅草までの切符は１６０円です。三枚一緒に買いましょう。はい、こっちに来て下さい。

2) あ、電車が来ましたね。

3) ただいま！

4) お帰りなさい。今日は学校どうだった？

5) 今日？

6) そうよ。学校の後でダンス教室に行ったりメールをしたり、忙しかったでしょう。

7) 変ですね。午後四時に学校が終わって、今六時だから。。。

8) 僕達の旅は二時間ほどだけでした。

9) 本当に不思議ですね。長い旅だと思っていました。

10) さあ、晩ご飯にしましょう！

11) やっぱり家が一番。

12) でも、今、お腹がペコペコだから、いただきましょう。

13) あら、ベンはまるで友さんみたいですね。『類は友を呼ぶ』と言うから。

14) 友さんはどうしているでしょうね。

15) いただきます！

会話 Dialog

(Setting: The group is at the ticket machines purchasing tickets.)

1. じゅん ：秋葉原駅から浅草までの切符は160円です。三枚一緒に買いましょう。はい、こっちに来て下さい。

2. ベン ：あ、電車が来ましたね。

(Entering Jun's house)

3. 皆 ：ただいま！

4. じゅんの母 ：お帰りなさい。今日は学校どうだった？

5. 皆 ：今日？

6. じゅんの母 ：そうよ。学校の後でダンス教室に行ったりメールをしたり、忙しかったでしょう。

7. じゅん ：変ですね。午後四時に学校が終わって、今六時だから…

8. ベン ：僕達の旅は二時間ほどだけでした。

9. キアラ ：本当に不思議ですね。長い旅だと思っていました。

10. じゅんの母 ：さあ、晩ご飯にしましょう！

11. じゅん ：やっぱり家が一番。

12. ベン ：でも、今、お腹がペコペコだから、いただきましょう。

13. キアラ ：あら、ベンはまるで友さんみたいですね。「*類は友を呼ぶ」と言うから。

14. じゅん ：友さんはどうしているでしょうね。

15. 皆 ：いただきます！

* 類 – sort, kind

単語 New Words

えいきょう 影響 (*n*) – influence, effect

えいきょうする 影響する (*v*) – influence (to), effect (to)

よぶ 呼ぶ (*v*) – call (to); call out (to)

みつかる 見つかる (*v*) – round (to be), discovered (to be)

文化箱 Culture Chest

諺 – Proverbs

The Japanese language abounds with 諺 (proverbs). Some of these closely resemble English sayings, or those found in other languages and cultures, but others represent a uniquely Japanese perspective. For example, can you guess what this 諺 means?

一石二鳥
いっせき に ちょう

In the 会話 above, Jun says: 類は友を呼ぶ
How would you say this in English?

How about these two:

1. 出る杭はうたれる　　　　　　(杭 – nail; 打たれる – to hit)
2. 終わりよければすべてよし。　(〜ければ – if; すべて – all; よ – a form of 良い)

* One translation of Jun's proverb is "birds of a feather flock together."
Literally, those who have similar interests tend to call each other friends.
1. The nail that sticks out gets hit.
2. If the finish is good, it is all good.

🔊 メール

This is the first entry in Jun's journal. He is excited about his future career decisions.

Points to consider as you read:

❶ What influenced Jun's decision in his career choice?

❷ What or who has influenced your possible career choices?

❸ Do you think Jun will be successful? Why or why not?

ジャーナルへ、

今日、僕は一大決心をした。僕は将来*作家になる。絶対になるんだ。僕は今まで自分が何になりたいのか、全然分からなかったけど、やっと自分の道が見つかったんだ。キアラとベンに会えて、本当に良かった。ラッキーだった。二人と友達になれて僕は本当に嬉しい。それに、紫式部と北斎！僕は、この二人に大きな影響を受けた。作家になりたいと思ったのは、キアラやベンに会って、色々な経験をしたから。そして、紫式部や石川啄木、樋口一葉や川端康成などの素晴らしい作家、北斎や手塚治虫などの世界的に有名なアーティストに出会えたからだと思う。それに、僕は友さんにもすごく感謝している。彼は人生について、そして歴史について本当にたくさんの事を教えてくれたんだ。キアラ、ベン、友さん。素晴らしい彼らの人生に、乾杯！

---

*作家 – author, writer
さっか

For the *Beginning Japanese* Kanji List, visit www.TimeForJapanese.com!

Kanji List

Kanji	Ch./ sect.	Pronunciation	Meaning	Example usage
漢	1-1	カン	Sino~, Han (Chinese dynasty)	漢字 – Chinese characters
字	1-1	ジ, あざ	character, letter, section of village	ローマ字 – Latin alphabet
子	1-1	シ, ス, ツ, こ, ～こ, ね	child, sign of the rat	子供 – child
森	1-1	シン, もり	forest, woods	森 – forest, woods; 森本 – Morimoto (family name)
川	1-1	セン, かわ, がわ	river	川 – river; 西川 – Nishikawa (family name)
州	1-1	しゅう	province, state	本州 – Honshu; イリノイ州 – state of Illinois
館	1-1	カン, たて, やかた	large building	函館 – Hakodate; 図書館 – library
雪	1-1	セツ, ゆき	snow	雪 – snow; 大雪 – heavy snow
才	1-1	サイ	genius, years old	三才 – three years old; 天才 – genius, natural gift
歳	1-1	サイ, セイ, とし, とせ, よわい	year-end, age, occasion	三歳 – three years old; 歳を取る – to grow old (alt.: 年を取る)
自	1-2	ジ, みずか(ら)	oneself, self	自動 – automatic; 自分 – myself, yourself
重	1-2	ジュウ, チョウ, え, おも(い), かさ(なる)	heavy, pile up	重い – heavy, massive, serious
動	1-2	ドウ, うご(く)	move, motion, change	動く – to move; 動物 – animal
働	1-2	ドウ, はたら(く)	work	働く – to work; 働かせる – to put some one to work
駅	1-2	エキ	station	駅 – station; 駅前 – in front of station
歩	1-2	ボ, ブ, フ, ある(く)	counter for steps; walk	歩く – to walk; 百歩 – 100 steps
杯	1-2	ハイ, バイ, パイ, さかずき	wine glass, glass, counter for cupfuls	一杯 – 1 cupful
読	1-3	ドク, よ(む)	read	読む – to read; 読書 – reading (n)
勉	1-3	ベン, つと(める)	exertion	勉強 – to study
王	1-4	オウ, ～ノウ	king, rule, magnate	王様 – king; 女王 – queen
主	1-4	シュ	lord, chief, master	主人 – head (of a household); 家主 – landlord
住	1-4	ジュウ, す(む)	dwell, reside, live	住みます – to live (in a place); 住所 – address
田	1-4	デン, た	rice field, field	田んぼ – paddy field, farm; 秋田犬 – Akita (breed of dog)
町	1-4	チョウ, まち	town, village, block	町 – town; 下町 – Shitamachi, downtown
教	1-5	キョウ, おし(える)	teach, faith, doctrine	教える – to teach; 教育 – training, education; 教科書 – textbook
習	1-5	シュウ, なら(う)	learn	習う – to learn; 自習 – self-study
入	1-5	ニュウ, い(れる), は(いる)	enter, insert	入る – to enter; 入り口 – entrance
出	1-5	シュツ, で(る), だ(す)	to appear, emerge; to pull out, stick out	出る – to go out; 出して下さい – please take out
北	2-1	ホク, きた	north	北 – north; 東北 – northeast or northeastern region of Japan
南	2-1	ナ, ナン, みなみ	south	南 – south; 南海 – southern sea
西	2-1	セイ, サイ, にし	west	西 – west; 西洋 – the west, Western countries
番	2-1	バン, つが(い)	turn, number in a series	一番 – number 1; 電話番号 – telephone number
右	2-2	ウ, ユウ, みぎ	right	右 – right; 右手 – right hand(ed)
左	2-2	サ, シャ, ひだり	left	左 – left; 左側 – left side

Kanji	Ch./ sect.	Pronunciation	Meaning	Example usage
乗	2-2	ジョウ, ショウ, の(る), 〜の(り), の(せる)	ride, power, board, multiplication	乗る – to get on, to ride in; 乗せる – to place on (something)
降	2-2	コウ, ゴ, お(りる), くだ(る), ふ(る)	descend, precipitate, fall from	降る – to precipitate; 降りる – to get down/descend (mountain, train, etc.)
首	2-2	シュ, くび	neck, counter for songs and poems	首 – neck; 首都 – capital city; 手首 – wrist
道	2-2	ドウ, トウ, みち	road-way, street, journey, teachings	道 – road, street; 神道 – Shinto religion
枚	2-3	マイ	sheet of…	一枚 – one sheet; 何枚 – how many sheets?
的	2-3	テキ, もと	bull's eye, goal, ending for adjectives	目的 – purpose, goal; 伝統的 – traditional
新	2-3	シン, あたら(しい)	new	新しい – new; 新聞 – newspaper
古	2-3	コ, ふる(い)	old (things), ancient, aged, out dated	古い – old (things); 中古車 – used car
線	2-3	セン	line, tack, string	二番線 – track/platform 2; 山の手線 – Yamanote Line
横	2-3	よこ, オウ	sideways, side, horizontal, width	横 – sideways, side, horizontal, width; 横浜 – (city of) Yokohama
個	2-3	コ, カ	individual, counter for pieces, smallish objects	一個 – one piece/smallish object
注	2-4	チュウ, そそ(ぐ), つ(ぐ)	pour, irrigate, focus on	注文 – order, request
文	2-4	ブン, モン, ふみ, あや	sentence, literature, art, script	文字 – letter (of alphabet), character; 文化 – culture, civilization
晩	2-4	バン	nightfall, night	今晩 – tonight; 晩ご飯 – dinner
宿	2-4	シュク, やど, やど(る)	inn, lodging, dwell(ing)	宿題 – homework; 民宿 – guest house
少	2-4	ショウ, すく(ない), すこ(し)	few, small	少ない – few, a little; 少し – small quantity, little, few
多	2-4	タ, おお(い)	many, frequent, much	多い – many, numerous; 多数 – countless, majority
調	2-4	チョウ, しら(べる), しら(べ), ととの(う)	tune, meter, prepare, investigate	調べる – to investigate, to inspect
皆	2-4	カイ, みな, みんな	all, everything	皆 – all, everything; 皆さん – everyone
階	2-4	カイ, きざはし	story, stair	一階 – first floor; 階段 – staircase
会	2-4	カイ, エ, あ(う)	meet(ing), association, join	会う – to meet; 社会 – social studies
付	2-5	つ(ける), つ(く)	attach, including	付け – fixed, bill; 付く – to be attached
肉	2-5	ニク	meat	筋肉 – muscle; 焼(き)肉 – yakiniku (Japanese dish with grilled meat), Korean barbeque
酒	2-5	シュ, さけ	Japanese sake, alcohol	日本酒 – Japanese sake; 甘酒 – sweet sake
公	3-1	コウ	public, official, governmental	公開 – open to the public; 公立 – public (institution)
園	3-1	エン, その	park, garden, farm	公園 – (public) park; 祇園 – entertainment district in Kyoto
紙	3-1	シ, かみ	paper	紙 – paper; 和紙 – Japanese (rice) paper; 手紙 – letter
絵	3-1	カイ, エ	picture, drawing, painting, sketch	浮世絵 – (colored) wood block print from Edo pd.; 絵本 – picture book
飛	3-1	ヒ, と(ぶ), 〜と(ばす)	fly, skip (pages), scatter	飛ばす – to fly; 飛行機 – airplane
刀	3-1	トウ, かたな	sword, saber	刀 – sword; 短刀 – short sword, dagger
方	3-2	ホウ, かた, 〜かた, 〜がた	direction, person, alternative	この方; 〜の方が …〜 is more than…
空	3-2	クウ, そら, あ(き)	empty, sky, void	空 – sky; 空港 – airport
地	3-2	チ, ジ	ground, earth	地震 – earthquake; 地方 – area, locality
竹	3-2	チク, たけ	bamboo	竹 – bamboo; 竹の子 – baby bamboo shoots

Kanji	Ch./ sect.	Pronunciation	Meaning	Example usage
所	3-2	ショ, ところ, 〜ところ, どころ	place	所 – place; 場所 – place, location
速	3-2	ソク, はや(い), はや〜, はや(める), すみ(やか)	quick, fast	速い – quick, fast
然	3-3	ゼン, ネン	sort of thing, so, if so	自然 – natural; 全然 – not at all
簡	3-4	カン	simplicity	簡単 – simple
単	3-4	タン	simple, one, single	簡単 – simple; 単語 – word, vocabulary
弱	3-4	ジャク, よわ(い), よわ(まる)	weak, frail, to weaken	弱い – weak; 弱気 – timid, faint-hearted
難	3-4	ナン, かた(い), むずか(しい)	difficult, impossible, trouble	難しい – hard, difficult; 難民 – refugees
早	3-5	はや(い), はや, はや〜	early	早い – early; 早く – early, soon
力	3-5	リョク, リキ, ちから	power, strong, exert	力 – power, strength; 力強い – powerful, strong
連	4-1	レン, つれ(る)	take along/escort, lead, connect	国連 – United Nations; 連れる – to take along/escort
形	4-2	ギョウ, ケイ, かた, かたち	shape, form	形 – shape or form; 人形 – doll
合	4-2	ゴウ, あう, 〜あ(う), あ(い), あ(わす), あ(わせる)	fit, suit, join	合わす – to match, to add up; 合う – to fit, to match
茶	4-3	サ, チャ	tea, brown	お茶 – green tea; 茶色 – brown color
変	4-3	ヘン, か(える), かわ(る)	to change, to alter, move, be different	変な – strange; 変わる – to change, to be different
品	4-3	ヒン, しな	goods, articles	用品 – parts, supplies; 食品 – food supplies
葉	4-4	ヨウ, は	leaf, foliage, plane	言葉 – words; 葉書 – postcard
忘	4-4	ボウ, わす(れる)	to forget	忘れる – to forget; 忘れ物 – a forgotten item
度	4-4	ド, たび	degree; time, repetition	一度 – one time; 32度 – 32 degrees
非	4-4	ヒ, あら(ず)	un-, mistake, negative, injustice	非ず – is not so, never mind; 非常 – emergency, extraordinary, unusual
悲	4-4	ヒ, かな(しい), 悲(しむ)	sad, to be sad, grieve, regret	悲しい – sad, to be sad
洗	5-1	セン, あら(う)	wash	洗う – to wash; 洗濯 – laundry, washing
散	5-1	サン, ち(る), ち(らす)	scatter, disperse, squander	散らす – to scatter, to distribute; 散る – to fall (leaves/ blossoms)
浴	5-1	ヨク; あ(びる)	to bathe/shower, (to) bask in the sun	浴びる – to bathe, to sunbathe, to shower; 浴衣 – light cotton kimono
湯	5-1	トウ, ゆ	hot water, bath, hot spring	お湯 – hot water; 茶の湯 – tea ceremony
氷	5-1	ヒョウ, こおり, ひ, こお(る)	icicle, ice, hail, freeze	氷 – shaved ice dessert; 氷点 – freezing point
泳	5-1	エイ, およ(ぐ)	swim	泳ぐ – to swim; 水泳 – swimming
女	5-2	ジョ, おんな, め	female	女の人 – woman, female; 女性 – woman, feminine gender
男	5-2	ナン, ダン, おとこ, お	male	男性 – man, males; 男の人 – man
温	5-2	オン, あたた(かい), あたた(める)	warm, to warm	温める – to warm/heat (usually liquids); 温度 – temperature
泉	5-2	セン, いずみ	spring, fountain	平泉 – Hiraizumi (town name); 温泉 – hot spring, spa
若	5-2	ジャク, ニャク, わ(かい)	young	若い – young; 若く見える – to look (seem) young
冷	5-2	レイ, さ(める), さ(ます), つめ(たい), ひ(やす)	cool, cold (liquid or person), chill	冷たい – cool, cold (liquid or aloof person); お冷や – cool water, cold sake
近	5-3	キン, ちか(い)	near, close	近い – near, close; 近所 – neighborhood
遠	5-3	エン, オン, とお(い)	far, distant	遠い – far, distant; 遠く – far away, at a distance

Kanji	Ch./ sect.	Pronunciation	Meaning	Example usage
暖	5-3	ダン, あたた(かい), あたた(める)	warmth	暖かい – warm, mild; 温暖 – warmth
比	5-3	ヒ, くら(べる)	compare	比べる – to compare, to make a comparison; 比較 – comparison
忙	5-3	ボウ, モウ, いそ(がしい), せわ(しい)	busy, occupied, restless	忙しい – busy; 大忙し – very busy (person or thing)
浜	5-4	ヒン, はま	seashore, beach	浜 – beach; 横浜 – city near Tokyo
止	5-5	シ, と(まる), と(める), や(める)	stop, halt	止まる – to stop; 禁止 – prohibition, ban
危	5-5	キ, あぶ(ない)	dangerous, fear	危ない – dangerous; 危険 – danger, hazard
夕	6-1	セキ, ゆう	evening	七夕 – Star Festival; 夕食 – evening meal, dinner
内	6-1	ナイ, ダイ, うち	inside, within, among, home	内 – home; 国内 – domestic
朝	6-1	チョウ, あさ	morning, dynasty	朝ご飯 – breakfast; 朝日 – morning sun, a popular newspaper
昼	6-1	チュウ, ひる	daytime, noon	昼ご飯 – lunch; 昼寝 – nap (noontime sleep)
夜	6-1	ヤ, よ, よる	night, evening	夜 – night, evening; 一夜 – one night, all night
正	6-1	ただ(しい), まさ, セイ, ショウ	correct, justice	正しい – right, correct; 正す – to correct, to amend
様	6-2	ヨウ, さま	way, manner, suffix	本田様 – Mr./Ms. Honda; この様 – this way
第	6-2	ダイ, テイ	number (#)	第一 – first, formost; 第一課 – Chapter 1
鬼	6-2	キ, おに	ghost, devil	鬼 – ghost, devil
怖	6-3	フ, こわ(い), こわ(がる)	scary, be frightened	怖い – dreadful, scary; 恐怖する – fear, dread
以	6-3	イ, も(って)	by means of, because, compared	以上 – not less than; 以下 – not exceeding, below
配	6-4	ハイ, くば(る)	distribute, apportion	心配 – worry; 配る – distribute, ration
知	6-5	チ, し(る), し(らせる)	know, wisdom	知る – to know; 知恵 – wisdom, sense, intelligence
治	7-1	ジ, おさ(める), おさ(まる)	reign, be at peace, calm down	明治 – Meiji reign period; popular brand of chocolates
代	7-1	ダイ, よ, か(える), か(わる)	to change, to substitute, period/age, decades	世代 – generation; 時代 – period, counter for era
疲	7-1	ヒ, つか(れる), ～づか(れ)	exhausted, tire	疲れ – tiredness
漫	7-2	マン	cartoon	漫画 – (Japanese) comic
画	7-2	ガ, エ, カク	brush-stroke, picture	漫画 – (Japanese) comic; 映画 – film
由	7-2	ユ, ユウ, よし	a reason, significance	自由 – free; 由来 – origin, history
庭	7-3	テイ, にわ	courtyard, garden	庭 – garden; 家庭 – household
松	7-3	ショウ, まつ	pine tree	松本 – family name; 赤松 – red pine (tree)
飯	7-4	ハン, めし	meal, cooked rice	ご飯 – meal, cooked rice
願	7-5	ガン, ねが(う), ～ねが(い)	request, petition	お願いします – to request, to beg; 願い出る – to apply for
初	7-5	ショ, はじ(め), はつ	first time, beginning	初め – start, beginning; 初めまして – How do you do?
関	8-1	カン, せき	barrier, gateway, related to	関東 – the Kanto (eastern) region; 関西 – the Kansai (western) region
開	8-1	カイ, ひら(く), ひら(ける), あ(く), あ(ける)	open, unfold	開ける – to open (a door or window); 開く – to open (book)
閉	8-1	ヘイ, と(じる), と(ざす), し(める), し(まる)	closed, shut	閉じる – to close (books, eyes, meetings, etc.); 閉める – to be shut/closed
台	8-1	タイ, ダイ	pedestal, platform, counter for vehicles and machines	台風 – typhoon; 車一台 – one vehicle

Kanji	Ch./ sect.	Pronunciation	Meaning	Example usage
始	8-1	シ, はじ(まる), はじ(める)	start, begin	始めましょう – let's begin; 開始 – to commence or begin
次	8-1	シ, ジ, つぎ	next, order or sequence	次男 – second son; 次に – next, and then
集	8-1	シュウ, あつ(める), あつ(まる)	to collect, to gather	集まる – to gather; 集合する – to meet, to assemble
伝	8-1	デン, つた(える), つた(え), つた(わる)	transmit, legend, communicate	手伝う – to help; 伝える – to transmit (relay a message)
考	8-2	コウ, かんが(える), かんが(え)	consider, think about	考え – thinking, thought, ideas
困	8-4	コン, こま(る)	become distressed, annoyed	困る – to be troubled, worried, or distressed
走	8-5	ソウ, はし(る)	run	走る – run; 走り書き – scribbling
覚	9-1	カク, おぼ(える), さ(ます), さ(める)	memorize, learn, remember	覚え – memory; 覚える – to remember/memorize
式	9-1	シキ	style, ceremony, rite	方式 – form, method; 卒業式 – graduation ceremony
急	9-1	キュウ, いそ(ぐ), いそ(ぎ)	hurry, emergency, sudden	急ぐ – to hurry, to rush; 急ぎ – haste, hurry, speed
牛	10-2	ギュウ, うし	cow	牛乳 – (cow's) milk; 牛肉 – beef
匹	10-2	ヒツ, ひき	counter for small animals	一匹 – one animal (small)
馬	10-2	バ, うま	horse	馬 – horse; 馬車 – horse cart/carriage
鳥	10-2	チョウ, とり	bird, chicken	鳥居 – Shinto gate; 白鳥 – swan
虎	10-2	コ, とら	tiger	虎の尾 – tiger's tail

Appendix
Grammar References

Verb Conjugation Summary

Type 1 Verbs

Non-Past (〜ます)	Dictionary (Infinitive)	Plain Past (〜た)	Plain Negative (〜ない)	Plain Negative Past (〜なかった)	〜て form	Potential (〜える)	Conditional (〜えば)	English meaning
聞きます	聞く	聞いた	聞かない	聞かなかった	聞いて	聞ける	聞けば	to listen, to ask
待ちます	待つ	待った	待たない	待たなかった	待って	待てる	待てば	to wait
乗ります	乗る	乗った	乗らない	乗らなかった	乗って	乗れる	乗れば	to ride
会います	会う	会った	会わない	会わなかった	会って	会える	会えば	to meet

Type 2 Verbs

Non-Past (〜ます)	Dictionary (Infinitive)	Plain Past (〜た)	Plain Negative (〜ない)	Plain Negative Past (〜なかった)	〜て form	Potential (〜られる)	Conditional (〜えば)	English meaning
見ます	見る	見た	見ない	見なかった	見て	見られる	見れば	to look, to see
上げます	上げる	上げた	上げない	上げなかった	上げて	上げられる	上げれば	to give (to an equal or superior)

Irregular Verbs

Non-Past (〜ます)	Dictionary (Infinitive)	Plain Past (〜た)	Plain Negative (〜ない)	Plain Negative Past (〜なかった)	〜て form	Potential (〜られる)	Conditional (〜えば)	English meaning
します	する	した	しない	しなかった	して	できる	すれば	to do
来ます	来る	来た	来ない	来なかった	来て	来られる	来れば	to come

2011s	過ごす	pass time (to)
2011s	貯める	save money (to)
2012	歩いて行く	go by walking (to)
2012	歩いて帰る	return by walking (to)
2012	歩いて来る	come by walking (to)
2012	歩く	walk (to)
2012	運転(を)する	drive (to)
2012s	掛かる	take time, money, etc. (to)
2012s	通う	commute (to)
2012	勤める	employed [at] (to be)
2012	乗る	ride (to)
2012	働く	work (to)
2013	頂戴(する)	receive (to), be given (to)
2014s	追い掛ける	chase after (to), pursue (to)
2015	影響する	influence (to), effect (to)
2015	教える	teach (to), tell/inform (to)
2015	固める	harden (to), solidify (to)
2015	空く	empty (to become)
2015	スノーボード(を)する	snowboard (to)
2015	習う	learn (to)
2015s	ならぶ	line up (to)
2021	上がる	ascend (to), rise (to), climb (to)
2021s	思い出す	remember (to)
2021	似る	resemble (to), similar (to be), (common usage: 似ている)
2021s	貼り出す	post (to), display (to)
2021s	回る	rotate (to), revolve (to)
2022	降りる	disembark (to), get off (a vehicle)
2022s	感動する	feel like (to), give a sense of (to)
2022	下がる	descend (to), go back (to), hang down (to)
2022	上る	ascend (to), rise (to), climb (to)
2022	曲がる	turn (to)
2022s	焼けてしまう	burn down completely (to)

2022	渡る	cross over (to), to go across
2023s	組む	assemble (to), put together (to)
2023	弾く	pull (to), play (a stringed instrument) (to)
2023	混ぜる	mix (to), stir (to)
2023	わくわく(する)	tremble (to), get nervous (to), thrilled (to be)
2024s	空いている	is open, is free
2024	会う	meet (to)
2024s	ググって	Google (to), search on the internet (to)
2024	注文する	order (to)
2024	泊まる	stay at [e.g., hotel] (to)
2024	乗り換える	transfer (to)
2024	予約する	reserve (to)
2025	釣る	fish (to)
2031s	続ける	continue (to)
2031	飛ぶ	fly (to), jump (to), leap (to)
2031s	離れる	separate (to)
2031s	彫る	carve (to)
2032s	繰り返す	repeat (to)
2032s	残す	let remain (to)
2032s	引っ越しする	move home/office (to), change residence (to)
2033s	驚く	surprise (to)
2033s	変わる	change (to)
2033	過ぎる	pass (to), exceed (to), above (to be)
2033s	伝える	report (to), communicate (to)
2034s	信じる	believe (to)
2034	年を取る	grow old (to), age (to)
2034s	慣れる	become familiar with (to)
2035s	喜ぶ	make happy (to)
2041	出発する	depart (to)
2041	着く	arrive at (to)
2041s	続く	continue (to)
2041	始まる	begin (to) [intrans.]

2042	合う	come together (to), fit (to), match (to)
2042	合わせる	match (to), mix (to)
2042	動かす	move (to), set in motion (to)
2042	動く	move (to), operate (to)
2042	踊る	dance (to)
2042	出来る	able to do (to be)
2043	演じる	perform (to)
2043	休憩(を)する	take a break (to)
2043	咲く	bloom (to)
2043	参る	go (to), come (to), visit (to) a grave or shrine (humble for 行きます・来ます)
2043	見せる	show (to)
2044	致す	do (to) [humble for します]
2044	いらっしゃる	come (to), go (to), somewhere (to be) [honorific for 行きます or います]
2044	借りる	borrow (to), rent (to)
2044	御座います	be (to), exist (to), [formal]
2044	出掛ける	depart (to), set out [on an excursion] (to)
2044s	召し上がる	eat (to) [formal]
2044	忘れる	forget (to)
2045	払う	pay (to)
2045	求める	seek (to), request (to)
2051	洗う	wash (to)
2051	乾く	dry (to)
2051s	敷く	spread out (to), lay out (to)
2052	浴びる	shower (to), bask in the sun (to), bathe (to)
2053s	置かれる	place (to), put (to)
2055	亡くなる	pass away (to) [formal for 死ぬ (cannot be used for one's own death)]
2061	祝う	celebrate (to)
2061	感謝(を)する	give thanks (to)
2062s	諦める	give up (to)

062s	気が付く	notice (to)
062	逃げる	escape (to), run away (to)
062s	折れない	break (to)
063	誘う	invite (to)
064s	お辞儀する	bow (to)
064s	隠れる	hide completely (to)
064s	泣く	cry [animals] (to)
064s	ほっとする	relieved (to be)
065	祈る	pray (to), wish (to)
065s	写す	photographed (to be), copy (to)
065s	興奮する	excited (to be)
065s	凧揚げをする	fly a kite (to)
065	助かる	saved (to be), rescued (to be)
065	助ける	save (to), rescue (to)
065s	引っ掛かる	tangled up in (to be)
071	叱る	scold (to)
071	疲れる	become tired (to)
071	任せる	entrust (to), leave to a person (to)
073	ビックリする	surprised (to be), amazed (to be)
074	タバコを吸う	smoke tobacco (to)
081	開く	open (to)

2081	開ける	open (to) (eyes, doors, etc.)
2081	集まる	meet (to), congregate (to)
2081	集める	collect (to), put together (to)
2081	起こす	wake someone up (to), rise (to)
2081	閉まる	close (to)
2081	閉める	close (to)
2081	渡す	hand over (to), pass along (to)
2082	準備(を)する	prepare (to)
2084	困る	have trouble (to), be in difficulty
2084	止まる	stop (to), halt (to)
2084	止める	stop (something or someone) (to), turn off (to)
2084s	破壊される	cause destruction (to), cause disruption (to)
2084s	避難される	criticized (to be)
2084s	予知する	predict (to), know beforehand (to)
2085	ガードする	guard (to), protect (to)
2085	走る	run (to)
2085	学ぶ	study (in depth) (to), learn or take lessons in (to)
2091	急ぐ	hurry (to)

2091	覚える	remember (to), memorize (to)
2091	考える	think (to), consider (to)
2091	聞く	ask (to), listen (to)
2091	建てる	build (to)
2092	置く	put (to), place (to)
2092s	協力する	cooperate (to)
2092s	理解する	grasp (to), comprehend (to)
2093s	押さえ付ける	press down (to)
2093s	出来上がる	complete (to), finish (to)
2093s	溶く	dissolve (to)
2094s	込み合う	crowded (to be)
2094	煮る	boil (to)
2094	測る	measure (to)
2094	蒸す	steam (to)
2094	焼く	fry (to)
2101	選ぶ	choose (to), select (to)
2101s	選べる	select (to), choose (to)
2101	決める	decide (to)
2101s	卒業(を)する	graduate (to)
2102	調べる	investigate (to)
2105	見つかる	find (to)
2105	呼ぶ	call (by a name) (to)

Adjective Conjugation Summary

い Adjectives

Non-Past (formal ～いです/ informal ～い)	Past (formal ～かったです/ informal ～かった)	Negative (formal ～くありません/ informal ～くない)	Negative Past (formal ～くありませんでした/ informal ～くなかった)	～て-form (～くて)	English meaning
正しいです/正しい	正しかったです/ 正しかった	正しくありません/ 正しくない	正しくありませんでした/ 正しくなかった	正しくて	correct, right
速いです/速い	速かったです/速かった	速くありません/速くない	速くありませんでした/ 速くなかった	速くて	fast, quick
ぬるいです/ぬるい	ぬるかったです/ ぬるかった	ぬるくありません/ ぬるくない	ぬるくありませんでした/ ぬるくなかった	ぬるくて	lukewarm

な Adjectives

Non-Past (formal 〜です/ informal 〜だ)	Past (formal 〜でした/ informal 〜だった)	Negative (formal 〜ではありません/ informal 〜じゃない)	Negative Past (formal 〜ではなかった/ informal 〜じゃなかった)	〜て-form (〜で)	English meaning
簡単です かんたん	簡単でした	簡単ではありません/ 簡単ではない/ 簡単じゃありません/ 簡単ではない	簡単ではありませんでした/ 簡単ではなかったです/ 簡単じゃありませんでした/ 簡単じゃなかったです	簡単で	simple
複雑です ふくざつ	複雑でした	複雑ではありません/ 複雑ではない/ 複雑じゃありません/ 複雑ではない	複雑ではではありませんでした/ 複雑ではなかったです/ 複雑じゃありませんでした/ 複雑じゃなかったです	複雑で	complex, complicated

Irregular Adjective

Non-Past (formal 〜です/ informal 〜だ)	Past (formal 〜でした/ informal 〜だった)	Negative (formal 〜ではありません/ informal 〜じゃない)	Negative Past (formal 〜ではなかった/ informal 〜じゃなかった)	〜て-form (〜で)	English meaning
いいです or 良いです/いい/良い よ	良かったです/ 良かった	良くありません/良くない	良くありませんでした/ 良くなかった	良くて	good

い Adjectives & な Adjectives

い Adjectives

2014s	仲の悪い なか わる	unfriendly
2023	遅い おそ	slow, late
2023	速い はや	fast, quick
2025	甘い あま	sweet
2025s	うらやましい	jealous
2025	辛い から	spicy
2025	酸っぱい す	sour
2025	苦い にが	bitter
2031	多い おお	many, numerous
2031	少ない すく	few, a little
2032	厚い あつ	thick, heavy (coating), deep (color)
2032	薄い うす	light, thin
2033s	細かい こま	detailed
2034	若い わか	young
2043	可笑しい おか	strange, funny, ridiculous
2043	珍しい めずら	unusual, rare
2044	よろしい	good, OK, fine
2051	冷たい	cold (to the touch)
2052	暖かい あたた	warm
2052	ぬるい	lukewarm
2052	恥ずかしい は	shy, embarrassed, ashamed
2053	温かい あたた	warm
2061	正しい ただ	correct, right, proper
2064	恐ろしい おそ	afraid
2064	寂しい さび	lonely, lonesome
2072s	濃い こ	thick, dark
2074	面倒くさい めんどう	bother(some) to do, tiresome
2084	重い おも	heavy (weight)
2084	軽い かる	light (weight)
2095	貧しい まず	poor, needy

な Adjectives

2021	簡単 かんたん	simple
2021	複雑 ふくざつ	complex, complicated
2021	バラバラ	scattered, in pieces, disconnected
2022	まっすぐ	straight (ahead)
2022s	のどか	calm, peaceful
2022s	便利 べん り	useful
2023	伝統的 でんとうてき	traditional
2023	日本的 てき	Japanese (typically)
2025	幸せ しあわ	happiness, good fortune
2025s	大変 たいへん	extreme, problematic
2031s	さまざま	various, assorted
2032	平 たいら	flat
2043	変 へん	unusual, strange
2053	気楽 きらく	relaxing
2053s	健康的 けんこうてき	healthy
2054	めちゃくちゃ	messy, disorderly, absurd
2063	賑やか にぎ	bustling, busy
2071	迷惑 めいわく	trouble, bother
2073	平気 へいき	coolness, calmness, unconcern
2081	不幸 ふ こう	unhappiness, misfortune
2092	大切 たいせつ	important, valuable

Adverbs

2011	中 なか	in, inside, middle, center	2024s	多分 た ぶん	maybe, possibly	2044	まず	first (of all), anyway, well then
2021s	いつか	at some time, sometime	2024s	なるべく	as much as possible	2044	ぎりぎり	just barely, at the last moment/grinding sound
2021s	特に とく	especially, particularly	2033	かなり	considerably, quite	2054	ほかほか	steamy hot food, warm(ly)
2021s	やっぱり	after all, same as やはり	2033	逆に ぎゃく	conversely, on the contrary	2054	わいわい	noisily, clamorously
2023	必ず かなら	always, without exception	2033	なかなか	very, considerably, easily, by no means (with neg. verb)	2061	ほとんど	mostly, almost
2023	普通 ふ つう	usual, normal	2035	遅く おそ	slowly	2074	以外 い がい	with the exception of
2023s	わくわく	thrilled, excited	2035	早く はや	early (in the day)	2101	いったい	generally, in general
2024s	一応 いち おう	at least, for the present	2043	きっと	surely, undoubtedly			

Conjunctions

2032	だから/ ですから	so, therefore	2041	それとも	or, or else	2064	すると	therefore, then, and (then) [used predominately in written language]
2032	ですから/ だから	so, therefore	2044	それで	and, because of that (at beginning of sentence)	2095	為に ため	or, on behalf of
2033	しかし	however, but	2044	ので	since, given that..., because of...	2101s	なら	if, in case, if it is the case
2034s	そろそろ	before long, soon	2053	から	because	2101	なら/ならば	if, in case, if it is true that

Counters

Counting Basic Numbers

-10 1021	11-20 1022	Above 20 1022	Hundreds 1023s	Thousands 1052	Ten Thousands	One Hundred Thousands 1091
一 いち	11 十一 じゅういち	21 二十一 にじゅういち	100 百 ひゃく	1,000 千 せん	10,000 一万 いちまん	110,000 十一万 じゅういちまん
二 に	12 十二 じゅうに	22 二十二 にじゅうに	200 二百 にひゃく	2,000 二千 にせん	20,000 二万 にまん	120,000 十二万 じゅうにまん
三 さん	13 十三 じゅうさん	30 三十 さんじゅう	300 三百 さんびゃく	3,000 三千 さんぜん	30,000 三万 さんまん	130,000 十三万 じゅうさんまん
四 よん/し	14 十四 じゅうよん/し	40 四十 よんじゅう	400 四百 よんひゃく	4,000 四千 よんせん	40,000 四万 よんまん	140,000 十四万 じゅうよんまん
五 ご	15 十五 じゅうご	50 五十 ごじゅう	500 五百 ごひゃく	5,000 五千 ごせん	50,000 五万 ごまん	150,000 十五万 じゅうごまん
六 ろく	16 十六 じゅうろく	60 六十 ろくじゅう	600 六百 ろっぴゃく	6,000 六千 ろくせん	60,000 六万 ろくまん	160,000 十六万 じゅうろくまん
七 しち/なな	17 十七 じゅうしち/なな	70 七十 ななじゅう	700 七百 ななひゃく	7,000 七千 ななせん	70,000 七万 ななまん	170,000 十七万 じゅうななまん
八 はち	18 十八 じゅうはち	80 八十 はちじゅう	800 八百 はっぴゃく	8,000 八千 はっせん	80,000 八万 はちまん	180,000 十八万 じゅうはちまん
九 く/きゅう	19 十九 じゅうく/きゅう	90 九十 きゅうじゅう	900 九百 きゅうひゃく	9,000 九千 きゅうせん	90,000 九万 きゅうまん	190,000 十九万 じゅうきゅうまん
十 じゅう	20 二十 にじゅう				100,000 十万 じゅうまん	200,000 二十万 にじゅうまん 210,000 二十一万 にじゅういちまん

	Hours 1032	Minutes 1032	Grade Levels 1031	Class Periods 1033	Times/Temp. 1101	People 1021	Small Animals 1022	Ages 1022	Generic Counters 1024	Pages 1042	Flat Objects 1042
1	一時 いちじ	一分 いっぷん	Elem./Primary 小学一年生 しょうがくいちねんせい	一時間目 いちじかんめ	一度 いちど	一人 ひとり	一匹 いっぴき	一歳 いっさい	一つ ひと	一ページ いち/ひとページ	一枚 いちまい
2	二時 にじ	二分 にふん	小学二年生 しょうがくにねんせい	二時間目 にじかんめ	二度 にど	二人 ふたり	二匹 にひき	二歳 にさい	二つ ふた	二ページ にページ	二枚 にまい
3	三時 さんじ	三分 さんぷん	小学三年生 しょうがくさんねんせい	三時間目 さんじかんめ	三度 さんど	三人 さんにん	三匹 さんびき	三歳 さんさい	三つ みっ	三ページ さんページ	三枚 さんまい
4	四時 よじ	四分 よんぷん	小学四年生 しょうがくよねんせい	四時間目 よじかんめ	四度 よんど	四人 よにん	四匹 よんひき	四歳 よんさい	四つ よっ	四ページ よんページ	四枚 よんまい
5	五時 ごじ	五分 ごふん	小学五年生 しょうがくごねんせい	五時間目 ごじかんめ	五度 ごど	五人 ごにん	五匹 ごひき	五歳 ごさい	五つ いつ	五ページ ごページ	五枚 ごまい
6	六時 ろくじ	六分 ろっぷん	小学六年生 しょうがくろくねんせい	六時間目 ろくじかんめ	六度 ろくど	六人 ろくにん	六匹 ろっぴき	六歳 ろくさい	六つ むっ	六ページ ろくページ	六枚 ろくまい
7	七時 しち/ななじ	七分 ななふん	MS/Jr. High 中学一年生 ちゅうがくいちねんせい	七時間目 ななじかんめ	七度 ななど	七人 しち/ななにん	七匹 ななひき	七歳 ななさい	七つ なな	七ページ しち/ななページ	七枚 しち/ななまい
8	八時 はちじ	八分 はちふん/はっぷん	中学二年生 ちゅうがくにねんせい		八度 はちど	八人 はちにん	八匹 はっぴき	八歳 はっさい	八つ やっ	八ページ はち/やっページ	八枚 はちまい
9	九時 くじ	九分 きゅうふん	中学三年生 ちゅうがくさんねんせい		九度 きゅうど	九人 きゅうにん	九匹 きゅうひき	九歳 きゅうさい	九つ ここの	九ページ きゅうページ	九枚 きゅうまい
10	十時 じゅうじ	十分 じゅっ/じっぷん	Senior High 高校一年生 こうこういちねんせい		十度 じゅうど	十人 じゅうにん	十匹 じゅう/じっぴき	十歳 じゅっさい	十 とお	十ページ じゅっページ	十枚 じゅうまい
11	十一時 じゅういちじ	十一分 じゅういっぷん	高校二年生 こうこうにねんせい			十一人 じゅういちにん	十一匹 じゅういっぴき	十一歳 じゅういっさい	十一 じゅういち	十一ページ じゅういちページ	十一枚 じゅういちま…
12	十二時 じゅうにじ	十二分 じゅうにふん	高校三年生 こうこうさんねんせい			十二人 じゅうににん	十二匹 じゅうにひき	十二歳 じゅうにさい	十二 じゅうに	十二ページ じゅうにページ	十二枚 じゅうにま…

Dates 1053						Cylindrical Objects 1092	Cupfuls 1092	Bound Volumes 1092
1st 一日 ついたち	11th 十一日 じゅういちにち	21st 二十一日 にじゅういちにち		1	一本 いっぽん	一杯 いっぱい	一冊 いっさつ
2nd 二日 ふつか	12th 十二日 じゅうににち	22nd 二十二日 にじゅうににち		2	二本 にほん	二杯 にはい	二冊 にさつ
3rd 三日 みっか	13th 十三日 じゅうさんにち	23rd 二十三日 にじゅうさんにち		3	三本 さんぼん	三杯 さんばい	三冊 さんさつ
4th 四日 よっか	14th 十四日 じゅうよっか	24th 二十四日 にじゅうよっか		4	四本 よんほん	四杯 よんはい	四冊 よんさつ
5th 五日 いつか	15th 十五日 じゅうごにち	25th 二十五日 にじゅうごにち		5	五本 ごほん	五杯 ごはい	五冊 ごさつ
6th 六日 むいか	16th 十六日 じゅうろくにち	26th 二十六日 にじゅうろくにち		6	六本 ろっぽん	六杯 ろっぱい	六冊 ろくさつ
7th 七日 なのか	17th 十七日 じゅうしちにち	27th 二十七日 にじゅうしちにち		7	七本 ななほん	七杯 ななはい	七冊 ななさつ
8th 八日 ようか	18th 十八日 じゅうはちにち	28th 二十八日 にじゅうはちにち		8	八本 はちほん/はっぽん	八杯 はっぱい	八冊 はっさつ
9th 九日 ここのか	19th 十九日 じゅうくにち	29th 二十九日 にじゅうくにち		9	九本 きゅうほん	九杯 きゅうはい	九冊 きゅうさつ
10th 十日 とおか	20th 二十日 はつか	30th 三十日 さんじゅうにち		10	十本 じゅっ/じっぽん	十杯 じゅっ/じっぱい	十冊 じゅっさつ
		31st 三十一日 さんじゅういちにち					

#__ 2011	Smallish objects 2022	The #th 2023	Night's stay 2024	Floor 2024	Large animals 2102	Birds 2102
一番 いちばん	一個 いっこ	一番目 いちばんめ	一泊 いっぱく	一階 いっかい	一頭 いっとう	一羽 いちわ
二番 にばん	二個 にこ	二番目 にばんめ	二泊 にはく	二階 にかい	二頭 にとう	二羽 にわ
三番 さんばん	三個 さんこ	三番目 さんばんめ	三泊 さんぱく	三階 さんかい/がい	三頭 さんとう	三羽 さんわ
四番 よんばん	四個 よんこ	四番目 よんばんめ	四泊 よんはく	四階 よんかい	四頭 よんとう	四羽 よんわ
五番 ごばん	五個 ごこ	五番目 ごばんめ	五泊 ごはく	五階 ごかい	五頭 ごとう	五羽 ごわ
六番 ろくばん	六個 ろっこ	六番目 ろくばんめ	六泊 ろっぱく	六階 ろっかい	六頭 ろくとう	六羽 ろくわ
七番 ななばん	七個 ななこ	七番目 ななばんめ	七泊 ななはく	七階 ななかい	七頭 ななとう	七羽 ななわ
八番 はちばん	八個 はちこ	八番目 はちばんめ	八泊 はっぱく	八階 はちかい	八頭 はち/はっとう	八羽 はちわ
九番 きゅうばん	九個 きゅうこ	九番目 きゅうばんめ	九泊 きゅうはく	九階 きゅうかい	九頭 きゅうとう	九羽 きゅうわ
十番 じゅうばん	十個 じゅっ/じっこ	十番目 じゅうばんめ	十泊 じゅっぱく	十階 じゅっかい	十頭 じゅっとう	十羽 じっぱ/じゅうわ

Onomatopoetic Expressions

064	いらいら	イライラ	nervous	
054s	こんこん	コンコン	tap, wrap	
054	さくさく		crunchy, crisp	
064	どきどき	ドキドキ	excited, go pitter-patter	
051	どろどろ		syrupy, muddled	
054	どんどん	ドンドン	steadily, drumming (noise), boom boom	
051	びしょびしょ		sopping wet, drenched	

2044	ぎりぎり		just barely, at the last moment/grinding sound	
2054	ほかほか		steamy hot food, warm(ly)	
2054	わいわい		noisily, clamorously	
2023s	わくわく		thrilled, excited	
2054	あつあつ	熱々	piping hot, passionately in love	
2021	ばらばら	バラバラ	scattered, in pieces, disconnected	
2054	めちゃくちゃ		messy, disorderly, absurd	

Particles

	signifies a question	1014
	in; at; used after a location or time word	1015
	possession; replaces a noun	1021, 1093
	new information marker; "but"; conjunction; used to combine two sentences	1021, 1071, 1073, 1095
	"and" used to connect more than one noun, quotation particle, used after a direct quotation	1022
	used after the direct object	1023
	too; also; replaces particles は、が、 and を	1024
ら	from (a place or a time); from (used with spec. times or locations)	1031, 1032
も	but/however - at the beginning of a sentence	1034
	sentence ending for a rhetorical question or when seeking agreement	1035
え	sentence ending that can be exclamatory or express surprise	1035
	sentence ending for a strong declarative statement or for emphasis	1035

で	by means of a "tool"; at; for (used for shopping or ordering food)	1043, 1063, 1092
まで	until (used with spec. locations or times)	1053
など	et cetera, and so forth	1101
へ/に	either of these can be used to mean "to" and comes after a place of destination	1023
かな	I wonder (sentence ending part.), should I? / is it? (question part.), I wish that… (with a negative)	2023
から	because	2032
～より	than ~	2032
ので	that being the case, because of …	2043
～くらい	about ~	2043
だけ	only, just, as	2062
など	et cetera, and the like	2062
より	from (in the conclusion of a letter)	2062
ばかり	only, just	2062

Japanese-English Glossary

This glossary has simplified abbreviations to make it easier to use. The following abbreviations are used for parts of speech:

い *adj.*	い adjective	*interj.*	interjection
な *adj.*	な adjective	*n*	noun
ir. adj.	irregular adjective	*ono.*	onomatopoetic exp.
adv.	adverb	*part.*	particle
conj.	conjunction	*pn*	person or place name
exp.	expression	*pron.*	pronoun
inter.	interrogative	*v*	verb

The numbering system for location of vocabulary words in the chapters is made up of the volume numbe (the first digit; 2 is this volume, *Intermediate Japanese*); a two-digit chapter number; and the section numbe An "s" indicates words that are supplemental: they are not on the New Words lists, but are also include in the book (in the Dialogues, Journal entries, etc.). For example:

2025s

Vol. 2   Chapter 2   Section 5   supplementary (not in New Words)

Japanese	Location		English
ああ	1025	*interj.*	Ah!, Oh!
あい・愛	1022s	*n*	love
あいこ・愛子	1015s	*pn*	Aiko (female name)
あいすくりーむ・アイスクリーム	App.	*n*	ice cream
あいだ・間	2023	*n*	interval, space [between]
あいたい・会いたい	1044s	*v*	want to meet
あいでぃあ・アイディア	1051s	*n*	idea
あいている・空いている	2024s	*v*	is open, is free
あいぬ・アイヌ	2013	*n*	peoples indigenous to Hokkaido, Sakhalin, and the Kuril Islands
あう・会う	2024	*v*	meet (to)
あう・合う	2042	*v*	come together (to), fit (to), match (to)
あう・会う	1054s	*v*	meet (to)
あお・青	1074	*n*	blue
あおい・青い	1082	い *adj.*	blue-colored
あおのり・青のり	2093s	*n*	green seaweed
あか・赤	1074	*n*	red
あかい・赤い	1082	い *adj.*	red-colored
あかふじ・赤富士	2035s	*pn*	Red Mt. Fuji (woodblock print)
あがる・上がる	2021	*v*	ascend (to), rise (to), climb (to)
あかるい・明るい	1093	い *adj.*	bright, light
あき・秋	1101	*n*	fall, autumn
あきた・秋田	2061	*pn*	Akita (prefecture)
あきらめる・諦める	2062s	*v*	give up (to)
あく・開く	2081	*v*	open (to)

Japanese	Location		English
あくしゅ	1042	*n*	handshake
あくま・悪魔	2034s	*n*	devil, demon
あける・開ける	2081	*v*	open (to) (eyes, doors, etc.)
あける・開ける/あけます・開けます	1034	*v*	open (to) [door/window]
あげる・上げる/あげます・上げます	1094	*v*	give (to) [to equals or superior
あさ・朝	1025	*n*	morning
あさごはん・朝ご飯	1025	*n*	breakfast
あさって・明後日	1102	*n*	day after tomorrow
あさって・明後日	2022	*n*	the day after tomorrow
あし・足	1061	*n*	leg, foot
あした・明日	1032	*n*	tomorrow
あしんめとりっくでざいん・アシンメトリックデザイン	2032	*n*	asymmetric design
あそこ	1024	*pron.*	over there
あそぶ・遊ぶ/あそびます・遊びます	1103	*v*	play (to)
あたたかい・暖かい	2052	い *adj.*	warm
あたたかい・温かい	2053	い *adj.*	warm
あたま・頭	1061	*n*	head
あたらしい・新しい	1081	い *adj.*	new
あちこち	1054s	*adv.*	here and there
あちら	1014s	*pn*	that (person) over there
あっち	2011	*prn*	that way (direction distant fro both speaker and listener), over there [informal for あち

342   Intermediate Japanese

Japanese	Location		English
あっ	1031	interj.	oh
あっ	2051	interj.	A! (exp. of surprise)
あつい・暑い	1034	い adj.	hot (weather)
あつあつ・熱々	2054	n/ono.	piping hot, passionately in love
あつい・厚い	2032	い adj.	thick, heavy (coating), deep (color)
あつまる・集まる	2081	v	meet (to), congregate (to)
あつめる・集める	2081	v	collect (to), put together (to)
あと・跡	2021s	n	ruins, remains
あと・後	1033		after
あとで・後で	1033	adv.	later, afterwards
あなた	1041s	pron.	you [best not used too often]
あに・兄	1021	n	older brother (my)
あにめ・アニメ	1011	n	animated cartoons/films
あね・姉	1021	n	older sister (my)
あの	1023		that (thing) over there
あびる・浴びる	2052	v	shower (to), bask in the sun (to), bathe (to)
あぶない・危ない	1081	い adj.	dangerous
あまのはしだて・天橋立	1082	pn	Amanohashidate (place)
あまい・甘い	2025	い adj.	sweet
あまり	1074	adv.	not very
あめ・雨	1101	n	rain
あめ・飴	1023s	n	candy/sweets
アメリカぐん・アメリカ軍	2065s	n	American army
アメフト, あめりかんふっとぼーる・アメリカンフットボール	1071	n	American football
あめりか・アメリカ	1041	pn	United States of America (place)
あめりかし・アメリカ史	1032	n	American history
あめりかじん・アメリカ人	1041	n	American (person)
アメリカぐんきちのへいたい・アメリカ軍基地の兵隊	2061s	n	soldier on an American military base
アメリカぐんのちゅうりゅうじだい・アメリカ軍の駐留時代	2034s	n	American Occupation (the)
ありがとう	1023	exp.	thanks
あらう・洗う	2051	v	wash (to)
あらすじ	2043s	n	outline, summary
ある/あります	1021	v	exist (to) [inanimate things]
あるいていく・歩いて行く	2012	v	go by walking (to)
あるいてかえる・歩いて帰る	2012	v	return by walking (to)
あるいてくる・歩いて来る	2012	v	come by walking (to)
あるく・歩く	2012	v	walk (to)
あるばいと・アルバイト	1025s	n	part time job
アルバイト	2011s	n	part-time job
あれ	1015	pron.	that (over there)
あわせる・合わせる	2042	v	match (to), mix (to)
あんぜん・安全	2084	n	safe
あんない・案内	2061s	n	guidance, information
あんぱん・あんパン	2071	n	roll or bun filled with sweet red bean paste (anko)
いい/よい・良い	1041s	ir. adj.	good
いいえ	1014		no
いいえ、ちがいます。・違います。	1014	exp.	No, it is not/different.
いいえ、わかりません。・わかりません。	1016s	exp.	No, I don't understand.
いう・言う/いいます・言います	1041	v	say (to)
いうとおり・言う通り	2032s	exp.	as you say
いえ/うち・家	1022	n	house, home
いか・以下	2063	n	not more than; ... and less than/below
いがい・以外	2074	adv.	with the exception of
いきましょう・行きましょう	1035	exp.	let's go
いぎりす・イギリス	1041	pn	England (place)
いぎりすけい・イギリス系	1041	n	English (descent)
いぎりすじん・イギリス人	1041	n	English (person)
いく・行く/いきます・行きます	1044	v	go
いくつ	1021	inter.	how many (things)?
いくつ・(お)いくつ	1022s	inter.	how old (animate beings), how many
いくつ・(お)いくつ	2011	inter.	how old, how many years (old)?
いくら	1092	inter.	how much?
いけ・池	1101s	n	pond
いけばな・生け花	1071	n	flower arranging
いけん・意見	2092	n	opinion, view
いし・石	1101	n	stone, rock
いし・石	2031	n	stone; rock
いしゃ・医者	1063	n	doctor
いしょう・衣装	2033s	n	clothing
いじょう・以上	2063	n	not less than, ... and more than, above
いす・椅子	App.	n	chair
イスラムきょう・イスラム教	2062	n	Islam
いぜな・伊是名	2021s	pn	Izena, small island in n.e. Okinawa Prefecture
いそがしい・忙しい	1054	い adj.	busy
いそぐ・急ぐ	2091	v	hurry (to)
いたい・痛い	1063	い adj.	painful
いたす・致す	2044	v	do (to) [humble for します]
いただく/いただきます	1092	v	receive (to) [very polite], lit.: I will receive.
いたち	2014s	n	weasel
いたりあ・イタリア	1041	pn	Italy (place)
いたりあご・イタリア語	1042	n	Italian (language)
いたりあじん・イタリア人	1041	n	Italian (person)
いち・一	1021	counter	one
いちおう・一応	2024s	adv.	at least, for the present
いちがつ・一月	1052	n	January
いちご・イチゴ	App.	n	strawberry
いちじ・一時	1032	counter	one o'clock
いちじかんめ・一時間目	1033	counter	first period
いちど・一度	1101	counter	one time
いちねんせい・一年生	1031s	counter	first year student
いちばん・一番	2011	counter	first, number one
いちばんめ・一番目	2023	counter	the first
いちばんうえの あに/あね・一番上の 兄/姉	1021	n	oldest brother/sister (my)
いちばんしたのおとうと/いもうと・一番下の 弟/妹	1021	n	youngest brother/sister (my)
いちびょう・一秒	1032	counter	one second
いち/いっぺーじ・一ページ	1042	counter	one page/page one
いちまい・一枚	1042	counter	one sheet/piece
いちまん・一万	1091	counter	ten thousand
いちわ・一羽	2102	counter	one bird

Japanese	Location		English
いつ	1052	inter.	when?
いつか	2021s	adv.	at some time; sometime
いつか・五日	1053	counter	fifth (day of the month)
いっかい・一階	2024	counter	first floor
いっこ・一個	2022	counter	one piece/smallish object
いっさい・一歳/才	1052	counter	one year old
いったい	2101	n/adv.	What the heck?, What on earth?; (adv.) generally, in general
いっさつ・一冊	1092	counter	one volume
いっしょ・一緒	1043s	n	together, at the same time, same
いっしょに・一緒に	1044s	exp.	together, at the same time, same
いつつ・五つ	1024	counter	five (things)
いっとう・一頭	2102	counter	one large animal
いっぱい・一杯	1092	counter	one cupful
いっぱく・一泊	2024	counter	stopping one night
いっぴき・一匹	1092	counter	one small animal
いっぷん・一分	1032	counter	one minute
いっぽん・一本	1092	counter	one cylindrical object
いつも	1061	n/adv.	always
いなか・田舎	2032s	n	countryside, rural
いなりずし・稲荷寿司	1103s	n	sushi wrapped in fried tofu (abura-age)
いぬ・犬	1021	n	dog
いぬどし・犬年, 戌年	2014	n	year of the dog
いのこり・居残り	2074s	n	detention
いのしし・猪	2013	n	wild boar
いのる・祈る	2065	v	pray (to), wish (to)
いま・今	1032	n/adv.	now
いみ・意味	2031s	n	meaning, significance
いもうと・妹	1021	n	younger sister (my)
いもうとさん・妹さん	1022	n	younger sister (someone else's)
いやいや	1094s		by no means, reluctantly
いやだ・嫌だ	2021s	n	disagreeable, unpleasant
いやりんぐ・イヤリング	1064	n	earring
いらいら・イライラ	2064	ono.	nervous
いらっしゃいませ	1043	exp.	welcome (usually used at a place of business)
いらっしゃる	2044	v	come (to), go (to), somewhere (to be), honorific for 行きます or います
いらんじん・イラン人	1041	n	Iranian (person)
いる/います	1021	v	exist (to) [animate beings]
いれる・入れる/いれます・入れます	1061	v	put into (to)
いろ・色	1074	n	color
いろいろ・色々	1074	adv.	various
いろり	2061s	n	open, central fire pit used for cooking and heat in houses in n. Japan
いわう・祝う	2061	v	celebrate (to)
いんさつ・印刷	2031s	n	printing
いんさつき・印刷機	2031s	n	printing press
いんしょうがか・印象画家	2033s	n	Impressionists
いんぷれっしょにずむ・インプレッショニズム	2032	pn	Impressionism
いんどねしあ・インドネシア	1041	pn	Indonesia (place)
うぃんどうしょっぴんぐ・ウィンドウショッピング(を)する/します	1091s	n	window-shop (to)
いんどねしあご・インドネシア語	1042	n	Indonesian (language)

Japanese	Location		English
いんどねしあじん・インドネシア人	1041	n	Indonesian (person)
うえ・上	2022	n	above, up
うぇいとれす・ウェイトレス	1084s	n	waitress
うきよえ・浮世絵	1091	n	woodblock print (prior to and through the Edo Period)
うごかす・動かす	2042	v	move (to), set in motion (to)
うごく・動く	2042	v	move (to), operate (to)
うさぎ・兎	2013	n	rabbit
うし・牛	2012	n	cow
うしろ・後ろ	2015	n	behind, back
うすい・薄い	2032	い adj.	light, thin
うそ・嘘	1104	n	lie
うた・歌	1071	n	song
うたう・歌う/うたいます・歌います	1071	v	sing (to)
うたうこと・歌う事	1071	n	singing
うたまろ・歌麿	2032	pn	Kitagawa Utamarou, artist
うち・内	2061	n	inside, within, (of the) home
うち/いえ・家	1022s	n	home/house
うちのこども・うちの子供	2061	n	children (my/our)
うちのひと・うちの人	2061	n	husband (my)
うちゅうひこうし・宇宙飛行士	2104	n	astronaut
うつくしい・美しい	1081	い adj.	beautiful
うつす・写す	2065s	v	photographed (to be), copy (to be)
うで・腕	1061	n	arm
うでどけい・腕時計	2015	n	wristwatch
うなぎ・鰻	2043	n	eel
うま・馬	1082	n	horse
うまれる/・生まれるうまれます・生まれます	1052	v	born (to be)
うみ・海	1081	n	ocean, sea
うら・裏	2065		back(side), reverse
うらやましい	2025s	い adj.	jealous
うらしまたろう・浦島太郎	1084s	pn	Urashima Taro (folktale character
うる・売る/うります・売ります	1091	v	sell (to)
うるさい	1081	い adj.	noisy, loud
うれしい・嬉しい	1081	い adj.	glad, happy
え・絵	1091	n	painting, drawing
えあこん・エアコン	1035	n	airconditioning
えいが・映画	1091	n	movie
えいきょう・影響	2015	n	influence, effect
えいきょう・影響する	2015	v	influence (to), effect (to)
えいご・英語	1032	n	English (language)
えいごで いってください。・英語で言って下さい。	1016s	exp.	Please say it in English.
ええ/はい	1032s		yes
ええっ/え?	1033s	inter.	huh?
ええと	1033s	interj.	let me see, well…
えき・駅	2012	n	station (subway/rail)
えさ・餌	2095s	n	animal food
えすさいず・Sサイズ	1092	n	small (S) size
えど・江戸	1044s	pn	Edo, former name of Tokyo (place)
えぬえいちけー・NHK	2085	n	Japan Broadcasting Corporatic (TV network: 日本放送協会)
えむさいず・Mサイズ	1092	n	medium (M) size
えむぴーすりーぷれーやー・MP3プレーヤー	1031	n	MP3 player

Japanese	Location		English
えらぶ・選ぶ	2101	v	choose (to), select (to)
えらべる・選べる	2101s	v	select (to), choose (to)
えるさいず・Lサイズ	1092	n	large (L) size
うんてん・運転(を)する	2012	v	drive (to)
えんじる・演じる	2043	v	perform (to)
えんそう・演奏	2023	n	musical performance
えんぴつ・鉛筆	1024	n	pencil
えんりょ・遠慮	2102	n/な adj.	tact, thoughtfulness
おーすとらりあ・オーストラリア	1041	pn	Australia (place)
おーすとらりあじん・オーストラリア人	1041	n	Australian (person)
おいかける・追い掛ける	2014s	v	chase after (to); pursue (to)
おいしい・美味しい	1081	い adj.	delicious
おうさま・王様	2021s	n	king, ruler
おうふく・往復	2024	n	round trip, return ticket
おおい・多い	2031	い adj.	many, numerous
おおあめ・大雨	1101	n	heavy rain
おおきい・大きい	1031	い adj.	big, large
おおさか・大阪	1083s	pn	Osaka (place)
おおみそか・大晦日	2061	n	New Year's Eve
おかあさん・お母さん	1022	n	mother (someone else's)
おかえりなさい・お帰りなさい	1015	exp.	welcome home
おかげ・お蔭	2063	n	thanks to or owing to, assistance
おかし・(お)菓子	1095	n	Japanese traditional sweets
おかしい・可笑しい	2043	い adj.	strange, funny, ridiculous
おかず	2025s	n	side dishes
おかず	2025s	n	accompaniment for rice dishes, main dish or side dish
おかれる・置かれる	2053s	v	place (to), put (to)
おかわり・お代わり	2061	n	second helping, substitute, alternate
おきょう・お経	1052s	n	scriptures
おきなわ・沖縄	2011	pn	Okinawa (island of or island chain of)
おきゃくさん・お客さん	2045	n	customer, guest
おきる・起きる/おきます・起きます	1051	v	wake (up) (to)
おく・置く	2092	v	put (to), place (to)
おくりもの・贈り物	2083	n	gift
おくる・送る/おくります・送ります	1051	v	send (to)
おこす・起こす	2081	v	wake someone up (to), rise (to)
おこづかい・お小遣い	2024s	n	allowance
おごりで	2071s	n	treat (someone to a meal)
おさえつける・押さえ付ける	2093s	v	press down (to)
おじ	2065	n	uncle
おじいさん	1022	n	grandfather (someone else's)
おしえる・教える	2015	v	teach (to), tell/inform (to)
おしえて ください・教えて 下さい	1032s	exp.	tell me/teach me, please
おじぎする・お辞儀する	2064s	v	bow (to)
おじさん	1022	n	uncle or man quite a bit older than you
おしゃかさま・お釈迦様	2014s	pn	Buddha
おしゃべり	2054	n	chatter, gossip
おしゃれ	1062	な adj	fashionable
おしょうがつ・お正月	2061	n	New Year, New Year's Day
おすすめ・お勧め	2042s	n	recommendation

Japanese	Location		English
おせちりょうり・お節料理	2061	n	food served during New Year's Holidays
おせわ・お世話	2063	n	help, assistance
おそい・遅い	2023	い adj.	slow, late
おそく・遅く	2035	adv.	slowly
おそろしい・恐ろしい	2064	い adj.	afraid
おだやか	1084	な adj	calm, peaceful
おちゃ・お茶	1024s	n	green tea
おちゃのみず・お茶の水	1024s	pn	Ochanomizu (section of Tokyo)
おっと	1083	interj.	oops, sorry
おつり	1092	n	change (cash)
おてあらいへ いっても・お手洗いへ 行っても いいですか。	1016s	exp.	May I go to the restroom/W.C.?
おでん	1091s	n	oden (various ingredients stewed in soy-flavored dashi)
おと・音	2054	n	sound
おとうさん・お父さん	1022	n	father (someone else's)
おとうと・弟	1021	n	younger brother (my)
おとうとさん・弟さん	1022	n	younger brother (someone else's)
おとこ・男	1064s	n	man, male
おとこのこ・男の子	1064	n	boy
おとこのひと・男の人	1064	n	man, male
おととい・一昨日	2022	n	day before yesterday
おととい・一昨日	1102	n	day before yesterday
おとな・大人	2062	n	adult
おどり・踊り	1071	n	dancing
おどる・踊る	2042	v	dance (to)
おどろく・驚く	2033s	v	surprise (to)
おなか・お腹	1061	n	stomach
おなか(が) いっぱい・お腹(が)一杯	1104	exp.	have a full stomach
おなじ・同じ	1044s	n	same
おに・鬼	2062	n	ghost, devil
おにいさん・お兄さん	1022	n	older brother (someone else's)
おにぎり	1105s	n	rice balls
おねえさん・お姉さん	1022	n	older sister (someone else's)
おねがい・お願い/おねがいします・お願いします	1013s	exp.	please
おばあさん	1022	n	grandmother (someone else's)
おばさん	1022	n	aunt or woman quite a bit older than you
おはよう	1015	exp.	good morning [informal]
おはよう ございます	1015	exp.	good morning [formal]
おふろ・お風呂	1093s	n	bath
おび・帯	2023s	n	tie, belt for a kimono
おひゃくしょうさん・お百姓さん	2065s	n	farmers
おぼえる・覚える	2091	v	remember (to), memorize (to)
おほーつくかい・オホーツク海	2015s	pn	Sea of Okhotsk
おみずを のんでも・お水を 飲んでもいいですか。	1016s	exp.	May I drink (some) water?
おみやげ・お土産	1023	n	souvenir(s)
おもい・重い	2084	い adj.	heavy (weight)
おもいだす・思い出す	2021s	v	remember (to)
おもいで・思い出	2064s	n	memory, remembrance
おもう・思う/おもいます・思います	1072	v	think (to)
おもしろい・面白い	1082	い adj.	interesting
おやすみ・お休み	1015	exp.	good night [informal]

Japanese	Location		English
おやすみなさい・お休みな さい	1015	*exp.*	good night [formal]
おやつ	App.	*n*	snack
およぐ・泳ぐ/およぎます・ 泳ぎます	1071	*v*	swim (to)
およぐこと・泳ぐ事	1071	*n*	swimming
おらんだ・オランダ	1041	*pn*	Holland (place)
おらんだご・オランダ語	1042	*n*	Dutch (language)
おらんだじん・オランダ人	1041	*n*	Dutch person
おりる・降りる	2022	*v*	disembark (to), get off (a vehicle)
おれない・折れない	2062s		will not break
おわん・お碗	2065s	*n*	bowl
おれんじ・オレンジ	1074	*n*	orange
おれんじじゅーす・オレン ジジュース	1043s	*n*	orange juice
おわる・終わる/おわり ます・終わります	1052	*v*	finish (to)
おんかい・音階	2023s	*n*	musical scale
おんがく・音楽	1032	*n*	music
おんがくかい・音楽会	1052s	*n*	concert, recital
おんせん・温泉	2015	*n*	hot spring
おんど・温度	1101	*n*	temperature
がーどする・ガードする	2085	*v*	guard (to), protect (to)
おんな・女	1064s	*n*	woman, female
おんながた・女形	2042	*n*	male actor in female Kabuki role
おんなのこ・女の子	1064	*n*	girl
おんなのひと・女の人	1064	*n*	woman, female
か	1014	*part.*	signifies a question
が	1021s	*part.*	new information marker, used to
"but",	1071s	*conj.*	combine two sentences
がーどする・ガードする	2085	*v*	guard (to), protect (to)
かい・回	2021s	*counter*	times
かい・〜階	2054	*counter*	floors/stories
かいがい・海外	2091	*n*	foreign, overseas
がいこく・外国	1041	*n*	foreign country
がいこくじん・外国人	1041	*n*	foreigner
かいしゃ・会社	2024	*n*	company
かいしゃいん・会社員	1025s	*n*	company employee
かいたくのむら・開拓の村	2013s	*n*	pioneer village
かいだん・階段	2022	*n*	stairs, staircase
がいねん・概念	2031s	*n*	concept, idea
かいはつ・開発	2031s	*n*	advancement, expansion
かいふくをねがう・回復を 願う	2091s	*exp.*	hope for recovery [from an illness] (to)
かいもの・買い物	1091	*n*	shopping
かいもの・買い物(を)する /します	1091	*v*	go shopping (to)
かいわ・会話	1013s	*n*	dialogue
かう・買う/かいます・ 買います	1091	*v*	buy (to)
かえる・蛙	1072	*n*	frog
かえる・帰る/かえります・ 帰ります	1044	*v*	return (to)
かお・顔	1061	*n*	face
かがく・科学	1032	*n*	science
ががく・雅楽	1075	*n*	gagaku, ancient Japanese court music
かかる・掛かる	2012s	*v*	take time (to)
かく・描く/かきます・ 描きます	1054s	*v*	draw (to)

Japanese	Location		English
かく・書く/かきます・ 書きます	1013	*v*	write (to)
かくにん・確認	2044s	*n*	confirmation
がくせい・学生	1031	*n*	student
かくれる・隠れる	2064s	*v*	hide completely (to)
かける/かけます	1064	*v*	wear glasses or sunglasses (to)
かこ・過去	2085s	*n*	past (the), bygone days
かざり・飾り	2062s	*n*	decoration
かざん・火山	2055	*n*	volcano
かし (お)・(お)菓子	1095s	*n*	Japanese traditional sweets
かしこい	1081	い *adj.*	bright, wise
かしパン・菓子パン	2025s	*n*	sweet bread
かぜ・風	1035	*n*	wind
かぜ・風邪	1063	*n*	cold (a)
かぜ(を) ひく/ひきます・ 風邪(を) 引く/引きます	1063	*v*	catch a cold
かぞく・家族	1021	*n*	family (my)
かすてら・カステラ	2071	*n*	sponge cake
かた・肩	1061	*n*	shoulder
かた・〜方	2093	*n*	method of "~ing"
かたな・刀	2031	*n*	sword, saber
かたみち・片道	2024	*n*	one-way (trip)
かためる・固める	2015s	*v*	harden (to); solidify (to)
がっき・楽器	2023s	*n*	musical instrument
かっこいい	1062	い *adj.*	cool (look/appearance)
がっこう・学校	1031	*n*	school
がっしょう・合唱	1033	*n*	chorus, choir
がっせん・合戦	2012s	*n*	battle
かっぷけーき・カップケーキ	App.	*n*	cupcake
かていか・家庭科	1032	*n*	family consumer science
かど・角	2022	*n*	corner
かな	2023	*part.*	I wonder (sentence ending); should I?/is it? (question prt.); I wish that… (w/ a negative)
かない・家内	2061	*n*	wife (my)
かなざわ・金沢	1101s	*pn*	Kanazawa (place)
かなしい・悲しい	1061	い *adj.*	sad
かなだ・カナダ	1041	*pn*	Canada (place)
かなだじん・カナダ人	1041	*pn*	Canadian (person)
かならず・必ず	2023	*adv.*	always, without exception
かなり	2033	*adv.*	considerably, quite
かに	1083	*n*	crab
かね (お)・(お)金	1092s	*n*	money
かのじょ・彼女	2052	*pron.*	she, girlfriend
かのじょ・彼女	1074	*pron.*	she, girlfriend
かばん・鞄	1024	*n*	briefcase, bag
かぶき・歌舞伎	1075	*n*	kabuki theater
かぶる・被る/かぶります・ 被ります	1064	*v*	wear on the head (to)
かべ・壁	2021s	*n*	wall
かみ・神	2013	*n*	God, god, spirit
かみ・紙	1024	*n*	paper
かみ(のけ)・髪(の毛)	1061	*n*	hair
かみがた・髪型	2021s	*n*	hairstyle
かみさま・神様	2013	*n*	God, god, spirit
かみしばい・紙芝居	2041	*n*	picture story show
かみなり・雷	1101	*n*	lightning
がむ・ガム	App.	*n*	gum
かめ・亀	1082	*n*	turtle
がめん・画面	2104	*n*	screen

Japanese	Location		English
かもく・科目	1032	n	school subject
かもしれない	2065	exp.	may, might, perhaps [informal]
かもしれません	2065	exp.	may, might, perhaps
かよう・通う	2012s	v	commute (to)
かようび・火曜日	1051	n	Tuesday
から	1032	part.	from (used with spec. times or locations)
から	2053	conj.	because (introduced as particle earlier)
から	2032	part.	because
からい・辛い	2025	い adj.	spicy
からおけ・カラオケ	1105s	n	karaoke
からおけ・カラオケ(を)する/します	1091	v	karaoke (to sing/do)
がらす・ガラス	2085	n	glass
からだ・体	1061	n	body
からて・空手	1011	n	karate (martial art)
かりる・借りる	2044	v	borrow (to), rent (to)
かりる・借りる/かります・借ります	1063s	v	borrow (to)
かるい・軽い	2084	い adj.	light (weight)
かれーらいす・カレーライス	2071	n	curry and rice
かれ・彼	1074	pron.	he, boyfriend
かれら・彼ら	1082	pron.	they, them
かわいい	1081	い adj.	cute
かわいそう	2014s	exp.	pitiful; pathetic
かわく・乾く	2051	v	dry (to)
かわる・変わる	2033s	v	change (to)
かんがえ・考え	2091	n	an idea
かんがえる・考える	2091	v	think (to), consider (to)
かんきょう・環境	2102	n	environment, circumstance
かんこく・韓国	1041	pn	South Korea (place)
かんこくけい・韓国系	1041s	n	Korean (descent)
かんこくご・韓国語	1042	n	Korean (language)
かんこくじん・韓国人	1041	n	Korean (person)
かんごし・看護師	1063	n	nurse
かんじ・感じ	2022	n	sense, feeling, sensation
かんじ・漢字	1012s	n	Chinese characters (used in Japan)
かんしゃ・感謝	2061	n	thanks, gratitude
かんしゃ・感謝(を)する	2061	v	give thanks (to)
かんしゃさい・感謝祭	2061	n	Thanksgiving
かんそう・感想	2043s	n	impressions, thoughts
かんたん・簡単	2021	な adj.	simple
がんたん・元旦	2061	n	New Year's Day
がんばる・頑張る/がんばります・頑張ります	1073	v	do one's best (to)
かんとう・関東	2055	pn	Kantou (region of Japan including Tokyo and the surrounding area)
かんどうする・感動する	2022s	v	feel like (to), give a sense of (to)
き・木	1011s	n	tree
きいろ・黄色	1074	n	yellow
きいろい・黄色い	1082	い adj.	yellow-colored
きかい・機械	2024s	n	machine
きがする・気がする	2021s	exp.	feel inclined toward
きがつく・気が付く	2062s	v	notice (to)
きく・聞く	2091	v	ask (to); listen (to)
きく・聞く/ききます・聞きます	1013	v	listen (to)
きこえる・聞こえる/きこえます・聞こえます	1104s	v	hear (can)
きっさてん・喫茶店	2071	n	coffee house (traditional), coffee lounge
ぎじゅつ・技術	2031s	n	art, craft, technique
きせつ・季節	1101	n	season
きそく・規則	2074	n	rules, regulations
きた・北	2021	n	north
ぎたー・ギター	1071	n	guitar
ぎたーを ひく/ひきます・ギターを 弾く/弾きます	1071	v	play guitar (to)
きっと	2043	adv	surely, undoubtedly
きたない	1081	い adj.	dirty, messy
きつね・狐	1035s	n	fox
きつね・狐	2044	n	fox
きねんび・記念日	2082s	n	anniversary
きのう・昨日	1032	n/adv.	yesterday
きびしい	1081	い adj.	strict
きっぷ・切符	2012	n	ticket
きぼう・希望	2051s	n	hope, aspiration
きもの・着物	1011	n	kimono (Japanese traditional clothing)
きもち・気持ち	2053	n	mood, feelings
きめる・決める	2101	v	decide (to)
ぎゃくに・逆に	2033	adv.	conversely, on the contrary
きゃんでぃ・キャンディ,	1023	n	candy/sweets
きゃんべら・キャンベラ	1021s	pn	Canberra (place)
きゅうかい・九階	2024	counter	ninth floor
きゅうきゅうしゃをよんで・救急車を呼んで	1063	n	Call an ambulance!
きゅうけい・休憩	2043	n	rest, break
きゅうけい・休憩(を)する/します	2043	v	take a break (to)
きゅうこ・九個	2022	counter	nine pieces/smallish objects
きゅうさい・九歳	1052	counter	nine years old
きゅうさつ・九冊	1092	counter	nine volumes
きゅうしゅう・九州	1041s	pn	Kyushu (place)
きゅうしゅう・九州	2011	pn	Kyushu (southernmost of the four main islands of Japan)
きゅうじゅう・九十	1022	counter	ninety
きゅうせん・九千	1052	counter	nine thousand
きゅうど・九度	1101	counter	nine times/degrees
きゅうとう・九頭	2102	counter	nine large animals
ぎゅうどん・牛丼	2025s	n	beef on rice
ぎゅうにゅう・牛乳	2015	n	milk
きゅうわ・九羽	2102	counter	nine birds
きゅうにん・九人	1021	counter	nine people
きゅうはい・九杯	1092	counter	nine cupfuls
きゅうはく・九泊	2024	counter	stopping nine nights
きゅうばん・九番	2011	counter	ninth, number nine
きゅうばんめ・九番目	2023	counter	the ninth
きゅうひき・九匹	1092	counter	nine small animals
きゅうひゃく・九百	1023s	counter	nine hundred
きゅうびょう・九秒	1032	counter	nine seconds
きゅうふん・九分	1032	counter	nine minutes
きゅうぺーじ・九ページ	1042	counter	nine pages, page nine
きゅうほん・九本	1092	counter	nine cylindrical objects
きゅうまい・九枚	1042	counter	nine sheets
きゅうまん・九万	1091	counter	ninety thousand
きょう・今日	1032	n	today
きょうかい・教会	2062	n	church
きょうかしょ・教科書	1013	n	textbook

Japanese	Location		English
きょういんしつ・教員室	2031s	n	teacher's office
ぎょうざ	1043s	n	pot stickers
きょうしつ・教室	1032	n	classroom
きょうだい・兄弟	1021	n	siblings
きょうと・京都	1013s	pn	Kyoto (place)
きょうどう・共同	2051s	n	co-ed, shared/common (facilities)
きょうみ・興味	2031s	n	interest (in)
きょうみ(を)もつ・興味(を)持つ	2081	n	interest (to have an)
きょうりょくする・協力する	2092s	v	cooperate (to)
きょく・曲	2023s	n	song, tune, melody
きょねん・去年	1054	n	last year
きらい・嫌い	1072	な adj.	dislike
きらく・気楽	2053	な adj.	relaxing
ぎりぎり	2044	adv. ono.	just barely, at the last moment grinding sound
きりすときょう・キリスト教	2062	n	Christianity
きりたんぽ	2062	n	regional (Akita) dish of cooked and pounded rice, grilled on skewers
きりつ。・起立。	1016s	exp.	stand up
ぎりの〜	1021		step-
きれながい・切れ長い	2033s		sharply slanted
きる・着る/きます・着ます	1064	v	wear above the waist (to)
きろく・記録	2032s	n	record
きれい	1081	な adj	clean, pretty
きんいろ・金色	1074	n	gold
ぎんいろ・銀色	1074	n	silver
きんえん・禁煙	2024	n	non-smoking
ぎんこう・銀行	2011s	n	bank
ぎんざ・銀座	1033s	pn	Ginza (place)
きんにく・筋肉	1061	n	muscle
きんたろう・金太郎	2034s	pn	Kintarou, mythical strong man
きんぱつ・金髪	1074	n	blond (hair)
きんようび・金曜日	1051	n	Friday
きをつける・気を付ける	2025	exp.	take care, be careful
く/きゅう・九	1021	counter	nine
ぐあいが わるい・具合が悪い	1063	exp.	sick, feel bad
くうかい・空海	1052s	pn	Kukai (person's name)
くうかん・空間	2032	n	space
くうこう・空港	2012	n	airport
ぐうぜん・偶然	2074	exp.	(by) chance, suddenly
くがつ・九月	1052	n	September
ぐぐって・ググッて	2024s	v	Google (to); search on the internet (to)
くさのね・草の根	2095	n	grassroots, rank and file
くじ・九時	1032	counter	nine o'clock
くすり・薬	1063	n	medicine
くすり(を) のむ/のみます・薬(を)飲む/飲みます	1063	v	take medicine (to)
ぐぜん・偶然	2061s	n	coincidentally
くだもの・果物	1075s	n	fruit
くち・口	1061	n	mouth
くつ・靴	1064	n	shoes
くっきー・クッキー	App.	n	cookie
くつした・靴下	1064	n	socks
くに・国	1041	n	country
くに・国	2013	n	country
くび・首	1061	n	neck

Japanese	Location		English
くま・熊	2013	n	bear
くむ・組む	2023s	v	assemble (to), put together (to)
くもり・曇り	1101	n	cloudy
くもる・曇る/くもります・曇ります	1101	n	become cloudy
くらい・暗い	1093	い adj.	dark
くらい	2043	part.	about ~
くらし・暮らし	2013s	n	living, livelihood
くらす・クラス	1032	n	class
くる・来る/きます・来ます	1044	v	come (to)
くるま・車	1043	n	car, vehicle
くりかえす・繰り返す	2032s	v	repeat (to)
くりすます・クリスマス	2061	n	Christmas
ぐれい・グレイ	1074	n	gray
くれる/くれます	1095	v	give (to) [to me or a family member]
くろ・黒	1074	n	black
くろい・黒い	1082	い adj.	black-colored
くろず・黒酢	2025s	n	black vinegar
くろふね・黒船	2033s	n	black ships (American ships that first went to Japan)
くろぶね・黒舟	2033s	n	Black Ships
くわんざ・クワンザ	2061	n	Kwanzaa
くん (〜)・〜君	1013	suffix	suffix AFTER a boy's name
ぐん・軍	2022s	n	army
けーき・ケーキ	1094	n	cake
けいぐ・敬具	2064	n	closing for written letters
けいけん・経験	1065	n	experience
けいご・敬語	2044	n	polite speech
けいざい・経済	1032s	n	economy
けいざいがく・経済学	1032	n	economics
げいじゅつ・芸術	2031s	n	arts; crafts
げいじん・芸人	2031s	n	performer
けいたい(でんわ)・携帯(電話)	1031	n	cellular phone
けが・怪我(を) する/します	1063	v	injure, hurt oneself (to)
けさ・今朝	1051s	n/adv.	this morning
けしき・景色	2033	n	scenery, landscape
けっか・結果	2021s	n	results
けっこう	2033	n/な adj.	splendid, nice [n]; sufficient, (I'm) fine, no thank you [な adj.]
		adv.	reasonably, fairly
けしごむ・消しゴム	1024	n	eraser
げつようび・月曜日	1051	n	Monday
けど	1041s	conj.	but
けにあ・ケニア	1041	pn	Kenya (place)
けにあじん・ケニア人	1041	n	Kenyan (person)
けんか・喧嘩(を) する/します	1091	v	fight (to)
げんかん・玄関	2044	n	entranceway, foyer
げんき・元気	1015	n/な adj.	healthy, energetic
げんきで・(お)元気で	2015	exp.	take care, go in good health
けんきゅうかい・研究会	2035s	n	study workshop
けんこう・健康	1063	n	health
けんこうてき・健康的	2053s	な adj.	healthy
けんこう・健康に いい です	1063	exp.	good for your health
げんだい・現代	2034s	n	modern, today
けんちょう・県庁	2022s	n	prefectural offices
けんどう・剣道	1033s	n	kendo
けんどうぶ・剣道部	1033	n	kendo club

Japanese	Location		English
けんろくえん・兼六園	1102s	pn	Kenroku Park (place)
ご・五	1021	n	five
ごーぎゃん・ゴーギャン	2032	pn	Gauguin, Paul
こーら・コーラ	1043	n	cola
こい・鯉	1031s	n	koi (carp)
こい・濃い	2072s	い adj.	thick, dark
こううん・幸運	2065s	n	good luck
こうえん・公演	2043	n	performance (public)
こうえん・公園	2013	n	park
こうけんてんのう・孝謙天皇	1053s	pn	Emperor Kouken
こうこう・高校	1031	n	high school
こうこういちねんせい・高校一年生	1031	counter	tenth grader
こうこうさんねんせい・高校三年生	1031	counter	twelfth grader
こうこうせい・高校生	1031	n	high school student
こうこうにねんせい・高校二年生	1031	counter	eleventh grader
こうさてん・交差点	2022	n	intersection, crossing
こうぼうだいし・弘法大師	1052s	pn	Kobo Daishi (person's name)
こうふんする・興奮する	2065s	v	excited (to be)
こうやさん・高野山	1052s	pn	Mt. Koya (place)
こうりゅう・交流	2095	n	exchange (cultural), networking
こえ・声	1061	n	voice
こおり・氷	2011	n	ice, shaved ice (snow cone)
ごかい・五階	2024	counter	fifth floor
ごかぞく・ご家族	1021	n	someone else's family
ごがつ・五月	1052	n	May
こくさい・国際	2081	n	international
こくさいこうりゅう・国際交流	2081	n	international exchange
こくご・国語	1032	n	national language (Japanese language)
こくばん・黒板	1024	い adj.	blackboard
ここ	1024	pron.	here
ごこ・五個	2022	counter	five pieces/smallish objects
ごご・午後	1032	n	p.m.
ここのか・九日	1053	counter	ninth (day of the month)
ここのつ・九つ	1024	counter	nine (things)
こころ・心	1061	n	heart (not one's physical heart), soul
ごさい・五歳	1052	counter	five years old
ございます・御座います	2044	v	be (to), exist (to), [formal]
ごさつ・五冊	1092	counter	five volumes
ごじ・五時	1032	counter	five o'clock
ごじかんめ・五時間目	1033	counter	fifth period
こしょう	2093	n	pepper
ごじゅう・五十	1022	counter	fifty
こすちゅーむ・コスチューム	2043	n	costume
こぜに・小銭	2041s	n	small change (money)
ごせん・五千	1052	counter	five thousand
ごぜん・午前	1032	n	a.m.
ごちそうさまでした	2022	exp.	It was a feast. (said at the end of a meal)
こっち	2011	pron.	this way (close to or toward the speaker) this direction, [informal for こちら]
ごっほ・ゴッホ	2032	pn	Van Gogh, Vincent
こちら	1014	pron.	this person (polite)
こと・事	1071s	n	thing (tangible)
こと・事	2023	n	an intangible thing
こと・琴	1105s	n	koto, Japanese zither/harp
こと・琴	2023	n	koto, Japanese zither/harp
ごど・五度	1101	counter	five times/degrees
ごとう・五頭	2102	counter	five large animals
ことし・今年	1054	n	this year
ことば・言葉	2043	n	language, dialect, words
ことば・言葉	1101s	n	language, dialect, words
こども・子供	1082	n	child, children
こども・子供	2013	n	child, children
こどもたち・子供達	1082	n	children
こどものひ・子供の日	2091	n	Children's Day (holiday)
ごにん・五人	1021	counter	five people
この	1023		this (thing)
ごはい・五杯	1092	counter	five cupfuls
ごはく・五泊	2024	counter	stopping five nights
ごはん・ご飯	1015	n	cooked rice, a meal
ごばん・五番	2011	counter	fifth, number five
ごばんめ・五番目	2023	counter	the fifth
こぴー・コピーする/します	1062	v	copy, photocopy (to)
ごひき・五匹	1092	counter	five small animals
ごひゃく・五百	1023s	counter	five hundred
ごびょう・五秒	1032	counter	five seconds
ごふん・五分	1032	counter	five minutes
ごぺーじ・五ページ	1042	n	page five
ごほん・五本	1092	counter	five cylindrical objects
ごまい・五枚	1042	counter	five sheets, five pages
こまかい・細かい	2033s	い adj.	detailed
こまる・困る	2084	v	have trouble (to); be in difficulty
ごまん・五万	1091	counter	fifty thousand
こみあう・混み合う	2094s	v	crowded (to be)
ごめん [informal], ごめんなさい [formal]	1072s		excuse me, I'm sorry, beg your pardon
ごめんください・ごめん下さい	1092s	exp.	May I come in?, please forgive me
ごゆっくり/ゆっくり	2044	exp.	slowly, at ease, restful
ごらん・ご覧	2044	n	seeing, watching, perusing; [honorific for 見る]
ごるふ・ゴルフ	1071	n	golf
これ	1015	pron.	this (one)
ごわ・五羽	2102	counter	five birds
ころ or ごろ	1032		about
こわい	1081	い adj.	scary
こんくーる・コンクール	2015s	n	competition
こんげつ・今月	1054	n	this month
こんさーと・コンサート	1052s	n	concert
こんしゅう・今週	1054	n	this week
こんど・今度	2043	n	now, this time, next time
こんにちは・今日は	1015	exp.	hello
こんばんは・今晩は	1015	exp.	good evening
こんびに・コンビニ/こんびにえんすすとあ・コンビニエンスストア	2024	n	convenience store
こんぴゅーたーらぼ・コンピューターラボ	1033		computer lab
さあ	1035	inter.	well...
さいがい・災害	2084s	n	calamity, disaster
さいきん・最近	2073	n	nowadays, most recent
さいご・最後	2045	n	last, conclusion
さいじつ・祭日	2062	n	holiday
さいしょ・最初	2045	n	first, beginning

Japanese	Location		English
さいのうがある・才能がある	2083s	exp.	have an aptitude for, a genius for
さいん・サイン	1042	n	signature
さがす・探す/さがします・探します	1093	v	search (to)
さかな・魚	1101	n	fish
さがる・下がる	2022	v	descend (to), go back (to), hang down (to)
さき(に)・先(に)	2043	n	before, ahead, future
さく・咲く	2043	v	bloom (to)
さくさく	2054	ono.	crunchy, crisp
さくひん・作品	2033s	n	works
さくぶん・作文	1032	n	essay
さくら・桜	1105	n	cherry tree/blossom
さけ・酒	2025s	n	rice wine
さじ	2094		spoonful
ざせき・座席	2044	n	seat [formal]
さそう・誘う	2063	v	invite (to)
さっか・作家	2105s	n	author, writer
さっかー・サッカー(を)する/します	1091	v	play soccer (to)
さっき	2093s	n	some time ago
ざっし・雑誌	2013	n	magazine
さっぽろ・札幌	2011	pn	Sapporo (city in Hokkaido)
さつま・薩摩	1041s	pn	Satsuma (place)
さて	1091s	interj.	well, now
さて	2023	interj.	well, now then
さとう・砂糖	App.	n	sugar
さどう/ちゃどう・茶道	1071	n	tea ceremony
さびしい・寂しい	1061s	い adj.	lonely
さびしい・寂しい	2064	い adj.	lonely, lonesome
ざぶとん・座布団	2044	n	flat cushion (used when sitting or kneeling on the floor)
さま・〜様	2013	suffix	polite suffix for Mr., Miss, or Mrs. when writing letters
さまざま	2031s	な adj.	various, assorted
さむい・寒い	1034	い adj.	cold (weather)
さむらい・侍	1061	n	samurai
さようなら	1015	exp.	goodbye
さる・猿	2014s	n	monkey
さん(〜)・〜さん	1013	suffix	suffix AFTER a name
さん・三	1021	counter	three
さんかい/さんがい・三階	2024	counter	third floor
さんがつ・三月	1052	n	March
さんこ・三個	2022	counter	three pieces/smallish objects
さんさい・三歳	1052	counter	three years old
さんさつ・三冊	1092	counter	three volumes
さんしん・三線	2023s	n	Okinawa instrument, like a shamisen
さんじ・三時	1032	counter	three o'clock
さんじかんめ・三時間目	1033	counter	third period
さんじゅう・三十	1022	counter	thirty
さんじゅういちにち・三十一日	1053	counter	thirty-first (day of the month)
さんじゅうにち・三十日	1053	counter	thirtieth (day of the month)
さんせっと・サンセット	1104s	n	sunset
さんぜん・三千	1052	counter	three thousand
さんだん・三段	1033s	counter	third degree (belt)
さんど・三度	1101	counter	three times/degrees
さんとう・三頭	2102	counter	three large animals
さんにん・三人	1021	counter	three people

Japanese	Location		English
ざんねん・残念	1093	n/な adj.	regrettably, unluckily
さんねんせい・三年生	1031s	counter	third year student
さんばい・三杯	1092	counter	three cupfuls
さんぱく・三泊	2024	counter	stopping three nights
さんばん・三番	2011	counter	third, number three
さんばんめ・三番目	2023	counter	the third
さんびき・三匹	1092	counter	three small animals
さんびゃく・三百	1023s	counter	three hundred
さんびょう・三秒	1032	counter	three seconds
さんぷん・三分	1032	counter	three minutes
さんぺーじ・三ページ	1042	counter	three pages, page three
さんぽ・散歩	1054	n	walk
さんぽ・散歩(を)する/します	1054	v	take a walk (to)
さんぼん・三本	1092	counter	three cylindrical objects
さんまい・三枚	1042	counter	three sheets
さんまん・三万	1091	counter	thirty thousand
さんわ・三羽	2102	counter	three birds
じーんず・ジーンズ	1064	n	jeans
しあわせ・幸せ	2025	な adj.	happiness, good fortune
じぇすちゃー・ジェスチャー	2043	n	gesture
しお・塩	2093		salt
しお・塩	App.	n	salt
しか・鹿	2095s	n	deer
しかし	2033	conj.	however, but
しかたがない・仕方がない	2022s		futile, there is no use
しがつ・四月	1052	n	April
しかる・叱る	2071	v	scold (to)
じかんわり・時間割	1032	n	schedule, timetable
しき・式	2091	n	ceremony, rite
しく・敷く	2051s	v	spread out (to), lay out (to)
しけん・験	1032	n	test, exam
しこく・四国	2011	pn	Shikoku (smallest of the four main islands of Japan)
しごと・仕事	2012	n	job, occupation
しごと・仕事	1025	n	job, occupation
しごと・仕事(を)する/します	1052s	v	work (to)
じしょ・辞書	App.	n	dictionary
じしん・地震	1101	n	earthquake
しじん・詩人	2032s	n	poet
しずか・静か	1061	な adj	quiet
しずかに して ください。・静かに して 下さい。	1016s	exp.	Please be quiet.
しぜん・自然	2033	n/な adj.	nature
		adv.	naturally
した・下	2022	n	below, down
じだい・時代	2071	n	period, era
じだい・時代	1071s	n	era, period, age
したぎ・下着	1064	n	underwear
したじき・下敷き	1024	n	writing pad, mat
しち/なな・七	1021	counter	seven
しち/なながつ・七月	1052	n	July
しち/ななじ・七時	1032	counter	seven o'clock
しち/ななにん・七人	1021	counter	seven people
しちめんちょう・七面鳥	2102	n	turkey
じこしょうかい・自己紹介	2011	n	self-introduction
しつぎおうどう・質疑応答	2035s	n	question and answer (period)
じっさい・実際	2043	n	practically, practical, reality
じつは・実は	1104	adv.	by the way, actually

Japanese	Location		English
しっぱい・失敗	2071	n	failure, mistake
しつもん・質問	2102	n	question
しつもん・質問	1032s	n	question
しつもんおうとう・質問応答	2035s	n	question-and-answer
しつれいします・失礼します	1022	exp.	excuse me, I'm sorry to bother you.
じてんしゃ・自転車	2012	n	bicycle
じどうしゃ・自動車	2012	n	car, automobile
しなもの・品物	2033s	n	items, products
しばい・芝居	2044	n	play, drama
しぶい・渋い	1062	い adj.	tasteful, cool
じぶん・自分	2011	n	myself, yourself, oneself
しま・島	1083	n	island
しまいこうこう・姉妹高校	2011s	n	sister school
しまいとし・姉妹都市	2091s	n	sister city
しまる・閉まる	2081	v	close (to)
しみんかいかん・市民会館	2024s	n	City Hall
しめだいこ・締め太鼓	2023s	n	small Japanese drum
しめる・閉める	2081	v	close (to)
じむしょ・事務所	1032	n	office
しめる・閉める/しめます・閉めます	1034	v	close (to), shut (to) [doors/windows]
じゃ/じゃあ	1033s		well then…
じゃーなる・ジャーナル	1011s	n	journal
じゃあ また	1015	exp.	see you later [informal]
しゃかい・社会	1032	n	social studies, society
じゃがいも・ジャガイモ	1042s	n	potato
じゃかるた・ジャカルタ	1042s	pn	Jakarta (place)
しゃくはち・尺八	2025	n	shakuhachi (end-blown bamboo flute)
じゃけっと・ジャケット	1064	n	jacket
しゃこうダンス・社交ダンス	2081s	n	social dancing
しゃしん・写真	1021	n	photograph
しゃしん(を)とる/とります・写真(を)撮る/撮ります	1042	v	take a photo (to)
しやすい・〜しやすい	2074s	n	easy to make, easy to do
しゃつ・シャツ	1064	n	shirt
しゃわー・シャワー(を)する/します	1091	v	take a shower (to)
しゃみせん・三味線	2023	n	shamisen (musical stringed instrument)
しゃんぷー・シャンプー(を)する/します	1091	v	shampoo (to)
じゅーす・ジュース	1063	n	juice
じゅう・十	1021	counter	ten
じゆう・自由	1105s	な adj.	freedom, liberty
じゅう・銃	2074	n	gun, arms
じゅういち・十一	1022	counter	eleven
じゅういちがつ・十一月	1052	n	November
じゅういっこ・十一個	2022	counter	eleven pieces/smallish objects
じゅういちじ・十一時	1032	counter	eleven o'clock
じゅういちにち・十一日	1053	counter	eleventh (day of the month)
じゅういちまん・十一万	1091	counter	one hundred ten thousand
じゅういっさい・十一歳/才	1052	counter	eleven years old
じゅういっぷん・十一分	1032	counter	eleven minutes
しゅうがくりょこう・修学旅行	2013s	n	school excursion
じゅうがつ・十月	1052	n	October
しゅうかん・習慣	2075s	n	custom, tradition
じゅうきゅうまん・十九万	1091	counter	one hundred ninety thousand
しゅうきょう・宗教	1052s	n	religion
じゅうく/じゅうきゅう・十九	1022	counter	nineteen
じゅうくにち・十九日	1053	counter	nineteenth (day of the month)
じゅうご・十五	1022	counter	fifteen
じゅうごにち・十五日	1053	counter	fifteenth (day of the month)
じゅうごまん・十五万	1091	counter	one hundred fifty thousand
じゅうさん・十三	1022	counter	thirteen
じゅうさんさい・十三歳/才	1052	counter	thirteen years old
じゅうさんにち・十三日	1053	counter	thirteenth (day of the month)
じゅうさんぷん・十三分	1032	counter	thirteen minutes
じゅうさんまん・十三万	1091	counter	one hundred thirty thousand
じゅうじ・十時	1032	counter	ten o'clock
じゅうしちにち・十七日	1053	counter	seventeenth (day of the month)
じゅうど・十度	1101	counter	ten times/degrees
じゅうどう・柔道	1033	n	judo
じゅうなな/じゅうしち・十七	1022	counter	seventeen
じゅうななまん・十七万	1091	counter	one hundred seventy thousand
じゅうに・十二	1022	counter	twelve
じゅうにがつ・十二月	1052	n	December
じゅうにこ・十二個	2022	counter	twelve pieces/smallish objects
じゅうにさい・十二歳	1052	counter	twelve years old
じゅうにし・十二支	2014s	n	twelve zodiac animals
じゅうにじ・十二時	1032	counter	twelve o'clock
じゅうににち・十二日	1053	counter	twelfth (day of the month)
じゅうにふん・十二分	1032	counter	twelve minutes
じゅうにまん・十二万	1091	counter	one hundred twenty thousand
じゅうにん・十人	1021	counter	ten people
じゅうはち・十八	1022	counter	eighteen
じゅうはちにち・十八日	1053	counter	eighteenth (day of the month)
じゅうはちまん・十八万	1091	counter	one hundred eighty thousand
じゅうばん・十番	2011	counter	tenth, number ten
じゅうばんめ・十番目	2023	counter	the tenth
じゅうびょう・十秒	1032	counter	ten seconds
じゅうまい・十枚	1042	counter	ten sheets
しゅうまつ・週末	1054	n	weekend
じゅうまん・十万	1091	counter	one hundred thousand
じゅうよっか・十四日	1053	counter	fourteenth (day of the month)
じゅうよん/じゅうし・十四	1022	counter	fourteen
じゅうよんさい・十四歳/才	1052	counter	fourteen years old
じゅうよんまん・十四万	1091	counter	one hundred forty thousand
じゅうろく・十六	1022	counter	sixteen
じゅうろくにち・十六日	1053	counter	sixteenth (day of the month)
じゅうろくまん・十六万	1091	counter	one hundred sixty thousand
じゅうわ・十羽	2102	counter	ten birds
じゅぎょう・授業	1032	n	class
しゅくだい・宿題	1032	n	homework
しゅくだい・宿題(を)する/します	1091	v	do homework (to)
しゅじん・主人	2061	n	head (of household), one's husband
じゅっかい・十階	2024	counter	tenth floor
じゅっ/じっこ・十個	2022	counter	ten pieces/smallish objects
じゅっさい・十歳/才	1052	counter	ten years old
じゅっ/じっさつ・十冊	1092	counter	ten volumes
しゅっしん・出身	2011	n	person's origin (hometown, country, etc.)
じゅっとう・十頭	2102	counter	ten large animals
じゅっ/じっぱい・十杯	1092	counter	ten cupfuls
じゅっぱく・十泊	2024	counter	stopping ten nights
しゅっぱつ・出発	2041	n	departure
しゅっぱ・出発する	2041	v	depart (to)

Japanese	Location		English
じゅっ/じっぴき・十匹	1092	*counter*	ten small animals
じゅっ/じっぷん・十分	1032	*counter*	ten minutes
じゅっ/じっぺーじ・十ページ	1042	*counter*	ten pages, page ten
じゅっ/じっぽん・十本	1092	*counter*	ten cylindrical objects
しゅりじょう・首里城	2022s	*pn*	Shurijo, castle in Naha, Okinawa
しゅと・首都	1052s	*n*	capital
しゅみ・趣味	1071	*n*	hobby
しゅわ・手話	1042	*n*	sign language
しゅれいもん・守礼門	2022s	*pn*	Shuremon, a famous gate at Shurijo castle
じゅん・順	2014s	*n*	in order of ~
じゅんばん・順番	2062s	*n*	order (sequential)
じゅんび・準備	2035s	*n*	preparation
じゅんび・準備(を)する	2082	*v*	prepare (to)
しょーとぱんつ・ショートパンツ	1064s	*n*	short pants, shorts
じょう・〜畳	2054	*counter*	tatami mats
しょうかい・紹介	2011	*n*	introduction
しょうかい・紹介 して 下さい	1021	*v*	introduce (please)
しょうかい・紹介 する/します	1021	*v*	introduce (to)
しょうがくいちねんせい・小学一年生	1031	*n*	elementary school first grader
しょうがくさんねんせい・小学三年	1031	*n*	elementary school third grader
しょうがくせい・小学生	1031	*n*	elementary school student
しょうがくにねんせい・小学二年生	1031	*n*	elementary school second grader
しょうがくよねんせい・小学四年生	1031	*n*	elementary school fourth grader
しょうがくろくねんせい・小学六年生	1031	*n*	elementary school sixth grader
しょうがっこう・小学校	1031	*n*	elementary school
じょうぎ・定規	App.	*n*	ruler
しょうぐん・将軍	1051s	*n*	military leader
じょうず・上手	1062	*な adj*	skillful
しょうたい・招待	2023	*n*	invitation
じょうだん・冗談	1072	*n*	joke
しょうてすと・小テスト	1032	*n*	small test, quiz
じょうば・乗馬	1071	*n*	horseback riding
じょうひん・上品	2082s	*n*	elegant, refined
しょうめん・正面	2044s	*n*	front, main
しょうらい・将来	2104	*n*	future (near)
しょうゆ・醤油	1015	*n*	soy sauce
しょうわ・昭和	2061	*pn*	reign period of Emperor Hirohito (1926 – 1989)
じょぎんぐ・ジョギング	1071	*n*	jogging
しょくじ・食事(を)する/します	1091	*v*	meal (to have a), dine (to)
しょうがくごねんせい・小学校五年生	1031	*n*	elementary school fifth grader
しょくつき・食事付き	2024	*exp.*	with meals (included)
しょくひん・食品	2043	*n*	food supplies, foodstuff
しょっき・食器	2033s	*n*	foods
しょどう・書道	2015	*n*	calligraphy
しらべる・調べる	2102	*v*	investigate (to)
しりません・知りません	1016s	*exp.*	I don't know.
しる・知る/しります・知ります	1042	*v*	know something/someone (to)

Japanese	Location		English
しりょう・資料	2035s	*n*	resources
しる・汁	2065s	*n*	soup, broth
しるし・印	2062s	*n*	a sign
じれったい	1081	*い adj.*	irritating
しろ・白	1074	*n*	white
しろ・城	1101	*n*	castle
しろい・白い	1082	*い adj.*	white-colored
じんぎすかん・ジンギスカン	2015s	*n*	Mongolian stirfry barbeque
しんごう・信号	2022	*n*	traffic light, signal
じんこう・人口	2011	*n*	population
しんさい・震災	2084s	*n*	earthquake disaster
しんじる・信じる	2034s	*v*	believe (to)
じんじゃ・神社	1033	*n*	shrine
しんせつ・親切	2022s	*n*	gentleness, kindness
しんちょう・身長	2071s	*n*	height (of someone), stature
しんとう・神道	2062	*n*	Shinto religion
しんとう・神道	1052s	*pn*	Shinto (religion)
しんぶん・新聞	2013	*n*	newspaper
しんぱい・心配(を) する/します	1063	*v*	worry (to)
しんはんが・新版画	1091	*n*	woodblock print (new), art print (new)
しんぷる・シンプル	1064	*な adj*	simple
しんめとりっくでざいん・シンメトリックデザイン	2032	*n*	symmetric design
すいぎゅうしゃ・水牛車	2022s	*n*	water buffalo cart
しんりがく・心理学	1032	*n*	psychology
すーつ・スーツ	1064	*n*	suit
すいえい・水泳	1071	*n*	swimming
すいようび・水曜日	1051	*n*	Wednesday
すうがく・数学	1032	*n*	math
すいじゅん・水準	2031s	*n*	standard
すうひゃく・数百	2031s	*n*	several hundreds
すきやき・すき焼き	2074	*n*	thin slices of beef, cooked with vegetables
すかーと・スカート	1064	*n*	skirt
すき・好き	1072	*な adj*	like
すぎ (〜)・〜すぎ	1032		past, after
すきー・スキー	1071	*n*	skiing
すきやき・すき焼き	App.	*n*	thin slices of beef, cooked with vegetables
すぎる・過ぎる	2033	*v*	pass (to), exceed (to), above (to be)
すく・空く	2015	*v*	empty (to become)
すくない・少ない	2031	*い adj.*	few, a little
すぐ	1082		immediately, at once
すぐしたの おとうと/いもうと・すぐ下の 弟/妹	1021	*n*	next youngest brother/sister (my...
すごす・過ごす	2011s	*v*	pass time (to)
すけじゅーる・スケジュール	1032	*n*	schedule
すけっちぶっく・スケッチブック	1062s	*n*	sketchbook
すけぼー・スケボー(を) する/します	1071	*v*	skateboard (to)
すごい	1035	*い adj.*	amazing, great, terrible
すこし・少し	1031	*adv.*	little
すすきの	2015s	*pn*	Susukino, town in Hokkaido
すし・寿司	1011	*n*	sushi
すっぱい・酸っぱい	2025	*い adj.*	sour
すずしい・涼しい	1034	*い adj.*	cool (weather)
ずっと	1083		continuously, throughout

Japanese	Location		English
すてーき・ステーキ	App.	n	steak
すてき・素敵	1064	な adj.	wonderful, nice
すとーりー・ストーリー	2044	n	story
すのーぼーど・スノーボード(を)する	2015	v	snowboard (to)
すると	2064	conj.	therefore, then, and (then) [used predominately in written language]
すぱげてぃ・スパゲティ	1043s	n	spaghetti
すばらしい・素晴しい	1065	い adj.	wonderful
すぺいん・スペイン	1041	pn	Spain (place)
すぺいんご・スペイン語	1042	n	Spanish (language)
すぺいんじん・スペイン人	1041	n	Spaniard
すぽーつ・スポーツ	1071	n	sports
ずぼん・ズボン	1064	n	pants, trousers
すまーと・スマート	1062	な adj	slim, stylish
すみません	1033s	interj.	excuse me, I'm sorry
すむ・住む/すみます・住みます	1064	v	live/reside (to)
すもう・相撲	1011	n	Japanese sumo wrestling
すりっぱ・スリッパ	1093s	n	slipper(s)
する/します (して)	1044	v	do (to), wear (to)
ずるい	1081	い adj.	cunning
ずるい	1081	い adj.	cunning
すると	1082s	conj.	thereupon
せいき・世紀	2013s	n	century
すわひりご・スワヒリ語	1042	n	Swahili (language)
すわる・座る/すわります・座ります	1013	v	sit (to)
せ/せい・背	1061	n	height, stature
せいき・世紀	1041s	n	century, era
せき・席	2024	n	seat, place
せいせき・成績	1033	n	score, grade
せいと・生徒	1031	n	student
せいふく・制服	1025s	n	uniform (school)
せいぶつがく・生物学	1032	n	biology
せかい・世界	1032s	n	world (the), society
せかいし・世界史	1032	n	world history
せっけん・石鹸	2052	n	soap
せなか・背中	2014s	n	back; backbone
せっと・セット	1103s	n	set
せまい・狭い	1083	い adj.	narrow
せりふ・セリフ	2041s	n	script
せん・線	2032	n	line
せんこう・専攻	2101	n	major subject, special study
せん・千	1052	counter	one thousand
せんげつ・先月	1054	n	last month
せんす・扇子	2031	n	folding fan
せんそう・戦争	2092	n	war
せんぱい・先輩	2022s	n	a senior; an elder
せんしゅう・先週	1054	n	last week
せんしゅうのかようび・先週の火曜日	1054	n	last week Tuesday
せんせい・先生、〜せんせい・〜先生	1011	n	teacher, suffix AFTER a teacher's, lawyer's, or doctor's name
ぜんぜん・全然	1074	adv.	not at all
ぜんぶっきょう・禅仏教	2062s	n	Zen Buddhism
ぜんぶ・全部	1083	n	all, entire, altogether
せんめんき・洗面器	2052s	n	sink, wash basin
ぜんぶで・全部で	1092	exp.	in all, total, all together
せんもん・専門	2101	n	subject of study, specialty
ぞう・像	2091	n	statue, figure
せんべい・煎餅	1094	n	rice crackers
そう	1033s	adv.	so, really, seeming
そうそう	2043	interj.	Oh, yes!, that's right
そうそふ・曾祖父	2061s	n	great grandfather
そつぎょう・卒業(を) する	2101s	v	graduate (to)
そうぶ・総武	1024s	pn	Soubu (train line)
そこ	1024	pron.	there
そして	1071	conj.	then, and then
そちら	1014s	pron.	that (person)
そっち	2011	pron.	that way (distant from the speaker, close to the listener), that direction (close to listener), [informal for そちら]
そで・袖	2023s	n	sleeve
そと・外	2023	n	outside
そば・傍	2031	n	nearby, side
そと・外	1045s	n	outside
その	1023		that (thing)
そば	1103s	n	buckweat noodles
そら・空	2032	n	sky
そふ・祖父	1021	n	grandfather (my)
そぼ・祖母	1021	n	grandmother (my)
それで	2044	conj.	and, because of that (at beginning of sentence)
それ	1015	pron.	that (one)
それから	1071	conj.	then, and then
それとも	2041	conj.	or, or else
そろそろ	2034s	conj.	before long, soon
それに	1071	conj.	moreover, furthermore
たいけん・体験	2085s	n	experience
たいいく・体育	1032	n	physical education
たいいくかん・体育館	1033	n	gymnasium
だいがく・大学	1031	n	college/university
だいがくいちねんせい大学一年生・	1031	n	first year college/university student
だいがくせい・大学生	1031	n	college/university student
だいきらい・大嫌い	1072	な adj.	dislike a lot, hate
たいこ・太鼓	2023	n	drum
たいせつ・大切	2092	な adj.	important, valuable
だいじ・大事	1051	な adj	important
たいしかん・大使館	1022s	n	embassy
だいじょうぶ・大丈夫	1063	な adj.	all right, safe, OK
だいすき・大好き	1072	な adj	love, really like
だいすきです。・大好きです	1025s	exp.	I love you
だいどころ・台所	2063	n	kitchen
だいだいいろ・橙色	1074	n	orange
だいにじせかいたいせん・第二次世界大戦	2034s	pn	World War II
たいへん・大変	2025s	な adj.	extreme, problematic
たいてい	1072	adv.	usually
だがし・駄菓子	2041s	n	sweets (traditional Japanese)
たいふう・台風	1101	n	typhoon
だいみょう・大名	1045s	n	feudal lord
たいむかぷせる・タイムカプセル	1094s	n	time capsule
たいわん・台湾	1041	pn	Taiwan (place)
たいわんじん・台湾人	1041	n	Taiwanese (person)
たかい・高い	1061	い adj.	high, tall, expensive

Japanese	Location		English
たかしまや・高島屋	2073s	pn	Japanese department store
だから	2032	conj.	so, therefore
たくしー・タクシー	2012	n	taxi
だから	1044	conj.	because of that
たくさん・たくさん	1031	n	many, a lot
たけ・竹	2032	n	bamboo
だけ	2062	part.	only, just, as
たこあげ・凧揚げをする	2065s	v	fly a kite (to)
たこ	1025		octopus
だし	2093s	n	soup stock (fish-based)
たこす・タコス	1025	n	tacos (Mexican)
たすかる・助かる	2065	v	saved (to be), rescued (to be)
たすける・助ける	2065	v	save (to), rescue (to)
ただしい・正しい	2061	い adj.	correct, right, proper
たこやき・たこ焼き	1104s	n	breaded octopus balls
だす・出す/だします・出します	1013	v	take (it) out (to)
ただいま	1015	exp.	I'm home
たたみ・畳	2054	n	tatami mat, rush straw-reed floor mat
たてもの・建物	2022	n	building
たつ・立つ/たちます・立ちます	1013	v	stand (to)
たっきゅうぶ・卓球部	1033	n	Ping-Pong club
たってください・立って下さい	1013	exp.	Stand please.
たつまき・竜巻	1101	n	tornado
たてもの・建物	1051s	n	building
たてる・建てる	2091	v	build (to)
たのしみにしています・〜楽しみにしています	2011s	exp.	looking forward to ~
たぬき・狸	1035s	n	raccoon dog, tanuki
たのしい・楽しい	1032	い adj.	fun, enjoyable
たばこをすう・タバコを吸う	2074	v	smoke tobacco (to)
たび・旅	1071s	n	trip, travel
たび・旅	2032s	n	trip
たびげいにん・旅芸人	2054	n	traveling performer
たひち・タヒチ	2031	pn	Tahiti
たぶん・多分	2024s	adv.	maybe, possibly
ために・為に	2095	conj.	for, on behalf of
たべもの・食べ物	1043	n	food(s)
たべる・食べる/たべます・食べます	1043	v	eat (to)
たべること・食べる事	1071	n	eating
たまご・卵	1015	n	egg
だめ	1034	な adj.	is bad
ためる・貯める	2011s	v	save money (to)
たり（〜）	2012s	part.	do things like ~
だんす・ダンス	2071	n	dance
だれ	1021	inter.	who
だれも	1102	exp.	no one
たろう・太郎	1014	n	Taro (male name)
たんご・単語	1013s	n	vocabulary
だんご	App.	n	dango (round sticky rice balls on a stick)
たんさく・探索	1013s	n	search, hunt
たんじょうび・誕生日	1052	n	birthday
ちかてつ・地下鉄	2012	n	subway
ちいさい・小さい	1031	い adj.	small
ちかい・近い	1061	い adj.	close, near

Japanese	Location		English
ちがう・違う/ちがいます・違います	1016s	v	is not right, incorrect
ちから・力	2035	n	power
ちきゅう・地球	2032	n	earth, globe
ちず・地図	2032	n	map
ちきん・チキン	1043	n	chicken
ちず・地図	App.	n	map
ちゃわん・茶碗	2053s	n	rice bowl
ちち・父	1014	n	father, dad
ちゃいろ・茶色	1074	n	brown
ちゃくせき。着席。	1016s	exp.	sit down
ちゅうしん・中心	2025s	n	center, middle
ちゃぱつ・茶髪	1074	n	brown (hair)
ちゅうがくいちねんせい・中学一年生	1031	counter	seventh grader
ちゅうがくさんねんせい・中学三年生	1031	counter	ninth grader
ちゅうがくせい・中学生	1031	n	middle school student
ちゅうがくにねんせい・中学二年生	1031	counter	eighth grader
ちゅうがっこう・中学校	1031	n	middle school
ちゅうごく・中国	1041	pn	China (place)
ちゅうごくけい・中国系	1041s	n	Chinese (descent)
ちゅうごくご・中国語	1042	n	Chinese (language)
ちゅうごくじん・中国人	1041	n	Chinese (person)
ちゅうもん・（ご）注文	2024	n	order, request
ちゅうもん・注文する	2024	v	order (to)
ちゅうりゅうじだい・駐留時代	2034s	n	occupation period
ちょうこく・彫刻	2035s	n	carving, carved sculpture
ちょーく・チョーク	1024	n	chalk
ちょうだい・頂戴（する）	2013	v	receive (to), be given (to)
ちょうちょう・蝶々	2031	n	butterfly
ちょうなん・長男	2011s	n	eldest son
ちょこれーと・チョコレート	2065	n	chocolate
	App.	n	
つかれる・疲れる	2071	v	become tired (to)
ちょっと	1032	adv.	little, somewhat
ちょっと まって ください。・ちょっと 待って 下さい。	1016s	exp.	Wait a minute please.
ちょっと…	1043	exp.	a little …
ちらしずし・散らし寿司	1103s	n	sushi in a box or bowl with a variety of ingredients
ついたち・一日	1053	counter	first (day of the month)
つかう・使う/つかいます・使います	1102	v	use (to)
つく・着く	2041	v	arrive at (to)
つぎ・次	1033	n/adv.	next
つたえる・伝える	2033s	v	report (to), communicate (to)
つくる・作る/つくります・作ります	1102	v	make (to)
つけもの・漬け物	1083	n	pickled vegetables (Japanese)
つづく・続く	2041s	v	continue (to)
つづける・続ける	2031s	v	continue (to)
つとめる・勤める	2012	v	employed [at] (to be)
つめたい・冷たい	2051	い adj.	cold (to the touch)
つなみ・津波	1011	n	tsunami, exceptionally large ocean wave
つもり	2043	n	intention, plan
つまらない	1082	い adj.	boring

Japanese	Location		English
つり・釣り	2021	n	fishing
つゆ・梅雨	1101	n	rainy season
つる・釣る	2025	v	fish (to)
ていしょく・定食	2025s	n	fixed menu lunch
つよい・強い	1061	い adj.	strong
つれて いく/いきます・連れて 行く/行きます	1105	v	take someone (to)
つれて かえる/かえります・連れて 帰る/帰ります	1105	v	return with someone (to)
つれて くる/きます・連れて 来る/来ます	1105	v	bring someone (to)
て・手	1061	n	hand
で	1043s, 1063s, 1092s	part.	by means of a "tool", at, for (used for shopping or ordering food)
でーと・デート(を) する/します	1091	v	date (to go on a)
てーぷ・テープ	App.	n	tape
てーぶる・テーブル	App.	n	table
てぃーしゃつ・Tシャツ	1023	n	t-shirt
てぃっしゅ・ティッシュ	App.	n	tissue
ていねいに・丁寧に	2093s	exp.	carefully, neatly
てーぶる・テーブル	2085	n	table
でかける・出掛ける	2044	v	depart (to), set out [on an excursion] (to)
できあがる・出来上がる	2093s	v	complete (to), finsh (to)
できる・出来る	2042	v	able to do (to be)
ですから	2032	conj.	so, therefore
できる・出来る/できます・出来ます	1016s	v	be able (to)
です	1013	copula	helping verb/linking verb, used similarly to "is" or "am"
てっぱんやき・鉄板焼き	2093	n	teppan'yaki (Japanese cooking prepared on a hot steel plate/table)
てすと・テスト	1032	n	test
てつだう・手伝う/てつだいます・手伝います	1041	v	help (to), assist (to)
では また	1015	exp.	see you later [formal]
てぬぐい・手ぬぐい	2052s	n	hand towel
では	2094	interj.	then, well then, so
デパちか・デパ地下	2024s	n	department store basement (often housing food stands)
てまえ・手前	2031	n	before, this side (of)
てんかす・天かす	2093s	n	fried dough (bits of)
てまきずし・手巻き寿司	1103s	n	sushi wrapped in nori
でも	1034	part.	"but" or "however" at the beginning of a sentence
てら・(お)寺	1033	n	temple (Buddhist)
てりやき・照り焼き	App.	n	teriyaki (meat or fish marinated in sweet soy sauce and broiled)
でる・出る/でます・出ます	1061	v	go out (to), leave (to), get out (to)
てれび・テレビ	1103s	n	television, TV
てんいん・店員	1092	n	shopkeeper, clerk
てんのう・天皇	1052s	n	emperor
でんしゃ・電車	2012	n	electric train
てんき・天気	1101	n	weather
でんき・電気	App.	n	lights, electricity
てんきよほう・天気予報	1101	n	weather report
でんとう・伝統	2023	n	tradition, convention
でんとうてき・伝統的	2023	な adj.	traditional

Japanese	Location		English
でんぴょう・伝票	2075s	n	bill (the), check (the)
てんぼうだい・展望台	2015s	n	overlook
でんしめーる・電子メール	1051	n	e-mail
てんぷら・天ぷら	1021s	n	tenpura (battered and deep fried fish or vegetable)
どあ・ドア	2022	n	door
でんわ・電話	1021	n	telephone
でんわ・電話(を) する/します	1091	v	telephone (to)
と	1022	part.	and (used to connect more than one noun, quotation particle, used after a direct quotation)
どあ・ドア	1034	n	door
といあわせ・問い合わせ	2051s	n	inquiry, interrogation
とう・頭	2102	counter	counter for large animals
どいつ・ドイツ	1041	pn	Germany (place)
どいつご・ドイツ語	1042	n	German (language)
どいつじん・ドイツ人	1041	n	German (person)
どう	1035	inter.	how
とうかいどう・東海道	2032s	pn	Tokaidou Road
どう でしたか。	1065	exp.	How was it?
どう ですか	1092	exp.	how about it?
どういたしまして	1023	exp.	you are welcome
とうき・冬季	2015s	n	winter season
とうじつけん・当日券	2042s	n	ticket (same day)
とうきょう・東京	1011	n	Tokyo (place)
とうきょうこくさいだいがく・東京国際大学	1022s	pn	Tokyo International University
とうきょうだいがく・東京大学	1031s	pn	Tokyo University
どうして or なぜ	1042	inter.	why
とうちゃく・到着	2041	n	arrival
どうぞ	1015	adv.	please (here you go), by all means
どうぞ よろしく	1013	exp.	best regards, treat me favorably (same meaning as よろしく おねがいします)
どうぞ よろしく おねがいします・お願いします	1013	exp.	polite for よろしく お願いします
とうだいじ・東大寺	1051s	pn	Todaiji Temple (in Nara)
どうやって	2012s	exp.	how do you do ~
とうふ・豆腐	1011	n	tofu
どうぶつ・動物	1072	n	animal
どうも ありがとう	1023	exp.	thank you
どうも ありがとうございます	1023	exp.	thank you very much (polite for どうも ありがとう)
どうろ・道路	2045	n	road, highway
どーなつ・ドーナツ	2071	n	doughnuts
とおり・通り	2022	n	avenue, street, way
とお・十	1024	counter	ten (things)
とおい 遠い	1061	い adj.	far, distant
とおか・十日	1053	counter	tenth (day of the month)
とかい・都会	2021s	n	city
とおる・通る/とおります・通ります	1051s	v	pass through, to
どきどき・ドキドキ	2064	ono.	excited, go pitter-patter
とき・時	1035s	n	time, hour
ときどき・時々	1032	n/adv.	sometimes
とく・溶く	2093s	v	dissolve (to)
ときのもん・時の門	1041s	n	time gate
とくに・特に	2021s	adv.	especially, particularly

Japanese	Location		English
とくい・得意	1073	な adj.	skilled at
とくがわ・徳川	1041s	pn	Tokugawa (family name)
どくしょ・読書	1071	n	reading
とけい・時計	2015	n	clock, watch
とくべつ・特別	1092	n/な adj.	special
とけい・時計	App.	n	clock
とけいだい・時計台	2015s	n	clock tower
ところ・所	2084	n	place, location, spot
どこ	1024	inter.	where?
どこでも	1054s	n	anywhere
どこにも	1102	adv.	nowhere (w. neg. verb), everywhere, anywhere, anyplace
どこへも	1102	adv.	nowhere, not anywhere, not any place (w. neg. verb) (ex: どこへも行きません。 = He is not going any place.)
どこも	1102	adv.	everywhere, wherever
としこしそば・年越しそば	2062	n	special New Year's soba
ところ・所	1052s	n	place
ところで	1041	exp.	by the way
としだま・(お)年玉	2061	n	New Year's gift (usually money)
としをとる・年を取る	2034	v	grow old (to); age (to)
とどうじに(へ)・～と同時に	2035s	exp.	at the same time as ~
とし(を)とる・年(を)取る	1101s	v	grow old (to), age (to)
とじて ください・閉じて 下さい	1013	exp.	close/Shut (it) please.
としょかん・図書館	1033	n	library
とじる・閉じる/とじます・閉じます	1013	v	close (to), shut (to) [bound paper objects]
とつぜん・突然	1104s	adv.	abrupt, sudden, unexpected
とても	1031	adv.	very
となり・隣	2022	n	neighboring
とぶ・飛ぶ	2031	v	fly (to), jump (to), leap (to)
とにかく	1044s	adv.	anyway, at any rate
どの	1023	inter.	which (thing)
とまる・止まる	2084	v	stop (to), halt (to)
とまと・トマト	App.	n	tomato
ともだち・友達	1022	n	friend
とまる・泊まる	2024	v	stay at [e.g., hotel] (to)
とめる・止める	2084	v	stop (something or someone) (to), turn off (to)
とら・虎	2013	n	tiger
どようび・土曜日	1051	n	Saturday
どろどろ	2051	ono.	syrupy, muddled
とらんぷ・トランプ	1071	n	playing cards, card game
とり・鳥	2102	n	bird
とりい・鳥居	1035	n	torii (Shinto shrine gate)
とりにく・鶏肉	1043	n	chicken
どれ	1015	inter.	which (one)
どれす・ドレス	1064	n	dress (a)
とろろ	2093s	n	grated yam
どんどん・ドンドン	2054	ono.	steadily, drumming (noise), boom boom
とんこつラーメン	1043s	n	pork ramen
とんでもない	1094	exp.	Don't be ridiculous! Not a chance! My pleasure
なか・中	2011	n/adv.	in, inside, middle, center
どんな	1062	inter.	what/which kind of
トンネル	1041s	n	tunnel
ながいき・長生き	2025s	n	long-lived
ながい・長い	1061	い adj.	long

Japanese	Location		English
なかなか	2033	adv.	very, considerably, easily, by no means (with neg. verb)
ながさき・長崎	1041s	pn	Nagasaki (place)
なかなおり・仲直り(を)する/します	1091	v	make up (to), reconcile
なかのわるい・仲の悪い	2014s	い adj.	unfriendly
なかま・仲間	2085s	n	circle of friends, group, partner
なかみ・中身	2062	n	contents, interior
なく・泣く	2064s	v	cry [animals] (to)
なくなる・亡くなる	2055	v	pass away (to), [formal for 死ぬ (cannot be used for one's own death)]
なつかしい・懐かしい	2082s	n	dear, missed
なし・梨	App.	n	Asian pear
なぜ or どうして	1042	inter.	why
なつ・夏	1101	n	summer
など	2062	part.	et cetera, and the like
ななかい・七階	2024	counter	seventh floor
など	1101s	part.	et cetera, and so forth
ななこ・七個	2022	counter	seven pieces/smallish objects
ななさい・七歳/才	1052	counter	seven years old
ななさつ・七冊	1092	counter	seven volumes
ななじゅう・七十	1022	counter	seventy
ななせん・七千	1052	counter	seven thousand
ななとう・七頭	2102	counter	seven large animals
ななつ・七つ	1024	counter	seven (things)
ななはく・七治	2024	counter	stopping seven nights
ななど・七度	1101	counter	seven times/degrees
ななはい・七杯	1092	counter	seven cupfuls
ななばん・七番	2011	counter	seventh, number seven
なな/しちばんめ・七番目	2023	counter	the seventh
ななわ・七羽	2102	counter	seven birds
ななひき・七匹	1092	counter	seven small animals
ななひゃく・七百	1023s	counter	seven hundred
ななびょう・七秒	1032	counter	seven seconds
ななふん・七分	1032	counter	seven minutes
なな/しちぺーじ・七ページ	1042	counter	seven pages, page seven
ななほん・七本	1092	counter	seven cylindrical objects
なな/しちまい・七枚	1042	counter	seven sheets
ななまん・七万	1091	counter	seventy thousand
なにどしですか・何年ですか	2014s	exp.	what zodiac animal are you?
なにいろ・何色	1074	inter.	what color
なにか・何か	1103		something
なにけい・何系	1041	inter.	what ethnicity or heritage
なは・那覇	2022	pn	prefectural capital of Okinawa
なにじん・何人	1041	inter.	what nationality
なにも・何も	1053	pron.	nothing
なのか・七日	1053	counter	seventh (day of the month)
なまけもの・怠け者	2062	n	lazy person
なまえ・名前	1013	n	name
なまたまご・生卵	2053s	n	raw egg
なまはげ	2062	n	folklore demon of Oga Peninsul seen on New Year's Eve
なみ・波	2032s	n	wave
なら	2101s	conj.	if, in case, if it is the case
なら/ならば	2101	conj.	if, in case, if it is true that
なら・奈良	1051s	pn	Nara (place)
ならう・習う	2015	v	learn (to)
ならぶ	2015s	v	line up (to)

Japanese	Location		English
ならう・習う/ならいます・習います	1065	v	learn (to)
ならじだい・奈良時代	1054s	pn	Nara Period
なるべく	2024s	adv.	as much as possible
なりたくうこう・成田空港	1011s	pn	Narita International Airport
なる/なります	1055	v	become (to)
なれる・慣れる	2034s	v	become familiar with (to)
なるほど	1042s	exp.	That makes sense.
なんかい/がい・何階	2024	inter.	what floor?
なん/なに・何	1021	inter.	what
なんだか・何だか	2043s	n	somehow, somewhat
なんがつ・何月	1052	inter.	what month
なんさい・何歳/才	1022s	inter.	how old (animate beings)
なんさつ・何冊	1092	inter.	how many volumes
なんじ・何時	1032	inter.	what time
なんじかんめ・何時間目	1033	inter.	what period
なんぜん・何千	1052	inter.	how many thousands
なんでも・何でも	1043s	pn	anything
なんとう・何頭	2102	inter.	how many large animals?
なんの・何の	2041	exp.	what kind of?
なんぱく・何泊	2024	inter.	stopping how many nights?
なんど・何度	1101	inter.	how many times/degrees
なんにち・何日	1053	inter.	what day of the month
なんにん・何人	1021	inter.	how many people
なんねん・何年	1054	inter.	what year
なんねんせい・何年生	1031	inter.	what grade/year
なんばい・何杯	1092	inter.	how many cupfuls
なんばん・何番	2011	inter.	what number?
なんめい・何名	2024	inter.	how many people?
なんびき・何匹	1092	inter.	how many small animals?
なんびょう・何秒	1032	inter.	How many seconds?
なんぷん・何分	1032	inter.	how many minutes
なんぺーじ・何ページ	1042	inter.	how many pages, what page
なんべい・南米	1042s	pn	South America (place)
なんぼん・何本	1092	inter.	how many cylindrical objects
なんまい・何枚	1042	inter.	how many sheets
なんまん・何万	1091	inter.	how many ten-thousands?
なんめいさま・何名様	2024	inter.	how many people? (polite)
なんわ・何羽	2102	inter.	how many birds?
なんめいさま・何名様	1103s	inter.	how many people (polite)
なんようび・何曜日	1051	inter.	what day of the week
にかい・二階	2024	counter	second floor
に	1015	part.	in, at, used after a location or time word
に・二	1021	counter	two
に	1023	part.	particle after a place word to mean "to" before a verb of motion (similar to the particle へ)
に よろしく	1065	exp.	Say hello to . . .
にがい・苦い	2025	い adj.	bitter
にぎやか・賑やか	2063	な adj.	bustling, busy
にく・肉	2025s	n	meat
にげる・逃げる	2062	v	escape (to), run away (to)
にこ・二個	2022	counter	two pieces/smallish objects
にがつ・二月	1052	n	February
にがて・苦手	1073	な adj.	unskilled at
にし・西	2021	n	west
にさい・二歳/才	1052	counter	two years old
にさつ・二冊	1092	counter	two volumes
にしょくつき・二食付き	2024	exp.	with 2 meals included
にじ・二時	1032	counter	two o'clock
にじかんめ・二時間目	1033	counter	second period
にじゅう・二十	1022	counter	twenty
にじゅういち・二十一	1022	counter	twenty-one
にじゅういちにち・二十一日	1053	counter	twenty-first (day of the month)
にじゅういちまん・二十一万	1091	counter	two hundred ten thousand
にじゅういっぷん・二十一分	1032	counter	twenty-one minutes
にじゅうくにち・二十九日	1053	counter	twenty-ninth (of the month)
にじゅうごにち・二十五日	1053	counter	twenty-fifth (day of the month)
にじゅうさんにち・二十三日	1053	counter	twenty-third (day of the month)
にじゅうしちにち・二十七日	1053	counter	twenty-seventh (day of the month)
にじゅうににち・二十二日	1053	counter	twenty-second (day of the month)
にじゅうはちにち・二十八日	1053	counter	twenty-eighth (day of the month)
にじゅうまん・二十万	1091	counter	two hundred thousand
にじゅうよっか・二十四日	1053	counter	twenty-fourth (day of the month)
にじゅうろくにち・二十六日	1053	counter	twenty-sixth (day of the month)
にじゅっぷん・二十分	1032	counter	twenty minutes
にせん・二千	1052	counter	two thousand
にちじょうせいかつ・日常生活	2032s	n	daily life
について	2051	exp.	concerning, per
にちようび・日曜日	1051	n	Sunday
にっけいじん・日系人	1041	n	Japanese descent
について（〜）	2013s	part.	about; per
にとう・二頭	2102	counter	two large animals
にはく・二泊	2024	counter	stopping two nights
にど・二度	1101	counter	two times/degrees
にねんせい・二年生	1031s	counter	second year student
にはい・二杯	1092	counter	two cupfuls
にばん・二番	2011	counter	second, number two
にばんめ・二番目	2023	counter	the second
にほんてき・日本的	2023	な adj.	Japanese (typically)
にばんめの あに/あね・二番目の 兄/姉	1021	n	second oldest brother/sister (my)
にひき・二匹	1092	counter	two small animals
にひゃく・二百	1023s	counter	two hundred
にびょう・二秒	1032	counter	two seconds
にふん・二分	1032	counter	two minutes
にぺーじ・二ページ	1042	counter	two pages, page two
にほん・日本	1011	pn	Japan (place)
にほん・二本	1092	counter	two cylindrical objects
にほんご・日本語	1011	n	Japanese language
にほんし・日本史	1032	n	Japanese history
にほんじん・日本人	1014	n	Japanese person
にほんぶよう・日本舞踊	2082s	n	traditional Japanese dance
にる・似る	2021	v	resemble (to), similar (to be); (common usage: 似ている)
にまい・二枚	1042	counter	two sheets
にまん・二万	1091	counter	twenty thousand
にゅーじーらんど・ニュージーランド	1041	pn	New Zealand (place)
にゅーじーらんどじん・ニュージーランド人	1041	n	New Zealander
にる・煮る	2094	v	boil (to)
にわ・二羽	2102	counter	two birds
にわとり・鶏	2014s	n	rooster, chicken
にわ・庭	1101	n	garden
にわとり・鶏	2014s	n	rooster, chicken
にんき・人気	2024s	n	popularity

Japanese	Location		English
ぬる・塗る	2062	n	spread (to), smear (to)
ぬるい	2052	い adj.	lukewarm
ね	1035	part.	sentence ending for a rhetorical question or when seeking agreement
ねえ	1035	part.	sentence ending that can be exclamatory or express surprise
ねくたい・ネクタイ	1064	n	necktie
ねこ・猫	1021	n	cat
ねずみ・鼠	1072	n	rat, mouse
ねずみいろ・鼠色	1074	n	gray (mouse colored)
ねつ・熱	1063	n	fever
ねむい・眠い	1053s	い adj.	sleepy
ねる・寝る/ねます・寝ます	1051	v	sleep (to)
ねること・寝る事	1071	n	sleeping
ねんがじょう・年賀状	2061	n	New Year's card
ねんかん・年間	1032s	n	period of years, duration
ねんごう・年号	1053s	n	reign year
ねんまつ・年末	2024s	n	year-end
の	1021	part.	possession, replaces a noun
のーと・ノート	1024	n	notebook
のあいだに（〜）・〜の間に	2014s	part.	between ~
のう・能	1075	n	Noh (a type of theater)
のこす・残す	2032s	v	let remain (to)
ので	2043	part.	that being the case, because of ...
ので	2044	conj.	since, given that..., because of...
のど・咽喉	1061	n	throat
のどか	2022s	な adj.	calm, peaceful
のときに（〜）・〜の時に	1055s	conj.	when
のぼる・上る	2022	v	ascend (to), rise (to), climb (to)
のみもの・飲み物	1043	n	drink(s)
のむ・飲む/のみます・飲みます	1043	v	drink (to)
のり	App.	n	seaweed
のり	2093	n	seaweed
のりかえる・乗り換える	2024	v	transfer (to)
のる・乗る	2012	v	ride (to)
のれん	1043s	n	noren curtain
は	1013	part.	denotes a sentence topic
ぱーてぃ・パーティ	1073s	n	party
はい	1014		yes, OK, here (roll call)
はい、そう です。	1014	exp.	yes it is
はい、わかります。・分かります。	1016s	exp.	Yes, I understand
はいいろ・灰色	1074	n	gray, ash (color)
はいく・俳句	1101	n	haiku (poem)
はいけい・拝啓	2064	n	opening for written letters
ばいてん・売店	2044	n	shop, stand
ばいばい・バイバイ	1015		bye-bye
はいる・入る/はいります・入ります	1061	v	come in (to), go in (to), enter (to)
はか・(お)墓	2021s	n	grave (a)
はかいされる・破壊される	2084s	v	cause destruction (to), cause distruption (to)
はかせ・博士	2015s		professor
ばかばかしい	1081	い adj.	foolish, silly
ばかり	2062	part.	only, just
はかる・測る	2094	v	measure (to)
はく・履く/はきます・履きます	1064	v	wear below the waist (to)

Japanese	Location		English
はくちょう・白鳥	2102	n	swan
はくぶつかん・博物館	2071	n	museum
はこ・箱	1081	n	box
はこだて・函館	2011	pn	Hakodate (city in Hokkaido)
はさみ	App.	n	scissors
はし・端	2044s	n	edge, border
はし・橋	2022	n	bridge
はし（お）・(お)箸	1015	n	chopsticks
はじまる・始まる	2041	v	begin (to) |intrans.|
ばしょ・場所	2104	n	place, location, position
はじめまして・初めまして	1013	exp.	How do you do?
はじめましょう・始めましょう	1011	exp.	Let's begin.
はじめる・始める/はじめます・始めます	1052	v	begin (to)
はしる・走る	2085	v	run (to)
はず	2043	n	expectation that something has taken or will take place, expected to be
ばす・バス	2012	n	bus
はずかしい・恥ずかしい	2052	い adj.	shy, embarrassed, ashamed
ばすけ・バスケ, ばすけっとぼーる・バスケットボール	1033	n	basketball
ばすけ・バスケ(を) する/します	1091	v	play basketball (to)
ばすけぶ・バスケ部	1033	n	basketball club (team)
はた・旗	App.	n	flag
はだし・裸足	2052	n	barefoot
はたち・二十歳	1052	counter	twenty years old
はたらく・働く	2012	v	work (to)
はち・八	1021	counter	eight
はちがつ・八月	1052	n	August
はちじ・八時	1032	counter	eight o'clock
はちじゅう・八十	1022	counter	eighty
はちど・八度	1101	counter	eight times/degrees
はちにん・八人	1021	counter	eight people
はちばん・八番	2011	counter	eighth, number eight
はちびょう・八秒	1032	counter	eight seconds
はちふん/はっぷん・八分	1032	counter	eight minutes
はち/はっぺーじ・八ページ	1042	counter	eight pages, page eight
はちほん/はっぽん・八本	1092	counter	eight cylindrical objects
はちまい・八枚	1042	counter	eight sheets
はちまん・八万	1091	counter	eighty thousand
はっかい・八階	2024	counter	eighth floor
はつか・二十日	1053	counter	twentieth (day of the month)
はったつ・発達	2031s	n	development, growth
ばっぐ・バッグ	1023s	n	bag/sack
ばっくぱっく・バックパック	1024	n	backpack
はっさい・八歳/才	1052	counter	eight years old
はっさつ・八冊	1092	counter	eight volumes
はっせん・八千	1052	counter	eight thousand
はちわ・八羽	2102	counter	eight birds
はっぱい・八杯	1092	counter	eight cupfuls
はっぱく・八泊	2024	counter	stopping eight nights
はっぴき・八匹	1092	counter	eight small animals
はっぴゃく・八百	1023s	counter	eight hundred
はな・鼻	1061	n	nose
はな・花	1101	n	flower
はなす・話す/はなします・話します	1042	v	speak (to)

Japanese	Location		English
はなな・バナナ	1023s	n	banana
はなみ・花見	1105	n	cherry blossom viewing, flower viewing
はなれる・離れる	2031s	v	separate (to)
はにわ・埴輪	1041s	n	haniwa
はぬか・ハヌカ	2061	pn	Hanukkah
はねつき・羽根つき	2065s	n	Japanese badminton
はは・母	1014	n	mother, mom
はま・浜	1081	n	beach
はやい・早い	1054s	い adj.	early
はやい・速い	2023	い adj.	fast, quick
はやく・速く	1035	adv.	quickly
はやく・早く	2035	adv.	early (in the day)
はらう・払う	2045	v	pay (to)
ばらばら・バラバラ	2021	な adj./ono.	scattered, in pieces disconnected
はりだす・貼り出す	2021s	v	post (to), display (to)
はる・春	1101	n	spring
はれ・晴れ	1101	n	clear (skies)
ばれーぼーるぶ・バレーボール部	1033	n	volleyball club (team)
はれる・晴れる/はれます・晴れます	1101	v	become clear (weather)
はん・〜半	1032	n	half hour
ばん・晩	1021s	n	evening
ぱん・パン	1043	n	bread
はんが・版画	1091	n	woodblock print
はんぎ・版木	2031s	n	woodblock print block
ばんぐみ・番組	2044	n	program (e.g., a TV program)
ばんごう・番号	2024s	n	number
ばんごはん・晩ご飯	1025	n	dinner, evening meal
はんさむ・ハンサム	1064	な adj	handsome, good-looking
ぱんつ・パンツ	1064	n	underwear
はんばーがー・ハンバーガー	1043	n	hamburger
ばんめ (〜)・〜番目	2014s	counter	number ~
ぱんや・パン屋	1043	n	bakery
びーち・ビーチ	1081	n	beach
ピア	2024s	pn	entertainment ticket sales venue
ぴあの・ピアノ	1071	n	piano
ひがし・東	2021	n	east
ひき (〜)・〜匹	1022s	counter	small animals counter
ひく・弾く	2023	v	pull (to), play (a stringed instrument) (to)
ひく・弾く/ひきます・弾きます	1071	v	play [a stringed instrument] (to)
ひくい・低い	1061	い adj.	low, short (height)
ひげ・髭	1061	n	mustache, beard
ひこうき・飛行機	2012	n	airplane
ひざ・膝	1061	n	knee
ぴざ・ピザ	1043s	n	pizza
ひさしぶり・久しぶり	2084s	n	it's been a while/long time since I saw you
びじゅつ・美術	1032	n	art, fine arts
びしょびしょ	2051	ono.	sopping wet; drenched
ひそかに	2081s	n	secretly
ひだり・左	2022	n	left
ひっかかってしまう・引っかかってしまう	2065s		get completely tangled up in
ひっくりかえす・ひっくり返す	2093s	n	turn over (to), flip (to)

Japanese	Location		English
びっくり・ビックリする/します	1105s	v	be surprised (to), be amazed (to)
びっくり・ビックリする	2073	v	surprised (to be), amazed (to be)
ひっこし・引越し	2032s	n	relocate, move
ひっこし・引っ越しする	2032s	v	move home/office (to), change residence (to)
ひつじどし・羊年/未年	2014	n	year of the sheep
ひつよう・必要	2035s	n	necessary, required
ひなん・避難される	2084s	v	criticized (to be)
びでおげーむ・ビデオゲーム	1071	n	video games
びでおげーむ・ビデオゲーム(を) する/します	1091	v	play video games (to)
ひと・人	1022	n	person
ひどい	1081	い adj.	terrible
ひとつ・一つ	1024	counter	one (thing)
ひとり・一人	1021	counter	one person
ひとりで・一人で	1104	exp.	alone, by oneself
ひま	1084	な adj	free (time)
ひみつ・秘密	1061	n	secret
ひゃく・百	1022	counter	one hundred
びょういん・病院	1063	n	hospital
びょうき・病気	1063	n	illness, sickness
ひょうしぎ・拍子木	2044s	n	wooden clappers
ひら・平	2032	な adj.	flat
ひらいずみ・平泉	1061s	pn	Hiraizumi (place)
ひらく・開く/ひらきます・開きます	1013	v	open (to) |book/bound object
ひる・昼	1025	n	daytime, noon
ひるごはん・昼ご飯	1025	n	lunch
ひるね・昼寝	1063	n	nap
ひるね・昼寝(を) する/します	1063	v	nap (to)
ひるやすみ・昼休み	1032	n	lunch break
ひろい・広い	1083	い adj.	wide, spacious
ひろお・広尾	1022s	pn	Hiroo (section of Tokyo)
ひろしげ・広重	2032	pn	Utagawa Hiroshige, artist
ひろしま・広島	1083s	pn	Hiroshima (place)
ぴんく・ピンク	1074	n	pink
ヒンズーきょう・ヒンズー教	2062	n	Hinduism
ふぁっしょん・ファッション	1074s	n	fashion
ふぁん・ファン	1065s	n	fan, supporter
ふぃるむ・フィルム	2085	n	film (coating)
ぷえるとりこじん・プエルトリコ人	1041	n	Puerto Rican (person)
ふうけい・風景	2032s	n	scenery
ふえ・笛	2025	n	flute
フェリー	2095s	n	ferry
ふがくさんじゅうろっけい・富嶽三十六景	2033s	pn	Thirty-six Views of Mt. Fuji by Hokusai
ぶかつ・部活	1033	n	club activity
ふく・服	1064	n	clothes
ぶざー・ブザー	2044	n	buzzer
ふしぎ・不思議	1081	な adj	mysterious
ふくざつ・複雑	2021	な adj.	complex, complicated
ふじさん・富士山	1094s	pn	Fuji (Mt.)
ぶた・豚	2013	n	pig, pork
ふたご・双子	1022s	n	twins
ふたつ・二つ	1024	counter	two (things)
ふたり・二人	1021	counter	two people

Japanese	Location		English
ふつう・普通	1064	adj./adv.	usual, normal
ふつう・普通	2023	n/adv.	usual; normal
ふつか・二日	1053	counter	second (day of the month)
ぶっか・物価	2102	n	price of comodities, cost of living
ぶっきょう・仏教	2062	n	Buddhism
ぶっきょう・仏教	1052s	n	Buddhism (religion)
ぶつりがく・物理学	1032	n	physics
ふで・筆	1033s	n	brush
ふでばこ・筆箱	App.	n	pencil box
ふとっています・太ってい ます	1062		fat/plump (is)
ふとる・太る/ふとります・ 太ります	1062	v	fat (to get)
ふとん・布団	1063	n	futon
ふこう・不幸	2081	な adj.	unhappiness, misfortune
ふね・舟	1045s	n	ship, boat
ふね・船	2012	n	boat, ship
ぶぶん・部分	2071	n	portion, section, part
ふゆ・冬	1101	n	winter
ぶらじるじん・ブラジル人	1041	n	Brazilian (person)
ぶらすばんど・ブラスバンド	1033	n	brass band
ふらんす・フランス	1041	pn	France
ふらんすご・フランス語	1042	n	French (language)
ふらんすじん・フランス人	1041	n	French (person)
ぷらんな－・プランナー	App.	n	planner, hand-book
ふる・降る/ふります・降り ます	1101	v	precipitate (to)
ふるーつ・フルーツ	1075s	n	fruit
ふるい・古い	1081	い adj.	old (used for things)
ぷれぜんと・プレゼント	2015	n	present, gift
ぷれぜんと・プレゼント	1094	n	a gift, a present
ぶんか・文化	1065	n	culture
ぶんぼうぐや・文房具屋	2073s	n	stationery store
へ	1023	part.	particle after a place word to mean "to" before a verb of motion (similar to the particle に)
へ/に	1104	part.	used with verbs of movement after place of destination
べーすぼーる・ベースボール	1033	n	baseball
へいき・平気	2073	な adj.	coolness, calmness, unconcern
へいし・兵士	2065s	n	soldier
へいわ・平和	2091	n	peace
へいじょうきょう・平城京	1051s	pn	Heijoukyou (ancient name for Kyoto)
ぺこぺこ・ペコペコ	1025		hunger (mimetic expression for)
へた・下手	1073	な adj	not good at
べつ・別	1092	n/な adj.	separate
べっど・ベッド	2031	n	bed
べつべつ・別々	1092	n/な adj.	separately, individually
べつべつ・別々にする	2014s	exp	separate (to)
へび・蛇	2013	n	snake
へびどし/みどし・巳年	2061	n	year of the snake
へや・部屋	1015	n	room (a)
ぺるーじん・ペルー人	1041	n	Peruvian (person)
ぺん・ペン	1024	n	pen
へん・辺	2011	n	vicinity
へん・変	2043	な adj.	unusual, strange
べんきょう・勉強する/します	1052	v	study (to)
べんけい・弁慶	1061s	pn	Benkei (famous samurai name)
へんじ・返事	2012s	n	reply, response

Japanese	Location		English
べんてんどう・弁天堂	2031s	pn	Bentendou, a Buddhist temple dedicated to the goddess Benten
べんとう・弁当	1011	n	box lunch (Japanese), bento
べんり・便利	2022s	な adj.	useful
ほーむしっく・ホームシック	2021s	n	homesick
ほーむすてい・ホームステ イ	2063	n	homestay
ほーむるーむ・ホームルー ム	1032	n	homeroom
ぼーるぺん・ボールペン	1024	n	ballpoint pen
ほいくえん・保育園	1031	n	nursery school
ほう・方	2032		direction (prev. learned as かた for person as in この方)
ほうかご・放課後	1033	n/adv.	time after school
ほうげん・方言	2053s	n	dialect
ぼうさい・防災	2085	n	disaster prevention
ほうさく・豊作	2063s	n	harvest
ぼうし	1023	n	hat/cap
ほうちょうとおけ・包丁と桶	2064s	n	knife and bucket
ほうほう・方法	2094	n	method
ほか・他	2023	n	other, another
ほかほか	2054	adv./ono.	steamy hot food, warm(ly)
ぼく・僕	1013	pron.	I, me (used by males only)
ほけんたいいく・保健体育	1032	n	health (class)
ほすとふぁみりー・ホスト ファミリー	2063	n	host family
ほっかいどう・北海道	2011	pn	Hokkaido (northernmost of the four main islands of Japan)
ほっちきす・ホッチキス	App.	n	stapler
ほっとする	2064s	v	relieved (to be)
ほてる・ホテル	2051	n	hotel
ほとんど	2061	adv.	mostly, almost
ほね・骨	2021s	n	bone
ほら！	1081s	interj.	look, Look out!
ほる・彫る	2031s	v	carve (to)
ぽるとがる・ポルトガル	1041	pn	Portugal (place)
ぽるとがるご・ポルトガル語	1042	n	Portuguese (language)
ぽるとがるじん・ポルトガ ル人	1041	n	Portuguese (person)
ほわいとぼーど・ホワイト ボード	App.	n	whiteboard
ほん・本	1011	n	book
ほんしゅう・本州	1041s	pn	Honshu (place)
ほんしゅう・本州	2011	pn	Honshu (largest of the four main islands of Japan)
ほんだな・本棚	App.	n	bookshelves
ほんとう・本当	2021s	n	original/main island (lit.)
ほんとう・本当	1104	n	truth, reality
ほんもの・本物	1091	n	real thing, genuine article
ほんや・本屋	1043	n	bookstore
ほんやさん・本屋さん	1043	n	bookstore
ま・〜間	2054	counter	rooms
まあまあ	1062	adv.	so so, not bad, moderate
まいしゅう・毎週	1054	n	every week
まいつき・毎月	1054	n	every month
まいとし/まいねん・毎年	1054	n	every year
まいにち・毎日	1032	n	every day
まいねん/まいとし・毎年	1054	n	every year

Japanese	Location		English
まいる・参る	2043	v	go (to), come (to), visit (to) a grave or shrine (humble for 行きます・来ます)
まえ・前	1032	n/adv.	front, in front, before
まかせる・任せる	2071	v	entrust (to), leave to a person (to)
まがる・曲がる	2022	v	turn (to)
まきずし・巻き寿司	1043s	n	rolled sushi
まじっく・マジック	App.	n	marker
まず	2044	adv.	first (of all), anyway, well then
まずい	1081	い adj.	not tasty, not good
まずしい・貧しい	2095	い adj.	poor, needy
まぜる・混ぜる	2023	v	mix (to), stir (to)
また	1092s	prefix	again, also, and
まだ	1043	adv.	not yet (with negative verb)
まち・町	2014	n	town, city block
まち・街	2031s	n	town
まつ・待つ/まちます・待ちます	1061	v	wait (to)
まつおばしょう・松尾芭蕉	1102s	pn	Basho Matsuo (Japanese poet)
まっすぐ	2022	な adj.	straight (ahead)
まったく・全く	1084	adv.	really, indeed, truly
まつり・祭り	1051	n	festival
まで	1053	part.	until (used with spec. locations or times)
まど・窓	1034	n	window
まなぶ・学ぶ	2085	v	study (in depth) (to), learn (to) or take lessons in
まやく・麻薬	2074	n	drugs, narcotic
まらそん・マラソン	2085	n	marathon
まわり・周り	2043	n	circumference, edge
まわりのひと・周りの人	2052s	n	surrounding people
まわる・回る	2021s	v	rotate (to); revolve (to)
まん・万	1091	counter	ten thousand
まんが・漫画	1011	n	Japanese comics
まんなか・真ん中	2031	n	middle, center, mid-way
みぎ・右	2021	n	right
みぎ・右	1104s	n	right
みじかい・短い	1061	い adj.	short (length)
みず・水	1024	n	water
みずぎ・水着	2052	n	swimming suit
みずげい・水芸	2031s	n	water magic performance
みせる・見せる	2043	v	show (to)
みせ・店	1091	n	shop, store
みそしる・味噌汁	1104s	n	miso soup
みたい（〜）	2021s	exp.	looks like ~
みち・道	2022	n	road, path, street
みっか・三日	1053	counter	third (day of the month)
みつかる・見つかる	2105	v	find (to)
みっつ・三つ	1024	counter	three (things)
みてください・見て下さい。	1013	exp.	Look/Watch please.
みどり・緑	1074	n	green
みなさん・皆さん	1031	n	everyone (polite)
みなと・港	2021s	n	port, harbor
みなみ・南	2021	n	south
みなみあふりか・南アフリカ	1041	pn	South Africa (place)
みにくい	1081	い adj.	ugly
みみ・耳	1061	n	ear
みらい・未来	2104	n	future (distant)
みる・見る/みます・見ます	1013	v	look/see (to)
みるく・ミルク	1043s	n	milk
みんしゅく・民宿	2024	n	guest house
みんぞくかん・民族間	2021s	n	folk museum
みんな・皆	1031	pron.	everyone, all
むいか・六日	1053	counter	sixth (day of the month)
むかし・昔	1082	n	long ago
むかしばなし・昔話	2013	n	folktale
むかしむかし・昔々	1082	n	long long ago
むぎちゃ・麦茶	1103s	n	barley tea
むこう・向こう	2031	n	across, opposite, over there
むしあつい・蒸し暑い	1034	い adj.	humid (weather)
むす・蒸す	2094	v	steam (to)
むずかしい・難しい	1032	い adj.	difficult
むすこ・息子	2061	n	son
むっつ・六つ	1024	counter	six (things)
むすめ・娘	2061	n	daughter
むら・村	2014	n	village
むらさき・紫	1074	n	purple
むらさきしきぶ・紫式部	1071s	pn	Shikibu, Murasaki (Heian Pd. author)
むり・無理	1063	な adj.	impossible, overdoing
むり しないで ください・無理 しないで 下さい	1063	exp.	Don't overexert.
め・目	1061	n	eye
めーる・メール	1051	n	e-mail
めいく・メイク	1064	n	make up (facial)
めいじじだい・明治時代	2071	n	Meiji Period (1868-1912)
めいわく・迷惑	2071	な adj.	trouble, bother
めがね・眼鏡	1064	n	eyeglasses
めきしこ・メキシコ	1041	pn	Mexico (place)
めきしこけい・メキシコ系	1041s	n	Mexican descent
めきしこじん・メキシコ人	1041	n	Mexican (person)
めしあがる・召し上がる	2044s	v	eat (to) [formal]
めずらしい・珍しい	2043	い adj.	unusual, rare
めだまやき・目玉焼き	2093s	n	sunny-side up fried egg
めちゃくちゃ	2054	な adj./ono	messy, disorderly, absurd
めも・メモ	1083	n	memo, note
めろん・メロン	1023s	n	melon (honeydew)
めんど（う）・面倒くさい	2074	い adj.	bother(some) to do, tiresome
も	1024	part.	too, also, replaces particles は、が、and を
もう	1104	adv./interj.	already
もういちど いって ください。・もう一度言って 下さい。	1016s	exp.	Say it again please.
もうすぐ	2063	exp.	very soon
もくようび・木曜日	1051	n	Thursday
もじ・文字	2031s	n	letter, characters
もしかして	2101	exp.	perhaps, possibly
もち・餅	1064	n	sticky rice cake (mochi)
もち・(お)餅	1064	n	sticky rice cake
もちろん	1105	exp.	of course
もつ持つ/もちます・持ちます	1061	v	have (to), hold (to), carry (to)
もって いく/いきます・持って 行く/行きます	1105	v	take something (to)
もって かえる/かえります・持って 帰る/帰ります	1105	v	return with something (to)
もって くる/きます・持って 来る/来ます	1105	v	bring something (to)

Japanese	Location		English
もとめる・求める	2045	v	seek (to), request (to)
もっと	1093	adv.	more
もの・物	1043	n	thing
もほう・摸倣	2033s	n	copy, imitation
ももいろ・もも色	1074	n	pink (peach) color
もやし	2093s	n	bean sprouts
もらう/もらいます	1094	v	receive (to) (very polite), lit.: I will receive.
もり・森	1101s	n	forest
もん・門	1033s	n	gate
もんだい・問題	1045s	n	problem
やきそば・焼きそば	1102s	n	fried noodles, yakisoba
やきとり・焼き鳥	2043	n	grilled chicken (kebab)
やきゅう・野球	1033	n	baseball
やく・焼く	2094	v	fry (to)
やくそく・約束	1105s	n	promise
やけてしまう・焼けてしまう	2022s	n	completely burn (to), burn down completely (to)
やさい・野菜	2065s	n	vegetable(s)
やさしい・優しい	1081	い adj.	easy, simple, kind, gentle
やすい・安い	1082	い adj.	cheap
やすむ・休む	1015s	v	rest (to), take a break (to)
やせています	1062		slim/skinny (is)
やせる/やせます	1062	v	thin (to become)
やった！	2021	exp.	We did it!
やっつ・八つ	1024	counter	eight (things)
やってみる/やってみます	1073	v	see if you can do (something), try to do (something) (to)
やっぱり	2021s	adv.	after all; same as やはり
やね・屋根	2084	n	roof
やま・山	1031	n	mountain
やまのて・山の手	1024s	pn	Yamanote (train line)
やまもと・山本	1031	pn	Yamamoto (family name)
やる/やります	1073	v	do (to)
ゆうがた・夕方	2063	n	evening
ゆうめい・有名	1061	な adj	famous
ゆうやけ・夕焼け	1104s	n	sunset
ゆうらんせん・遊覧船	2063s	n	excursion boat, sightseeing boat
ゆかた・浴衣	2052	n	yukata (light cotton) kimono worn in summer or in the evenings in ryokan or homes
ゆき/いき・行き	2024	n	bound for
ゆき・雪	1101	n	snow
ゆきがっせん・雪合戦	2012s	n	snowball fight
ゆだやきょう・ユダヤ教	2062	n	Judaism
ゆっくり	1016s	adv.	slowly, restful
ゆっくり おねがいします。・ゆっくり お願いします。	1016s	exp.	Please say it more slowly.
ゆっくり/ごゆっくり	2044	exp.	slowly, at ease, restful
ゆび・指	1061	n	finger(s)
よ	1035	part.	sentence ending for a strong declarative statement or for emphasis
ヨーロッパ	1042s	pn	Europe (place)
よーろっぱ・ヨーロッパ	2032	pn	Europe
よい（よく）・良い（良く）	1082	い adj.	well
よい/いい・良い	1041s	ir. adj.	good
よいおとしを・よいお年を	2063	exp.	have a good New Year
よいしょ・ヨイショ	2021	exp.	effort or strain (expression of)
よう・様	2095	n	way, manner
ようか・八日	1053	counter	eighth (day of the month)
ようこそ	1014	exp.	Welcome!, Nice to see you.
ようしき・様式	2035s	n	style
ようしつ・洋室	2024	n	Western-style room
ようしょく・洋食	2024	n	Western-style meal
ようす・様子	2031s	n	appearance
ようちえん・幼稚園	1031	n	kindergarten
ようひん・用品	2043	n	articles, supplies, parts
ようふう・洋風	2024	n	Western style
ようふく・洋服	1064	n	clothes, Western clothes
よく	1103s	adv.	well, nicely
よくそう・浴槽	2052s	n	bathtub
よくできました。・良く出来ました。	1016s	exp.	Well done.
よけい・余計	2043	n	too much, unnecessary, excess
よこ・横	2023	n	side (beside), sideways
よこはま・横浜	1031s	pn	Yokohama (place)
よじ・四時	1032	counter	four o'clock
よじかんめ・四時間目	1033	counter	fourth period
よちする・予知する	2084s	v	predict (to), know beforehand
よっか・四日	1053	counter	fourth (day of the month)
よっつ・四つ	1024	counter	four (things)
よてい・予定	2051s	n	plan, expectation
よにん・四人	1021	counter	four people
よぶ・呼ぶ	2105	v	call (by a name) (to)
よむ・読む/よみます・読みます	1013	v	read (to)
よやく・予約	2024	n	reservation
よやくする・予約する	2024	v	reserve (to)
より	2032	part.	than ~
より	2062	part.	from (in the conclusion of a letter
よろこぶ・喜ぶ	2035s	v	make happy (to)
よろしい	2044	い adj.	good, OK, fine
よろしく	1013s	adv.	best regards, please remember me (favorably)
よろしく おねがいします・お願いします	1013	exp.	best regards, treat me favorably
よわい・弱い	1061	い adj.	weak
よん/し・四	1021	counter	four
よんかい・四階	2024	counter	fourth floor
よんこ・四個	2022	counter	four pieces/smallish objects
よんさい・四歳/才	1052	counter	four years old
よんさつ・四冊	1092	counter	four volumes
よんじゅう・四十	1022	counter	forty
よんじゅうさんぷん・四十三分	1032	counter	forty-three dollars
よんせん・四千	1052	counter	four thousand
よんとう・四頭	2102	counter	four large animals
よんど・四度	1101	counter	four times/degrees
よんはい・四杯	1092	counter	four cupfuls
よんぱく・四泊	2024	counter	stopping four nights
よんばん・四番	2011	counter	fourth, number four
よんばんめ・四番目	2023	counter	the fourth
よんひき・四匹	1092	counter	four small animals
よんひゃく・四百	1023s	counter	four hundred
よんびょう・四秒	1032	counter	four seconds
よんぷん・四分	1032	counter	four minutes
よんぺーじ・四ページ	1042	counter	four pages, page four
よんほん・四本	1092	counter	four cylindrical objects
よんまい・四枚	1042	counter	four sheets
よんまん・四万	1091	counter	forty thousand

Japanese	Location		English
よんわ・四羽	2102	counter	four birds
らーめん・ラーメン	1043s	n	ramen
らいげつ・来月	1054	n	next month
らいしゅう・来週	1054	n	next week
らいねん・来年	1054	n	next year
らいぶ・ライブ	2023	n	"live" performance (concert, show, etc.)
らしい	2023s	suf.	seemingly, looks like ~, resembles ~
りかいする・理解する	2092s	v	grasp (to), comprehend (to)
りきし・力士	2034s	n	sumo wrestler
りくじょうぶ・陸上部	1033	n	track and field club
りゅう・龍	2013	n	dragon
りゅうがくせい・留学生	2102	n	exchange student, overseas student
りゅうきゅうおうこく・琉球王国	2022s	pn	Ryukyu Kingdom
りょう・寮	2012s	n	dormitory
りょうきん・料金	2024s	n	price
りょうり・料理	1071	n	cooking
りょうしん・両親	2011	n	parents
りょかん・旅館	2051	n	ryokan, Japanese inn/hotel
りょかん・旅館	1044s	n	ryokan, Japanese inn/hotel
りょこう・旅行	1071	n	trip, travel
りょこうがいしゃ・旅行会社	2024	n	travel agency/company
りょこう（・旅行（を）する/します	1091	v	take a trip (to), travel (to)
りんご	1023s	n	apple
れい・例	2034s	n	example
れい・礼	1016s	exp.	bow
れきし・歴史	1032	n	history
れすとらん・レストラン	1043	n	restaurant
れもねーど・レモネード	2071	n	lemonade
れんしゅう・練習（を）する/します	1051	v	practice (to)
ろうか・廊下	2022	n	corridor, hallway
ろうそく	2094s	n	candle
ろく・六	1021	counter	six
ろくがつ・六月	1052	n	June
ろくさい・六歳	1052	counter	six years old
ろくさつ・六冊	1092	counter	six volumes
ろくじ・六時	1032	counter	six o'clock
ろくじかんめ・六時間目	1033	counter	sixth period
ろくじゅう・六十	1022	counter	sixty
ろくせん・六千	1052	counter	six thousand
ろくとう・六頭	2102	counter	six large animals
ろくど・六度	1101	counter	six times/degrees
ろくにん・六人	1021	counter	six people
ろくばん・六番	2011	counter	sixth, number six
ろくばんめ・六番目	2023	counter	the sixth
ろくびょう・六秒	1032	counter	six seconds
ろくぺーじ・六ページ	1042	counter	six pages, page six
ろくまい・六枚	1042	counter	six sheets
ろくまん・六万	1091	counter	sixty thousand
ろくわ・六羽	2102	counter	six birds
ろしあ・ロシア	1041	pn	Russia (place)
ろしあご・ロシア語	1042	n	Russian (language)
ろしあじん・ロシア人	1041	n	Russian (person)

Japanese	Location		English
ろっかーへ いっても いい ですか。・ロッカーへ行っ ても いいですか。	1016s	exp.	May I go to my locker?
ろっかい・六階	2024	counter	sixth floor
ろっくんろーる・ロックン ロール	1105	n	rock and roll (music)
ろっこ・六個	2022	counter	six pieces/smallish objects
ろっぱい・六杯	1092	counter	six cupfuls
ろっぱく・六泊	2024	counter	stopping six nights
ろっぴき・六匹	1092	counter	six small animals
ろっぴゃく・六百	1023s	counter	six hundred
ろっぷん・六分	1032	counter	six minutes
ろっぽん・六本	1092	counter	six cylindrical objects
ろっぽんぎ・六本木	1024s	pn	Roppongi section of Tokyo
ろてんぶろ・露天風呂	2051s	n	open air (outdoor) bath
わ・羽	2102	counter	counter for birds
わいわい	2054	adv./ono.	noisily, clamorously
わか・和歌	1072s	n	waka (classic Japanese poem)
わかい・若い	2034	い adj.	young
わがまま	1081	な adj.	selfish
わかる・分かる/わかりま す・分かります	1016s	v	understand (to)
わくわく	2023s	adv./ono.	thrilled, excited
わくわく（する）	2023	v	tremble (to), get nervous (to), thrilled (to be)
わさび	1015	n	wasabi, Japanese horseradish
わしつ・和室	2024	n	Japanese-style room
わしょく・和食	2024	n	Japanese-style meal
わすれる・忘れる	2044	v	forget (to)
わたし・私	1013	pron.	me, I
わたしたち・私達	1013	pron.	we, us
わたす・渡す	2081	v	hand over (to), pass along (to)
わたる・渡る	2022	v	cross over (to), to go across
わっ！	1035	interj.	wow!
わふう・和風	2024	n	Japanese style
わらでできたみの	2064s	n	straw raincoat
わるい・悪い	1082	い adj.	bad
を	1023	part.	used after the direct object

English-Japanese Glossary

This glossary has simplified abbreviations to make it easier to use. The following abbreviations are used for parts of speech:

い adj.	い adjective	interj.	interjection
な adj.	な adjective	n	noun
ir. adj.	irregular adjective	ono.	onomatopoetic exp.
adv.	adverb	part.	particle
conj.	conjunction	pn	person or place name
exp.	expression	pron.	pronoun
inter.	interrogative	v	verb

The numbering system for location of vocabulary words in the chapters is made up of the volume number (the first digit; 2 is this volume, *Intermediate Japanese*); a two-digit chapter number; and the section number. An "s" indicates words that are supplemental: they are not on the New Words lists, but are also included in the book (in the Dialogues, Journal entries, etc.). For example:

2025s

Vol. 2　Chapter 2　Section 5　supplementary (not in New Words)

English	Location		Japanese
A! (exp. of surprise)	2051	*interj.*	あっ
a.m.	1032	*n*	ごぜん・午前
able to do (to be)	2042	*v*	できる・出来る
about ~	2043	*part.*	くらい
about	1032		ごろ or ころ
about; per	2013s	*part.*	について (～)
above, up	2022	*n*	うえ・上
abrupt, sudden, unexpected	1104s	*adv.*	とつぜん・突然
accompaniment for rice dishes, main dish or side dish	2025s	*n*	おかず
across, opposite, over there	2031	*n*	むこう・向こう
actually	1104	*adv.*	じつは・実は
adult	2062	*n*	おとな・大人
advancement, expansion	2031s	*n*	かいはつ・開発
afraid	2064	い *adj.*	おそろしい・恐ろしい
after all; same as やはり	2021s	*adv.*	やっぱり
after	1033		あと・後
afterwards, later	1033	*adv.*	あとで・後で
again, also, and	1092s	*prefix*	また
Ah!, Oh!	1025	*interj.*	ああ
Aiko (female name)	1015s	*pn*	あいこ・愛子
airconditioning	1035	*n*	えあこん・エアコン
airplane	2012	*n*	ひこうき・飛行機
airport	2012	*n*	くうこう・空港
Akita (prefecture)	2061	*pn*	あきた・秋田
allowance	2024s		おこづかい・お小遣い

English	Location		Japanese
all right, safe, OK	1063	な *adj.*	だいじょうぶ・大丈夫
all, entire, altogether	1083	*n*	ぜんぶ・全部
alone, by oneself	1104	*exp.*	ひとりで・一人で
already	1104	*adv./interj.*	もう
already	1104	*adv./interj.*	もう
always, every time	2031	*adv.*	いつも
always, without exception	2023	*adv.*	かならず・必ず
always	1061	*n/adv.*	いつも
Amanohashidate (place)	1082	*pn*	あまのはしだて・天橋立
amazing, great, terrible, to a great extent	1035	い *adj.*	すごい
American (person)	1041	*n*	あめりかじん・アメリカ人
American football	1071	*n*	あめふと・アメフト, あめりかんふっとぼーる・アメリカンフットボール
American history	1032	*n*	あめりかし・アメリカ史
American army	2065s	*n*	アメリカぐん・アメリカ軍
American Occupation (the)	2034s	*n*	アメリカぐんのちゅうりゅうじだい・アメリカ軍の駐留時代
used like "and" or "with" to connect nouns, used imm. after a direct quotation	1022	*part.*	と
and, because of that (at beginning of sentence)	2044	*conj.*	それで
animal	2014s	*n*	どうぶつ・動物

English	Location		Japanese
animal	1072	n	どうぶつ・動物
animal food	2095s	n	えさ・餌
animated cartoons/films	1011	n	あにめ・アニメ
anniversary	2082s	n	きねんび・記念日
anything	1043s	pron.	なんでも・何でも
anyway, at any rate	1044s	adv.	とにかく
anywhere	1054s	n	どこでも
appearance	2031s	n	ようす・様子
apple	1023s	n	りんご
April	1052	n	しがつ・四月
arm	1061	n	うで・腕
arrival	2041	n	とうちゃく・到着
arrive at (to)	2041	v	つく・着く
art, craft, technique	2031s	n	ぎじゅつ・技術
army	2022s	n	ぐん・軍
art, fine arts	1032	n	びじゅつ・美術
articles, supplies, parts	2043	n	ようひん・用品
arts; crafts	2031s	n	げいじゅつ・芸術
as much as possible	2024s	adv.	なるべく
as you say	2032s	exp.	いうとおり・言う通り
ascend (to), rise (to), climb (to)	2022	v	のぼる・上ぼる
ascend (to), rise (to), climb (to)	2021	v	あがる・上がる
Asian pear	App.	n	なし・梨
ask (to); listen (to)	2091	v	きく・聞く
assemble (to), put together (to)	2023s	v	くむ・組む
astronaut	2104	n	うちゅうひこうし・宇宙飛行士
asymmetric design	2032	n	あしんめとりっくでざいん・アシンメトリックデザイン
at least, for the present	2024s	adv.	いちおう・一応
at some time; sometime	2021s	adv.	いつか
at the same time as ~	2035s	exp.	どどうじに（〜）・〜と同時に
August	1052	n	はちがつ・八月
aunt or woman quite a bit older than you	1022	n	おばさん
Australia (place)	1041	pn	おーすとらりあ・オーストラリア
Australian (person)	1041	n	おーすとらりあじん・オーストラリア人
author, writer	2105s	n	さっか・作家
autumn, fall	1101	n	あき・秋
avenue, street, way	2022	n	とおり・通り
back; backbone	2014s	n	せなか・背中
backpack	1024	n	ばっくぱっく・バックパック
back(side), reverse	2065		うら・裏
bad	1082	い adj.	わるい・悪い
bag/sack	1023s	n	ばっぐ・バッグ
bakery	1043	n	ぱんや・パン屋
ballpoint pen	1024	n	ぼーるぺん・ボールペン
bamboo	2032	n	たけ・竹
banana	1023s	n	ばなな・バナナ
bank	2011s	n	ぎんこう・銀行
barefoot	2052	n	はだし・裸足
barley tea	1103s	n	むぎちゃ・麦茶
baseball	1033	n	べーすぼーる・ベースボール, やきゅう・野球
Basho Matsuo (Japanese poet)	1102s	pn	まつおばしょう・松尾芭蕉
basketball	1033	n	ばすけ・バスケ, ばすけっとぼーる・バスケットボール
basketball club (team)	1033	n	ばすけぶ・バスケ部

English	Location		Japanese
bath	1093s	n	おふろ・お風呂
bathtub	2052s	n	よくそう・浴槽
battle	2012s	n	がっせん・合戦
be (to), exist (to), [formal]	2044	v	ございます・御座います
be able (to)	1016s	v	できる/できます・出来る/出来ます
be surprised (to), be amazed	1105s	v	びっくり・ビックリ する/します
beach	1081	n	はま・浜, びーち・ビーチ
bean sprouts	2093s	n	もやし
bear	2013	n	くま・熊
beautiful	1081	い adj.	うつくしい・美しい
because	2032	part.	から
because (introduced as particle earlier)	2053	conj.	から
because of that	1044	conj.	だから
become (to)	1055	v	なる/なります
become clear (weather)	1101	v	はれる/はれます・晴れる/晴れます
become cloudy	1101	v	くもる・曇る/くもります・曇ります
become familiar with (to)	2034s	v	なれる・慣れる
become tired (to)	2071	v	つかれる・疲れる
bed	2031	n	べっど・ベッド
beef on rice	2025s	n	ぎゅうどん・牛丼
before, front, in front	1051	n/adv.	まえ・前
before long, soon	2034s	conj.	そろそろ
before, ahead, future	2043	n	さき(に)・先(に)
before, this side (of)	2031	n	てまえ・手前
begin (to) [intrans.]	2041	v	はじまる・始まる
begin (to)	1052	v	はじめる・始める/はじめます・始めます
behind, back	2015	n	うしろ・後ろ
believe (to)	2034s	v	しんじる・信じる
below, down	2022	n	した・下
Benkei (famous samurai name)	1061s	pn	べんけい・弁慶
Bentendou, a Buddhist temple dedicated to the goddess Benten	2031s	pn	べんてんどう・弁天堂
best regards, please remember me (favorably)	1013s	adv.	よろしく
best regards, treat me favorably	1013	exp.	よろしく おねがいします・お願いします
best regards, treat me (same favorably meaning as よろしく おねがいします)	1013	exp.	どうぞ よろしく
between ~	2014s	part.	のあいだに（〜）・〜の間に
bicycle	2012	n	じてんしゃ・自転車
big, large	1031	い adj.	おおきい・大きい
bill (the), check (the)	2075s	n	でんぴょう・伝票
biology	1032	n	せいぶつがく・生物学
bird	2102	n	とり・鳥
birthday	1052	n	たんじょうび・誕生日
bitter	2025	い adj.	にがい・苦い
black	1074	n	くろ・黒
black-colored	1082	い adj.	くろい・黒い
blackboard	1024	n	こくばん・黒板
Black Ships	2033s	n	くろぶね・黒舟
Black ships	2033s	n	くろぶね・黒船
black vinegar	2025s	n	くろず・黒酢
blond (hair)	1074	n	きんぱつ・金髪

English	Location		Japanese
bloom (to)	2043	v	さく・咲く
blue	1074	n	あお・青
blue-colored	1082	い adj.	あおい・青い
boat, ship	2012	n	ふね・船
body	1061	n	からだ・体
boil (to)	2094	v	にる・煮る
bone	2021s	n	ほね・骨
book	1011	n	ほん・本
bookshelves	App.	n	ほんだな・本棚
bookstore	1043	n	ほんや・本屋
bookstore	1043	n	ほんやさん・本屋さん
boring	1082	い adj.	つまらない
born (to be)	1052	v	うまれる・生まれる/うまれます・生まれます
borrow (to)	1063s	v	かりる・借りる/かります・借ります
borrow (to), rent (to)	2044	v	かりる・借りる
bother(some) to do, tiresome	2074	い adj.	めんど(う)くさい・面倒くさい
bound for	2024	n	ゆき/いき・行き
bow (to)	2064s	v	おじぎ・お辞儀する
bow	1016s	exp.	れい・礼
bowl	2065s	n	おわん・お碗
box	1081	n	はこ・箱
box lunch (Japanese), bento	1011	n	べんとう・弁当
boy	1064	n	おとこのこ・男の子
boyfriend, he	1074	pron.	かれ・彼
brass band	1033	n	ぶらすばんど・ブラスバンド
Brazilian (person)	1041	n	ぶらじるじん・ブラジル人
bread	1043	n	ぱん・パン
breaded octopus balls	1104s	n	たこやき・たこ焼き
breakfast	1025	n	あさごはん・朝ご飯
bridge	2022	n	はし・橋
briefcase, bag	1024	n	かばん・鞄
bright, light	1093	い adj.	あかるい・明るい
bright, wise	1081	い adj.	かしこい
bring someone (to)	1105	v	つれて くる/きます・連れて 来る/来ます
bring something (to)	1105	v	もって くる/きます・持って 来る/来ます
brown	1074	n	ちゃいろ・茶色
brown (hair)	1074	n	ちゃばつ・茶髪
brush	1033s	n	ふで・筆
buckwheat noodlcs	1103s	n	そば
Buddha	2014s	pn	おしゃかさま・お釈迦様
Buddhism (religion)	1052s	n	ぶっきょう・仏教
Buddhism	2062	n	ぶっきょう・仏教
build (to)	2091	v	たてる・建てる
building	2022	n	たてもの・建物
building	1051s	n	たてもの・建物
burn down completely (to)	2022s	v	やけてしまう・焼けてしまう
bus	2012	n	ばす・バス
bustling, busy	2063	な adj	にぎやか・賑やか
busy	1054	い adj.	いそがしい・忙しい
but	1041s	conj.	けど
but/however - at the beginning of a sentence	1034	part.	でも
butterfly	2031	n	ちょうちょう・蝶々
buy (to)	1091	v	かう・買う/かいます・買います

English	Location		Japanese
buzzer	2044	n	ぶざー・ブザー
by chance, suddenly	2074	exp.	ぐうぜん・偶然
by means of a "tool", at, for (used for shopping or ordering food)	1043s	part.	で
by no means, reluctantly	1094s		いやいや
by the way	1041	exp.	ところで
bye-bye	1015		ばいばい・バイバイ
cake	1094	n	けーき・ケーキ
calamity, disaster	2084s	n	さいがい・災害
call (by a name) (to)	2105	v	よぶ・呼ぶ
Call an ambulance!	1063	n	きゅうきゅうしゃを よんで・救急車を 呼んで
calligraphy	2015	n	しょどう・書道
calm, peaceful	2022s	な adj.	のどか
calm, peaceful	1084	な adj.	おだやか
Canada (place)	1041	pn	かなだ・カナダ
Canadian (person)	1041	n	かなだじん・カナダ人
Canberra (place)	1021s	pn	きゃんべら・キャンベラ
candle	2094s	n	ろうそく
candy/sweets	1023	n	きゃんでぃ・キャンディ, あめ・飴
capital	1052s	n	しゅと・首都
car, automobile	2012	n	じどうしゃ・自動車
car, vehicle	1043	n	くるま・車
card game; playing cards	1071	n	とらんぷ・トランプ
carefully, neatly	2093s	exp.	ていねいに・丁寧に
carve (to)	2031s	v	ほる・彫る
carving, carved sculpture	2035s	n	ちょうこく・彫刻
castle	1101	n	しろ・城
cat	1021	n	ねこ・猫
catch a cold	1063	v	かぜ(を)ひく/ひきます・風邪(を)引く/引きます
cause destruction (to), cause distruption (to)	2084s	v	はかい・破壊 される
celebrate (to)	2061	v	いわう・祝う
cellular phone	1031	n	けいたい(でんわ)・携帯(電話)
center, middle	2025s	n	ちゅうしん・中心
century	2013s	n	せいき・世紀
century, era	1041s	n	せいき・世紀
ceremony, rite	2091	n	しき・式
certainly		adv.	きっと
chair	App.	n	いす・椅子
chalk	1024	n	ちょーく・チョーク
chance (by), suddenly	2074	exp.	ぐうぜん・偶然
change (to)	2033s	v	かわる・変わる
change (cash)	1092	n	おつり
chase after (to); pursue (to)	2014s	v	おいかける・追い掛ける
chatter, gossip	2054	n	おしゃべり
cheap	1082	い adj.	やすい・安い
cherry blossom viewing, flower viewing	1105	n	はなみ・花見
cherry tree/blossom	1105	n	さくら・桜
chicken	1043	n	ちきん・チキン, とりにく・鶏肉
child, children	1082	n	こども・子供
child, children	2013	n	こども・子供
children	1082	n	こどもたち・子供達
children (my/our)	2061	n	うちのこども・内の子供
Children's Day (holiday)	2091	n	こどものひ・子供の日

English	Location		Japanese
China (place)	1041	pn	ちゅうごく・中国
Chinese (descent)	1041s	n	ちゅうごくけい・中国系
Chinese (language)	1042	n	ちゅうごくご・中国語
Chinese (person)	1041	n	ちゅうごくじん・中国人
Chinese characters (used in Japan)	1012s	n	かんじ・漢字
chocolate	App.	n	ちょこれーと・チョコレート
chocolate	2065	n	ちょこれーと・チョコレート
choose (to), select (to)	2101	v	えらぶ・選ぶ
choir, chorus	1015	n	がっしょう・合唱
chopsticks	1015	n	はし（お）・（お）箸
chorus, choir	1033	n	がっしょう・合唱
Christianity	2062	n	きりすときょう・キリスト教
Christmas	2061	n	くりすます・クリスマス
church	2062	n	きょうかい・教会
circle of friends, group, partner	2085s	n	なかま・仲間
circumference, edge	2043	n	まわり・周り
city	2021s	n	とかい・都会
City Hall	2024s	n	しみんかいかん・市民会館
class	1032	n	くらす・クラス
class	1032	n	じゅぎょう・授業
classroom	1032	n	きょうしつ・教室
clean, pretty	1081	な adj.	きれい
clear (skies)	1101	n	はれ・晴れ
clock	App.	n	とけい・時計
clock tower	2015s	n	とけいだい・時計台
clock, watch	2015	n	とけい・時計
close (to)	2081	v	しまる・閉まる
close (to)	2081	v	しめる・閉める
close (to), shut (to) [bound paper objects]	1013	v	とじる・閉じる/とじます・閉じます
close (to), shut (to) [doors/windows]	1034	v	しめる・閉める/しめます・閉めます
close, near	1061	い adj.	ちかい・近い
Close/Shut (it) please.	1013	exp.	とじて ください・閉じて 下さい
closing for written letters	2064	n	けいぐ・敬具
clothes	1064	n	ふく・服
clothes, Western clothes	1064	n	ようふく・洋服
clothing	2033s	n	いしょう・衣装
cloudy	1101	n	くもり・曇り
club activity	1033	n	ぶかつ・部活
co-ed, shared/common (facilities)	2051s	n	きょうどう・共同
coffee house (traditional), coffee lounge	2071	n	きっさてん・喫茶店
coincidentally	2061s	n	ぐぜん・偶然
cola	1043	n	こーら・コーラ
cold (a)	1063	n	かぜ・風邪
cold (to the touch)	2051	い adj.	つめたい・冷たい
cold (weather)	1034	い adj.	さむい・寒い
collect (to), put together (to)	2081	v	あつめる・集める
college/university	1031	n	だいがく・大学
college/university student	1031	n	だいがくせい・大学生
color	1074	n	いろ・色
come (to)	1044	v	くる・来る/きます・来ます
come (to), go (to), somewhere (to be), [honorific for 行きます or います]	2044	v	いらっしゃる

English	Location		Japanese
come in (to), go in (to), enter (to)	1061	v	はいる・入る/はいります・入ります
come by walking (to)	2012	v	あるいてくる・歩いて来る
come together (to), fit (to), match (to)	2042	v	あう・合う
come, come now	2041	interj.	さあ
commute (to)	2012s	v	かよう・通う
company	2024	n	かいしゃ・会社
company employee	1025s	n	かいしゃいん・会社員
competition	2015s	n	こんくーる・コンクール
complete (to), finsh (to)	2093s	v	できあがる・出来上がる
completely burn (to)	2022s	n	やけてしまう・焼けてしまう
complex, complicated	2021	な adj.	ふくざつ・複雑
computer lab	1033	n	こんぴゅーたーらぼ・コンピューターラボ
concept, idea	2031s	n	がいねん・概念
concerning, per	2051	exp.	に ついて
concert	1052s	n	こんさーと・コンサート
concert, receital	1052s	n	おんがくかい・音楽会
confirm	2044s	n	かくにん・確認
considerably, quite	2033	adv.	かなり
contents, interior	2062	n	なかみ・中身
continue (to)	2041s	v	つづく・続く
continue (to)	2031s	v	つづける・続ける
continuously; throughout	1083		ずっと
convenience store	2024	n	こんびに・コンビニ/こんびにえんすすとあ・コンビニエンスストア
conversely, on the contrary	2033	adv.	ぎゃくに・逆に
cooked rice, a meal	1015	n	ごはん・ご飯
cookie	App.	n	くっきー・クッキー
cooking	1071	n	りょうり・料理
cool (look/appearance)	1062	ir. adj.	かっこいい
cool (weather)	1034	い adj.	すずしい・涼しい
cool, tasteful	1062	い adj.	しぶい・渋い
coolness, calmness, unconcern	2073	な adj.	へいき・平気
cooperate (to)	2092s	v	きょうりょく・協力 する/します
copy, photocopy (to)	1062	v	こぴー・コピー する/します
copy, imitation	2033s	n	もほう・摸倣
corner	2022	n	かど・角
correct, right, proper	2061	い adj.	ただしい・正しい
corridor, hallway	2022	n	ろうか・廊下
costume	2043	n	こすちゅーむ・コスチューム
counter for birds	2102	counter	わ・羽
counter for floors/stories	2054	counter	かい・〜階
counter for large animals	2102	counter	とう・頭
counter for number ~	2014s	counter	ばんめ（〜）・〜番目
counter for rooms	2054	counter	ま・〜間
counter for tatami mats	2054	counter	じょう・〜畳
counter for times	2021s	counter	かい・回
country	2013	n	くに・国
country	1041	n	くに・国
countryside, rural	2032s	n	いなか・田舎
cow	2012	n	うし・牛
crab	1083	n	かに・
criticized (to be)	2084s	v	ひなん・非難される
cross over (to), to go across	2022	v	わたる・渡る
crowded (to be)	2094s	v	こみあう・混み合う
crunchy, crisp	2054	ono.	さくさく

English	Location		Japanese
cry [animals] (to)	2064s	v	なく・泣く
culture	1065	n	ぶんか・文化
cunning	1081	い adj.	ずるい
cupcake	App.	n	かっぷけーき・カップケーキ
curry and rice	2071	n	かれーらいす・カレーライス
custom, tradition	2075s	n	しゅうかん・習慣
customer, guest	2045	n	おきゃくさん・お客さん
cute	1081	い adj.	かわいい
daily life	2032s	n	にちじょうせいかつ・日常生活
dance	2071	n	だんす・ダンス
dance (to)	2042	v	おどる・踊る
dancing	1071	n	おどり・踊り
dangerous	1081	い adj.	あぶない・危ない
dango (round sticky rice balls on a stick)	App.	n	だんご
dark	1093	い adj.	くらい・暗い
date (to go on a)	1091	v	でーと・デート(を)する/します
daughter	2061	n	むすめ・娘
day after tomorrow	1102	n	あさって・明後日
day before yesterday	2022	n	おととい・一昨日
day before yesterday	1102	n	おととい・一昨日
daytime, noon	1025	n	ひる・昼
dear, missed	2082s	n	なつかしい・懐かしい
December	1052	n	じゅうにがつ・十二月
decide (to)	2101	v	きめる・決める
decoration	2062s	n	かざり・飾り
deer	2095s	n	しか・鹿
delicious	1081	い adj.	おいしい・美味しい
denotes a sentence topic	1013	part.	は
depart (to)	2041	v	しゅっぱつ・出発する/します
depart (to), set out [on an excursion] (to)	2044	v	でかける・出掛ける
department store basement (often housing food stands)	2024s	n	でぱちか・デパ地下
departure	2041	n	しゅっぱつ・出発
descend (to), go back (to), hang down (to)	2022	v	さがる・下がる
detailed	2033s	adj.	こまかい・細かい
detention	2074s	n	いのこり・居残り
development, growth	2031s	n	はったつ・発達
devil, demon	2034s	n	あくま・悪魔
dialect	2053s	n	ほうげん・方言
dialogue	1013s	n	かいわ・会話
dictionary	App.	n	じしょ・辞書
difficult	1032	い adj.	むずかしい・難しい
dine (to), have a meal (to)	1091	v	しょくじ・食事(を)する/します
dinner, evening meal	1025	n	ばんごはん・晩ご飯
direction (prev. learned as かた for person as in この方)	2032	n	ほう・方
directly, immediately, nearby	2022	n	すぐ
dirty, messy	1081	い adj.	きたない
disagreeable, unpleasant	2021s	n	いやだ・嫌だ
disaster prevention	2085	n	ぼうさい・防災
disembark (to), get off (a vehicle)	2022	v	おりる・降りる
dislike	1072	な adj.	きらい・嫌い
dislike a lot, hate	1072	な adj.	だいきらい・大嫌い
dissolve (to)	2093s	v	とく・溶く
do (to)	1073	v	やる/やります
do (to), humble for します	2044	v	いたす・致す
do (to), wear (to)	1044	v	する/します (して)
do homework (to)	1091	v	しゅくだい・宿題(を)する/します
do one's best (to)	1073	v	がんばる・頑張る/がんばります・頑張ります
do things like ~	2012s	part.	たり(〜)
do us a favor of allowing us to (to)	2023s	v	させてくれる
doctor	1063	n	いしゃ・医者
dog	1021	n	いぬ・犬
Don't be ridiculous! Not a chance! My pleasure	1094	exp.	とんでもない
Don't overexert.	1063	exp.	むり しないで ください・無理 しないで 下さい
door	1034	n	どあ・ドア
door	2022	n	どあ・ドア
dormitory	2012s	n	りょう・寮
doughnuts	2071	n	どーなつ・ドーナツ
dragon	2013	n	りゅう・龍
draw (to)	1054s	v	かく・描く/かきます・描きます
dress (a)	1064	n	どれす・ドレス
drink (to)	1043	v	のむ・飲む/のみます・飲みます
drink(s)	1043	n	のみもの・飲み物
drive (to)	2012	v	うんてん・運転(を)する
drugs, narcotic	2074	n	まやく・麻薬
drum	2023	n	たいこ・太鼓
drumming (noise), boom boom, steadily	2054	ono.	どんどん・ドンドン
dry (to)	2051	v	かわく・乾く
Dutch (language)	1042	n	おらんだご・オランダ語
Dutch (person)	1041	n	おらんだじん・オランダ人
e-mail	1051	n	でんしめーる・電子メール/めーる・メール
ear	1061	n	みみ・耳
early	1054s	い adj.	はやい・早い
early	2035	い adj.	はやい・早い
early (in the day)	2035	adv.	はやく・早く
earring	1064	n	いやりんぐ・イヤリング
earth, globe	2032	n	ちきゅう・地球
earthquake	1101	n	じしん・地震
earthquake disaster	2084s	n	しんさい・震災
east	2021	n	ひがし・東
easy, simple, kind, gentle	1081	い adj.	やさしい・優しい
easy to make, easy to do	2074s	n	しやすい・〜しやすい
eat (to) [formal]	2044s	v	めしあがる・召し上がる
eat (to)	1043	v	たべる・食べる/たべます・食べます
eating	1071	n	たべること・食べる事
economics	1032	n	けいざいがく・経済学
economy	1032s	n	けいざい・経済
edge, border	2044s	n	はし・端
edge, circumference	2015s	n	まわり・周り
Edo (former name of Tokyo)	1044s	pn	えど・江戸
eel	2043	n	うなぎ・鰻
effort or strain (expression of)	2021	exp.	よいしょ・ヨイショ
egg	1015	n	たまご・卵
eight	1021	counter	はち・八

English	Location		Japanese
flat cushion (used when sitting or kneeling on the floor)	2044	n	ざぶとん・座布団
flower	1101	n	はな・花
flower arranging	1071	n	いけばな・生け花
flute	2025	n	ふえ・笛
fly (to), jump (to), leap (to)	2031	v	とぶ・飛ぶ
fly a kite (to)	2065s	v	たこあげ・凧揚げ をする
folding fan	2031	n	せんす・扇子
folk museum	2021s	n	みんぞくかん・民族間
folklore demon of Oga Peninsula, seen on New Year's Eve	2062	n	なまはげ
folktale	2013	n	むかしばなし・昔話
food served during New Year's holidays	2061	n	おせちりょうり・お節料理
food supplies, foodstuff	2043	n	しょくひん・食品
foods	2033s	n	しょっき・食器
food(s)	1043	n	たべもの・食べ物
foolish, silly	1081	い adj.	ばかばかしい
foot, leg	1061	n	あし・足
for, on behalf of	2095	conj.	ために・為に
foreign, overseas	2091	n	かいがい・海外
foreign country	1041	n	がいこく・外国
foreigner	1041	n	がいこくじん・外国人
forest	1101s	n	もり・森
forest	2012s	n	もり・森
forget (to)	2044	v	わすれる・忘れる
four	1021	counter	よん/し・四
fox	1035s	n	きつね・狐
fox	2044	n	きつね・狐
France (place)	1041	pn	ふらんす・フランス
free; freely	2025s	n	じゆう・自由
free (time)	1084	な adj	ひま
freedom, liberty	1105s	な adj.	じゆう・自由
French (language)	1042	n	ふらんすご・フランス語
French (person)	1041	n	ふらんすじん・フランス人
Friday	1051	n	きんようび・金曜日
fried dough (bits of)	2093s	n	てんかす・天かす
fried noodles, yakisoba	1102s	n	やきそば・焼きそば
friend	1022	n	ともだち・友達
frog	1072	n	かえる・蛙
from (in the conclusion of a letter)	2062	part.	より
from (used with spec. times or locations)	1032	part.	から
front, in front, before	1032	adv.	まえ・前
front, main	2044s	n	しょうめん・正面
fruit	1075s	n	くだもの・果物/ふるーつ・フルーツ
Fuji (Mt.)	1094s	pn	ふじさん・富士山
fun, enjoyable	1032	い adj.	たのしい・楽しい
fry (to)	2094	v	やく・焼く
futile, there is no use	2022s	n	しかたがない・仕方がない
futon	1063	n	ふとん・布団
future (distant)	2104	n	みらい・未来
future (near)	2104	n	しょうらい・将来
gagaku, ancient Japanese court music	1075	n	ががく・雅楽
garden	1101	n	にわ・庭
gate	1033s	n	もん・門
gather (to)	2033s	v	あつめる・集める
Gauguin, Paul	2032	pn	ごーぎゃん・ゴーギャン

English	Location		Japanese
general, ordinary [n]; normally, generally [adv.]	2023	n	ふつう・普通
gentleness, kindness	2022s	n	しんせつ・親切
genuine article; real thing	1091	n	ほんもの・本物
German (language)	1042	n	どいつご・ドイツ語
German (person)	1041	n	どいつじん・ドイツ人
Germany (place)	1041	pn	どいつ・ドイツ
gesture	2043	n	じぇすちゃー・ジェスチャー
get completely tangled up in	2065s		ひっかかってしまう・引っかかってしまう
ghost, devil	2062	n	おに・鬼
gift	2083	n	おくりもの・贈り物
gift, present	1094	n	ぷれぜんと・プレゼント
Ginza (place)	1033s	pn	ぎんざ・銀座
girl	1064	n	おんなのこ・女の子
give (to) [to equals or superiors]	1094	v	あげる・上げる/あげます・上げます
give (to) [to me or a family member]	1095	v	くれる/くれます
give thanks (to)	2061	v	かんしゃ・感謝 (を) する
give up (to)	2062s	v	あきらめる・諦める
glad, happy	1081	い adj.	うれしい・嬉しい
glass	2085	n	がらす・ガラス
globe (the), earth (the)	2092s	n	ちきゅう・地球
go	1044	v	いく・行く/いきます・行きます
go (to), come (to), visit (to) a grave or shrine [humble for 行きます・来ます]	2043	v	まいる・参る
go by walking (to)	2012	v	あるいていく・歩いて行く
go out (to), leave (to), get out (to)	1061	v	でる・出る/でます・出ます
go shopping (to)	1091	v	かいもの・買い物 (を)する/します
God, god, spirit	2013	n	かみ・神
God, god, spirit	2013	n	かみさま・神様
gold	1074	n	きんいろ・金色
golf	1071	n	ごるふ・ゴルフ
good	1041s	ir. adj.	いい/よい・良い
good, OK, fine	2044	い adj.	よろしい
good evening	1015	exp.	こんばんは・今晩は
good luck	2065s	n	こううん・幸運
good for your health	1063	exp.	けんこう・健康に いい で
good morning [formal]	1015	exp.	おはよう ございます
good morning [informal]	1015	exp.	おはよう
good night [formal]	1015	exp.	おやすみなさい・お休みなさい
good night [informal]	1015	exp.	おやすみ・お休み
good-looking, handsome	1064	な adj	はんさむ・ハンサム
goodbye	1015	exp.	さようなら
Google (to); search on the internet (to)	2024s	v	ぐぐって・ググッて
graduate (to)	2101s	v	そつぎょう・卒業 (を)す
grandfather (my)	1021	n	そふ・祖父
grandfather (someone else's)	1022	n	おじいさん
grandmother (my)	1021	n	そぼ・祖母
grandmother (someone else's)	1022	n	おばあさん
grasp (to), comprehend (to)	2092s	v	りかい・理解 する
grassroots, rank and file	2095	n	くさのね・草の根
grated yam	2093s	n	とろろ
grave (a)	2021s	n	はか・(お)墓
gray	1074	n	ぐれい・グレイ

English	Location		Japanese
gray (mouse colored)	1074	n	ねずみいろ・鼠色
gray, ash (color)	1074	n	はいいろ・灰色
great grandfather	2061s	n	そうそふ・曾祖父
green	1074	n	みどり・緑
green seaweed	2093s	n	あおのり・青のり
green tea	1024s	n	おちゃ・お茶
grilled chicken (kebab)	2043	n	やきとり・焼き鳥
grow old (to); age (to)	2034	v	としをとる・年を取る
grow old (to), age (to)	1101s	v	とし(を)とる・年(を)取る
guard (to), protect (to)	2085	v	がーど・ガード する
guest house	2024	n	みんしゅく・民宿
guidance, information	2061s	n	あんない・案内
guitar	1071	n	ぎたー・ギター
gum	App.	n	がむ・ガム
gymnasium	1033	n	たいいくかん・体育館
gun, arms	2074	n	じゅう・銃
haiku (poem)	1101	n	はいく・俳句
hair	1061	n	かみ(のけ)・髪(の毛)
hairstyle	2021s	n	かみがた・髪型
Hakodate (city in Hokkaido)	2011	pn	はこだて・函館
half hour	1032	n	はん・〜半
hamburger	1043	n	はんばーがー・ハンバーガー
hand	1061	n	て・手
hand over (to), pass along (to)	2081	v	わたす・渡す
handshake	1042	n	あくしゅ・あくしゅ
handsome, good-looking	1064	な adj	はんさむ・ハンサム
hand towel	2052s	n	てぬぐい・手ぬぐい
haniwa	1041s	n	はにわ・埴輪
Hanukkah	2061	pn	はぬか・ハヌカ
happiness, good fortune	2025	な adj.	しあわせ・幸せ
happy, glad	1081	い adj.	うれしい・嬉しい
harden (to); solidify	2015s	v	かためる・固める
harvest	2063s	n	ほうさく・豊作
hat/cap	1023	n	ぼうし
have (to), hold (to), carry (to)	1061	v	もつ/もちます・持つ/持ちます
have a full stomach	1104	exp.	おなか(が) いっぱい・お腹(が)一杯
have a good New Year	2063	exp.	よいおとしを・よいお年を
have a meal (to), dine (to)	1091	v	しょくじ・食事(を) する/します
have an aptitude for, a genius for	2083s	exp.	さいのう・才能 がある
have trouble (to); be in difficulty	2084	v	こまる・困る
he, boyfriend	1074	pron.	かれ・彼
head	1061	n	あたま・頭
head (of household), one's husband	2061	n	しゅじん・主人
health	1063	n	けんこう・健康
health (class)	1032	n	ほけんたいいく・保健体育
healthy	2053s	な adj	けんこうてき・健康的
healthy, energetic	1015	n/な adj.	げんき・元気
hear (can)	1104s	v	きこえる・聞こえる/きこえます・聞こえます
heart (not one's physical heart), soul	1061	n	こころ・心
heavy rain	1101	n	おおあめ・大雨
heavy (weight)	2084	い adj.	おもい・重い
height (of someone), stature	2071s	n	しんちょう・身長
height, stature	1061	n	せ/せい・背

English	Location		Japanese
Heijoukyou (ancient name for Kyoto)	1051s	pn	へいじょうきょう・平城京
hello	1015	exp.	こんにちは・今日は
help (to), assist (to)	1041	v	てつだう・手伝う/てつだいます・手伝います
help, assistance	2063	n	おせわ・お世話
helping verb/linking verb used similarly to "is" or "am"	1013	copula	です
here	1024	pron.	ここ
here and there	1054s	adv.	あちこち
hide completely (to)	2064s	v	かくれる・隠れる
high school	1031	n	こうこう・高校
high school student	1031	n	こうこうせい・高校生
high, tall, expensive	1061	い adj.	たかい・高い
Hinduism	2062	n	ひんずーきょう・ヒンズー教
Hiraizumi (place)	1061s	pn	ひらいずみ・平泉
Hiroo (section of Tokyo)	1022s	pn	ひろお・広尾
Hiroshima (place)	1083s	pn	ひろしま・広島
history	1032	n	れきし・歴史
hobby	1071	n	しゅみ・趣味
Hokkaido (northernmost of the four main islands of Japan)	2011	pn	ほっかいどう・北海道
holiday	2062	n	さいじつ・祭日
Holland (place)	1041	pn	おらんだ・オランダ
home, house	1022	n	いえ/うち・家
homeroom	1032	n	ほーむるーむ・ホームルーム
homesick	2021s	n	ほーむしっく・ホームシック
homestay	2063	n	ほーむすてい・ホームステイ
homework	1032	n	しゅくだい・宿題
honorific suffix for 〜さん	2024s		〜さま・〜様
Honshu (largest of the four main islands of Japan)	2011	pn	ほんしゅう・本州
Honshu (place)	1041s	pn	ほんしゅう・本州
hope for recovery [from an illness] (to)	2091s	exp.	かいふくをねがう・回復を願う
hope, aspiration	2051s	n	きぼう・希望
horse	1082	n	うま・馬
horseback riding	1071	n	じょうば・乗馬
hospital	1063	n	びょういん・病院
host family	2063	n	ほすとふぁみりー・ホストファミリー
hot spring	2015	n	おんせん・温泉
hot (weather)	1034	い adj.	あつい・暑い
hotel	2051	n	ほてる・ホテル
how	1035	inter.	どう
how about it?	1092	exp.	どう ですか
how do you do?	1013	exp.	はじめまして・初めまして
how do you do 〜	2012s	exp.	どうやって
how many (things)?	1021	inter.	いくつ
how many birds?	2102	inter.	なんわ・何羽
how many cupfuls	1092	inter.	なんばい・何杯
how many cylindrical objects	1092	inter.	なんぼん・何本
how many large animals?	2102	inter.	なんとう・何頭
how many minutes	1032	inter.	なんぷん・何分
how many pages, what page	1042	inter.	なんぺーじ・何ページ
how many people?	2024	inter.	なんめい・何名
how many people	1021	inter.	なんにん・何人
how many people (polite)	1103s	inter.	なんめいさま・何名様
how many people? (polite)	2024	inter.	なんめいさま・何名様

English	Location		Japanese
how old, how many years (old)?	2011	*inter.*	いくつ・(お)いくつ
how many seconds?	1032	*inter.*	なんびょう・何秒
how many sheets	1042	*inter.*	なんまい・何枚
how many small animals?	1092	*inter.*	なんびき・何匹
how many ten-thousands?	1091	*inter.*	なんまん・何万
how many thousands	1052	*inter.*	なんぜん・何千
how many times/degrees	1101	*inter.*	なんど・何度
how many volumes	1092	*inter.*	なんさつ・何冊
how much?	1092	*inter.*	いくら
how old (animate beings)	1022s	*inter.*	なんさい・何歳 [less formal] or (お)いくつ
How was it?	1065	*exp.*	どう でしたか。
however, but	2033	*conj.*	しかし
huh?	1033s	*inter.*	ええっ/え?
humid (weather)	1034	い *adj.*	むしあつい・蒸し暑い
hunger (mimetic expression for)	1025		ぺこぺこ・ペコペコ
hurry (to)	2091	*v*	いそぐ・急ぐ
husband (my)	2061	*n*	うちのひと・内の人
I don't know.	1016s	*exp.*	しりません・知りません
I love you	1025s	*exp.*	だいすき・大好き です
I, me (used by males only)	1013	*pron.*	ぼく・僕
I, me	1013	*pron.*	わたし・私
I'm sorry, excuse me	1033s	*inter.*	すみません
I'm home	1015	*exp.*	ただいま
I wonder (sentence ending); should I?/is it? (question prt.); I wish that… (w/ a neg.)	2023	*part.*	かな
ice, shaved ice (snow cone)	2011	*n*	こおり・氷
ice cream	App.	*n*	あいすくりーむ・アイスクリーム
idea	1051s	*n*	あいでぃあ・アイディア
idea	2091	*n*	かんがえ・考え
if, in case, if it is true that	2101	*conj.*	なら/ならば
illness, sickness	1063	*n*	びょうき・病気
immediately, at once	1082		すぐ
important	1051	な *adj.*	だいじ・大事
important, valuable	2092	な *adj.*	たいせつ・大切
impossible, overdoing	1063	な *adj.*	むり・無理
Impressionism	2032	*pn*	いんぷれっしょにずむ・インプレッショニズム
Impressionists	2033s	*n*	いんしょうがか・印象画家
impressions, thoughts	2043s	*n*	かんそう・感想
in all, total, all together	1092	*exp.*	ぜんぶで・全部で
in, at, used after alocation or time word	1015	*part.*	に
in, inside, middle, center	2011	*n/adv.*	なか・中
indeed, truly, really	1084	*adv.*	まったく・全く
Indonesia (place)	1041	*pn*	いんどねしあ・インドネシア
Indonesian (language)	1042	*n*	いんどねしあご・インドネシア語
Indonesian (person)	1041	*n*	いんどねしあじん・インドネシア人
in front of, before	2021	*n*	まえ・前
influence (to), effect (to)	2015	*v*	えいきょう・影響 する
influence, effect	2015	*n*	えいきょう・影響
information, guidance	2061s	*n*	あんない・案内
injure, hurt (oneself) (to)	1063	*v*	けが・怪我(を) する/します
in order of ~	2014s	*n*	じゅん・順
inquiry, interrogation	2051s	*n*	といあわせ・問い合わせ
insect, bug	2035	*n*	むし・虫

English	Location		Japanese
inside, within, (of the) home	2061	*n*	うち・内
intangible thing	2023	*n*	こと・事
intention, plan	2043	*n*	つもり
interest (in)	2031s	*n*	きょうみ・興味
interest (to have an)	2081	*n*	きょうみ(を)もつ・興味(を)持つ
international	2081	*n*	こくさい・国際
international exchange	2081	*n*	こくさいこうりゅう・国際交流
intersection, crossing	2022	*n*	こうさてん・交差点
interval, space [between]	2023	*n*	あいだ・間
interesting	1082	い *adj.*	おもしろい・面白い
introduce (please)	1021	*v*	しょうかい して ください・紹介 して 下さい
introduce (to)	1021	*v*	しょうかい・紹介 する/します
introduction	2011	*n*	しょうかい・紹介
investigate (to)	2102	*v*	しらべる・調べる
invitation	2023	*n*	しょうたい・招待
invite (to)	2063	*v*	さそう・誘う
Iranian (person)	1041	*n*	いらんじん・イラン人
irritating	1081	い *adj.*	じれったい
is bad	1034	な *adj.*	だめ
is not right, incorrect	1016s	*v*	ちがう・違う/ちがいます・違います
is open, is free	2024s	*v*	あいている・空いている
Islam	2062	*n*	イスラムきょう・イスラム教
It was a feast. (said at the end of a meal)	2022	*exp.*	ごちそうさまでした
island	1083	*n*	しま・島
Italian (language)	1042	*n*	いたりあご・イタリア語
Italian (person)	1041	*n*	いたりあじん・イタリア人
Italy (place)	1041	*pn*	いたりあ・イタリア
items, products	2033s	*n*	しなもの・品物
Izena, small island in n.e. Okinawa Prefecture	2021s	*pn*	いぜな・伊是名
jacket	1064	*n*	じゃけっと・ジャケット
Jakarta (place)	1042s	*pn*	じゃかるた・ジャカルタ
January	1052	*n*	いちがつ・一月
Japan (place)	1011	*pn*	にほん・日本
Japan Broadcasting Corporation (TV network: 日本放送協会), NHK	2085	*n*	えぬえいちけー/NHK
Japanese (typically)	2023	な *adj.*	にほんてき・日本的
Japanese badminton	2065s	*n*	はねつき・羽根つき
Japanese comics	1011	*n*	まんが・漫画
Japanese department store	2073s	*pn*	たかしまや・高島屋
Japanese descent	1041	*n*	にっけいじん・日系人
Japanese history	1032	*n*	にほんし・日本史
Japanese language	1011	*n*	にほんご・日本語
Japanese person	1014	*n*	にほんじん・日本人
Japanese style	2024	*n*	わふう・和風
Japanese-style meal	2024	*n*	わしょく・和食
Japanese-style room	2024	*n*	わしつ・和室
Japanese sumo wrestling	1011	*n*	すもう・相撲
Japanese traditional sweets	1095	*n*	(お)かし・(お)菓子
jealous	2025s	い *adj.*	うらやましい
jeans	1064	*n*	じーんず・ジーンズ
job, occupation	1025	*n*	しごと・仕事
job, occupation	2012	*n*	しごと・仕事
jogging	1071	*n*	じょぎんぐ・ジョギング

English	Location		Japanese
joke	1072	n	じょうだん・冗談
Jomon Period (10,500 BCE-300 BCE)	????	pn	じょうもんじだい・縄文時代
journal	1011s	n	じゃーなる・ジャーナル
judo	1033	n	じゅうどう・柔道
juice	1063	n	じゅーす・ジュース
Judaism	2062	n	ゆだやきょう・ユダヤ教
July	1052	n	しちがつ/なながつ・七月
June	1052	n	ろくがつ・六月
just barely, at the last moment [adv.], grinding sound [ono.]	2044	adv./ono.	ぎりぎり
kabuki theater	1075	n	かぶき・歌舞伎
Kanazawa (place)	1101s	pn	かなざわ・金沢
Kantou (region of Japan including Tokyo and the surrounding area)	2055	pn	かんとう・関東
karaoke (to sing/do)	1091	v	からおけ・カラオケ (を)する/します
karate (martial art)	1011	n	からて・空手
karaoke	1105s	n	からおけ・カラオケ
Katsushika Hokusai, artist	2032	pn	ほくさい・北斎
kendo	1033s	n	けんどう・剣道
kendo club	1033	n	けんどうぶ・剣道部
Kenroku Park (place)	1102s	pn	けんろくえん・兼六園
Kenya (place)	1041	pn	けにあ・ケニア
Kenyan (person)	1041	n	けにあじん・ケニア人
kimono (Japanese traditional clothing)	1011	n	きもの・着物
king, ruler	2021s	n	おうさま・王様
kind, gentle, easy, simple	1081	い adj.	やさしい・優しい
kindergarten	1031	n	ようちえん・幼稚園
Kintarou, mythical strong man	2034s	pn	きんたろう・金太郎
Kitagawa Utamarou, artist	2032	pn	うたまろ・歌麿
kitchen	2063	n	だいどころ・台所
knee	1061	n	ひざ・膝
knife and bucket	2064s	n	ほうちょうとおけ・包丁と桶
know something/someone (to)	1042	v	しる・知る/しります・知ります
Kobo Daishi (person's name)	1052s	pn	こうぼうだいし・弘法大師
koi (carp)	1031s	n	こい・鯉
Korean (descent)	1041s	n	かんこくけい・韓国系
Korean (language)	1042	n	かんこくご・韓国語
Korean (person)	1041	n	かんこくじん・韓国人
koto, Japanese zither/harp	1105s	n	こと・琴
koto, Japanese zither/harp	2023	n	こと・琴
Kukai (person's name)	1052s	pn	くうかい・空海
Kwanzaa	2061	n	くわんざ・クワンザ
Kyoto (place)	1013s	pn	きょうと・京都
Kyushu (place)	1041s	pn	きゅうしゅう・九州
Kyushu (place)	2011	pn	きゅうしゅう・九州
language, dialect, words	1101s	n	ことば・言葉
language, dialect, words	2043	n	ことば・言葉
large (L) size	1092	n	えるさいず・Lサイズ
large, big	1031	い adj.	おおきい・大きい
last, conclusion	2045	n	さいご・最後
last month	1054	n	せんげつ・先月
last week	1054	n	せんしゅう・先週
last week Tuesday	1054	n	せんしゅうのかようび・先週の火曜日
last year	1054	n	きょねん・去年
later, afterwards	1033	adv.	あとで・後で

English	Location		Japanese
lazy person	2062	n	なまけもの・怠け者
learn (to)	2015	v	ならう・習う
learn (to)	1065	v	ならう・習う/ならいます・習います
left	2022	n	ひだり・左
leg, foot	1061	n	あし・足
lemonade	2071	n	れもねーど・レモネード
let me see, well…	1033s	interj.	ええと
let remain (to)	2032s	v	のこす・残す
let's go	1035	exp.	いきましょう・行きましょう
Let's begin.	1011	exp.	はじめましょう・始めましょう
letter, characters	2031s	n	もじ・文字
library	1033	n	としょかん・図書館
lie	1104	n	うそ・嘘
light (weight)	2084	い adj.	かるい・軽い
light, bright	1093	い adj.	あかるい・明るい
light, thin	2032	い adj.	うすい・薄い
lights, electricity	App.	n	でんき・電気
like	1072	な adj.	すき・好き
line	2032	n	せん・線
line up (to)	2015s	v	ならぶ
listen (to)	1013	v	きく・聞く/ききます・聞きます
little	1031	adv.	すこし・少し
little, somewhat	1032	adv.	ちょっと
(something is) a little …	1043	exp.	(〜は) ちょっと・・・
live/reside (to)	1064	v	すむ・住む/すみます・住みます
live performance (concert, show, etc.)	2023	n	らいぶ・ライブ
lonely	1061s	い adj.	さびしい・寂しい
living, livelihood	2013s	n	くらし・暮らし
long	1061	い adj.	ながい・長い
long ago	1082	n	むかし・昔
long long ago	1082	n	むかしむかし・昔々
lonely, lonesome	2064	い adj.	さびしい・寂しい
long time since I saw you/it's been a while	2084s		ひさしぶり・久しぶり
long-lived	2025s	n	ながいき・長生き
look, Look out!	1081s	interj.	ほら!
look/see (to)	1013	v	みる・見る/みます・見ます
Look/Watch please.	1013	exp.	みてください・見て下さい。
looking forward to ~	2011s	exp.	たのしみにしています〜楽しみにしています
looks like ~	2021s	exp.	みたい(〜)
looks like ~; resembles ~	2023s		〜らしい
love	1022s	n	あい・愛
love, really like	1072	な adj.	だいすき・大好き
low, short (height)	1061	い adj.	ひくい・低い
lukewarm	2052	い adj.	ぬるい
lunch	1025	n	ひるごはん・昼ご飯
lunch break	1032	n	ひるやすみ・昼休み
make (to)	1102	v	つくる・作る/つくります・作ります
make happy (to)	2035s	v	よろこぶ・喜ぶ
make up (facial)	1064	n	めいく・メイク
make up (to), reconcile (to)	1091	v	なかなおり・仲直り(を)する/します
male actor in female Kabuki role	2042	n	おんながた・女形
man, male	1064s	n	おとこ・男

English	Location		Japanese
man, male	1064	n	おとこのひと・男の人
many, a lot	1031	n	たくさん・たくさん
many, numerous	2031	い adj.	おおい・多い
map	2032	n	ちず・地図
map	App.	n	ちず・地図
March	1052	n	さんがつ・三月
marker	App.	n	まじっく・マジック
marathon	2085	n	まらそん・マラソン
match (to), mix (to)	2042	v	あわせる・合わせる
math	1032	n	すうがく・数学
May	1052	n	ごがつ・五月
may do ~	2021s		～かもしれない
May I come in?, please forgive me	1092s	exp.	ごめんください・ごめん下さい
May I drink (some) water?	1016s	exp.	おみずを のんでも いいですか。・お水を 飲んでも いいですか。
May I go to my locker?	1016s	exp.	ろっかーへ いっても いいですか。・ロッカーへ 行っても いいですか。
May I go to the restroom/W.C.?	1016s	exp.	おてあらいへ いっても いいですか。・お手洗いへ 行ってもいいですか。
may, might, perhaps	2065	exp.	かもしれません・かも知れません
may, might, perhaps [informal]	2065	exp.	かもしれない・かも知れない
maybe, possibly	2024s	adv.	たぶん・多分
me, I	1013	pron.	わたし・私
meaning, significance	2031s	n	いみ・意味
measure (to)	2094	v	はかる・測る
meat	2025s	n	にく・肉
medicine	1063	n	くすり・薬
medium (M) size	1092	n	えむさいず・Mサイズ
meet (to)	1054s	v	あう・会う
meet (to)	2024	v	あう・会う
meet (to), congregate (to)	2081	v	あつまる・集まる
meet, want to	1044s	v	あいたい・会いたい
Meiji Period (1868-1912)	2071	n	めいじじだい・明治時代
melon (honeydew)	1023s	n	めろん・メロン
memo, note	1083	n	めも・メモ
memory, remembrance	2064s	n	おもいで・思い出
messy, disorderly, absurd	2054	な adj./ ono.	めちゃくちゃ
method	2094	n	ほうほう・方法
method of "~ing"	2093	n	かた・～方
Mexican (person)	1041	pn	めきしこじん・メキシコ人
Mexican descent	1041s	n	めきしこけい・メキシコ系
Mexico (place)	1041	pn	めきしこ・メキシコ
middle, center, mid-way	2031	n	まんなか・真ん中
middle school	1031	n	ちゅうがっこう・中学校
middle school student	1031	n	ちゅうがくせい・中学生
military leader	1051s	n	しょうぐん・将軍
milk	1043s	n	ミルク
milk	2015	n	ぎゅうにゅう・牛乳
miso soup	1104s	n	みそしる・味噌汁
mix (to), stir (to)	2023	v	まぜる・混ぜる
mochi (sticky rice cake)	App.	n	もち・餅
modern, today	2034s	n	げんだい・現代
Monday	1051	n	げつようび・月曜日
money	1092s	n	(お)かね ・(お)金

English	Location		Japanese
Mongolian stirfry barbeque	2015s	n	じんぎすかん・ジンギスカン
monkey	2014s	n	さる・猿
mood, feelings	2053	n	きもち・気持ち
more	1093	adv.	もっと
more than ~	2012s		いじょう・以上
More slowly please.	1013	exp.	ゆっくり おねがいします。・お願いします。
moreover, furthermore	1071	conj.	それに
morning	1025	n	あさ・朝
mostly, almost	2061	adv.	ほとんど
mostly, generally	2031	adv.	たいてい
mother (someone else's)	1022	n	おかあさん・お母さん
mother, mom	1014	n	はは・母
mountain	1031	n	やま・山
mouth	1061	n	くち・口
move (to), operate (to)	2042	v	うごく・動く
move (to), set in motion (to)	2042	v	うごかす・動かす
move home/office (to), change residence (to)	2032s	v	ひっこし・引っ越しする
movie	1091	n	えいが・映画
MP3 player	1031	n	えむぴーすりー ぷれーやー・MP3 プレーヤー
Mt. Koya (place)	1052s	pn	こうやさん・高野山
Murasaki Shikibu (Heian Pd. author)	1071s	pn	むらさきしきぶ・紫式部
muscle	1061	n	きんにく・筋肉
museum	2071	n	はくぶつかん・博物館
music	1032	n	おんがく・音楽
musical instrument	2023s	n	がっき・楽器
musical performance	2023	n	えんそう・演奏
musical scale	2023s	n	おんかい・音階
mustache, beard	1061	n	ひげ・髭
myself, yourself, oneself	2011	n	じぶん・自分
mysterious	1081	な adj	ふしぎ・不思議
Nagasaki (place)	1041s	pn	ながさき・長崎
name	1013	n	なまえ・名前
nap	1063	n	ひるね・昼寝
nap (to)	1063	v	ひるね・昼寝(を) する/します
Nara (place)	1051s	pn	なら・奈良
Nara Period	1054s	n	ならじだい・奈良時代
Narita International Airport	1011s	pn	なりたくうこう・成田空港
narrow	1083	い adj.	せまい・狭い
national language (Japanese language)	1032	n	こくご・国語
naturally	2033	adv.	しぜん・自然
nature	2033	n/な adj	しぜん・自然
near, close	1061	い adj.	ちかい・近い
nearby, side	2031	n	そば・傍
necessary, required	2035s	n	ひつよう・必要
neck	1061	n	くび・首
necktie	1064	n	ねくたい・ネクタイ
neighboring	2022	n	となり・隣
nervous	2064	ono.	いらいら・イライラ
new	1081	い adj.	あたらしい・新しい
new information marker, "but", conjunction, used to combine two sentences	1021s, 1071s, 1073s, 1095s	part.	が
New Year, New Year's Day	2061	n	おしょうがつ・お正月
New Year's card	2061	n	ねんがじょう・年賀状

English	Location		Japanese
New Year's Day	2061	n	がんたん・元旦
New Year's Eve	2061	n	おおみそか・大晦日
New Year's gift (usually money)	2061	n	としだま・(お)年玉
New Zealand (place)	1041	pn	にゅーじーらんど・ニュージーランド
New Zealander (person)	1041	pn	にゅーじーらんどじん・ニュージーランド人
newspaper	2013	n	しんぶん・新聞
next	1033	n/adv.	つぎ・次
next month	1054	n	らいげつ・来月
next week	1054	n	らいしゅう・来週
next year	1054	n	らいねん・来年
next youngest brother/sister (my)	1021	n	すぐしたの おとうと/いもうと・すぐ下の 弟/妹
nice, wonderful	1064	な adj.	すてき・素敵
nine	1021	counter	く/きゅう・九
no	1014		いいえ
no one	1102	exp.	だれも
No, I don't understand.	1016s	exp.	いいえ、わかりません。・分かりません。
No, it is not/different.	1014	exp.	いいえ、ちがいます。・違います。
Noh (a type of theater)	1075	n	のう・能
noisily, clamorously	2054	adv./ono.	わいわい
noisy, loud	1081	い adj.	うるさい
non-smoking	2024	n	きんえん・禁煙
noon, daytime	1025	n	ひる・昼
noren curtain	1043s	n	のれん
normal, usual	1064	adj./adv.	ふつう・普通
north	2021	n	きた・北
nose	1061	n	はな・鼻
not at all	1074	adv.	ぜんぜん・全然
not good at	1073	な adj.	へた・下手
not less than, ... and more than, above	2063	n	いじょう・以上
not more than; ... and less than/below	2063	n	いか・以下
not tasty, not good	1081	い adj.	まずい
not very	1074	adv.	あまり
not yet (w. neg. verb)	1043	adv.	まだ
notebook	1024	n	のーと・ノート
nothing	1053	pron.	なにも・何も
notice (to)	2062s	v	きがつく・気が付く
November	1052	n	じゅういちがつ・十一月
now	1032	n/adv.	いま・今
now, this time, next time	2043	n	こんど・今度
nowadays, most recent	2073	n	さいきん・最近
nowhere (w. neg. verb), every-where, anywhere, anyplace	1102	adv.	どこにも
nowhere, not anywhere, not any place (w. neg. verb)	1102	adv.	どこへも
number	2024s	n	ばんごう・番号
nurse	1063	n	かんごし・看護師
nursery school	1031	n	ほいくえん・保育園
occupation, job	1025	n	しごと・仕事
occupation period	2034s	n	ちゅうりゅうじだい・駐留時代
ocean, sea	1081	n	うみ・海
Ochanomizu (section of Tokyo)	1024s	pn	おちゃのみず・お茶の水
October	1052	n	じゅうがつ・十月
octopus	1025	n	たこ
oden (various ingredients stewed in soy-flavored dashi)	1091s	n	おでん
of course	1105	exp.	もちろん
office	1032	n	じむしょ・事務所
oh	1031	interj.	あっ
Oh, yes!, that's right	2043	interj.	そうそう
Okinawa (island of or island chain of)	2011	pn	おきなわ・沖縄
Okinawa instrument, like a shamisen	2023s	n	さんしん・三線
old (used for things)	1081	い adj.	ふるい・古い
older brother (my)	1021	n	あに・兄
older brother (someone else's)	1022	n	おにいさん・お兄さん
older sister (my)	1021	n	あね・姉
older sister (someone else's)	1022	n	おねえさん・お姉さん
oldest brother/sister (my)	1021	n	いちばんうえの あに/あね・一番上の 兄/姉
one	1021	counter	いち・一
one-way (trip)	2024	n	かたみち・片道
only, just	2062	part.	ばかり
only, just, as	2062	part.	だけ
oops, sorry	1083	interj.	おっと
open (to)	2081	v	あく・開く
open (to) [book/bound object]	1013	v	ひらく・開く/ひらきます・開きます
open (to) [door/window]	1034	v	あける・開ける/あけます・開けます
open (to) (eyes, doors, etc.)	2081	v	あける・開ける
open air (outdoor) bath	2051s	n	ろてんぶろ・露天風呂
open, central fire pit used for cooking and heat in houses in n. Japan	2061s	n	いろり
opening for written letters	2064	n	はいけい・拝啓
opinion, view	2092	n	いけん・意見
or, or else	2041	conj.	それとも
orange	1074	n	おれんじ・オレンジ
orange juice	1043s	n	おれんじじゅーす・オレンジジュース
order (sequential)	2062s	n	じゅんばん・順番
order (to)	2024	v	ちゅうもん・注文 する
order, request	2024	n	(ご)ちゅうもん・(ご)注文
original/main island (lit.)	2021s	n	ほんとう・本当
Osaka (place)	1083s	pn	おおさか・大阪
other, another	2023	n	ほか・他
outline, summary	2043s	n	あらすじ
outside	2023	n	そと・外
outside	1045s	n	そと・外
over there	1024	pron.	あそこ
overlook	2015s	n	てんぼうだい・展望台
p.m.	1032	n	ごご・午後
painful	1063	い adj.	いたい・痛い
painting, drawing	1091	n	え・絵
pants, trousers	1064	n	ずぼん・ズボン
paper	1024	n	かみ・紙
parents	2011	n	りょうしん・両親
park	2013	n	こうえん・公園
part, component	2034s	n	ぶぶん・部分
part time job	1025s	n	あるばいと・アルバイト
part-time job	2011s	n	アルバイト

English	Location		Japanese
particle after a place word to mean "to" before a verb of motion (similar to the particle に)	1023	part.	へ
particle after a place word to mean "to" before a verb of motion (similar to the particle へ)	1023	part.	に
party	1073s	n	ぱーてぃ・パーティ
pass (to), exceed (to), above (to be)	2033	v	すぎる・過ぎる
pass away (to), [formal for 死ぬ (cannot be used for one's own death)]	2055	v	なくなる・亡くなる
pass time (to)	2011s	v	すごす・過ごす
pass through, to	1051s	v	とおる・通る/とおります・通ります
past (the), bygone days	2085s		かこ・過去
past, after	1032		すぎ (〜)
pay (to)	2045	v	はらう・払う
peace	2091	n	へいわ・平和
peaceful, calm	1084	な adj.	おだやか
pen	1024	n	ぺん・ペン
pencil	1024	n	えんぴつ・鉛筆
pencil box	App.	n	ふでばこ・筆箱
pencil box	App.	n	ほっちきす・ホッチキス
peoples indigenous to Hokkaido, Sakhalin, and the Kuril Islands	2013	n	あいぬ・アイヌ
pepper	2093	n	こしょう
perform (to)	2043	v	えんじる・演じる
performance (public)	2043	n	こうえん・公演
performer	2031s	n	げいじん・芸人
perhaps, possibly	2101	exp.	もしかして
period, era	2071	n	じだい・時代
period of years, duration	1032s	n	ねんかん・年間
person	1022	n	ひと・人
person's origin (hometown, country, etc.)	2011	n	しゅっしん・出身
Peruvian (person)	1041	n	ぺるーじん・ペルー人
photograph	1021	n	しゃしん・写真
photographed (to be), copy (to be)	2065s	v	うつす・写す
physical education	1032	n	たいいく・体育
physics	1032	n	ぶつりがく・物理学
piano	1071	n	ぴあの・ピアノ
pickled vegetables (Japanese)	1083	n	つけもの・漬け物
picture story show	2041	n	かみしばい・紙芝居
pig, pork	2013	n	ぶた・豚
Ping-Pong club	1033	n	たっきゅうぶ・卓球部
pink	1074	n	ぴんく・ピンク
pink (peach) color	1074	n	ももいろ・もも色
pioneer village	2013s	n	かいたくのむら・開拓の村
piping hot, passionately in love	2054	n/ono.	あつあつ・熱々
pitiful; pathetic	2014s	exp.	かわいそう
pizza	1043s	n	ぴざ・ピザ
place	1052s	n	ところ・所
place (to), put (to)	2053s	v	おかれる・置かれる
place, location, position	2104	n	ばしょ・場所
place, location, spot	2084	n	ところ・所
plan, expectation	2051s	n	よてい・予定
planner, hand-book	App.	n	ぷらんなー・プランナー
play (to)	1103	v	あそぶ・遊ぶ/あそびます・遊びます

English	Location		Japanese
play [a stringed instrument] (to)	1071	v	ひく・弾く/ひきます・弾きます
play basketball (to)	1091	v	ばすけ・バスケ (を) する/します
play, drama	2044	n	しばい・芝居
play guitar (to)	1071	v	ぎたーを ひく/ひきます・ギターを 弾く/弾きます
play soccer (to)	1091	v	さっかー・サッカー(を) する/します
play video games (to)	1091	v	びでおげーむ・ビデオゲーム (を) する/します
playing cards, card game	1071	n	とらんぷ・トランプ
please	1013s	exp.	おねがい・お願い/おねがいします・お願いします
please (here you go), by all means	1015	adv.	どうぞ
Please be quiet.	1016s	exp.	しずかに して ください。・静かに して 下さい。
Please say it in English.	1016s	exp.	えいごで いって ください。・英語で 言って 下さい。
poet	2032s	n	しじん・詩人
polite for よろしく お願いします	1013	exp.	どうぞ よろしく おねがいします・お願いします
polite speech	2044	n	けいご・敬語
polite suffix for Mr., Miss, or Mrs. when writing letters	2013	suffix	さま・〜様
pond	1101s	n	いけ・池
poor, needy	2095	い adj.	まずしい・貧しい
popularity	2024s	n	にんき・人気
population	2011	n	じんこう・人口
pork ramen	1043s	n	とんこつラーメン
port, harbor	2021s	n	みなと・港
portion, section, part	2071	n	ぶぶん・部分
Portugal	1041	pn	ぽるとがる・ポルトガル
Portuguese (language)	1042	n	ぽるとがるご・ポルトガル語
Portuguese (person)	1041	n	ぽるとがるじん・ポルトガル人
possession, replaces a noun	1021	part.	の
post (to), display (to)	2021s	v	はりだす・貼り出す
pot stickers	1043s	n	ぎょうざ
potato	1042s	n	じゃがいも・ジャガイモ
power	2035	n	ちから・力
practically, practical, reality	2043	n	じっさい・実際
practice (to)	1051	v	れんしゅう・練習 (を)する/します
pray (to), wish (to)	2065	v	いのる・祈る
precipitate (to)	1101	v	ふる・降る/ふります・降ります
predict (to), know beforehand	2084s	v	よち・予知 する
prefectural capital	2022s	n	けんちょう・県庁
prefectural capital of Okinawa	2022	pn	なは・那覇
prefectural offices	2022s	n	けんちょう・県庁
preparation	2035s	n	じゅんび・準備
prepare (to)	2082	v	じゅんび・準備(を)する
present, gift	2015	n	ぷれぜんと・プレゼント
present (a), a gift	1094	n	ぷれぜんと・プレゼント
press down (to)	2093s	v	おさえつける・押さえ付ける
pretty, clean	1081	な adj.	きれい
price	2024s	n	りょうきん・料金
price of comodities, cost of living	2102	n	ぶっか・物価
printing	2031s	n	いんさつ・印刷
printing press	2031s	n	いんさつき・印刷機

English	Location		Japanese
problem	1045s	n	もんだい・問題
professor	2015s	n	はかせ・博士
program (e.g., a TV program)	2044	n	ばんぐみ・番組
promise	1105s	n	やくそく・約束
psychology	1032	n	しんりがく・心理学
Puerto Rican (person)	1041	n	ぷえるとりこじん・プエルトリコ人
pull (to), play (a stringed instrument) (to)	2023	v	ひく・弾く
purple	1074	n	むらさき・紫
put (to), place (to)	2092	v	おく・置く
put into (to)	1061	v	いれる・入れる/いれます・入れます
question	1032s	n	しつもん・質問
question	2102	n	しつもん・質問
question and answer (period)	2035s	n	しつぎおうとう・質疑応答
question-and-answer	2035s	n	しつもんおうとう・質問応答
quickly	1035	adv.	はやく・速く
quiet	1061	な adj.	しずか・静か
rabbit	2013	n	うさぎ・兎
raccoon dog, tanuki	1035s	n	たぬき・狸
rain	1101	n	あめ・雨
rainy season	1101	n	つゆ・梅雨
ramen	1043s	n	らーめん・ラーメン
rat, mouse	1072	n	ねずみ・鼠
raw egg	2053s	n	なまたまご・生卵
read (to)	1013	v	よむ・読む/よみます・読みます
reading	1071	n	どくしょ・読書
real thing, genuine article	1091	n	ほんもの・本物
really, indeed, truly	1084	adv.	まったく・全く
reasonably, fairly	2033	adv.	けっこう
receive (to), be given (to)	2013	v	ちょうだい・頂戴(する)
receive (to) (very polite), lit.: I will receive.	1092	v	いただく/いただきます
receive (to), lit.: I will receive.	1094	v	もらう/もらいます
recommendation	2042s	n	おすすめ・お勧め
reconcile (to), make up (to)	1091	v	なかなおり・仲直り（を）する/します
record	2032s	n	きろく・記録
red	1074	n	あか・赤
red-colored	1082	い adj.	あかい・赤い
Red Mt. Fuji (woodblock print)	2035s	pn	あかふじ・赤富士
regional (Akita) dish of cooked and pounded rice, grilled on skewers	2062	n	きりたんぽ
regrettably, unluckily	1093	n/な adj.	ざんねん・残念
reign period of Emperor Hirohito (1926 – 1989)	2061	pn	しょうわ・昭和
reign year	1053s	n	ねんごう・年号
relaxing	2053	な adj	きらく・気楽
relieved (to be)	2064s	v	ほっとする
religion	1052s	n	しゅうきょう・宗教
relocate, move	2032s	n	ひっこし・引越し
remember (to)	2021s	v	おもいだす・思い出す
remember (to), memorize (to)	2091	v	おぼえる・覚える
repeat (to)	2032s	v	くりかえす・繰り返す
reply, response	2012s	n	へんじ・返事
report (to), communicate (to)	2033s	v	つたえる・伝える

English	Location		Japanese
resemble (to), similar (to be); (common usage: 似ている)	2021	v	にる・似る
resemble X (to), be like X~.	2095	suffix	よう・様
reservation	2024	n	よやく・予約
reserve (to)	2024	v	よやく・予約 する
resources	2035s	n	しりょう・資料
rest (to), take a break (to)	1015s	v	やすむ・休む
rest, break	2043	n	きゅうけい・休憩
results	2021s	n	けっか・結果
restaurant	1043	n	れすとらん・レストラン
return (to)	1044	v	かえる・帰る/かえります・帰ります
return by walking (to)	2012	v	あるいてかえる・歩いて帰る
return with someone (to)	1105	v	つれて かえる/かえります・連れて 帰る/帰ります
return with something (to)	1105	v	もって かえる/かえります・持って 帰る/帰ります
rice balls	1105s	n	おにぎり
rice bowl	2053s	n	ちゃわん・茶碗
rice crackers	1094	n	せんべい・煎餅
rice wine	2025s	n	さけ・酒
ride (to)	2012	v	のる・乗る
right	2021	n	みぎ・右
right	1104s	n	みぎ・右
road, highway	2045	n	どうろ・道路
road, path, street	2022	n	みち・道
rock and roll (music)	1105	n	ろっくんろーる・ロックンロール
rock, stone	1101	n	いし・石
roll or bun filled with sweet red bean paste (anko)	2071	n	あんぱん・あんパン
rolled sushi	1043s	n	まきずし・巻き寿司
roof	2084	n	やね・屋根
room (a)	1015	n	へや・部屋
rooster, chicken	2014s	n	にわとり・鶏
Roppongi (section of Tokyo)	1024s	pn	ろっぽんぎ・六本木
rotate (to); revolve (to)	2021s	v	まわる・回る
round trip, return ticket	2024	n	おうふく・往復
ruins, remains	2021s	n	あと・跡
ruler	App.	n	じょうぎ・定規
rules, regulations	2074	n	きそく・規則
run (to)	2085	v	はしる・走る
Russia (place)	1041	pn	ろしあ・ロシア
Russian (language)	1042	n	ろしあご・ロシア語
Russian (person)	1041	n	ろしあじん・ロシア人
ryokan, Japanese inn/hotel	1044s	n	りょかん・旅館
ryokan, Japanese inn/hotel	2051	n	りょかん・旅館
Ryukyu Kingdom	2022s	pn	りゅうきゅうおうこく・琉球王国
sad	1061	い adj.	かなしい・悲しい
safe	2084	n	あんぜん・安全
salt	2093	n	しお・塩
salt	App.	n	しお・塩
same	1044s	n	おなじ・同じ
samurai	1061	n	さむらい・侍
Sapporo (city in Hokkaido)	2011	pn	さっぽろ・札幌
Satsuma (place)	1041s	pn	さつま・薩摩
Saturday	1051	n	どようび・土曜日
save (to)	2011s	v	ためる・貯める
save (to), rescue (to)	2065	v	たすける・助ける

English	Location		Japanese
save money (to)	2011s	v	ためる・貯める
saved (to be), rescued (to be)	2065	v	たすかる・助かる
say (to)	1041	v	いう・言う/いいます・言います
Say hello to . . .	1065	exp.	に よろしく (…)
Say it again please.	1016s	exp.	もういちど いって ください。・もう一度 言って 下さい。
scary	1081	い adj.	こわい
scary	2064	い adj.	こわい・怖い
scattered, in pieces, disconnected	2021	な adj./ ono.	ばらばら・バラバラ
scenery	2032s	n	ふうけい・風景
scenery, landscape	2033	n	けしき・景色
schedule	1032	n	すけじゅーる・スケジュール
schedule, timetable	1032	n	じかんわり・時間割
school	1031	n	がっこう・学校
school excursion	2013s	n	しゅうがくりょこう・修学旅行
school subject	1032	n	かもく・科目
science	1032	n	かがく・科学
scissors	App.	n	はさみ
scold (to)	2071	v	しかる・叱る
score, grade	1033	n	せいせき・成績
screen	2104	n	がめん・画面
script	2041s	n	せりふ・セリフ
scriptures	1052s	n	おきょう・お経
sea, ocean	1081	n	うみ・海
Sea of Okhotsk	2015s	pn	オホーック海
search (to)	1093	v	さがす・探す/さがします・探します
search, hunt	1013s	n	たんさく・探索
season	1101	n	きせつ・季節
seat [formal]	2044	n	ざせき・座席
seat, place	2024	n	せき・席
seaweed	2093	n	のり
seaweed	App.		
second helping, substitute, alternate	2061	n	おかわり・お代わり
second oldest brother/sister (my)	1021	n	にばんめの・あに/あね・二番目の 兄/姉
secret	1061	n	ひみつ・秘密
secretly	2081s	n	ひそかに
see if you can do (something), try to do (something) (to)	1073	v	やってみる/やってみます
seeing, watching, perusing [honorific for 見る]	2044	n	ごらん・ご覧
see you later [formal]	1015	exp.	では また
see you later [informal]	1015	exp.	じゃあ また
selfish	1081	な adj.	わがまま
seek (to), request (to)	2045	v	もとめる・求める
seemingly, looks like ~, resembles ~	2023s	suf.	らしい
select (to), choose (to)	2101s	v	えらべる・選べる
self-introduction	2011	n	じこしょうかい・自己紹介
sell (to)	1091	v	うる・売る/うります・売ります
send (to)	1051	v	おくる・送る/おくります・送ります
senior; an elder	2022s	n	せんぱい・先輩
sense, feeling, sensation	2022	n	かんじ・感じ

English	Location		Japanese
sentence ending for a rhetorical question or when seeking agreement	1035	part.	ね
sentence ending for a strong declarative statement or for emphasis	1035	part.	よ
sentence ending that can be exclamatory or to express surprise	1035	part.	ねえ
separate	1092	n/な adj.	べつ・別
separate (to)	2031s	v	はなれる・離れる
separate (to)	2014s	exp.	べつべつ・別々 に する
separately, individually	1092	n/な adj.	べつべつ・別々
September	1052	n	くがつ・九月
set	1103s	n	せっと・セット
seven	1021	counter	しち/なな・七
several hundreds	2031s	n	すうひゃく・数百
shakuhachi (end-blown bamboo flute)	2025	n	しゃくはち・尺八
shamisen (musical stringed instrument)	2023	n	しゃみせん・三味線
shampoo (to)	1091	v	しゃんぷー・シャンプー (を) する/します
sharply slanted	2033s		きれなが・切れ長
she, girlfriend	2052	pron.	かのじょ・彼女
she, girlfriend	1074	pron.	かのじょ・彼女
Shikoku (smallest of the four main islands of Japan)	2011	pn	しこく・四国
Shinto religion	2062	n	しんとう・神道
Shinto (religion)	1052s	n	しんとう・神道
ship, boat	1045s	n	ふね・舟
shirt	1064	n	しゃつ・シャツ
shoes	1064	n	くつ・靴
shop, stand	2044	n	ばいてん・売店
shop, store	1091	n	みせ・店
shopkeeper, clerk	1092	n	てんいん・店員
shopping	1091	n	かいもの・買い物
short (length)	1061	い adj.	みじかい・短い
short pants, shorts	1064s	n	しょーとぱんつ・ショートパンツ
shoulder	1061	n	かた・肩
show (to)	2043	v	みせる・見せる
shower (to), bask in the sun (to), bathe (to)	2052	v	あびる・浴びる
shrine	1033	n	じんじゃ・神社
Shuremon, a famous gate at Shurijo castle	2022s	pn	しゅれいもん・守礼門
Shurijo, castle in Naha, Okinawa	2022s	pn	しゅりじょう・首里城
shy, embarrassed, ashamed	2052	い adj.	はずかしい・恥ずかしい
siblings	1021	n	きょうだい・兄弟
sick, feel bad	1063	exp.	ぐあいが わるい・具合が 悪い
sickness, illness	1063	n	びょうき・病気
side (beside), sideways	2023	n	よこ・横
side dishes	2025s	n	おかず
sign	2062s	n	しるし・印
sign language	1042	n	しゅわ・手話
signature	1042	n	さいん・サイン
signifies a question	1014	part.	か
silly, foolish	1081	い adj.	ばかばかしい
silver	1074	n	ぎんいろ・銀色
simple	1064	な adj.	しんぷる・シンプル

English	Location		Japanese
simple	2021	な adj.	かんたん・簡単
since, given that..., because of...	2044	conj.	ので
sing (to)	1071	v	たう・歌う/うたいます・歌います
singing	1071	n	うたうこと・歌う事
sink, wash basin	2052s	n	せんめんき・洗面器
sister city	2091s	n	しまいとし・姉妹都市
sister school	2011s	n	しまいこうこう・姉妹高校
sit (to)	1013	v	すわる・座る/すわります・座ります
sit down	1016s	exp.	ちゃくせき・着席
six	1021	counter	ろく・六
skateboard (to)	1071	v	すけぼー・スケボー (を) する/します
sketchbook	1062s	n	すけっちぶっく・スケッチブック
skiing	1071	n	すきー・スキー
skilled at	1073	な adj.	とくい・得意
skillful	1062	な adj.	じょうず・上手
skirt	1064	n	すかーと・スカート
sky	2032	n	そら・空
sleep (to)	1051	v	ねる・寝る/ねます・寝ます
sleeping	1071	n	ねること・寝る事
sleepy	1053s	い adj.	ねむい・眠い
sleeve	2023s	n	そで・袖
slim, stylish	1062	な adj.	すまーと・スマート
slim/skinny (is)	1062	v	やせる/やせています
slipper(s)	1093s	n	すりっぱ・スリッパ
slow, late	2023	い adj.	おそい・遅い
slowly	2035	adv.	おそく・遅く
slowly, restful	1016s	adv.	ゆっくり
slowly, at ease, restful	2044	exp.	ごゆっくり/ゆっくり
small	1031	い adj.	ちいさい・小さい
small (S) size	1092	n	えすさいず・Sサイズ
small animals counter	1022s	counter	ひき (〜)・〜匹
small change (money)	2041s	n	こぜに・小銭
small Japanese drum	2023s	n	しめだいこ・締め太鼓
small test, quiz	1032	n	しょうてすと・小テスト
smoke tobacco (to)	2074	v	たばこをすう・タバコを吸う
snack	App.	n	おやつ
snake	2013	n	へび・蛇
snow	1101	n	ゆき・雪
snowball fight	2012s	n	ゆきがっせん・雪合戦
snowboard (to)	2015	v	すのーぼーど・スノーボード (を)する
so so, not bad, moderate	1062	adv.	まあまあ
so, therefore	2032	conj.	だから/ですから
so, really, seeming	1033s	adv.	そう
soap	2052	n	せっけん・石鹸
social dancing	2081s	n	しゃこうダンス・社交ダンス
social studies, society	1032	n	しゃかい・社会
socks	1064	n	くつした・靴下
soldier	2065s	n	へいし・兵士
soldier on an American military base	2061s	n	あめりかぐんきちのへいたい・メリカ軍基地の兵隊
some time ago	2093s	n	さっき
somehow, somewhat	2043s	n	なんだか・何だか
someone else's family	1021	n	ごかぞく・ご家族
something	1103		なにか・何か

English	Location		Japanese
sometimes	1032	n/adv.	ときどき・時々
somewhat, little	1032	adv.	ちょっと
son	2061	n	むすこ・息子
song	1071	n	うた・歌
song, tune, melody	2023s	n	きょく・曲
sopping wet; drenched	2051	ono.	びしょびしょ
Soubu (train line)	1024s	pn	そうぶ・総武
sound	2054	n	おと・音
soup stock (fish-based)	2093s	n	だし
soup, broth	2065s	n	しる・汁
sour	2025	い adj.	すっぱい・酸っぱい
south	2021	n	みなみ・南
South Africa (place)	1041	pn	みなみあふりか・南アフリカ
South America (place)	1042s	pn	なんべい・南米
South Korea (place)	1041	pn	かんこく・韓国
souvenir(s)	1023	n	おみやげ・お土産
soy sauce	1015	n	しょうゆ・醤油
space	2032	n	くうかん・空間
spaghetti	1043s	n	すぱげてぃ・スパゲティ
Spain (place)	1041	pn	すぺいん・スペイン
Spaniard (person)	1041	n	すぺいんじん・スペイン人
Spanish (language)	1042	n	すぺいんご・スペイン語
speak (to)	1042	v	はなす・話す/はなします・話します
special	1092	n/な adj.	とくべつ・特別
special New Year's soba	2062	n	としこしそば・年越しそば
spicy	2025	い adj.	からい・辛い
splendid, nice	2033	n	けっこう
sponge cake	2071	n	かすてら・カステラ
spoonful	2094		さじ
sports	1071	n	すぽーつ・スポーツ
spread (to), smear (to)	2062	n	ぬる・塗る
spread out (to), lay out (to)	2051s	v	しく・敷く
spring	1101	n	はる・春
stairs, staircase	2022	n	かいだん・階段
stand (to)	1013	v	たつ・立つ/たちます・立ちます
Stand please.	1013	exp.	たってください・立って下さい
stand up	1016s	exp.	きりつ・起立
standard	2031s	n	すいじゅん・水準
stapler	App.	n	ほっちきす・ホッチキス
start (to)	2081	v	はじめる・始める
station (subway/rail)	2012	n	えき・駅
stationery store	2073s	n	ぶんぼうぐや・文房具屋
statue, figure	2091	n	ぞう・像
stay at [e.g., hotel] (to)	2024	v	とまる・泊まる
steak	App.	n	すてーき・ステーキ
steam (to)	2094	v	むす・蒸す
steamy hot food, warm(ly)	2054	adv./ono.	ほかほか
step-	1021		ぎりの〜・
sticky rice cake	1064	n	もち・餅
stomach	1061	n	おなか・お腹
stone, rock	1101	n	いし・石
stone; rock	2031	n	いし・石
stop (something or someone) (to), turn off (to)	2084	v	とめる・止める
stop (to), halt (to)	2084	v	とまる・止まる
stopping how many nights?	2024	inter.	なんぱく・何泊
store, shop	2025s	n	ばいてん・売店

English	Location		Japanese
store, shop	1091	n	みせ・店
story	2044	n	すとーりー・ストーリー
straight (ahead)	2022	な adj.	まっすぐ
strange, funny, ridiculous	2043	い adj.	おかしい・可笑しい
straw raincoat	2064s	n	わらでできたみの
strawberry	App.	n	いちご・イチゴ
strict	1081	い adj.	きびしい
strong	1061	い adj.	つよい・強い
student	1031	n	がくせい・学生, せいと・生徒
study (to)	1052	v	べんきょう・勉強 (を) する/します
study (in depth) (to), learn (to) or take lessons in	2085	v	まなぶ・学ぶ
study workshop	2035s	n	けんきゅうかい・研究会
style	2035s	n	ようしき・様式
subject of study, specialty	2101	n	せんもん・専門
subway	2012	n	ちかてつ・地下鉄
sufficient, (I'm) fine, no thank you	2033	な adj.	けっこう
suffix AFTER a boy's name	1013	suffix	くん (〜)・〜君
suffix AFTER a name	1013	suffix	さん・〜さん
sugar	App.	n	さとう・砂糖
suit	1064	n	すーつ・スーツ
summer	1101	n	なつ・夏
sumo wrestler	2034s	n	りきし・力士
sumo wrestling	2034s	n	すもう・相撲
Sunday	1051	n	にちようび・日曜日
sunny-side up fried egg	2093s	n	めだまやき・目玉焼き
surely, undoubtedly	2043	adv	きっと
surprise (to)	2033	v	おどろく・驚く
surprised (to be), amazed (to be)	2073	v	びっくり・ビックリ する
surrounding people	2052s	n	まわりのひと・周りの人
sunset	1104s	n	さんせっと・サンセット/ゆうやけ・夕焼け
sushi	1011	n	すし・寿司
sushi in a box or bowl with a variety of ingredients	1103s	n	ちらしずし・散らし寿司
sushi wrapped in fried tofu (abura-age)	1103s	n	いなりずし・稲荷寿司
sushi wrapped in nori	1103s	n	てまきずし・手巻き寿司
Susukino, town in Hokkaido	2015s	pn	すすきの
Swahili (language)	1042	n	すわひりご・スワヒリ語
swan	2102	n	はくちょう・白鳥
sweet	2025	い adj.	あまい・甘い
sweet bread	2025s	n	かしパン・菓子パン
sweets (traditional Japanese)	2041s	n	だがし・駄菓子
swim (to)	1071	v	およぐ・泳ぐ/およぎます・泳ぎます
swimming	1071	n	およぐこと・泳ぐ事/すいえい・水泳
swimming suit	2052	n	みずぎ・水着
sword, saber	2031	n	かたな・刀
symmetric design	2032	n	しんめとりっくでざいん・シンメトリックデザイン
syrupy, muddled	2051	ono.	どろどろ
t-shirt	1023	n	てぃーしゃつ・Tシャツ
table	2085 App.	n	てーぶる・テーブル
tacos (Mexican)	1025	n	たこす・タコス
tact, thoughtfulness	2102	n/な adj.	えんりょ・遠慮
Tahiti	2031	pn	たひち・タヒチ

English	Location		Japanese
Taiwan (place)	1041	pn	たいわん・台湾
Taiwanese (person)	1041	n	たいわんじん・台湾人
take (it) out (to)	1013	v	だす・出す/だします・出します
take a break (to)	2043	v	きゅうけい・休憩 (を) する
take a photo (to)	1042	v	しゃしん(を) とる/とります・写真(を) 撮る/撮ります
take a shower (to)	1091	v	しゃわー・シャワー (を) する/します
take a trip (to), travel (to)	1091	v	りょこう・旅行 (を) する/します
take a walk (to)	1054	v	さんぽ・散歩 (を) する/します
take care, be careful	2025	exp.	きをつける・気を付ける
take care, go in good health	2015	exp.	(お)げんきで・(お)元気で
take medicine (to)	1063	v	くすり(を) のむ/のみます・薬(を) 飲む/飲みます
take someone (to)	1105	v	つれて いく/いきます・連れて 行く/行きます
take something (to)	1105	v	もって いく/いきます・持って 行く/行きます
take time, money, etc. (to)	2012s	v	かかる・掛かる
tape	App.	n	てーぷ・テープ
Taro (male name)	1014	pn	たろう・太郎
tasteful, cool	1062	い adj.	しぶい・渋い
tatami mat, rush straw-reed floor mat	2054	n	たたみ・畳
taxi	2012	n	たくしー・タクシー
tea ceremony	1071	n	さどう/ちゃどう・茶道
teach (to), tell/inform (to)	2015	v	おしえる・教える
teacher, suffix AFTER a teacher's, lawyer's, or doctor's name	1011	n	せんせい・先生/〜せんせい・〜先生
teacher's office	2031s	n	きょういんしつ・教員室
technique	2031s	n	ぎじゅつ・技術
telephone	1021	n	でんわ・電話
telephone (to)	1091	v	でんわ・電話 (を) する/します
television, TV	1103s	n	てれび・テレビ
tell me/teach me, please	1032s	exp.	おしえて ください・教えて 下さい
temperature	1101	n	おんど・温度
temple (Buddhist)	1033	n	(お)てら・(お)寺
ten	1021	counter	じゅう・十
tenpura (battered and deep fried fish or vegetable)	1021s	n	てんぷら・天ぷら
tenth (day of the month)	1053	counter	とおか・十日
tenth grader	1031	counter	こうこういちねんせい・高校一年生
teppan'yaki (Japanese cooking prepared on a hot steel plate/table)	2093	n	てっぱんやき・鉄板焼き
teriyaki (meat or fish marinated in sweet soy sauce and broiled)	App.	n	てりやき・照り焼き
terrible	1081	い adj.	ひどい
terrible, amazing, wonderful	2013	い adj.	すごい
test	1032	n	てすと・テスト
test, exam	1032	n	しけん・験
textbook	1013	n	きょうかしょ・教科書
than ~	2032	part.	より
thank you	1023	exp.	どうも ありがとう

English	Location		Japanese
thank you very much	1023	*exp.*	どうも　ありがとう　ございます (polite for どうも　ありがとう)
thanks	1023	*exp.*	ありがとう
thanks to or owing to, assistance	2063	*n*	おかげ・お蔭
thanks, gratitude	2061	*n*	かんしゃ・感謝
Thanksgiving	2061	*n*	かんしゃさい・感謝祭
that (one)	1015	*pron.*	それ
that (over there)	1015	*pron.*	あれ
that (person)	1014s	*pron.*	そちら
that (person) over there	1014s	*pron.*	あちら
that (thing)	1023	*pron.*	その
that (thing) over there	1023	*pron.*	あの
that being the case, because of ...	2043	*part.*	ので
That makes sense.	1042s	*exp.*	なるほど
that way (direction distant from both speaker and listener), over there, [informal for あちら]	2011	*prn*	あっち
that way (distant from the speaker, close to the listener), that direction (close to listener), [informal for そちら]	2011	*pron.*	そっち
the day after tomorrow	2022	*n*	あさって・明後日
then, well then, so	2094	*interj.*	では
then, and then	1071	*conj.*	そして
then, and then	1071	*conj.*	それから
there	1024	*pron.*	そこ
therefore, then, and (then) [used predominately in written language]	2064	*conj.*	すると
thereupon	1082s	*conj.*	すると
they, them	1082	*pron.*	かれら・彼ら
thick, dark	2072s	い *adj.*	こい・濃い
thick, heavy (coating), deep (color)	2032	い *adj.*	あつい・厚い
thin (to become)	1062	*v*	やせる/やせます
thin slices of beef, cooked with vegetables	App.	*n*	すきやき・すき焼き
thin slices of beef, cooked with vegetables	2074	*n*	すきやき・すき焼き
thing	1043	*n*	もの・物
thing (in tangible)	1071s	*n*	こと・事
think (to)	1072	*v*	おもう・思う/おもいます・思います
think (to), consider (to)	2091	*v*	かんがえる・考える
third degree (belt)	1033s	*counter*	さんだん・三段
Thirty-six Views of Mt. Fuji by Hokusai	2033s	*pn*	ふがくさんじゅうろくけい・富嶽三十六景
this (one)	1015	*pron.*	これ
this (thing)	1023		この
this month	1054	*n*	こんげつ・今月
this morning	1051s	*n/adv.*	けさ・今朝
this (person [polite] or thing), here (place close to speaker)	1014	*pron.*	こちら
this way (close to or toward the speaker) this direction, [informal for こちら]	2011	*pron.*	こっち
this week	1054		こんしゅう・今週
this year	1054		ことし・今年
three	1021	*counter*	さん・三
thrilled, excited	2023s	*adv./ono.*	わくわく
throat	1061	*n*	のど・咽喉

English	Location		Japanese
throughout, continuously	1083		ずっと
thunder	1101	*n*	かみなり・雷
Thursday	1051	*n*	もくようび・木曜日
ticket	2012	*n*	きっぷ・切符
ticket (same day)	2042s	*n*	とうじつけん・当日券
tie, belt for a kimono	2023s	*n*	おび・帯
tiger	2013	*n*	とら・虎
time after school	1033	*n/adv.*	ほうかご・放課後
time capsule	1094s	*n*	たいむかぷせる・タイムカプセル
time gate	1041s	*n*	ときのもん・時の門
time, hour	1035s	*n*	とき・時
tissue	App.	*n*	てぃっしゅ・ティッシュ
Todaiji Temple (in Nara)	1051s	*pn*	とうだいじ・東大寺
today	1032	*n*	きょう・今日
tofu	1011	*n*	とうふ・豆腐
together, at the same time, same	1043s	*n*	いっしょ・一緒
together, at the same time, same	1044s	*exp.*	いっしょに・一緒に
Tokaidou Road	2032s	*pn*	とうかいどう・東海道
Tokugawa (family name)	1041s	*pn*	とくがわ・徳川
Tokyo (place)	1011	*pn*	とうきょう・東京
Tokyo International University	1022s	*pn*	とうきょうこくさいだいがく・東京国際大学
Tokyo University	1031s	*pn*	とうきょうだいがく・東京大学
tomato	App.	*n*	とまと・トマト
tomorrow	1032	*n*	あした・明日
too, also, replaces particles は, が, and を		*part.*	も
too much, unnecessary, excess	2043	*n*	よけい・余計
torii (Shinto shrine gate)	1035	*n*	とりい・鳥居
tornado	1101	*n*	たつまき・竜巻
total, all together, in all	1092	*exp.*	ぜんぶで・全部で
town	2031s	*n*	まち・街
town, city block	2014	*n*	まち・町
tradition, convention	2023	*n*	でんとう・伝統
traditional	2023	な *adj.*	でんとうてき・伝統的
traditional Japanese dance	2082s	*n*	にほんぶよう・日本舞踊
track and field club	1033	*n*	りくじょうぶ・陸上部
traffic light, signal	2022	*n*	しんごう・信号
transfer (to)	2024	*v*	のりかえる・乗り換える
travel agency/company	2024	*n*	りょこうがいしゃ・旅行会社
traveling performer	2054	*n*	たびげいにん・旅芸人
treat (someone to a meal)	2071s	*n*	おごりで
tree	1011s	*n*	き・木
tremble (to), get nervous (to), thrilled (to be)	2023	*v*	わくわく(する)
trip	2032s	*n*	たび・旅
trip, travel	1071	*n*	りょこう・旅行/たび・旅
trouble, bother	2071	な *adj.*	めいわく・迷惑
trousers, pants	1064	*n*	ずぼん・ズボン
truth, reality	1104	*n*	ほんとう・本当
tsunami, exceptionally large ocean wave	1011	*n*	つなみ・津波
Tuesday	1051	*n*	かようび・火曜日
tune, melody	2023s	*n*	きょく・曲
tunnel	1041s	*n*	トンネル
turn (to)	2022	*v*	まがる・曲がる

English	Location		Japanese
turn over (to), flip (to)	2093s	n	ひっくりかえす・ひっくり返す
turkey	2102	n	しちめんちょう・七面鳥
turtle	1082	n	かめ・亀
twelve zodiac animals	2014s	n	じゅうにし・十二支
twins	1022s	n	ふたご・双子
two	1021	counter	に・二
typhoon	1101	n	たいふう・台風
ugly	1081	い adj.	みにくい
uncle	2065	n	おじ
unusual, rare	2043	い adj.	めずらしい・珍しい
unusual, strange	2043	な adj.	へん・変
unskilled at	1073	な adj.	にがて・苦手
until (used with spec. locations or times)	1053	part.	まで
Urashima Taro (folktale character)	1084s	pn	うらしまたろう・浦島太郎
us, we	1013	pron.	わたしたち・私達
use (to)	1102	v	つかう・使う/つかいます・使います
used after the direct object	1023	part.	を
useful, convenient	2022s	な adj.	べんり・便利
usual; normal	2023	n/adv.	ふつう・普通
usual, normal	1064	adj./adv.	ふつう・普通
usually	1072	adv.	たいてい
Utagawa Hiroshige, artist	2032	pn	ひろしげ・広重
Van Gogh, Vincent	2032	pn	ごっほ・ゴッホ
uncle or man quite a bit older than you	1022	n	おじさん
understand (to)	1016s	v	わかる・分かる/わかります・分かります
underwear	1064	n	したぎ・下着, ぱんつ・パンツ
unfriendly	2014s	い adj.	なかのわるい・仲の悪い
unhappiness, misfortune	2081	な adj.	ふこう・不幸
uniform (school)	1025s	n	せいふく・制服
United States of America (place)	1041	pn	あめりか・アメリカ
university/college student	1031	n	だいがくせい・大学生
various	1074	adv.	いろいろ・色々
various, assorted	2031s	な adj.	さまざま
vegetable(s)	2065s	n	やさい・野菜
very	1031	adv.	とても
very soon	2063	exp.	もうすぐ
very, considerably, easily, by no means (w. neg. verb)	2033	adv.	なかなか
vicinity	2011	n	へん・辺
video games	1071	n	びでおげーむ・ビデオゲーム
village	2014	n	むら・村
vocabulary	1013s	n	たんご・単語
voice	1061	n	こえ・声
volcano	2055	n	かざん・火山
volleyball club (team)	1033	n	ばれーぼーるぶ・バレーボール部
wait (to)	1061	v	まつ・待つ/まちます・待ちます
Wait a minute please.	1016s	exp.	ちょっと まって ください。・ちょっと 待って 下さい。
waitress	1084s	n	うえいとれす・ウェイトレス
waka (classic Japanese poem)	1072s	n	わか・和歌
wake someone up (to), rise (to)	2081	v	おこす・起こす

English	Location		Japanese
wake (up) (to)	1051	v	おきる・起きる/おきます・起きます
walk	1054	n	さんぽ・散歩
walk (to)	2012	v	あるく・歩く
wall	2021s	n	かべ・壁
war	2092	n	せんそう・戦争
warm	2052	い adj.	あたたかい・暖かい
warm	2053	い adj.	あたたかい・温かい
wasabi, Japanese horseradish	1015	n	わさび
wash (to)	2051	v	あらう・洗う
wash basin	2052s	n	せんめんき・洗面器
water	1024	n	みず・水
water buffalo cart	2022s	n	すいぎゅうしゃ・水牛車
water magic performance	2031s	n	みずげい・水芸
wave	2032s	n	なみ・波
way, manner	2095	n	よう・様
we, us	1013	pron.	わたしたち・私達
We did it!	2021	exp.	やった！
weak	1061	い adj.	よわい・弱い
wear (to), do (to)	1064	v	する/します
wear above the waist (to)	1064	v	きる・着る/きます・着ます
wear below the waist (to)	1064	v	はく・履く/はきます・履きます
wear glasses or sunglasses (to)	1064	v	かける/かけます
wear on the head (to)	1064	v	かぶる・被る/かぶります・被ります
weasel	2014s	n	いたち
weather	1101	n	てんき・天気
weather report	1101	n	てんきよほう・天気予報
Wednesday	1051	n	すいようび・水曜日
weekend	1054	n	しゅうまつ・週末
welcome (usually used at a place of business)	1043	exp.	いらっしゃいませ
welcome home	1015	exp.	おかえりなさい・お帰りなさい
Welcome!, Nice to see you.	1014	exp.	ようこそ
well	1082	い adj.	よい（よく）・良い
well, now then	2023	interj.	さて
well, often	2031	adv.	よく
Well done.	1016s	exp.	よくできました。・良く出来ました。
well then…	1033s		じゃ/じゃあ
well, nicely	1103s	adv.	よく
well, now	1091s	interj.	さて
well…	1035	inter.	さあ
west	2021	n	にし・西
Western style	2024	n	ようふう・洋風
Western-style meal	2024	n	ようしょく・洋食
Western-style room	2024	n	ようしつ・洋室
what	1021	inter.	なん/なに・何
what color	1074	inter.	なにいろ・何色
what day of the month	1053	inter.	なんにち・何日
what day of the week	1051	inter.	なんようび・何曜日
what ethnicity or heritage	1041	inter.	なにけい・何系
what floor?	2024	inter.	なんかい/がい・何階
what grade/year	1031	inter.	なんねんせい・何年生
what kind of?	2041	exp.	なんの・何の
what month	1052	inter.	なんがつ・何月
what nationality	1041	inter.	なにじん・何人
what number?	2011	inter.	なんばん・何番

English	Location		Japanese
what period	1033	*inter.*	なんじかんめ・何時間目
What the heck?, What on earth?; (adv.) generally, in general	2101	*n/adv.*	いったい
what time	1032	*inter.*	なんじ・何時
what year	1054	*inter.*	なんねん・何年
what/which kind of	1062	*inter.*	どんな
what zodiac animal are you	2014s	*exp.*	なにどし・何年ですか
when	1055s	*conj.*	のときに・～の時に
when?	1052	*inter.*	いつ
where?	1024	*inter.*	どこ
which (one)	1015	*inter.*	どれ
which (thing)	1023	*inter.*	どの
which/what kind of	1062	*inter.*	どんな
white	1074	*n*	しろ・白
white-colored	1082	い *adj.*	しろい・白い
whiteboard	App.	*n*	ほわいとぼーど・ホワイトボード
who	1021	*inter.*	だれ
why	1042	*inter.*	どうして, なぜ
wide, spacious	1083	い *adj.*	ひろい・広い
wife (my)	2061	*n*	かない・家内
wild boar	2013	*n*	いのしし・猪
will not break	2062s		おれない・折れない
wind	1035	*n*	かぜ・風
window	1034	*n*	まど・窓
window-shop (to)	1091s	*n*	うぃんどうしょっぴんぐ・ウィンドウショッピング (を) する/します
winter	1101	*n*	ふゆ・冬
winter season	2015s	*n*	とうき・冬季
wise, bright	1081	い *adj.*	かしこい
with 2 meals included	2024	*exp.*	にしょくつき・二食付き
with meals (included)	2024	*exp.*	しょくつき・食事付き
with the exception of	2074	*adv.*	いがい・以外
woman, female	1064s	*n*	おんな・女
woman, female	1064	*n*	おんなのひと・女の人
wonderful	1065	い *adj.*	すばらしい・素晴らしい
wonderful, nice	1064	な *adj.*	すてき・素敵
woodblock print	1091	*n*	はんが・版画
woodblock print (new), art print (new)	1091	*n*	しんはんが・新版画
woodblock print (prior to and through the Edo Period)	1091	*n*	うきよえ・浮世絵
woodblock print block	2031s	*n*	はんぎ・版木
wooden clappers	2044s	*n*	ひょうしぎ・拍子木
word	2043	*n*	ことば・言葉
work (to)	1052s	*v*	しごと・仕事 (を) する/します
work (to)	2012	*v*	はたらく・働く
works	2033s	*n*	さくひん・作品
world (the), society	1032s	*n*	せかい・世界
world history	1032	*n*	せかいし・世界史
World War II	2034s	*pn*	だいにじせかいたいせん・第二次世界大戦
worry (to)	1063	*v*	しんぱい・心配(を) する/します
wow!	1035	*interj.*	わっ!
wristwatch	2015	*n*	うでどけい・腕時計
write (to)	1013	*v*	かく・書く/かきます・書きます

English	Location		Japanese
writing pad, mat	1024	*n*	したじき・下敷き
Yamamoto (family name)	1031	*pn*	やまもと・山本
Yamanote (train line)	1024s	*pn*	やまのて・山の手
year of the dog	2014	*n*	いぬどし・犬年/戌年
year of the sheep	2014	*n*	ひつじどし・羊年/未年
year of the snake	2061	*n*	へびどし/みどし・巳年
year-end	2024s	*n*	ねんまつ・年末
yellow	1074	*n*	きいろ・黄色
yellow-colored	1082	い *adj.*	きいろい・黄色い
yes	1032s		ええ/はい
yes it is	1014	*exp.*	はい、そう です。
Yes, I understand.	1016s	*exp.*	はい、わかります。・はい、分かります。
yes, OK, here (roll call)	1014		はい
yesterday	1032	*n/adv.*	きのう・昨日
Yokohama (place)	1031s	*pn*	よこはま・横浜
you [best not used too often]	1041s	*pron.*	あなた
you are welcome	1023	*exp.*	どういたしまして
young	2034	い *adj.*	わかい・若い
younger brother (my)	1021	*n*	おとうと・弟
younger brother (someone else's)	1022	*n*	おとうとさん・弟さん
younger sister (my)	1021	*n*	いもうと・妹
younger sister (someone else's)	1022	*n*	いもうとさん・妹さん
youngest brother/sister (my)	1021	*n*	いちばんしたの おとうと/いもうと・一番下の 弟/妹
yukata (light cotton) kimono worn in summer or in the evenings in ryokan or homes	2052	*n*	ゆかた・浴衣
Zen Buddhism	2062s	*n*	ぜんぶっきょう・禅仏教